RELUCTANT EUROPEANS

RELUCTANT EUROPEANS

Norway, Sweden, and Switzerland in the Process of Integration

Sieglinde Gstöhl

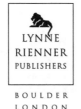

LYNNE
RIENNER
PUBLISHERS

BOULDER
LONDON

Published in the United States of America in 2002 by
Lynne Rienner Publishers, Inc.
1800 30th Street, Boulder, Colorado 80301
www.rienner.com

and in the United Kingdom by
Lynne Rienner Publishers, Inc.
3 Henrietta Street, Covent Garden, London WC2E 8LU

Library of Congress Cataloging-in-Publication Data
Gstöhl, Sieglinde, 1964–
    Reluctant Europeans : Norway, Sweden, and Switzerland in the process of integration /
Sieglinde Gstöhl.
        p. cm.
    Includes bibliographical references and index.
    ISBN 1-58826-036-4 (alk. paper)
    1. Europe—Economic integration.   2. European federation.   3. European Union—
Norway.   4. European Union—Sweden.   5. European Union—Switzerland.
6. Norway—Foreign relations—Europe.   7. Sweden—Foreign relations—Europe.
8. Switzerland—Foreign relations—Europe.   I. Title.
    HC241.G76   2002
    337.4048—dc21

                                                                    2001048637

British Cataloguing in Publication Data
A Cataloguing in Publication record for this book
is available from the British Library.

Printed and bound in the United States of America

The paper used in this publication meets the requirements
⊗ of the American National Standard for Permanence of
Paper for Printed Library Materials Z39.48-1984.

5   4   3   2   1

Contents

Tables

Preface

Il est difficile de tomber amoureux d'un marché commun.
—Jacques Delors

Today, Sweden looks back on a few years of membership in the European Union (EU), Norway is part of the European Economic Area (EEA), and Switzerland has stayed out of both but concluded bilateral sectoral agreements with the Union. All three countries were founding members of the European Free Trade Association (EFTA), which was intended as an alternative to the European Communities (EC: the European Community, the European Coal and Steel Community, and the European Atomic Energy Community) and as a bridge-building device between the two trading groups. Even though the EFTA countries easily fulfilled the accession criteria, they were either latecomers or still have not joined the EU.

In this book, I attempt to explain why small, rich, and open economies such as Norway, Sweden, and Switzerland, whose major trading partner has traditionally been the European Community, have been so reluctant toward supranational integration. In search of an answer to this puzzle, I trace the trajectory of their integration policies across five decades. An explanation is offered by combining an analysis of economic interests in market integration with ideational interests in protecting national identity. The approach thus lies at an intersection that currently engages the discipline of international relations, and it shifts the focus of European studies from integration theory to integration policy theory.

The inspiration to write the book stems from my involvement in the negotiations on the creation of a European Economic Area in the early 1990s, a project that finally accomplished what the Organization for European Economic Cooperation (OEEC) negotiations on a wider European free trade area failed to do in the late 1950s. Yet, when the EEA entered into force, most EFTA states had already applied for EU membership. This puzzle accompanied me on a stimulating stay at the Harvard Center for International Affairs and finally at the Graduate Institute of International Studies in Geneva, Switzerland. As I developed the project into a book, the manuscript moved with me to two more countries and academic institutions, thus prolonging the list of people to whom I am grateful. I wish to thank them all for their support and encouragement, in particular my family and friends and my academic mentors, David Sylvan and Andrew Moravcsik.

In light of the European Union's ongoing enlargements to the east and south of Europe that will add considerably not only to the number but to the diversity of its membership, and bearing in mind the EU's intrusion into increasingly sensitive areas of political integration, an understanding of the varying willingness of states to further integrate, to which I hope to contribute in this book, is becoming more and more salient.

1

Reluctant Europeans:
A Puzzle

Nothing will get your dinner-guests heading for the door faster than the subject of EFTA-EEC relations. Why is this worthy theme such a conversation-stopper? . . . Mainly because EFTA's identity is negative—its members are chiefly not-in-the-EEC . . . The topic becomes more interesting when it turns to particular EFTA countries and asks: what is it that prevents Austria or Sweden or Norway from joining the Community?
—The Economist, "Survey," p. 43

Since the 1950s, the European Union (EU) has become Europe's largest market and most important political actor. It has not only steadily deepened its scope of integration but also has widened its membership from the original six to fifteen states in 1995, with a queue of applicants that could double the Union's size in the not-too-distant future. Yet the demand for membership has varied over time and across countries: the original six "committed Europeans" who have been able and willing founding members of the European Communities (EC; the European Community, the European Coal and Steel Community, and the European Atomic Energy Agency); the able but not willing "reluctant Europeans";[1] and the "eager Europeans" who willingly applied for membership as soon as they felt remotely able to join. In this book, I deal with the second category.

Many former and current members of the European Free Trade Association (EFTA) are found among the reluctant Europeans. Countries such as the United Kingdom, Denmark, Norway, Sweden, and Switzerland would have fulfilled the eligibility criteria from the outset, but for a long time they aimed at a lower level of integration than full EC membership.[2] I seek to explain why Sweden, Norway, and Switzerland have been so reluctant. After briefly summarizing five decades of EC-EFTA relations, I review some theoretical approaches and then set out the framework of analysis.

Brief Laggards' History

The creation of the European Communities in the 1950s divided Western Europe into the Six (Belgium, France, Germany, Italy, Luxembourg, and the Netherlands) and the "non-Six" (see Chapter 3). The attempt to overcome this division by creating a comprehensive European free trade area within the framework of the Organization for European Economic Cooperation (OEEC) failed. As a result, the United Kingdom and its supporters (Austria, Denmark, Norway, Portugal, Sweden, and Switzerland) in 1960 founded the European Free Trade Association (EFTA). Whereas the EC-6 favored a supranational customs union with the long-term objective of a political union, the ambitions of the EFTA-7 amounted to nothing more than a classical free trade area in industrial goods with purely intergovernmental decisionmaking.

After only one year of EFTA's existence, however, the United Kingdom applied for EC membership, followed by Denmark, Norway, and Ireland (see Chapter 4). The rest of the EFTA countries sought closer economic association with the Communities in order to avoid trade distortions. Such aspirations failed in 1963 with the veto of British membership by French president Charles de Gaulle. In 1967, the four countries applied for the second time, with the same result. After de Gaulle's resignation two years later, the European Communities finally opened themselves toward the EFTA countries and revived the dormant applications. In 1973, Great Britain, Denmark, and Ireland joined, but Norway did not ratify the accession treaty after a negative referendum (see Chapter 5). At the same time, bilateral free trade agreements (FTAs) entered into force between the enlarged European Communities and the remaining EFTA countries, including Finland, which had been associated with EFTA since 1961, and Iceland, which became a member in 1970. Greece joined the EC in 1981 and Portugal and Spain in 1986.

The EC-EFTA free trade agreements proved to be real success stories, and in 1984, the last tariffs and almost all quantitative restrictions on trade in industrial goods were removed. In an attempt to keep up with the "deepening" of integration in the European Communities, the "Luxembourg process," a pragmatic sector-by-sector approach for cooperation, was launched in 1984 (see Chapter 6). In light of the dynamics toward the completion of the EC's internal market initiated by the 1985 White Paper, the Luxembourg process soon proved to be too cumbersome. In 1989, the idea was introduced to switch from a sectoral to a global approach toward cooperation (see Chapter 7). The outcome was the EC-EFTA agreement on the European Economic Area (EEA), which entered into force in 1994 and basically extended the internal market to the EFTA countries.

In spite of the EEA negotiations, however, Austria applied for EC membership in 1989, when the end of the Cold War was near. Within three years, Sweden, Finland, Switzerland, and Norway had joined the applicants' queue (see Chapter 7). Surprisingly, they submitted their membership bid at a time when the European Community (the Community) was moving toward a political union requiring increasing sacrifices of sovereignty, even though they were offered participation in the internal market through the EEA. Switzerland failed to ratify the EEA agreement in 1992 and decided to suspend its application for EC membership. Soon after the Maastricht Treaty entered into force in November 1993, the enlargement negotiations with the remaining applicants were successfully concluded. Austria, Finland, and Sweden joined the EU in 1995, but Norway once again failed to accede because of a negative referendum.

As the cases of Great Britain, Denmark, and Sweden show, reluctant integration policies do not easily disappear with EU membership. On the contrary, skepticism toward closer integration is likely to become even more salient in the future as efforts to further deepen integration encroach upon more sensitive areas and enlargements increase the EU's diversity. There is thus a compelling need to understand reluctant integration policies.

Puzzling Economic Theory

Economic theory leads us to expect that small and highly industrialized states are more likely to integrate than larger or less advanced countries. Regional integration allows small countries to obtain advantages similar to those large countries have through the opportunity to specialize in accord with comparative advantages, the ability to exploit economies of scale, and the stimulating effects of increased competition.

First, trade diversion generally threatens to reduce the welfare of nonmembers. From an EFTA point of view, not participating in the reduction of intra-EC barriers would have meant that Community members substitute EC goods for EFTA goods, thus deteriorating EFTA's terms of trade. The sales of EFTA-based firms in EC markets would be displaced without any offsetting increase in exports. Moreover, the likelihood that a preferential trading agreement increases the welfare of its members rises as more trade is concentrated in the region. Countries close to the Community have strong economic incentives to join, especially if the EC is their main customer—as has increasingly been the case with the EFTA countries.[3] The formation of a customs union would be particularly advisable for small countries that cannot individually affect the terms of trade.

Second, customs unions permit better exploitation of economies of scale that cannot be reaped in small domestic markets. Low unit-cost production is especially important for highly industrialized, specialized, and export-oriented market economies such as those of the EFTA states. Staying outside the EC meant that the EFTA countries' location of production would become less attractive and might require a depreciation of their national currencies, which would further worsen the terms of trade. For the latecomers, the larger the market they join, the better, since it implies a greater potential scope for division of labor and scale economies. At the same time, watching the community grow from the outside is becoming more and more costly in terms of forgone economic benefits, increasing discrimination, and a growing body of EC legislation that requires adaptation without influence.

Third, the benefits of increased competition are greater for countries with similar production, such as the intra-industry trade in manufactures typical for Western Europe. An increase in competition reduces monopoly distortions and increases efficiency and consumers' choice, which is expected to benefit small economies in particular. EC membership would also help avoid the problem of investment diversion, that is, EFTA firms investing in the Community rather than the association in order to improve access to the internal market.

In Search of Integration Policy Theory

The *acquis académique* on integration policy theory and enlargement theory is extremely scarce. None of the existing approaches is readily available to explain the long-standing aloofness of the "reluctant Europeans," their search for limited integration, or their hesitant policies once members of the Union.[4] The classical theories focus primarily on the deepening of integration and not on the conduct of integration policy. The neofunctionalist perspective vaguely suggests that successful integration will elicit a reaction from adversely affected outsiders, in particular from interest groups that fear the danger of discrimination and isolation, compelling them to closer ties. This "externalization" may finally lead to a "geographical spillover" in terms of an enlargement of the European Union.[5]

To explain integration preferences, a domestic perspective needs to be added. Simon Bulmer claims that different economic structures, domestic institutions, and political traditions produce different integration policies.[6] In fact, pluralist theories suggest that the preferences of interest groups and the dynamics of party systems should matter most; elite theories locate the sources of integration policies in the nature and beliefs of the national decisionmakers; and institutional theories focus on decisionmaking structures to explain national preferences. In contrast to these "rationalist" approaches, constructivism claims that identities shape preferences.[7] Both schools of thought are—to some extent—right.

Walter Mattli maintains that a country applies for EU membership after one or more years of growth rates below the average of the member states.[8] Obviously, a government may use integration to improve economic performance in view of its goal of reelection. Based on opinion polls, however, Christopher Anderson and Karl Kaltenthaler found that GDP growth has, unlike unemployment and inflation, no significant effects on public support for a country's EU membership.[9] In my view, export dependence and market access provide better indicators of economic incentives to join than performance gaps. Indeed, Mattli's hypothesis does not explain the integration policies of Norway, Sweden, Switzerland, and other EFTA countries that have either applied when their performance was above EU average, have failed to apply in spite of persistently low growth vis-à-vis the Union, or did apply but did not join after a negative referendum.[10] Moreover, as Mattli concedes, the argument does not apply to the candidate countries that were significantly poorer than the least wealthy member states but enjoyed higher growth rates (e.g., Portugal and Central and Eastern European countries).[11]

Regarding the Nordic countries, Christine Ingebritsen argues that the transformation of the international security system in 1989 made the changes in integration policy possible and that the variation with regard to EU membership can be explained by the leading economic sectors and their respective political influence.[12] More precisely, Sweden and Finland joined the European Union because manufacturing and forestry are export-dependent; Denmark remains because its agriculture and manufacturing benefit from EU subsidies and open markets; and Norway and Iceland stay out because fishing is threatened by EU policies and because Norway's oil revenues make nonmembership economically feasible. Hence, "the divergent paths to Europe conformed to the specificities of sectoral politics, not to the structure of the state, to membership in international institutions, or to class divisions within the society."[13] I can only partly agree with this argument. The results of the referenda in Switzerland in 1992 and in Sweden in 1994 were negative and uncertain, respectively, despite heavily pro-integration leading sectors and political elites. In Norway, the interests tied to the most important industry, oil and gas, were inconsequential in the membership issue, whereas marginal sectors such as fishing and farming mattered. Even if one concedes that the petroleum sector did not actively lobby the government on the membership issue but rather provided the revenues that allowed the state to dole out subsidies to agriculture and fisheries, which in turn enabled them to campaign against membership, the question remains why in 1972 those two sectors contributed to a "no" vote without the existence of oil-generated subsidies.[14] Opposition may not only arise from economic sectoral interests exercising pressure through political representation but can also originate in political institutions, societal cleavages, or historical constraints.

Mattli and Ingebritsen are basically in line with liberal intergovernmentalism, outlined below, which claims that economic interests sufficiently explain national integration preferences and that only where they are "weak, diffuse, or indeterminate could national politicians indulge the temptation to consider geopolitical goals."[15] I suggest that political factors of a domestic or geohistorical nature are relevant beyond those cases. They are not a foil against which to argue but a variable that helps explain national preferences. Although rationalist approaches are most useful in elucidating economic motives, they neglect the "hidden" impact of national identities on integration policy.[16] Hence, constructivist approaches, which claim that constructions of nation and statehood shape interests and thus also policies, might offer valuable insights.

In this vein, Martin Marcussen and colleagues examine the variation in the extent to which nation-state identities have become European.[17] They argue that new visions of European order need to resonate with preexisting collective identities embedded in political institutions and cultures in order to constitute a legitimate political discourse and that such new ideas can most easily be promoted by political elites during "critical junctures," when old identities are contested. I agree that the importance of political impediments to integration, as perceived by the elites, decreases when the old concepts are viewed as becoming irrelevant (e.g., neutrality policy after the Cold War) or having failed (e.g., the Nordic welfare model in the 1990s). Such an approach is helpful in understanding the countries' overall attitudes toward integration, but it cannot explain the timing or contents of their policy decisions. If Europe does not resonate well with British identity and if "statements show a remarkable continuity of British attitudes toward the EU and related identity constructions from the 1950s (and earlier) until the present time,"[18] why did Britain join the European Communities in 1973? Economic and political interests may not be dismissed as explanatory factors. One might also wonder why Norwegian and Swiss elites, in contrast to the Swedes, have not succeeded in using the "critical juncture" of the end of the Cold War to redefine national identity in a way that suited their perceived power interests (that is, in favor of EU membership).

Constructivist approaches run the danger of providing post hoc explanations in the sense that if integration policy has changed, national identity must have changed first. Given that "domestic politics, national myth and identity, economic strength or weakness, geographical position and security constraints, shape perception of interests,"[19] as William Wallace argues, the interesting question is not whether identities precede the definition of interests or matter more, but how they matter.[20] For instance, what difference do identity-related domestic institutions, societal cleavages, historical experiences, or traditions make with regard to integration policies? What are the distinct obstacles leaders face as they attempt to redefine the boundaries of community from the nation to Europe?

To conclude, we lack an integration policy theory to be able to explain the individual countries' varying willingness to integrate and to theorize the demand side of EU enlargement. Neither economic interests nor national identity alone are sufficient to explain integration policies, but both material and ideational factors must be considered. In the remainder of this chapter, I set out a new framework of analysis.

Incentives for, Impediments to, and Intent Regarding Integration

In order to explain the reluctance of the three EFTA countries, I choose as a dependent variable *the level of integration a policy aims at,* measured by the scope of integration and the degree of institutionalization. With regard to the scope of integration, nonmembers face different options ranging from sectoral integration (low scope: only one or very few specific issue areas of an integration scheme are covered) to a global approach (medium scope: most of the issue areas are covered) to full membership (high scope: all the issue areas of an integration scheme are covered). The degree of institutionalization varies because there are either no institutions, an intergovernmental setup (low degree: intergovernmental bodies with mainly unanimity voting), a quasi-supranational setup (medium degree: supranational bodies and intergovernmental bodies with mainly unanimity voting), or a supranational setup (high degree: supranational and intergovernmental bodies with a great extent of majority voting). The resulting index of the dependent variable is constructed so that the larger the scope and the tighter the institutionalization, the higher the level of integration the policy aims at.

To allow for interesting implications and as a means of validation, the level of integration aimed at is also assessed in terms of operational sovereignty (or the legal freedom to act in certain issue areas) and voice opportunities (that is, the state's opportunities to participate in the collective decisionmaking processes of an integration scheme). The two perspectives are kept separate for purely analytical reasons. The scope of integration touches mainly upon the concept of operational sovereignty, and the degree of institutionalization is more closely linked to the issue of voice. The specific mixture of sovereignty and voice of an integration option is part of the strategy to achieve goals such as wealth, security, or control over domestic policies and can, for instance, be traced in elite statements.

Preferences are explained by the economic and political incentives (or "gains") and impediments (or "costs") to integration, metaphorically understood as "net" positions. Governments consent to an international agreement only if they gain more than they lose. Again, each variable is measured by different indicators whose values are classified as either "low," "medium," or "high." Incentives could, for instance, include the benefits accruing from liberalization in different fields, the potential transfers from community funds, the aim of permanently reconciling historical enemies, the need to stabilize young democracies or market economies, or the desire to gain more prestige in Europe. Impediments may arise from the perceived threat to important economic sectors, political institutions, or traditions. In Sweden, Norway, and Switzerland, the typical aggregate balance sheet has been characterized by *economic incentives* and *political impediments* to integration. These two explanatory variables are further specified along the lines of the importance of market access and the importance of political constraints.

The Importance of Market Access

Choosing the importance of access to the integrating foreign markets implies a focus on the export sectors of the economy, which is justified because Sweden, Norway, and Switzerland are highly industrialized, export-oriented economies that have traditionally sold most of their products to the Western European market. The importance of market access is measured in terms of a country's overall export dependence on that market and the corresponding sensitivity of its main export sectors.[21] Overall export dependence refers to a country's exports to an integration scheme as a share of total exports (export ratio) as well as to the importance of these exports in relation to gross domestic product (GDP ratio).[22] Calculating the share of GDP reveals the market's relevance for the national income and discounts the effect of general economic expansion over time.

The leading sectors' export sensitivity assesses the potential of a sector being negatively affected by integrating markets. I define "leading sectors"—based on the two-digit Standard International Trade Classification (SITC) system—as those three sectors of an economy with the highest share of exports to an integration scheme of the total exports to that scheme (sector share). In addition, the sectors' exports to the integration area as a share of their total exports (sector export ratio) are calculated. For a more accurate assessment, the sectors' exports are complemented by the level of trade barriers which they (would have) encountered as outsiders.[23] Because of the usual problems of calculation, aggregation, and comparability, the data on trade barriers are, of course, only rough estimates. In the EC-EFTA context, the tariffs for industrial goods have gradually been abolished by the free trade agreements until 1984, whereas the nontariff barriers to trade (NTBs) became relevant thereafter, when the EC embarked upon the completion of the internal market by 1993. With the steady elimination of barriers to trade, in particular through the EEA, additional economic indicators (such as investment flows) might thus be of interest in the 1990s. To back up and validate the statistical data, statements of national elites are used.[24] They provide additional evidence on how the magnitude of export dependence was perceived at the time and on the expected economic effects of different integration options.

The Importance of Political Constraints

The importance of political impediments to integration depends on whether the required loss of operational sovereignty touches on a country's "national identity." According to William Bloom, national identity "describes that condition in which a mass of people have made the same identification with national symbols . . . so that they may act as one psychological group when there is a threat to, or the possibility of enhancement of, these symbols of national identity."[25] It is thus closely linked to ideas about sovereignty and statehood. Actors internalize national identity and embed it in domestic institutions, political culture, and traditions. Hence, national identities are relatively resistant to change. This comparative stability does not, however, exclude that the importance attributed to certain aspects of national identity may change over time. National identity is "context bound" in the sense that different components of it are invoked by different policy areas.[26] To assess the importance of identity-related constraints on integration, elites use implicit reference points (e.g., the international security environment) that are equally subject to change. The potential impediments comprise domestic and geohistorical constraints on integration.

A country's domestic structure comprises a certain institutional pattern and fragmentation of society. Domestic institutions are "the rules of the game in a society or, more formally, are the humanly devised constraints that shape human interaction."[27] They are sensitive to integration, if elites, based on a broad national consensus (or "intersubjective, shared understandings of identity that have become consensual among social groups"[28]), perceive them to be both significant and threatened by integration. "Cleavages are the criteria which divide the members of a community or subcommunity into groups, and the relevant cleavages are those which divide members into groups with important political differences at specific times and places."[29] Such societal divisions form part of national identity, if they belong to a nation's historical memories or mass public culture.[30] Although social stratification sets the structural conditions for cleavages, they become fully political through the processes of politicization and are visible in opinion polls, elections, and referenda. In order to become politicized, societal cleavages "have to develop, on the one hand, a collective identity, a sense of solidarity, and political consciousness, and, on the other hand, an organizational infrastructure."[31] Class-based cleavages, for instance, have in the past typically been capitalized on by political parties, yet the integration issue often crosscuts the party spectrum. In this study, I distinguish religious, ethnolinguistic, and regional cleavages. These societal cleavages are relevant if, based on evidence from elite statements, they are considered important and if their divisions take opposing positions on an integration issue. Such reinforcing cleavages ensure that those persons who are divided by one cleavage are (at least to some extent) also divided by another, even if cleavages are not logically related to the integration issue. By contrast, crosscutting cleavages entail cross-pressures that produce a moderating influence.

The historical experience of foreign rule, as perceived by the elites at a given time, and the "integration compatibility" of foreign policy serve as indicators for geohistorical constraints. Traditions of external relations and myths about the fight for independence may form part of national identity. Foreign rule may include former colonization, "satellization," or military occupation. The foreign policy tradition is compatible if it is unaffected by the proposed integration scheme, if it is perceived to be similar to the foreign policies of the member states, or if the further maintenance of a divergent national policy is not considered important. Evidence of a national consensus on the importance of maintaining the foreign policy tradition is, again, supplied by elites' statements.[32] In sum, the political impediments are high if either the domestic or the geohistorical constraints are strong. They are low if both the domestic and the geohistorical constraints are weak and medium if they show mixed constraints.[33]

Explaining National Preferences

The next step is to specify the process that translates these explanatory variables, which conflate economic and identity-related factors, into a country's integration preferences. In this book, I follow the Weberian maxim that material and ideational interests, rather than ideas, directly govern behavior, even though the worldviews created by ideas often determine the tracks along which the dynamics of interests have pushed action.[34] The analyses of material interests in market integration and ideational interests in protecting national identity complement each other. As Robert Keohane points out, "one can recognize that the social world has been socially constructed—by ideas and institutions—without denying the importance of state action, material forces, or rational calculation" because the real issue is "how these ideas are mixed with material forces, and embedded in enduring institutions, to produce the variations in outcomes that we observe."[35] Hence, an approach aiming to explain reluctant policies must consider how ideational interests (or political impediments) may curb material interests (or economic incentives) with regard to European integration.

In much of international relations literature, "cooperation is generally conceptualized as the product of a two-step process: first, actors form their preferences; second, they interact until they reach an outcome."[36] Andrew Moravcsik applies this concept to the study of European integration by means of liberal intergovernmentalism and adds an institutional dimension.[37] In the first stage, national preferences are shaped by the constraints and opportunities imposed by economic interdependence. In the second stage, the outcome of intergovernmental negotiations is determined by factors such as relative bargaining power. The third stage, the institutional delegation (or pooling) of sovereignty, is explained by the governments' search for more credible commitments. Hence, each stage requires its own theory: a liberal theory for the national preference formation, an intergovernmentalist approach to the interstate bargaining outcomes, and a regime-theoretical credibility explanation for the states' choices to transfer sovereignty to international institutions.

I focus exclusively on the first stage, analyzing the formation of national preferences.[38] I do not aspire to explain the final outcome of negotiations but only the level of integration aimed at by the EFTA countries. A liberal approach to the formation of national preferences may well take into account ideational factors such as collective ideas about national identity.[39] For analytical reasons, I distinguish two (simultaneous) aspects: the construction of national preferences as such, aiming at full or limited integration, and the selection of a "strategy" pinpointing a certain mixture of national sovereignty and international cooperation as the means to achieve the goals.

A Liberal Approach to Preference Formation

Peter Katzenstein shows that small European states, such as Norway, Sweden, and Switzerland, have adopted a dual strategy of international liberalization and domestic compensation based on corporatist political structures.[40] They have combined centralized decisionmaking with a high degree of societal penetration channeled through associations. Corporatist systems are particularly accessible to societal actors who wish to articulate their preferences, and the reelection constraint ensures that the government takes them into account. Hence, I assume that national preferences reflect the views of dominant domestic coalitions as aggregated and perceived by the government. This assumption holds true in particular for corporatist states since, as Thomas Risse-Kappen argues, "the stronger the organization of societal interest representation, and the greater the consensus requirements in state-society relations, the less capable are national governments to pursue independent and autonomous policies on the EU level."[41] In democracies, conceptions of national interests and national identity articulated by elites should be broadly similar to those of society as a whole. However, uncertainty and inadequate information may distort the government's ability to reliably assess the alternative courses of action (e.g., with regard to society's minimally acceptable terms of an agreement).

The influence of societal groups and state officials often follows from the properties of the issue areas concerned.[42] Different policy areas involve not only different policy instruments but also different distributional consequences and thus different key actors. With regard to economic affairs, "the state is relatively passive and lacks autonomy from the major producer groups."[43] Following endogenous tariff theory, it is assumed that coalitions are more likely to form according to economic sectors instead of factors.[44] Domestic producers organize by sectors on the basis of their calculations of the (expected) costs and benefits resulting from different options of integration. When factors of production are specific to certain sectors, which they usually are in the short and medium term, politics will not pit labor versus capital along class lines but rather produce cleavages, such as those between exporting and import-competing sectors or multinational and domestic firms. Import-competing firms tend to favor trade barriers, whereas export-dependent and multinational firms endorse free trade (or at least a strategic trade policy), whether they are owned locally or by foreign investors. Where adjustment to free trade is relatively costless (or, alternatively, where compensation is arranged for the losers), distributional effects need not create opposition to integration. Sweden, Norway, and Switzerland have, with some exceptions such as agriculture, traditionally been export-oriented free traders, and their corporatist systems make domestic compensation more likely. Finally, domestic organizations and collective-action costs may play a decisive role.[45] Actors with a concentrated interest are more likely to mobilize than those with a dispersed interest (such as consumers) or those with no direct access to the policymaking process (such as foreign producers). Existing organizations are more likely to defend their interests since the costs are much lower than for unorganized groups. The export industries in the EFTA countries have traditionally been organized in industrial federations or chambers of commerce, and corporatism has granted them a prominent place in the policymaking process (see Chapter 2). Thus they are likely to play an important role in the formulation of preferences regarding European integration.

By contrast, in political cooperation, the costs and benefits for societal actors are more diffuse and uncertain, so that the key actors remain the political elites. Moreover, they have the last word on integration policy, unless public referenda are held. Even though in small corporatist states, political and economic elites are closely interwoven, in this study I distinguish between political elites and economic associations, particularly the export-oriented sectors. The focus on elites remains justified because I deal with preference formation (not integration outcomes) and because the main role of public opinion in foreign policy is to influence the coalition-building processes among elite groups.[46]

In international regional integration, decisionmakers need to choose between maintaining operational sovereignty, or legal freedom of action for specific national policies, and obtaining international opportunities to make their voice heard by participating in the collective decisionmaking processes of international institutions. Normally, the two ambitions cannot be realized at the same time. Growing interdependence questions the effectiveness of national policies and promotes the convergence of national preferences. The opportunity costs of not integrating increase compared to the costs of sacrificing some freedom of action. In Europe, the ability to achieve national policy goals in the course of five decades of integration has come more and more to depend on the European Union's policies. Hence, "in a trade-off curve between keeping . . . sovereignty on the one hand and gaining access to bodies where decisions with a real impact are being taken on the other, more and more countries prefer to give up some part of their sovereignty."[47]

Full or Limited Integration?

For four decades since 1950, the reluctant countries have more or less consistently aimed at limited integration instead of full membership in the European Communities. I argue that the following hypothesis explains this puzzle: *the lower the economic incentives and the higher the political impediments to integration are, the more reluctant a country's integration policy will be.* In other words, when market access is less important and the domestic and geohistorical constraints are stronger, the level of integration aimed at will be lower in terms of the scope of integration and the degree of institutionalization. As a corollary of this hypothesis, I argue that the lower the economic incentives and the higher the political impediments are, *the more important will be the maintenance of operational sovereignty relative to the acquisition of international voice opportunities.* With regard to the two key actors, it can be specified that when economic elites and in particular export-oriented sectors are more favorable toward integration, the economic incentives will be higher. The political elites are, in addition, more favorable toward integration when the political impediments are lower.

Since political elites, who care about the political aspects of integration, are the final decisionmakers and since small countries and countries with corporatist structures tend to pursue a cautious foreign policy that does not easily sell cherished political institutions for economic gains, it can be presumed that high political impediments dominate economic incentives for integration.[48] Yet, strong economic benefits reinforce the search for alternatives to full membership. Based on these considerations, the hypothesis is transposed into Table 1.1.

Table 1.1   Hypothesis: Targeted Level of Integration

		Economic Incentives		
		High	*Medium*	*Low*
Political	*High*	Medium/Low	Low	Low/None
Impediments	*Medium*	Medium	Medium/Low	Low
	Low	High	Medium	Medium/Low

The method followed in this study is that of structured, focused comparison, which requires asking the same questions of each case and collecting data on the same variables across units.[49] In order to better assess the validity of the findings, data from different sources are used, a technique known as "triangulation." Michael Zürn distinguishes three methods of assessing preferences independent of the behavior to be explained by these preferences: applying theories, using documents, and asking experts.[50] In this study, I rely primarily on documents such as government reports, parliamentary records, statistics, and other sources as well as secondary literature.

Case Selection

Mediterranean countries and those in Central and Eastern Europe so far have been "eager" rather than "reluctant" Europeans. For a long time, they have faced economic and political obstacles to accession. They concluded association agreements with the European Community and applied for membership as soon as they deemed they fulfilled the conditions.[51] They needed support for their young democracies and weak economies. It remains to be seen what role their national identities will play in the future.

The "able but not willing" Europeans mainly comprise the countries that at some point in time were members of the European Free Trade Association, with the exception of Portugal. Great Britain and Denmark became members of the European Communities in 1973; Austria, Finland, and Sweden joined at the end of the Cold War; Switzerland and Norway applied but did not join; and Iceland and Liechtenstein have so far never applied for EU membership.

Both the United Kingdom and Denmark have become notorious for their reluctance as member states. Britain, for instance, renegotiated its terms of membership in 1975, and they were sanctioned by a referendum. Nevertheless, the question of British contributions to the Community budget overshadowed relations between the UK and the other EC states from 1979 to 1984. In 1991, the United Kingdom was granted an opt-out from the social chapter that was to be included in the Maastricht Treaty, until the Labour government finally signed up for it in June 1997. Another opt-out concerned the third stage of monetary union, that is, the single currency. British reluctance is rooted in the country's historical legacy: "the continuity of institutions since the English Civil War; former world-power status; the successful avoidance, as an island, of full-scale invasion; the position of having 'stood alone' in 1940 together with the prestige gained as a victor; the myth of parliamentary sovereignty."[52] With an insular outlook of remoteness from the European continent, Britain has often taken more interest first in the empire and then the Commonwealth. The English national myths center around the Magna Carta, common law, and 700-year-old parliamentary traditions. For a long time, parliamentary sovereignty has been considered hardly compatible with the EC legal system and in particular with the principle of supremacy of EC law over national law.[53] However, as the only large EFTA state, the United Kingdom in the 1960s increasingly faced political (and economic) incentives for accession that ruled out the identity-related impediments. Prime Minister Harold Macmillan's statement of 1962 speaks for itself:

> In the past, as a great maritime Empire, we might give way to insular feelings of superiority over foreign breeds and suspicion of our neighbours across the Channel. . . . Are we now to isolate ourselves from Europe at a time when our own strength is no longer self-sufficient and when the leading European countries are joining together to build a future of peace and progress instead of wasting themselves in war? . . . By joining this vigorous and expanding community and becoming one of its leading members,

as I am convinced we would, this country would not only gain a new
stature in Europe, but also increase its standing and influence in the councils of the world. . . . In renouncing some of our own sovereignty we
would receive in return a share of the sovereignty renounced by other
members.[54]

Denmark, like Norway, suffered German occupation in World War II
and thereafter decided to give up neutrality and become an unenthusiastic
member of NATO[55] while pursuing an internationalist foreign policy along
with its Scandinavian neighbors. It followed the policy lead of Great
Britain in joining EFTA, in the repeated applications for EC membership,
and finally in accession. Yet in contrast to Britain's political aspirations, the
Danish motivations were predominantly economic: "membership became,
in popular parlance, a question of 'pork prices.'"[56] Both Denmark and
Ireland followed the United Kingdom into the Community because Britain
was their major market and agricultural products were their principal
exports. Danish (and Irish) politicians had a long-standing propensity to
present the EC as advantageous from a strictly economic point of view, not
as an emerging political union. That is, the Danish ideas about the
Community's *finalité politique* were quite diffuse at the time of joining,
and the later "foot-dragging" posture, particularly since the mid-1980s, represented a mounting tension between European and national identity that
resulted in a preference for intergovernmental cooperation.[57]

Agriculture has played a central role in the Danish national myths. The
"traditional amorphous peasant feelings of community and solidarity" were
successfully transformed into modern times and influenced, for instance,
the establishment of Denmark's welfare state.[58] The Danish welfare model
has been less developed than in Sweden, Norway, or Finland, corresponding to the relative strength of the social democrats and the labor unions.[59]
In addition, two peculiarities of the Danish political system, the principle of
"cooperative democracy" with close parliamentary control of the government and the constitutional requirement of public referenda, often limit the
government's bargaining space.[60] In 1986, the ratification of the Single
European Act needed a positive referendum because the Danish Parliament
had opposed it on the grounds that it might hamper Danish social and environmental policies, included political cooperation, and gave more powers
to the European Parliament, among other things.[61] In 1992, the Danish people opted against the Maastricht Treaty in spite of the fact that Parliament
had approved it. After obtaining special treatment on the issues of
European citizenship, the single currency, defense cooperation, and justice
and home affairs, Danish voters ratified the Treaty in 1993.

The integration policies of Austria and Finland were, to a large extent,
constrained by the Cold War and their special relationships with the Soviet
Union. In both countries, neutrality had been imposed by the East-West

conflict, and the collapse of the bipolar system four decades later finally created a "window of opportunity" for them to join the EU.[62] After World War II, Austria was occupied by French, British, U.S., and Soviet forces for ten years. In order to achieve an agreement among the Allies, Austria offered not to join any military alliance or admit any foreign troops on its territory. In 1955, the State Treaty, restoring Austria's full sovereignty, and the Federal Constitutional Law on Neutrality entered into force. Austrian national identity has been marked by the turbulent history of the country: the proclamation of the Austrian empire in 1804, the option for an Austro-Slavism instead of an inclusion in the German empire in 1848, the definite dissolution from the German Confederation in 1866, the First Republic in 1918, the 1938 National Socialist *Anschluss*, and the founding of the Second Republic after World War II.[63]

The Austrian nation has thus been built on a series of defeats and in confrontation with a pan-Germanic ideology. Felix Kreissler depicts the country as rather "integration-friendly" in the sense that Austria has traditionally sought backing from other states and thus faced no major identity-related obstacles to political integration.[64] In fact, a certain lack of national self-confidence and a feeling of uneasiness about possible isolation made European integration look like an answer to the search for a new order. Unlike equally neutral Switzerland, the Austrian government had considered joining the European Coal and Steel Community in 1956 and throughout the 1960s sought for closer association with the EC, which constituted its major trading partner. Moreover, the compatibility between EU membership and the (weak) Austrian federalism has never been as controversial as in Switzerland. According to Alfred Nydegger, "Without the neutrality obligation and the Germany clause in the State Treaty, Austria would probably have become a full member of the EEC a long time ago."[65]

Since the beginning of the Middle Ages, Finland belonged to the Swedish crown. In 1809, Sweden had to cede Finland to Russia, where it became an autonomous grand duchy under the tsar. In the turmoil of the Bolshevik Revolution and a violent civil war, Finland finally won its independence in 1918. The Soviet attack on neutral Finland in the winter of 1939 ended with the cession of some Finnish territory to the Soviet Union. However, in 1941 Finland resumed hostilities in cooperation with Germany, until a peace agreement was reached in 1944. In the Treaty of Friendship, Cooperation, and Mutual Assistance of 1948, the Soviet Union acknowledged Finland's desire to remain outside the conflicts of the big powers.

Compared to Austria, Finland was far less involved economically with the EC and politically more constrained by its special relationship with the Soviet Union, with which it had to conclude trade agreements. Until the end of the Cold War, the issue of neutrality determined not only Finnish security policy but also its relations to European integration efforts. The breakup of the Soviet Union caused a deep economic recession as a result of the plunge in Soviet trade and generated new security concerns. The move from a strict policy of neutrality to EU membership at the end of the Cold War was thus consistent, if it is understood as a strategy to reinforce Finnish security.[66] Finland and Austria had strong economic and political incentives to join the Union, and their relatively integration-friendly policies as EU members since 1995 confirm that they are not "genuine" reluctant Europeans.

Because of their smallness and peculiar economic structures, Liechtenstein and Iceland have developed integration strategies characterized by a priority for the preservation of their main sources of national income. Liechtenstein's economy rests on the two pillars of a financial services sector (including strict bank secrecy) and highly specialized export industries, whereas the Icelandic economy is very dependent on fisheries.[67] The EU's Common Fisheries Policy and the prospects of tax harmonization come close to economic impediments to EU membership. Iceland and Liechtenstein are therefore not the same kind of "reluctant Europeans" as Sweden, Norway, and Switzerland. In addition, Iceland's long fight for independence, which it gained from Denmark at the end of World War II, and its remoteness have marked national identity. By contrast, the tiny principality of Liechtenstein, established in 1719, has traditionally depended on a larger country or confederation. It has thus handled identity-generating features such as direct democracy and neutrality much more pragmatically than the Swiss did. Because it entered into a customs and currency union with Switzerland, Liechtenstein's integration policy has been closely intertwined with Swiss policy, yet it joined the European Economic Area in 1995 without Switzerland.

In this book, I chose to study the three EFTA countries of Sweden, Norway, and Switzerland, which provide an interesting set of cases over a long period of time (1950–1995). All three had valid economic reasons to join in the integration process, but they also faced different political, identity-related impediments to EC membership (see Chapter 2). This case selection is based on variation in the explanatory variables but also considers policies aiming at different levels of integration. It controls for small country size, traditional free trade policies, corporatist democracies, the level of economic development, and open market economies, but it varies with regard to geopolitical situations, historical backgrounds, the periods of sovereign independence, security policies, foreign policy traditions, domestic structures, and sectoral economic interests. To be more precise, not the countries themselves but their policy decisions constitute the cases, with regard to the establishment of the European Coal and Steel Community in 1951, the negotiations on a wider European Free Trade Area within the OEEC in 1957–1958, the founding of the European Economic Community (and Euratom) in 1957 and the European Free Trade Association in 1960, the EC membership applications and association requests in 1961–1962, the EC membership applications in 1967, the first enlargement of the European Communities and the bilateral EC-EFTA free trade agreements in 1972–1973, the EC-EFTA "Luxembourg Process" from 1984 to 1993, the EC-EFTA negotiations on a European Economic Area in 1989–1993, and the EC membership applications of the early 1990s. Taken together, Sweden, Norway, and Switzerland yield thirty cases.

Objectives of the Book

In this book, I attempt to combine theoretical rigor with empirical richness. On the theoretical level, I aim first to contribute to the debate on European integration by shifting the analytical focus from integration theory to integration policy theory and from deepening toward widening the European Union. I do so from the nonmember's point of view. For a long time, little attention has been paid to the consequences of integration in general and to the impact of integration on outsiders in particular. The research question engages a central theoretical issue in the study of integration: why and under what conditions would small, rich, open economies resist participation in regional integration?

On the empirical level, my main goal is not primary research into the domestic politics of Norway, Sweden, and Switzerland. The book's originality lies rather in assembling and coding the overall record of some thirty policy decisions across three countries and five decades. It presents the ever-closer relationship between the EU and the EFTA states not as "snapshot" views but as a path-dependent process. The varying willingness of states to further integrate is becoming a more and more salient policy issue and calls for theoretical treatment. Although some reluctant former EFTA states such as the United Kingdom, Denmark, and Sweden are already members of the European Union, future enlargement rounds will further augment the diversity of member states and deeply affect the EU's development.

Chapter 2 identifies the potential impediments to integration and the key actors in the three countries; Chapters 3 to 7 provide detailed analyses of the cases in the five decades; and Chapter 8 examines the implications and places the argument within a broader context.

Notes

1. Miljan, *The Reluctant Europeans,* has originally suggested the notion of "reluctant Europeans" for the Nordic countries.

2. The Treaty on European Union states in Articles 6(1) and 49 that any European state respecting the principles of liberty, democracy, and respect for human rights, fundamental freedoms, and the rule of law may apply to become a member of the Union.

3. See Hösli, "Trade Flows in Western Europe."

4. Some speculations have been formulated about the roots of "Europhobia," yet without an attempt at operationalization. For example, Underdal, "Diverging Roads to Europe"; Ljung, "The EFTA Countries' European Integration Policies"; Haaland Matláry, "'And Never the Twain Shall Meet?'"; Pfetsch, "Tensions in Sovereignty," pp. 120–137; and Grindheim, "Die Europäische Union," pp. 145–167.

5. Haas, *The Uniting of Europe*, pp. 313–317; and Schmitter, "Three Neofunctional Hypotheses About International Integration," p. 165.

6. Bulmer, "Domestic Politics and European Community Policy-Making," pp. 349–363.

7. For example, Wendt, "Collective Identity Formation and the International State," p. 385; and Katzenstein, "Introduction," p. 30. Pollack argues in a recent review article that realist, liberal, and institutionalist approaches are converging around a dominant rationalist research program, whereas constructivism has become the primary rival, but less developed, approach to the study of European integration. Pollack, "International Relations Theory and European Integration."

8. In fact, he only considers the growth rates of the original EC-6. Mattli, *The Logic of Regional Integration*, pp. 80–83.

9. Anderson and Kaltenthaler, "The Dynamics of Public Opinion Toward European Integration," pp. 188–189.

10. Mattli, *The Logic of Regional Integration*, pp. 85–89, 93–94.

11. Ibid., pp. 94–95.

12. Ingebritsen, *The Nordic States and European Unity*. Ingebritsen defines the leading sector as "the largest single contributor to national revenue" (pp. 10, 36) while presenting each country's principal exports (p. 117). At least, however, her argument requires consideration of the leading export sectors with regard to the EU market. Yet even those export shares do not necessarily determine the winners and losers from accession, as long as the level of trade barriers is ignored. For example, why should the Norwegian petroleum industry lobby in favor of EU membership if it already enjoys free access to the internal market?

13. Ibid., p. 115.

14. Neumann, "The Nordic States and European Unity," p. 91.

15. Moravcsik, *The Choice for Europe*, p. 7.

16. In fact, Ingebritsen elsewhere admits that "a thorough understanding of why the EU was more controversial in Norway than in Finland requires an understanding of *both* national interest *and* identity." Ingebritsen and Larson, "Interest and Identity," p. 210.

17. Marcussen et al., "Constructing Europe?" The same argument is put forward by Risse, "A European Identity?"

18. Marcussen et al., "Constructing Europe?" p. 627.

19. Wallace, "Small European States and European Policy-Making," p. 14.

20. For instance, Walsh found with regard to European monetary integration that national preferences were driven by domestic politics (that is, political coalitions and domestic institutions) rather than idea diffusion. Walsh, "National Preferences and International Institutions."

21. The export data in this study rely on Organization for Economic

Cooperation and Development (OECD) statistics for 1950–1961 and on the United Nations Commodity Trade Statistics Database for the years from 1963 on. Double-checking the two sources as well as other statistical publications yielded consistent results. The GDP/GNP data are based on the OECD national accounts. Since European integration made only limited progress in the free movement of services before the EC's internal market was completed, a focus on trade in goods seems justified.

22. Throughout the time periods, the sources have revealed that elites most often compare their country's export dependence on a specific market to its stake in other markets, whereas the GDP ratio is less often referred to. Hence, the overall export dependence is coded according to a simple algorithm that values the export ratio twice as highly as the GDP ratio. As empirically derived cutoff points for all cases (except for the very limited ECSC), the export ratio is considered "high" if it exceeds 40 percent, "medium" if it falls between 20 and 40 percent, and "low" if it remains below 20 percent. The GDP ratio is considered "high" beyond 10 percent, "medium" for a range of 4–10 percent, and "low" for 0–4 percent.

23. The leading sectors' export sensitivity follows the same coding rule as the overall export dependence. As points of reference, the sector share is considered "high" if it passes 20 percent, "medium" if it falls within 10–20 percent, and "low" for not exceeding 10 percent. The sector export ratio is regarded as "high" if it lies above 50 percent, "medium" for 30–50 percent, and "low" for less than 30 percent. The level of tariff barriers is "high" for a difference of more than 10 percent, "medium" for 5–10 percent, and "low" for 0–5 percent. Finally, the economic incentives index values the overall export dependence twice as much as the sectors' export sensitivity.

24. I adhere to Haas's definition of "elites" as "the leaders of all relevant political groups who habitually participate in the making of public decisions, whether as policy-makers in government, as lobbyists or as spokesmen of organised labour, higher civil servants and active politicians." Haas, *The Uniting of Europe*, p. 17.

25. Bloom, *Personal Identity, National Identity and International Relations*, p. 52.

26. Risse, "A European Identity?" p. 201.

27. North, *Institutions, Institutional Change and Economic Performance*, p. 3.

28. Risse, "A European Identity?" p. 201. I prefer to speak about the importance attached to components of identity threatened by integration rather than the identity-related meanings or understandings attached to them.

29. Rae and Taylor, *The Analysis of Political Cleavages*, p. 1.

30. Smith, *National Identity*, p. 14.

31. Kriesi et al., *New Social Movements in Western Europe*, pp. 3–4.

32. Unlike many constructivist studies, in this book I focus not only on the discourse within political parties (Marcussen et al., "Constructing Europe?" p. 616, Risse, "A European Identity?" p. 199) or parliaments (Banchoff, "German Identity and European Integration," p. 270) but consider statements of the economic elites as well. However, a lot of evidence had to be cut in the process of turning a 800-page dissertation into a publishable book.

33. In order for the domestic impediments to be significant, at least one of the indicators (institutions or cleavages) must be considered highly sensitive, whereas for them to be low, both indicators must be low. The mixed combinations fall into the medium category. The same coding rule holds for the geohistorical constraints.

34. Weber, *Gesammelte Aufsätze zur Religionssoziologie I*, p. 252. Collective ideas about national identity are not mere "transmission belts" for material interests

but may have an exogenous impact on national preferences. In constructivist terms, this is a rationalist claim. Constructivists claim that preferences change due to persuasion and socialization, that is, autonomous changes in ideas. Checkel and Moravcsik, "A Constructivist Research Program in EU Studies?" p. 229.

35. Keohane, "Ideas Part-way Down," p. 130. A group's ideational interest may, of course, turn into its material interest as well if it tries to gain income from it. By defending national identity drawing on rural culture, Norwegian farmers and fishermen also keep out EC competition and preserve subsidies.

36. Legro, *Cooperation Under Fire*, pp. 1–2.

37. Moravcsik, *The Choice for Europe*, chap. 1.

38. Therefore, it does not really matter whether preferences and identities are fixed prior to strategic interaction, as rationalists assume, or whether preferences and identities are being formed in the process of interaction, as constructivists claim.

39. See Moravcsik, "Taking Preferences Seriously." Rationalist approaches do not require a materialist ontology, but utility functions may include both material and ideational factors.

40. Katzenstein, "The Small European States in the International Economy," pp. 91–130.

41. Risse-Kappen, "Exploring the Nature of the Beast," p. 64.

42. See Zimmerman, "Issue Area and Foreign-Policy Process"; Kite, *Scandinavia Faces Europe*, chap. 3; and Moravcsik, "Preferences and Power in the European Community," pp. 488–496.

43. Katzenstein, *Small States in World Markets*, p. 126.

44. Magee, Brock, and Young, *Black Hole Tariff and Endogenous Political Theory*, pp. 101–110.

45. See Alt and Gilligan, "The Political Economy of Trading States," pp. 165–191; and Nelson, "Endogenous Tariff Theory," pp. 796–837.

46. Risse-Kappen, "Public Opinion, Domestic Structure, and Foreign Policy in Liberal Democracies," pp. 479–512.

47. Wessels, "Deepening Versus Widening?" p. 21.

48. A slight endogeneity problem might arise between the variables, in that integration policy itself may cause changes in the importance of market access or of political constraints. For instance, economic dependence on the EU might in the long run be a consequence, rather than a cause, of the level of integration aimed at. This feedback effect may introduce a positive bias that means that the effect of the economic incentives on integration policy is in reality smaller than estimated.

49. George and McKeown, "Case Studies and Theories of Organizational Decision Making," pp. 21–58.

50. Zürn, "Assessing State Preferences and Explaining Institutional Choice," pp. 298–302.

51. See Gorman and Kiljunen, *The Enlargement of the European Community;* Redmond, *The Next Mediterranean Enlargement of the European Community*; van Ham, *The EC, Eastern Europe and European Unity*; and Avery and Cameron, *The Enlargement of the European Union*. In the case of Ireland, the most important political motive was the desire to reduce dependence on Britain. Laffan, "Sovereignty and National Identity," p. 188.

52. Bulmer, "Britain and European Integration," p. 9. See also Wallace, "Foreign Policy and National Identity in the United Kingdom."

53. See Petersmann, *Die Souveränität des Britischen Parlaments in den Europäischen Gemeinschaften*. According to the doctrine of parliamentary sover-

eignty, Parliament has the right to make or unmake any law, and no person or body has a right to override or set aside its legislation.

54. *Times*, "Equal Footing with Great Power Groups," p. 8.

55. Denmark did not permit the stationing of foreign forces on its territory (except for Greenland) in peacetime nor the deployment or storage of tactical nuclear weapons. In the European Union, it has made a reservation with regard to defense cooperation and remained an observer in the Western European Union.

56. Worre, "Danish Public Opinion and the European Community," p. 211.

57. Petersen, "Denmark and the European Union 1985–96," pp. 185–210; and von Dosenrode-Lynge, *Westeuropäische Kleinstaaten in der EG und EPZ*, pp. 298–299, 315. In 1992, the Danes voted "no" on the Maastricht Treaty on political union, and in 2001 the Irish rejected the Treaty of Nice, which dealt primarily with institutional reforms.

58. Østergård, "Peasants and Danes," p. 23.

59. Esping-Andersen and Korpi, "From Poor Relief to Institutional Welfare States," pp. 72–73.

60. See von Dosenrode, "Denmark," pp. 52–68.

61. The Danish Constitution envisages that a parliamentary minority may demand that a bill passed by the *Folketing* is first approved by a referendum before becoming law. Its purpose is to force the majority into taking account of public opinion. Fifty-six percent of the voters said "yes" to the Single European Act. Petersen, "Denmark and the European Union 1985–96," pp. 185–210.

62. See Luif, *On the Road to Brussels*.

63. Heer, *Der Kampf um die österreichische Identität*.

64. Kreissler, *L'Autriche, treizième de douze*, pp. 56–61.

65. Nydegger, "Die Einstellung der drei EFTA-Neutralen gegenüber der EWG," p. 14. In the "Germany clause," Austria renounces any unification with Germany.

66. Tiilikainen, *Europe and Finland*, p. 168.

67. Kristinsson, "Iceland," pp. 245–253; and Gstöhl, "Successfully Squaring the Circle."

2

Political Constraints

Is the nation-state still the terminal community in Western Europe? Does it still provide the dominant source of identity for its citizens? Is its national myth intact and unchallenged? . . . The weakening of national myths is least evident in Switzerland, the Nordic countries, and Britain.
—Ernst B. Haas, *The Limits of Liberal Nationalism in Western Europe,*
p. 347

Sweden's Domestic Structure and Foreign Policy Legacy

Two deeply rooted features have dominated postwar Swedish political life: "in the first place, the creation of a democratic, full-employment welfare state on the basis of a modernized, export-oriented industry and, secondly, the pursuit of a foreign policy that kept the country out of international confrontations by avoiding all binding commitments to great-power politics."[1] "Neutrality and *folkhemmet* [the people's home] were thus the pillars of Sweden's projection of itself into the world."[2] For a long time, supranational European integration threatened the successful record of the Swedish (or Nordic) model as well as Sweden's long-standing freedom from alliances (*alliansfrihet*) since the Catholic, conservative, and capitalist European Community (EC) countries pursued very different welfare policies and were members of NATO.[3]

Domestic Constraints

Among the distinct features of the Nordic model are the comprehensiveness of social policy, the high degree of institutionalization of the social entitlement principle, and the solidaristic and universalist nature of social legislation. The labor movements have unionized around 80 percent of all wage-

25

earners, and the Nordic states have generally been committed to full employment, a centralized system of wage bargaining, policies aiming at an egalitarian distribution of income, and access to comprehensive social benefits. These characteristics depended, on the one hand, on the historical compromise between trade unions and employers and, on the other hand, on the social democrats' alliance with the farmers, which allowed them to exchange agricultural subsidies for political support.[4]

The plans of the Swedish model originate in the Great Depression of the 1930s, and they were gradually put into effect after World War II by the social democratic governments.[5] Until the late 1980s, the Swedish *folkhemmet* has actively been maintained by the Social Democratic Party with the support of the nonsocialist parties. In fact, the "Social Democrats have captured the idea of the nation—they have successfully interpreted the national identity as one of an ever-reforming welfare state, a national social community always striving to make itself more of a community."[6] Even though it is primarily a postwar achievement, the institution of the welfare state, which fits into the specific Swedish concept of common rights, has acquired qualities of a national myth.[7] Moreover, the Social Democratic Party and the Swedish model have become so entangled that "the crisis of social democracy would be a crisis of national identity as well."[8]

All Scandinavian countries present a rather homogeneous religious structure dominated by the Lutheran state church. The fundamentalist Lutheran tradition in their hinterlands was less politicized in Sweden and Denmark than in Norway. The same is true for the issue of public control over alcohol consumption. The only notable division tending to supplement the political left-right split has been "the urban-rural axis, owing to: (a) the geographical size of the country; (b) its sparse population; (c) its uniquely rapid transition from agrarian to modern industrial society . . .; and (d) its large landed agrarian class."[9] This urban-rural cleavage has, however, been much less pronounced in Sweden than in Norway. The Swedish peasantry never suffered the yoke of feudalism but was traditionally entitled to free ownership of land and forest, and the *allemansrätt* (everyman's right) guarantees everybody free access to nature irrespective of ownership. Hence, no lasting cleavages have remained in Swedish society, and "the gospels of evangelism, nationalism, ethnicism and regional matters have had little impact on 20th century Swedish politics."[10]

Policymaking Process

One common characteristic of the political economies of Sweden, Norway, and Switzerland is their corporatist structure, even though it comes in different variants.[11] According to Peter Katzenstein, the three defining traits of democratic corporatism are (1) an ideology of social partnership (rather than class conflict), (2) a relatively centralized and concentrated system of interest groups, and (3) voluntary, informal coordination of conflicting objectives through continuous bargaining among interest groups, state bureaucracies, and political parties.[12] The liberal corporatism of Switzerland is characterized by strong, internationally oriented business and weak labor movements and the social corporatism of Norway by weak, nationally oriented business and strong labor unions. Sweden combines elements from both patterns—Swedish business is quite centralized, powerful, and international, and the labor unions are also strong and centralized.

The small countries' democratic corporatism was born amid the economic crisis of the 1930s, fascism, and World War II.[13] It provided them with the capacity to successfully combine economic flexibility with political stability. In Sweden, the truce between the business community and the labor movement, organized in the Swedish Confederation of Trade Unions (LO-Sweden),[14] resulted in the "Saltsjöbaden Agreement" of 1938. In exchange for labor peace, openness to the world economy, and continued private control over property and capital markets, the Swedish Employers' Federation (SAF) acquiesced in a social democratic government, higher labor costs, a relatively expansive fiscal policy, and growing welfare services.[15] Hence, the development of a corporatist system was closely linked to the institutionalization of the welfare state.

For more than fifty years, the corporatist relationships in Sweden seemed particularly close: unions, business, and other interest organizations were represented on publicly mandated boards, agencies, and commissions, and the organizations themselves provided important services to the public.[16] Moreover, the level of participation in representative organizations has been very high. As a result, these interest associations attained a quasi-legal status and a right to speak for their segments of society in the policy process. One of the most important industrial associations is the Federation of Swedish Industries (SI). It represents companies that account for approximately three-quarters of Sweden's industrial output and almost all of its visible exports. The Swedish Trade Council (Exportrådet) is an export-promoting authority that aims to help Swedish companies do business abroad. In addition, the National Board of Trade (Kommerskollegium), as an independent governmental agency, advises the Swedish government on trade policy.

The Scandinavian states are characterized by a unitary tradition with centralized political structures. Their political landscapes have long been dominated by five parties and two political blocs: the Conservative, Liberal, and Agrarian (or Center) Parties formed one cluster, and the Social Democratic (or Labor) and Communist Parties another.[17] Only the Agrarian Parties fit less neatly into the left-right continuum since they have mainly capitalized on the urban-rural cleavage. The Swedish party system has traditionally comprised—from left to right—the Communist Party, which became the Left Party (Vänsterpartiet); the Social Democratic Party (SAP); the Agrarian Party (Centerpartiet); the Liberal Party (FP); and the Conservative Party (Moderata Samlingspartiet, formerly Högerpartiet).[18] There are also some small parties, such as the Christian Democratic Party (KD, formerly Kristdemokratiska Samhällspartiet), which has had parliamentary representation since 1991; the Green Party (Miljöpartiet de Gröna), which first made it into the Riksdag (the Swedish parliament) in 1988; and the populist Discontent Party (NYD), which entered the Riksdag in 1991 (and disappeared from it again three years later).

Until 1988 the Riksdag (whose bicameral system was abandoned in 1971) was exclusively composed of the five major parties. This stability was in particular due to the balance between the two party blocs of the socialists (SAP, Vänsterpartiet) and the nonsocialists (Conservative Party, Agrarian Party, FP) and a 4 percent hurdle in national elections (the minimum share of votes needed to gain seats in parliament). The social democrats, who hold close bonds with the labor unions, had been in office without interruption for over forty years until 1976. The nonsocialist parties ruled only from 1976 to 1982 and 1991 to 1994. No other democracy has had such a dominant party as Sweden's Social Democratic Party.

Geohistorical Constraints

Sweden has not experienced any relevant periods of foreign rule or occupation. On the contrary, it had itself governed foreign lands in the past. In the seventeenth century, under King Gustav Adolph, Sweden conquered territories in the Baltic, Poland, and Prussia and played an important role in the Thirty Years' War. Moreover, the Swedish kingdom won the three provinces in the southern part of its peninsula from Denmark. Swedish great power politics ended with a defeat in the Great Northern War against the combined forces of Denmark, Poland, and Russia. In the Treaty of Nystad in 1721, Sweden lost most of its provinces on the other side of the Baltic Sea. During the Napoleonic wars, Sweden was forced to cede Finland to Russia in 1809, and it lost its last possessions in northern Germany. Nevertheless, Sweden in 1812 allied with Russia against Napoleon. After a successful invasion of Denmark, an ally of the French emperor, the Danish king had to cede Norway to Sweden in 1814.

Since then, Sweden has enjoyed peace as a "result of caution and opportunism of Sweden's leaders combined with a healthy dose of good fortune, rather than any vision in policy."[19] In 1848, Sweden and Norway provided the Danish king with troops against his rebellious subjects in Holstein. In 1864, however, the Swedish government refused to follow its king, who had promised support to Denmark when it tried to incorporate Schleswig. Constitutional reforms and the rapid growth of the liberals and social democrats increased domestic pressure against military adventures. At the beginning of the twentieth century, the left successfully promoted a benign acceptance of Norwegian independence and a general foreign policy of neutrality.

In 1912 and in 1938, Sweden, Norway, and Denmark jointly declared their commitment to neutrality. The Swedish government rejected Finland's appeal for intervention, both in its struggle for independence in 1917 and against the Soviet attack in the Winter War of 1939–1940 despite a strong public opinion in favor of assistance. After the German invasion of Denmark and Norway in 1940, the Swedish government ignored the popular movement in support of Norway and tried to adhere to strict neutrality. In order to stay out of the war, however, Sweden permitted the German military to sail through its territorial waters and to fly within its airspace, and Swedish industry supplied Germany with key war materials. Even though Sweden had earlier refused the transit of French and British troops, it allowed German troops to cross Sweden toward northern Norway as well as from Norway to Finland.

In contrast to the permanent neutrality of other Western European countries, Sweden's neutrality has not been based upon an international treaty. The Swedish policy of "nonalignment in peace aiming at neutrality in war" is self-proclaimed and self-maintained. International law does not prescribe a neutral state's behavior in peacetime, but a permanently neutral state may pursue a certain policy to enhance its trustworthiness. In the postwar period, Sweden has made a significant effort to maintain its military capability, and it has actively tried to project the image of a country taking an independent stand on the issues dividing the great powers. Its international ambitions have embraced strong support for the United Nations, international law, disarmament, foreign aid, and the global environment.[20] The commitment to a just and equitable world order has in many ways reflected salient features of the Swedish political system, such as the national consensus formation or the sacrosanct welfare system, and the moral superiority of this worldview was often defended with missionary enthusiasm.[21] Neutrality offered a "third-way identity" between East and West.[22] In the official reasoning on neutrality and EC membership during the Cold War, one argument was particularly decisive: the maintenance of an independent foreign policy.[23] Even though after the Cold War neutrality has lost much of its long-standing salience, "the strong ties between the policy of neutrality and Swedish national identity may explain why, in the debate on Sweden's future security arrangement, the idea of Sweden as a neutral power in world affairs still occupies an important position."[24]

Norway's Domestic
Structure and Foreign Policy Legacy

Norway's national identity has been marked by its long struggle for independence, its geography, and its social structure, which construct manifold obstacles to supranational integration.[25] Such constraints may in particular emanate from the traditional center-periphery cleavage, the Norwegian version of the Nordic model and the history of foreign rule.

Domestic Constraints

During the worldwide depression in the 1930s, the social democrats in Norway succeeded in forming a political alliance with the Agrarian Party to support their program for job creation, welfare reforms, and agricultural subsidies. In 1935, the Norwegian Confederation of Trade Unions (LO-Norway) and the Norwegian Employers' Federation (NAF) signed the "Basic Agreement" (*Hovedavtale*), which covered many pay and labor agreements. Since then, they have jointly determined wages and incomes. Ten years later, all political parties agreed on a common program for welfare policy (the *Folketrygd* program).[26] Norway lacked the internationalized, large-scale corporate structure of Sweden, which may help explain why the conservatives accepted state economic leadership. Norwegian business faced difficulties in mobilizing the necessary capital for industrialization, and the economy was characterized by extensive state ownership of industry and banks. In the "Golden Age" of the 1950s–1960s, Norway's welfare model was the one with the strongest element of economic planning, state control of money markets, and strong efforts at regional policies. Norwegian identity became closely tied to the establishment of the welfare state.[27]

Marked and persistent societal differences have been documented throughout the history of Norwegian politics: a geographical cleavage between the eastern center and the southwestern and northern peripheries; cultural conflicts over linguistic policy, alcohol policy, and the control of the church; and economic conflicts, such as the struggle of the working class against owners and employers.[28] Norway, like Sweden, does not have ethnic minorities except for a small group of Sami (about 45,000 people). However, there are two major Norwegian languages, the rural language *nynorsk* (or *landsmål*) and the standard *bokmål* (or *riksmål*) spoken in the cities. Out of dissatisfaction with the Danish standard for written Norwegian and as an element of nation building, *nynorsk* was created out of several oral dialects in the 1850s. Even though *bokmål* dominates today, both languages are still spoken and taught at school. In addition, an orthodox lay movement dating back to the eighteenth century established itself within the Lutheran state church. This pietistic fundamentalism has been strong in the west and south of the country. In the same areas, a popular movement against the consumption of alcohol emerged. It won a referendum campaign for total prohibition in 1919, but prohibition was repealed in 1926. Ever since, the teetotalers' movement has acted as a pressure group to maintain the strict public monopoly on the sale of wine and spirits.

Norwegian society has thus been influenced by three countercultures based on religion, language, and abstinence and has accordingly split up into the secularized central and urban regions where none of the countercultures were strong, the western periphery where all of them prevailed, and some mixed regions. In other words, western Norway has been marked by strong Lutheran orthodoxy, teetotalism, and the usage of *nynorsk*, whereas the rest of the country, in particular the center around Oslo, has been rather secularized and uses *bokmål* as a written language. Norwegian nationalism provides a good example of how nations may be "invented" with the creation of their own language, the transfer of certain aspects of peasant or fisherman culture into the urban context, and the selection of national symbols and customs.[29]

The center-periphery conflict represents the combined effect of the traditional linguistic, religious, and urban-rural cleavages.[30] The political coalitions with regard to Norway's membership in the European Communities have usually formed along this conflict line.[31] The societal cleavages reinforce each other, whereas the party lines are crosscut. This potential for politicization is especially visible in the results of opinion polls, elections, and referenda and, together with the "Norwegian model," produces latent domestic constraints on integration.

Policymaking Process

Norway's social corporatism is characterized by strong, centralized labor unions and politically weak and relatively decentralized business communities with a national orientation.[32] Executives are often in a bargaining situation, both within the governmental apparatus and with organized interests in society. This process of "integrated participation" can take many forms, such as interest groups' participation in the networks of governmental committees, commissions, councils, and boards that initiate, design, advise, decide upon, implement, and administer governmental policies.[33] As Kvavik points out, "Few political systems are distinguished by as elaborate and active a network of interest groups as one finds in Norway, and few polities have an interest group system as pervasive and highly formalized."[34]

The most important industrial associations are the Confederation of Norwegian Business and Industry (NHO), created in 1989 by a merger of the Federation of Norwegian Industries (NI), the Federation of Norwegian Craftsmen (Norges Håndverkerforbund), and the NAF. Its members represent a turnover of goods and services equivalent to half of Norway's GDP. The Norwegian Trade Council (Norges Eksportråd) is a semiprivate organization that promotes Norwegian exports and advises the Foreign Ministry in matters of trade policy. Other important interest groups are the Norwegian Shipowners' Association (Norges Rederiforbund) and Association of Commerce and Services (Handels- og Servicenæringens Hovedorganisasjon), which was created in 1990 by the merger of the Federation of Norwegian Retailers (Norges Handelsstands Forbund) and other organizations.

Norway is a rather unitary state, built up around the political center of Oslo, which enjoys economic dominance. In the 1970s, reforms were carried out to introduce more decentralization for the regional and local governments. Norway's political parties have gradually emerged around the traditional social divisions.[35] To a lesser extent than Sweden, Norway is characterized by a left-right division.[36] In general, the Labor Party and the Conservative Party have been at opposite poles on issues within the advanced corporate urban economy, but they tended to take the same side in territorial-cultural conflicts of center versus periphery, religious activism, or language. The latter issues differentiate the parties of the middle from those of the left and the right.

The Norwegian party system comprises both a socialist bloc, with the Labor Party (DNA) and the Socialist People's Party (SF), which in 1975 became the Socialist Left Party (SV); and a nonsocialist bloc, with the Conservative Party (Høyre), the agrarian Center Party (SP), the Christian Democratic Party (KRF), the Liberal Party (Venstre), which split into two parties as a result of the 1972 referendum but reunited again in 1988, the Green Party (Miljøpartiet De Grønne), established in 1989, as well as the populist, liberal Progress Party (FRP) created in 1973.[37] Since 1945, the Labor Party and the Conservatives have been the most important parties in terms of votes, members, economic resources, and seats in the Norwegian parliament, the Storting. In the postwar era, the Labor Party has usually constituted the government, except for short periods of bourgeois coalitions in 1963, 1965–1971, 1972–1973, 1981–1986, 1989–1990, 1997–2000, and since October 2001.

Geohistorical Constraints

After the establishment of Norway's dynastic union with Denmark in 1380, it was gradually incorporated as a "colonial" territory under the Danish crown and increasingly administered from the mother country. The real "Danish period" began in 1536, when Norway's national government disappeared and the Catholic Church was replaced by the Lutheran state church. In the Treaty of Kiel of 1814, Sweden acquired Norway, yet without the ancient Norse Atlantic possessions, which were retained by the Danish king (e.g., Iceland, the Faroe Islands, and Greenland). The Norwegians would have preferred independence, but they could not resist Sweden's military power. They succeeded, however, in adopting a constitution and obtaining relatively favorable terms in the 1815 Act of Union (*Riksakt*) with Sweden. The Swedish king became king of Norway and conducted its foreign policy, but Norway remained rather independent in domestic affairs.

Tensions began to arise in the 1860s over Swedish pressures for a revision of the *Riksakt* and an integration of both countries' defense forces.[38] In 1895, the two countries were on the verge of war but decided to pursue negotiations. These negotiations failed in 1905, and the Norwegian parliament unilaterally declared that the union with Sweden was dissolved. The Swedish government presented Norway with several conditions for recognition of Norwegian independence, among them a plebiscite, which was held shortly afterward. Separation was approved of almost by unanimity, and the terms of dissolution were laid down in a convention. The Norwegians elected and crowned a Danish prince as their new king in 1916, the first king of Norway in over five hundred years.

Norway managed to remain outside World War I, but it suffered great losses in its merchant marine. On the eve of World War II in 1938, the Scandinavian countries revised and amended their joint neutrality rules. On 9 April 1940, however, German troops invaded Denmark and Norway. Whereas Denmark capitulated almost immediately, the Norwegians preferred to fight. After the Allies left, the Norwegian army surrendered, and the king and the government fled to England. The Germans established a Norwegian puppet government but did not succeed in a large-scale Nazification. Instead, a resistance movement was organized, many Norwegian soldiers and police were trained abroad, and the considerable Norwegian merchant fleet sided with the Allies. The liberation of Norway began in the fall of 1944 and officially ended with the German capitulation.

Norway's experience as the weaker part of several "unions" with other countries led to strong opposition to any form of foreign interference in Norwegian affairs.[39] Norwegian nationalism suffered from a "double lopsidedness—it was directed against Swedish political dominance and against Danish cultural dominance,"[40] and it was strengthened by the saga of Norway's heroic resistance against German occupation in World War II. This historical experience and the efforts at nation building have made Norwegians view integration in a rather negative way.[41] Fears of losing the traditional Norwegian way of life in another "union" figured prominently in the EC debates. The association of national identity with a constant struggle for independence in connection with the cleavages in its society indicate that "historical circumstances have given Norway a 'double dose' of counter-culture identification."[42]

After World War II, Norway resumed a foreign policy that had some of the same traits as Sweden's "third way," focusing on development aid, disarmament, and environmental and other internationalist issues.[43] German occupation and the Soviet pressure on countries like Finland and Czechoslovakia taught Norway that neutrality was only second best to joining a powerful military alliance. It rejected the Swedish proposal for a Scandinavian defense union and joined the North Atlantic Treaty Organization.[44] In spite of clearly anchoring its security policy in the West, Norway's commitment has remained cautious. It has not permitted the stationing of foreign troops on Norwegian soil in peacetime or the deployment or storage of tactical nuclear weapons.[45] Regarding this reluctance, Nils Ørvik argues, "The deepest cause, which is also the most difficult to grasp, is the psychological heritage of 500 years of foreign rule."[46] As a NATO member since 1949, Norway's alignment policy has never constituted an obstacle to membership in the European Communities.[47] On the contrary, the Norwegian governments would have liked to participate in the European Political Cooperation (EPC), established in 1970, which was replaced in 1993 by the Common Foreign and Security Policy (CFSP), including the gradual formulation of a common defense policy, but participation was possible only for EC members.

Switzerland's Domestic Structure and Foreign Policy Legacy

The major components of Swiss identity are rather straightforward. It is marked by a nation-building history closely tied to a fight for independence, similar to Norway's, and a long, strong tradition of neutrality, similar to Sweden's. In addition, the institutions of federalism and direct democracy and an ethnolinguistic cleavage characterize Swiss politics. A great consensus seems to prevail that these features belong to the historical identity of Switzerland.[48]

Domestic Constraints

In contrast to Sweden and Norway, the welfare state has never posed a problem for Switzerland's integration policy because its social system lies within the tradition of continental welfare regimes. The country has, however, faced other specific obstacles toward joining the European Community, in particular direct democracy, federalism, and neutrality.[49]

Swiss federalism and direct democracy have old historical roots and were institutionalized in the Federal Constitution of 1848. Many Swiss have worried that EC membership would reduce the cantons' legal freedom of action, limit their influence on federal legislation, and lead to a transfer of power from the cantons to the federal level.[50] More important than the threat to federalism seem the constraints on direct democracy in the domains of EC competences. The two main features of direct democracy are the referendum and the initiative. Every bill approved by the Swiss parliament is open to a national referendum if within ninety days a petition is made against it bearing the signature of at least 50,000 citizens. Referenda on constitutional modifications and on certain international treaties, such as membership in the European Union (EU), are compulsory and need a double majority of voters and cantons. An initiative of 100,000 signatures can demand that the Federal Constitution be amended or partially revised. These popular rights encourage government and parliament to anticipate possible opposition and lead them to consult parties and interest organizations at an early stage of the decisionmaking process. In the case of EU membership, the range of possible initiatives and referenda would be restricted since Community law precedes national law.[51]

In comparison to Scandinavian countries, Swiss society is rather heterogeneous. With German-, French-, Italian-, and Romansh-speaking groups, Switzerland displays high ethnolinguistic fragmentation. The predominant language is German (or *Schwyzerdütsch*), spoken by roughly two-thirds of the population. About one-fifth speak French in western Switzerland, and Italian is restricted to the southern part and is spoken by about 10 percent of the population. Romansh is spoken by barely 1 percent in the mountainous southeast.

The urban-rural conflict still has a latent mobilizing capacity in both the French- and the German-speaking areas but to a greater extent in the latter, where it is reinforced by historical populist, antiestablishment feelings. Many referenda have been characterized by a gap between the liberal cities and the more conservative countryside. In addition, the border cantons have traditionally been more open toward their neighboring countries than the inner core of Switzerland. However, the country lacks a true center, and federalism is likely to have pacified any urban-rural conflict. Hence, "the centre-periphery cleavage is assumed to be relatively unsalient in the Swiss federal system."[52] The religious antagonism between Protestants and Catholics was pacified early on through the integration of both sides into national politics. It has had practically no influence on integration policy.[53]

Unlike Norway's societal divisions, Switzerland's linguistic, religious, and regional cleavages are to a large extent crosscutting. Not all Swiss Germans are Catholic, conservative, and rural, and not all French-speaking

Swiss are Protestant, liberal, and urban. An analysis of the results of national referenda over a period of more than 100 years revealed that language was a more important factor than religion, education, age, or party membership.[54] The ethnolinguistic cleavage is clearly the dominant political cleavage in Swiss society, in particular with regard to external relations. In general, the francophone Swiss (*Romands*) tend to have a more cosmopolitan and integration-friendly outlook, whereas the German-speaking majority is more oriented toward traditional values and is less socially egalitarian than their French- or Italian-speaking compatriots.[55]

Policymaking Process

As in Sweden and Norway, the economic and political crises of the mid-1930s led to a new national consensus in Switzerland. In 1937, the Swiss Watchmakers' and Metalworkers' Union (SMUV), the largest trade union, and the Swiss Federation of Commerce and Industry (SHIV; often referred to, according to its managing committee, as Vorort), the largest employers' association, concluded the "Peace Agreement" (*Friedensabkommen*). The employers recognized the union as an equal partner on questions of labor market and social policy, and the union replaced its unconditional right to strike with a system of mediation and arbitration. Since this first agreement, social partnership has become standard practice in all industrial sectors.

Switzerland embodies the liberal version of democratic corporatism with politically strong, internationally oriented, and centralized business communities and relatively decentralized and weak labor unions.[56] The Swiss economy is highly cartelized and has many professional organizations. Employers have been organized into two main associations, the Vorort and the Federation of Swiss Employers' Organizations (ZSAO). Other employers' organizations are the Swiss Union of Small and Medium Enterprises (SGV) and the Swiss Farmers' Union (SBV). The Vorort focuses on economic policy, and the ZSAO deals mainly with matters of social policy. The Vorort represents most professional associations and chambers of commerce and covers almost all exports. In 2000, it was transformed into a new association under the name of Economie Suisse. It maintains close contacts with the Swiss authorities and often assumes expert functions, in particular with regard to trade policy.

Swiss corporatism emerged as a result of the threat of war rather than out of the left's own power. Only about one-third of the workforce has been unionized, and the labor unions are split into several different federations. The major umbrella organization is the Swiss Confederation of Trade Unions (SGB), followed by the Swiss Federation of Salaried Employees (VSA) and the Swiss Confederation of Christian Trade Unions (CNG). In spite of their weakness, Swiss unions have been extensively co-opted into policy networks.[57] Since 1947 the Federal Constitution has contained a provision that promotes the direct consultation of "interested economic groups" in the legislative process. Compared to Sweden and Norway, Switzerland's industrial policy has been rather passive, its income policy almost nonexistent, and wage bargaining highly decentralized. Moreover, the Swiss arrangements between the unions, business, and the state administration have remained sector-specific.

In comparison to the unitary Scandinavian states, Switzerland's political structure is best described as a federalism imposed from below as a result of the voluntary historical association of the cantons. The Federal Council is elected by a joint session of the two chambers (Nationalrat and Ständerat) of the Swiss parliament, the Bundesversammlung. According to the principle of cabinet collegiality, all seven federal councilors are of equal rank, and the presidency of the confederation rotates on an annual basis. There is thus no influential prime minister and no government-versus-opposition pattern.

The Swiss party system is highly fragmented along religious, class, and territorial lines. The Constitution of 1848 was the result of a short civil war between the Protestant liberals and the Catholic conservatives. Against the dominant urban commercial and industrial forces that organized in the Radical Democratic Party (FDP), the defeated Catholics founded a conservative party that later became the Christian Democratic People's Party (CVP). Another part of the opposition was organized by the agrarian Swiss People's Party (SVP) in the Protestant cantons. The electoral potential of the Social Democratic Party (SPS) was restricted by the presence of the Catholic CVP. In the postwar period, these four main political parties have been represented in the Federal Council, according to the different languages and regions and more or less proportionally to the parties' electoral strength. This "magic formula" comprises two radicals, two Christian democrats, two socialists, and one member from the Swiss People's party. The other, smaller parties, appearing at different points on the left-right continuum, have been represented in parliament but not in the federal government.[58]

Geohistorical Constraints

In the thirteenth century, some Swiss German valleys had become well-established communities (*Talgenossenschaften*) of largely free peasants under the leadership of powerful families whose most important civic activity was the administration of justice. The head of the valley (*Ammann*) adjudicated in the name of the emperor, whose direct subjects the communities claimed to be. Several cantons had established communal self-government in the form of the *Landsgemeinden*, the assemblies of free citizens. To resist competing claims after the death of King Rudolf of Habsburg and to prevent conflicts among themselves, the valley communities of Uri, Schwyz, and Unterwalden formed a (defensive) league. In their famous oath taken on the Rütli meadow in 1291, which came to symbolize the birth of the Swiss Confederation (*Eidgenossenschaft*), they swore that "we shall accept no judge nor recognise him in any way if he exercise his office for any reward or for money or if he is not one of our own and an inhabitant of the valleys."[59] The confederation grew as the original cantons formed alliances with other areas. The Swiss were famous for their military capabilities, which expressed themselves in expansion abroad, civil wars at home, and considerable mercenary services. The legend of William Tell dates back to the late fifteenth century and is rooted in the Swiss indignation toward the increasing demands of the *landvogts*. The hardy mountaineer who defied the Habsburgs and refused to bow down to anybody became a symbol of Swiss liberty.[60]

The Swiss patchwork of independent political units was overrun by the French in 1798, when revolutionary troops occupied the confederation and established the "Helvetic Republic." Even though this reform introduced some achievements of the French Revolution such as equality before the law, the separation of powers, uniformity of weights and measures, and a single code of justice, the new centralized order lasted only for five years before Napoleon gave the Swiss a new constitution. The so-called Act of Mediation of 1802 restored the rights of the cantons under a loose confederation and elevated some previously subject or allied territories to cantons. In 1848, a federal state was established whose constitution made foreign policy a federal prerogative. Nine years later, Switzerland attained its final territorial integrity with the acquisition of the canton of Neuchâtel.

The desire for independence is deeply rooted in the collective memories of the Swiss. Switzerland has liberated itself from foreign rulers and has resisted subjugation by the European great powers. A profound mistrust of "foreign judges" provokes the same negative reactions in Switzerland as does the notion of a "union" in Norway. Switzerland's internal cohesion has been strengthened by the mobilization against a common enemy, starting with the Habsburg empire and continuing with Napoleon, Nazi Germany, and the communist threat during the Cold War. The national myth of Switzerland being a special case (*Sonderfall*) in Europe was further bolstered by the period of peace since the Napoleonic wars, an experience the Swiss share with the Swedes.

The roots of Swiss neutrality date back to the sixteenth century for four main reasons.[61] First, the Swiss cantons refused to give up their local autonomy for a common, centralized leadership, which would have been necessary to continue their expansive foreign policies after their defeats in

Italy at the beginning of the sixteenth century. Second, Swiss participation in the religious wars would have destroyed the confederation, which was split in half between Catholics and Protestants. Third, the European balance of power was a prerequisite for Swiss neutrality, and the latter became an important element for the maintenance of the balance. Fourth, without neutrality, Switzerland most probably would have turned into the great powers' theater of war because of its geopolitical position at a strategic north-south connection.

Since Switzerland, unlike Sweden, is not a nation defined by a common language, religion, or culture, but a nation by will (*Willensnation*), neutrality also fulfilled an internal function. Neutrality's domestic "predecessor" was the practice of *Stillesitzen* (to sit still) that had been used in different alliances between cantons since the late fourteenth century and obliged them not to intervene in the conflicts of other cantons. Swiss neutrality was formally recognized by the European great powers at the peace congresses of Vienna and Paris in 1815. The Federal Constitution of 1848 explicitly mentions neutrality as a means of foreign policy. Nevertheless, Switzerland, like Sweden, could give up its neutrality unilaterally since it never accepted an international legal obligation to remain neutral.

During World War II, Switzerland was completely surrounded by the Axis Powers. Swiss policy alternated between compliance with the new political reality in Europe and determined resistance.[62] The government accepted the transit of goods destined for the belligerents through its territory, but—unlike Sweden—not the transit of foreign troops or weapons. It continued to trade with all belligerents and exported war materials to both sides, in particular to Germany. Moreover, the Swiss government had to provide considerable financial credits to Germany and Italy.

According to the traditional Swiss conception, a permanently neutral state must aim at a policy that avoids any obligations in peacetime that might, in the case of war, prevent it from following the rules of neutrality law. Since World War II (and until recently), these so-called antecedent effects (*Vorwirkungen*) of neutrality have been interpreted as comprising not only abstention from military alliances but also an economic policy that prevents the country from being drawn into an international conflict.[63] The decisive criterion has been whether a commitment entered into during peace could be canceled during war to regain the independence necessary to sustain neutrality. With regard to EC membership, it has often been argued that the credibility of a policy of neutrality might be affected by the loss of treaty-making power in a customs union, the obligation to participate in economic sanctions, or the fact that basically all EC members belonged to the same military alliance.[64]

The idea that neutrality prevented war has reinforced its significance for national identity and contributed to Swiss skepticism about foreign influence. In contrast to Sweden and Norway, Switzerland has hesitated to join international political institutions (e.g., the Council of Europe) and is still not a member of the United Nations.

Cross-Country Comparison

Since World War II, all three countries have enjoyed relatively stable domestic situations. Their corporatist systems and the long dominance of the social democrats in Sweden, of Labor in Norway, and of the coalition governments in Switzerland have contributed to this stability. Although Sweden and Norway constitute competitive democracies with a marked political left-right contest, Switzerland is a consociational democracy with left-right coalition governments.

With regard to sociopolitical institutions, Switzerland shows a unique combination of federalism and direct democracy, whereas Sweden and Norway have maintained a particular Nordic model of the welfare state. In contrast to the rather homogeneous Nordic societies, Switzerland stands out as fragmented by language (and religion). All three countries show electoral differences between the cities and the countryside, but to varying degrees. Norwegian society has been characterized by a very strong center-periphery cleavage, of which the religious and linguistic splits are a part. The Swiss regional split is weaker and crosscut by other divisions, in particular the dominating ethnolinguistic cleavage. Sweden's society lacks any relevant cleavages, except for the relatively weak urban-rural divide.

Although occupation in World War II was crucial for the choice between return to neutrality or NATO membership, a "colonial" experience of foreign rule seems to have been more decisive for a country's attitude toward supranational integration. For the young nation-state Norway, a founding member of NATO, the "Euro-compatibility" of its foreign policy has not posed a problem. In Switzerland and Norway, resistance to foreign rule has played a crucial role in nation building. The fact that both Sweden and Switzerland have succeeded in staying out of World War II was likely to reinforce their belief in neutrality. In the postwar period, Swedish foreign policy has been particularly contingent upon the East-West conflict and has had a distinct internationalist orientation. Switzerland, whose neutrality has historically fulfilled a domestic cohesion function, has been more cautious, even though it is situated in the heart of the continent and the Scandinavian countries are located on the periphery of Europe.

Table 2.1 highlights (in *italics*) the potential impediments to integration generated by national identity. The following five chapters discuss the varying importance of these political constraints, together with the economic incentives for Sweden, Norway, and Switzerland to take integration steps in each decade, to explain these countries' national preferences.

Table 2.1   Potential Domestic and Geohistorical Constraints (shown in italics) on Integration

	Sweden	Norway	Switzerland
Welfare state model	*Nordic model*	*Nordic model*	Continental
Political system	Representational	Representational	*Direct democracy*
Governance structure	Centralized	Centralized	*Federalism*
Religious cleavage	—	Orthodox-liberal Lutheranism	Catholic-Protestant
Ethnolinguistic cleavage	—	Nynorsk-bokmål	*German-Romance*
Regional cleavage	Urban-rural	*Center-periphery*	Urban-rural
"Colonization" by	—	*Denmark until 1814, and Sweden until 1905*	*Habsburg Empire until fifteenth century*
Occupation in World War II by	—	*Germany, 1940–1945*	—
Alignment policy	*Freedom from alliances*	NATO membership	*Permanent neutrality*

Notes

1. Olssen, "The Swedish Social Democrats," p. 223.
2. Kronsell and Svedberg, "The Duty to Protect," pp. 154–155.
3. See de Stercke, "La Suède," p. 159; Stråth, *Folkhemmet mot Europa*, pp. 217, 240; and Jerneck, "Sweden," pp. 25–26.
4. Esping-Andersen, *Politics Against Markets*.
5. See Esping-Andersen and Korpi, "From Poor Relief to Institutional Welfare States," pp. 39-74; and Olsson, *Social Policy and Welfare State in Sweden*, in particular chap. 3.
6. Heclo and Madsen, *Policy and Politics in Sweden*, p. 27.
7. These values (*allemansrättigheter*) comprise, for instance, the right of access to private land, the right to see public documents, and welfare policies that allow everyone to benefit from public services and support independent of personal conditions. Gidlund, "Epilog," p. 196.
8. Ruth, "The Second New Nation," p. 55.
9. Bergström, "Sweden's Politics and Party System at the Crossroads," p. 8.
10. Olsson, *Social Policy and Welfare State in Sweden*, p. 204.
11. There is little disagreement among scholars that Sweden and Norway are at the top of the corporatism scale, whereas Switzerland is usually placed in the upper half. See Lijphardt and Crepaz, "Corporatism and Consensus Democracy in Eighteen Countries," pp. 238–239.

12. Katzenstein, *Small States in World Markets*, p. 32.

13. Ibid., pp. 136–190.

14. The Swedish Confederation of Trade Unions (LO-Sweden) organizes the blue-collar workers, the Swedish Confederation of Salaried Employees (TCO) organizes the white-collar workers, and most members of the small Swedish Confederation of Professional Associations (SACO) are employed within the public sector.

15. See de Geer, *The Rise and Fall of the Swedish Model*.

16. See Milner, *Sweden*, chap. 3. However, in the early 1990s, the leading employers' organization (SAF) decided that it would no longer be involved in wage negotiations with LO-Sweden, and it left the governing boards of all public authorities. Kurzer shows that until then, Sweden was able to withstand the external pressures of financial integration and capital mobility, which in other European countries corroded concerted social action. Kurzer, *Business and Banking*.

17. See Berglund and Lindström, *The Scandinavian Party System(s)*, pp. 16–18. Surveys of political attitudes confirm the principal antagonism between left and right in spite of a relatively even income distribution. Petersson and Valen, "Political Cleavages in Sweden and Norway," pp. 313–331.

18. Särlvik, "Sweden," pp. 371–434.

19. Logue, "The Legacy of Swedish Neutrality," pp. 41–42.

20. Goldmann, "The Swedish Model of Security Policy," pp. 122–143.

21. Sundelius, "Committing Neutrality in an Antagonistic World," p. 12.

22. Stråth, *Folkhemmet mot Europa*, p. 206.

23. Ruin, *Svensk neutralitetspolitik*, p. 37.

24. Kronsell and Svedberg, "The Duty to Protect," p. 155.

25. Sæter, "Norway and the European Union," p. 137; and Eikestøl, "Vesteuropeisk integrasjon etter 1945," p. 23.

26. Esping-Andersen and Korpi, "From Poor Relief to Institutional Welfare States," p. 71.

27. Gaarder and Christensen, "Den Nordiske Velferdsstatsmodellen i det Nye Europa," p. 148; and Knudsen, "Norsk Europa-politikk, EF og de historiske og kulturelle rammebetingelser," pp. 22–23.

28. Valen and Rokkan, "Norway," p. 326; Rokkan and Valen, "Regional Contrasts in Norwegian Politics," pp. 190–247; and Rokkan, "Geography, Religion, and Social Class," pp. 367–444.

29. See Seip, "Nation-building Within the Union," pp. 35–50; Hylland Eriksen, *Ethnicity and Nationalism*, pp. 101–104; and Knudsen, "Norsk Europapolitikk, EF og de historiske og kulturelle rammebetingelser," pp. 19–24.

30. Bjørklund, "Sentrum mot periferi," pp. 41–53.

31. See Valen, "National Conflict Structure and Foreign Politics," pp. 47–82; Rokkan, "Geography, Religion, and Social Class," p. 438; and Bjørklund, *Mot strømmen*, pp. 11–13. These alliances were to some extent a revival of the coalitions of the late nineteenth century in favor of independence and of a prohibition on alcohol in 1919.

32. Christensen and Egeberg, "Organized Group-Government Relations in Norway," pp. 239–259.

33. Olsen, *Organized Democracy*, in particular chap. 5.

34. Kvavik, *Interest Groups in Norwegian Politics*, p. 11.

35. See Valen and Rokkan, "Norway," pp. 315–370; and Converse and Valen, "Dimensions of Cleavage and Perceived Party Distances in Norwegian Voting," pp. 107–152.

36. Petersson and Valen, "Political Cleavages in Sweden and Norway," pp. 313–331; and Knutsen, "Political Cleavages and Political Realignment in Norway," pp. 235–263.

37. There are a few more small parties, such as the Communist Party (NKP); the Red Electoral Alliance (RV), established in 1973; or the Nonpartisan Coastal Party, which won one seat in 1997.

38. Lindgren, *Norway-Sweden*, chaps. 4–12.

39. Knudsen, "Norsk Europa-politikk, EF og de historiske og kulturelle rammebetingelser," pp. 24–27.

40. Hylland Eriksen, *Typisk norsk*, p. 48.

41. As Haga shows, the Norwegian history books clearly convey a negative attitude toward integration and portray the study of European history separate from the study of Norwegian history. Haga, *Identity and Inclination Towards Integration*.

42. Sollohub, *National Identity and the Norwegian EC Debate*, p. 34.

43. Lawler, "Scandinavian Exceptionalism and European Union," p. 580.

44. See Prebensen, *Norway and NATO*; and Skodvin, *Norden eller NATO?*

45. Prebensen, *Norway and NATO*, pp. 14–20; and Dörfer, "Scandinavia and NATO," pp. 17–22.

46. Ørvik, "Från halvneutralitet till halvallians," p. 38.

47. See Archer and Sogner, *Norway, European Integration and Atlantic Security*.

48. Feller et al., "Zusammenfassung und Versuch einer Synthese der wissenschaftlichen Diskussion," p. 39; Tanner and von Burg, "Arbeitsgruppe 'Politische Aspekte schweizerischer Identität,'" pp. 281–289; Schindler, "Auswirkungen der EG auf die schweizerische Staatsstruktur," pp. 1–3; Schwok, "Switzerland," pp. 24–32; and Kriesi, *Le système politique suisse*, p. 12.

49. Blankart, "Considérations sur la politique européenne de la Suisse," pp. 24–25; Melich, "Identité nationale," p. 54; and Switzerland, Federal Council, *Bericht des Bundesrates vom 18. Mai 1992 über einen Beitritt der Schweiz zur Europäischen Gemeinschaft*, Bern, 18 May 1992, p. 23.

50. See Jacot-Guillarmod, "Conséquences, sur le fédéralisme suisse, d'une adhésion de la Suisse à la Communauté européenne," pp. 7–37.

51. See Jacot-Guillarmod, "Conséquences, sur la démocratie suisse, d'une adhésion de la Suisse à la Communauté européenne," pp. 39–79; and Epiney and Siegwart, "Direkte Demokratie und Europäische Union," pp. 117–139.

52. Sciarini and Listhaug, "Single Cases or a Unique Pair?" p. 413.

53. This was, for instance, clearly the case in the referendum on Switzerland's joining the European Economic Area. Kriesi et al., *Analyse de la votation fédérale du 6 décembre 1992*, p. 36.

54. Kriesi et al., *Le clivage linguistique*.

55. Ruffieux and Thurler Muller, "L'opinion publique face à l'intégration européenne," pp. 237–252; Nef, "Die Schweizer Referendumsdemokratie," pp. 56–57; and Kriesi et al., *Analyse de la votation fédérale du 6 décembre 1992*, p. 32–34. Except for the young, populist Lega dei Ticinesi, no political party exists to explicitly defend the interests of a linguistic region.

56. Katzenstein, *Corporatism and Change*, chaps. 3–4.

57. Kriesi, "The Structure of the Swiss Political System," p. 155.

58. For example, the Liberal Party (LPS), the liberal-social Independent Alliance (LDU), the Protestant People's Party (EVP), the Green Party (GPS), the left-wing Labor Party (PDA) and the right-wing Swiss Democrats (SD; formerly Nationale Aktion).

59. Translation quoted from Steinberg, *Why Switzerland?* p. 13. Literally, *Eidgenossen* are "comrades of the oath," a German expression that is today still used as a synonym for "Swiss."

60. Swiss history schoolbooks attempt to inculcate "a love of liberty, resistance to tyranny, courage, shrewdness, and self-reliance." Schmid, *Conflict and Consensus in Switzerland*, p. 81.

61. Bonjour, *Geschichte der schweizerischen Neutralität*, vol. 1, pp. 19–42.

62. Ibid., vols. 4–6.

63. Schindler, "Die Lehre von den Vorwirkungen der Neutralität," pp. 563–582.

64. See Schindler, "Vereinbarkeit von EG-Mitgliedschaft und Neutralität," pp. 91–119; and Coftier, "L'adhésion de la Suisse à la Communauté européenne vue sous l'angle de la neutralité," pp. 122–142.

3

The Split-up of
Western Europe in the 1950s

*As the 1950s came to a close, Western Europe was truly and literally at
sixes and sevens. It had taken 10 years for the states definitely to decide
where they stood on the question of integration. . . . The EEC and EFTA
seemed determined to go their separate ways, and to regard each other as
a rival, not a partner.*
—Derek W. Urwin, *The Community of Europe*, p. 99

In this chapter, I present twelve cases in which I investigate the three countries' closely linked choices regarding the founding of the European Coal
and Steel Community (ECSC), the creation of the European Economic
Community (EEC), the negotiations on a wider European free trade area in
the framework of the Organization for European Economic Cooperation
(OEEC), and the establishment of the European Free Trade Association
(EFTA). Here and in the following four chapters, I first introduce the policy
options of each period and the economic data and then discuss the hypothesis separately for Sweden, Norway, and Switzerland. That is, I investigate
whether their integration policies are more reluctant when economic incentives for integration are lower and political impediments to integration are
higher.

The Founding of the
European Coal and Steel Community

In 1950, French foreign minister Robert Schuman proposed the pooling of
coal and steel resources in Western Europe.[1] The Schuman Plan, drafted by
Jean Monnet, was based on the conviction that stability and peace were
contingent on rapprochement between France and West Germany and that
greater progress could be made by a functional approach to cooperation
rather than a federal one. Coal and steel production was to be administered

both by the member states and an independent authority, and all tariffs in these heavy industries were to be gradually eliminated. Six states (France, Germany, Italy, Belgium, the Netherlands, and Luxembourg) participated in the negotiations, which in 1951 led to the Treaty of Paris. Britain, the Nordic states, and Switzerland declined an invitation to join the discussions because they were unwilling to accept the a priori principle of a supranational authority.

The High Authority was set up, composed of independent commissioners nominated by the member states. Its powers are moderated by the Council of Ministers, which has to agree, for instance, on output limitations because of overproduction or on an equitable distribution of supplies during a shortage in output. Some decisions of the Council require unanimity, some need an absolute or a qualified majority. The High Authority, located in Luxembourg and in 1967 succeeded by the European Commission, is further checked by the Common Assembly (which later became the European Parliament) and by the Consultative Committee, composed of producers, employees, and consumers. The Court of Justice, consisting of judges from all member countries, rules on the legality of any High Authority action on the basis of complaints submitted by governments or enterprises. The ECSC obtains its own source of revenue from an annual levy on coal and steel production. It can fix production quotas as well as minimum and maximum prices, impose fines on industries that unfairly reduce wages, and frame rules controlling cartels and concentrations.

The ECSC treaty constitutes a sectoral agreement governing the free movement of coal, steel, iron ore, coke, and scrap. Nevertheless, membership requires giving up considerable operational sovereignty in the coal and steel sector.[2] The shared competences include tariffs, commercial policy, rules of competition, transportation, energy, research, and certain economic and social affairs. The ECSC therefore qualifies as having a high level of integration in the field of coal and steel. As alternatives to full membership, sectoral agreements or association with the new ECSC were conceivable as low or medium forms of integration, even though the Treaty of Paris makes no such explicit provisions. When the ECSC treaty expires in July 2002, the coal and steel sectors will be placed under the EEC treaty.

Given the success of the ECSC, the six member states soon initiated two new projects in military and political cooperation. After the outbreak of the Korean War in 1950, the United States insisted on rearming West Germany within NATO. As an alternative, the French government proposed the creation of a European Defense Community (EDC). The so-called Pleven Plan suggested a common European army, with the underlying assumption that it would preclude a distinct German army under German command. Since a common army generally calls for a common foreign policy, the treaty on a European Political Community was drafted right after the EDC treaty was signed in 1952. To secure some influence, the British government suggested in 1952 that the Council of Europe should be turned into an (intergovernmental) umbrella organization for all the European projects such as the ECSC, the EDC, and the political community. However, in 1954 the French parliament refused to ratify the European Defense Community, causing all plans to collapse.

As an alternative, the United Kingdom proposed the Western European Union (WEU) which expanded the Brussels Treaty of 1948, a military assistance pact between the UK, France, and the Benelux countries, to West Germany and Italy. The WEU treaty was signed in Paris in 1954. Its loose structure comprises the WEU Council and a consultative parliamentary assembly. Britain promised to keep troops on the continent, and Germany, although restricted militarily, regained its sovereignty.

Incentives for and Impediments to Integration

The following three tables present the statistics that help to assess the economic incentives of Sweden, Norway, and Switzerland in considering integration. Table 3.1 provides the three countries' exports of coal and steel to the new Community (ECSC export ratio)[3] and their importance in relation to domestic production (GNP ratio). The ECSC came into being in 1952, and in 1958 all import barriers between member states, most national subsidies, and the double pricing for home and export sales had been abolished and the external tariffs had been harmonized within a certain range.

Table 3.2 identifies those three economic sectors with the highest shares of exports from Sweden, Norway, and Switzerland to the ECSC-6 (at a two-digit SITC level[4]) and the sector export ratio.

To assess the export sensitivity of the coal and steel products, Table 3.3 indicates the relative levels of trade barriers. The intra-ECSC barriers were gradually eliminated by 1959, and the Community streamlined national tariffs (percentage ad valorem) for imports of treaty products from third countries.

Opening the common market for coal did not require the removal of any tariffs within the Community. Coal had been rather scarce in Europe and could thus be imported duty-free. Iron ore met no obstacles either since the Community as a whole was a net importer. On coke, only Italy charged a tariff. Scrap became the subject of a Community-wide policy, and export controls had to be abolished within the common market. With the exception of the Benelux states, the ECSC countries charged sizable tariffs on imports of pig iron and steel.

By 1958, the Community's external duties on steel products were substantially lowered, ranging between 5 and 10 percent. Yet the main problems in the European steel trade were not tariffs: "the main market distor-

Table 3.1   Overall Export Dependence on the ECSC, 1952 and 1958
(estimates)

	ECSC export ratio (exports of coal and steel to the ECSC as % of total exports)	Sector export ratio (exports of coal and steel to the ECSC as % of total exports of coal and steel)	GNP ratio (exports of coal and steel to the ECSC as % of GNP)
Sweden			
1952	7.4	45.8	1.5
1958	8.2	53.8	1.5
Norway			
1952	4.2	39.1	0.8
1958	3.6	39.6	0.7
Switzerland			
1952	2.1	57.7	0.1
1958	1.7	69.3	0.08
ECSC-Six			
1952	6.0	35.6	0.8
1958	6.3	42.6	0.9

Sources: UN, *Statistical Papers: Commodity Trade Statistics*, Series D, January–December 1952 (New York, 1953); UN, *Statistical Papers: Commodity Trade Statistics*, Series D, January–December 1958 (New York, 1959); OEEC, *Statistical Bulletins: Foreign Trade*, Series IV, 1955, issues for Belgium/Luxembourg, France, Germany, Italy, Netherlands, Norway, Sweden, Switzerland (Paris: OEEC, 1956); OEEC, *Statistical Bulletins: Foreign Trade*, Analytical Abstracts, Series B, 1960, issue "O.E.E.C. Countries Combined" (Paris: OEEC, 1961); and OECD, *National Accounts of OECD Countries 1950–1968* (Paris: OECD, 1970). The UN data for coal, iron, and steel (Standard International Trade Classification [SITC] 281, 282, 311, 681) do not cover exactly the same range of products as the ECSC treaty. Since Switzerland was not a reporting country in the UN *Statistical Papers* of 1952 and 1958, the Swiss calculations are based on Eidgenössische Oberzolldirektion, *Jahresstatistik des Aussenhandels der Schweiz*, vol. 1 (Bern, 1953); and *Jahresstatistik des Aussenhandels der Schweiz 1958*, vol. 1 (Bern, 1959).

tions were artificial currency parities, the workings of officially mandated price controls, government subsidies, and differences in taxation, freight, and credit policies."[5] The ECSC tackled some of these issues, such as licenses and special formalities for purposes of exchange controls, statistical records, customs procedures, subsidies, national price fixing, and the national discrimination in transportation rates.[6] By the end of the transitional period, the High Authority regarded the remaining features of this "invisible tariff" as of relatively minor importance.[7]

Sweden.   For Sweden, the coal and steel sector was, with 7.4 percent of total exports and 1.5 percent of GNP, of medium importance (see Table 3.1). In comparison to its competitors, the Swedish iron and steel industry was in good shape after World War II. Next to France, Sweden was Europe's biggest producer of iron ore, and almost half of its exports (and about one-third of the iron and steel exports) went to the new Community.

Table 3.2   Sector Exports to the ECSC, 1952

	Leading Export Sectors to the ECSC (SITC number)	Sector Share (sector exports to ECSC as % of total exports to ECSC)	Sector Export Ratio (sector exports to ECSC as % of total sector exports)
Sweden			
Pulp and waste paper	(25)	26.3	40.4
Metalliferous ores	(28)	16.9	41.1
Wood and cork	(24)	14.3	39.4
Norway			
Base metals	(68)	19.6	26.3
Pulp and waste paper	(25)	19.1	31.4
Fish	(03)	11.4	16.3
Switzerland			
Nonelectrical machinery	(71)	22.3	40.6
Textile manufactures	(65)	13.3	38.2
Professional instruments	(86)	n.a.	n.a.
Other manufactures	(8)	17.2	20.3

Sources: OEEC, *Statistical Bulletins: Foreign Trade*, Series IV, 1952, issues for Sweden, Norway, Switzerland (Paris: OEEC, 1953). This source (pp. 6–7) turned out to be flawed for SITC 28. The Swedish estimate is therefore based on National Board of Trade/Kommerskollegium, *Sveriges officiella statistik: Handel berättelse för år 1952*, del I (Stockholm, 1954). Statistics for Switzerland are only available for all SITC sections (one-digit level) but not for all SITC divisions (two-digit level). Yet, the division "professional instruments, watches and clocks" (SITC 86) constitutes the main share of the section "other manufactures" (SITC 8).

Table 3.3   Barriers to Trade: ECSC Tariffs, 1952 and 1959 (percentage)

	France	Benelux Countries	Germany	Italy	ECSC Average
Coal					
1952	0.0	0.0	0.0	0.0	0.0
1959	0.0	0.0	0.0	0.0	0.0
Coke					
1952	0.0	0.0	0.0	5–10	1.9
1959	0.0	0.0	0.0	10.0	2.5
Iron ore					
1952	0.0	0.0	0.0	0.0	0.0
1959	0.0	0.0	0.0	0.0	0.0
Pig iron					
1952	5.0	0–1	12.0	11–20	8.25
1959	4.0	3.0	3.0	5.0	3.75
Crude and semifinished steel					
1952	7–10	1–2	15–18	11–15	10.0
1959	3–5	0–4	2–4	7–8	4.5
Finished steel products					
1952	10–22	1–8	15–28	15–23	15.2
1959	5–9	4–8	4–8	9–10	7.1

Source: The 1952 data are based on Horst Mendershausen, "First Tests of the Schuman Plan," *The Review of Economics and Statistics* 35 (1953): 273; and the 1959 data are based on *Tariffs and Trade in Western Europe* (London: Political and Economic Planning, 1959), pp. 6, 50–54. The product categories used in the two studies are not necessarily identical. The Italian tariff on coal was 0.0 percent, except for briquettes (4.0 percent).

All member states except France imported relatively large quantities of high-grade ore from third countries since their ore was too low in iron content to be exported long distances. In 1952, the ECSC imported around 40 percent of its iron ore from Sweden, of which two-fifths went to Germany in exchange for coal and coke.[8] Germany produced half of the ECSC's coal production, and Scandinavia, Austria, and Switzerland bought most of the German coal and coke exports.

Sweden's major exports to the ECSC countries in 1952 were raw materials, primarily forestry products (see Table 3.2). With a sectoral share of 16.9 percent and two-fifths sent to the Community, the metalliferous ores (mainly iron ore) reached a medium proportion. The common market threatened to divert the German demand from Sweden to France since the ECSC's harmonization of external tariffs obliged Germany to reintroduce higher duties on imports from third countries. Swedish export sensitivity was mitigated by the duty-free market access of iron ore (but not of pig iron and steel) and the overall reduction in the Community's external tariffs (see Table 3.3). The low sensitivity of iron ore and the economic recovery in Europe meant that the creation of the Community constituted "no serious threat to Swedish economic interests" as it "never resulted in tariff discriminations which seriously hurt Swedish producers and the stabilisation of the European industry, including steel prices, had beneficial effects."[9] Moreover, starting with the Korean boom, the international demand for steel was growing rapidly, and at least for a few years, there existed a veritable seller's market.

In 1952, the foreign minister affirmed that there was general agreement among the political parties that Sweden "should maintain a policy of freedom from alliances in spite of the fact that Norway and Denmark joined the Atlantic Pact."[10] The high significance attributed to an independent foreign policy made membership in the ECSC an unlikely option. The government was afraid that the transfer of decisionmaking power to a supranational body would negatively affect the credibility of its neutrality policy. Moreover,

> Sweden believed she could build her socialist welfare state more easily alone, working together with other countries only in specific and concrete cases, whilst the "Europeans" looked upon integration as a way of realising their hopes. . . . There was no alternative to the policy of non-alignment, and the conservative character of "Little Europe" made it easy for the Social Democrats to keep the party together behind the rather "isolationist" policy.[11]

As a result, Sweden faced relatively strong political constraints against full participation in the European Coal and Steel Community, and access to the ECSC market could best be described as being of medium importance.

Norway. In contrast to Sweden, Norway exported only a small share of coal and steel (4.2 percent) to the Community (see Table 3.1). With a sector export ratio of 39.1 percent and a GNP ratio of 0.8 percent, the situation of Norway was close to the average of the ECSC countries. Norway was less highly industrialized than many continental countries. It had its own iron ore and expected a substantial increase in domestic steel output.[12] In 1952, Norway exported mainly other raw materials such as base metals and pulp, as well as fish, to the common market (see Table 3.2).

The bad experience with neutrality in World War II and the Cold War climate made Norway turn to the Atlantic alliance in spite of its historical aversion to integration: "The fact is that both elite and public opinion, center and periphery, far down the line shared a common political culture which was strongly characterized by skepticism against the Continent in general and in many cases also by reluctance against certain aspects of the policy carried out there."[13] Norway's political elites saw no need to participate in an endeavor that involved a loss of sovereignty to supranational bodies dominated by countries adhering to doctrines "inferior" to their own welfare model.[14] In the words of the foreign minister, "the Norwegian people . . . are definitely skeptical of plans for integration, which once more place our economy at the mercy of continental cartels."[15] Hence, for the Norwegian economy, access to the ECSC market was not important, whereas identity-related political obstacles were strong.

Switzerland. Since the Swiss economy was a typical consumer of coal and steel, the creation of the European Coal and Steel Community had no significant impact. Swiss exports to the ECSC countries were already in the early 1950s concentrated on manufactures (see Table 3.2), and the exports of coal, iron, and steel to the ECSC were negligible (see Table 3.1). Switzerland worried more about the security of its imports from the Community as its main provider. Thus, "even if the economic policy of our country would only be inspired by economic considerations, that is even if it would only aim at our material prosperity, it would still be far from prescribing us to participate in the integration of Europe."[16]

Since the Community covered only the coal and steel sector, federalism and direct democracy would hardly have been touched upon, but membership was out of the question for neutrality reasons.[17] The guidelines on neutrality set out by the Swiss Foreign Ministry in 1954 explicitly declared that

> an economic neutrality exists only in so far as the permanently neutral state may not conclude a customs or economic union with another state, since this would mean that the neutral state would more or less renounce its independence in political matters as well. The prerequisite is that the neutral state constitutes the weaker part and would thus depend on its

stronger partner; in this case the legal possibility to give notice of the
union treaty or a special war clause would not change the situation.[18]

Skeptical of any supranational institutions and foreign influence, the government's main argument was that in order to maintain its political and economic independence, Switzerland must remain aloof from the ECSC.[19]
Thus the country had no export interests to defend but had strong political
reasons against joining the new Community.

Integration Policy Preferences

The preceding analysis has revealed that the economic advantages of ECSC
membership were medium for Sweden, low for Norway, and almost nonexistent for Switzerland, whereas the political constraints were prominent,
particularly for Switzerland. It can thus be expected that all three countries
would be reluctant to join the Community and prefer a low level of integration, or none at all. According to my analysis, they should value the preservation of sovereignty more than the acquisition of a voice in the ECSC.
Since Sweden endured the strongest economic incentives, it should be the
most motivated to look for a form of participation other than full membership, whereas Switzerland should be the most hesitant country.

Sweden. An analysis based on the archives of the Ministry for Foreign
Affairs shows that the Swedish government was not at all enthusiastic
about the Schuman Plan but clearly adopted a policy of wait and see.[20]
Even though the iron and steel industry was one of Sweden's primary
export sectors, the political and economic elites remained rather skeptical.
Swedish membership in the ECSC was never seriously discussed, but the
government aimed at good relations with the Community, which, some
people feared, might develop into a private cartel.[21] In 1952 the Swedish
government decided to establish a permanent delegation at the seat of the
ECSC, as the third country after Great Britain and the United States.

The government had apprehensions about close association with an
organ that was part of a system of cooperation connected to the plans for a
European Defense Community and a European Political Community.[22] It
wanted to negotiate with the ECSC in order to avoid higher tariff barriers
for its exports after the completion of the common market. However, only
the German government was interested in bargaining with Sweden about
the tariffs on quality steel.[23] The talks did not lead to formal negotiations
on tariff reductions, but in 1966 Sweden concluded a bilateral agreement
providing for reciprocal information with the ECSC.[24] Thanks to the favorable economic development, the ECSC's imports of iron and steel from

third countries doubled between 1951 and 1958, and Swedish exports to the Community increased by 15 percent between 1952 and 1955.[25]

For Sweden's government, as for most social democratic parties in Europe, a policy of planning, nationalization, and income redistribution was only considered feasible if it allowed unlimited freedom of action in economic and social affairs. Supranational integration would render such a policy more difficult, if not impossible, given the strong conservative forces on the continent. In Sweden, the Schuman Plan was publicly presented in the rather unfavorable light of the famous "four C's": conservatism, capitalism, Catholicism, and cartels.[26]

As expected, Sweden actively aimed at establishing a sectoral agreement with the ECSC. However, it did not succeed.

Norway. The Norwegian Labor government did not consider participation in the Schuman Plan either. It established a delegation in Luxembourg, but it did not pursue a closer rapprochement with the Community. An inquiry made by the Norwegian ambassador in 1954 as to whether Norway could enter a similar process of cooperation as the one the High Authority had proposed to Great Britain was given a negative response.[27] The Norwegian Federation of Industries cautioned that the Community's creation of a common market for special steel might constitute "a serious blow for our exports of ferromanganese if we are closed off from our old markets."[28] Such a cutoff was not very likely, however, given the boom in the European steel industry.

Already in the 1940s, Denmark, Iceland, Norway, and Sweden had studied the creation of a Scandinavian defense union and a customs union, but the Norwegian government had rejected the plans.[29] In response to a British initiative, however, they established *Uniscan* (a term combining parts of United Kingdom and Scandinavia) in 1949, a loose, consultative structure to coordinate economic policies. But that was as far as planning went: "Basically Norway did not have a policy apart from wishing that European integration would not take place, and supporting Britain on matters of principle within the OEEC and the Council of Europe."[30] Norway's suspicion of the conservative regimes on the continent made it follow the lead of the British Labour government. It criticized the fact that France, Italy, Belgium, and West Germany adhered to a laissez-faire policy and were opposed to income equalization, public investments, and control of investments. In Oslo's view, "The Anglo-Scandinavian system is largely the opposite of the continental European. The desire to maintain full employment and considerations of social justice have priority, [and] other goals are secondary. These primary goals imply a kind of governmental responsibility which is most often alien to the continental philosophy."[31]

Ergo, the Norwegian government chose sovereignty over influence in the ECSC and stayed aloof from the new Community.

Switzerland. The Swiss Federation of Commerce and Industry greeted the creation of the ECSC with great reservations and even hostility. It disapproved of its supranational structure and its dirigiste, protectionist philosophy.[32] Nevertheless, the economic interest groups agreed with the government that a modus vivendi needed to be found with the Community.[33] Based on the fact that 75 percent of Swiss imports of coal, iron, and steel originated in the six ECSC countries, the government feared that the security of supplies might be threatened in times of crisis, that higher export prices might lead to discrimination, and that the railway traffic through Switzerland might be diverted.[34] The High Authority tried to rebut these concerns as it did not want to grant Switzerland any special treatment.[35] The Swiss government accredited a delegation in Luxembourg and pushed for negotiations with the ECSC to guarantee the prices and the delivery of coal, iron, and steel in case of shortages. A consultation agreement featuring a joint committee was finally reached in 1956. A second agreement was concluded on the introduction of direct international railway tariffs for the transit of coal and steel through Swiss territory.[36]

Switzerland aimed at sectoral, intergovernmental agreements with the ECSC and thus at a low level of integration. Its policy turned out to be somewhat more active than expected due to the fact that import dependence is not one of the indicators used to measure the importance of market access. Yet the scope of the agreements was very limited and did not require any sovereignty losses.

The elites in Sweden, Norway, and Switzerland upheld the importance of national political constraints against ECSC membership, and their coal and steel sectors did not push for integration. Switzerland concluded two substantially very narrow agreements regarding supplies, Sweden's request for an export agreement remained without success, and Norway renounced any bilateral steps.

The Founding of the
European Economic Community (and Euratom)

After the failure of the political integration projects, the ECSC member states were eager to relaunch economic integration in 1955. The idea of a customs union was still in the air. In addition, the immense costs of the exploitation of atomic energy made nuclear cooperation a candidate for collective action. As the only nonmember state associated with the ECSC and belonging to the WEU, Great Britain was officially invited to participate in the work. The British government accepted the invitation but withdrew before the real negotiations began. The two Treaties of Rome, establishing the European Economic Community and the European Atomic Energy Community (Euratom), were signed in March 1957 and entered into force on 1 January 1958.

The EEC treaty aimed at establishing a common market for all goods and services. Going beyond a customs union, it postulated the free movement of capital and labor as well as several coordinated or joint policies, such as the Common Agricultural Policy (CAP). A transitional period of twelve years was laid down to eliminate tariffs, customs duties, and quantitative restrictions on intra-Community trade and to set up a common tariff on imports from nonmembers. The original timetable was considerably accelerated, and the customs union was completed ahead of schedule on 1 July 1968. The main EEC institutions included a Council of Ministers, a supranational Commission, an independent Court of Justice, an advisory Economic and Social Committee, and a Parliamentary Assembly with limited legislative powers.[37] The European Atomic Energy Community, which was to promote the speedy establishment of the nuclear industries necessary to satisfy the growing need for energy, did not fulfill the initial expectations. It largely became an organization for sponsoring research into the commercial development of nuclear power and supplementing nuclear research in the member states.

The Treaties of Rome provide three basic options for involvement with the Community: accession as a full member, association with separate institutions, or a classic trade agreement under international law and without an institutional setup. These alternatives essentially correspond to high, medium, and low levels of integration.

Incentives for and Impediments to Integration

Table 3.4 details the export dependence of Sweden, Norway, and Switzerland on the EEC for the years of the Messina conference in 1955, the entry into force of the Rome Treaties in 1958, and the completion of the EEC customs union ten years later. The pattern of trade flows in Western Europe in 1958 reveals two major trading groups: the EEC-6, with Switzerland and Austria, in which Germany was the pivotal country (i.e., a major export market for all other countries in the group), and the British Isles and the Nordic countries, in which the United Kingdom played the crucial role.[38] As long as Britain stayed outside the Community, the EEC could hardly gain overwhelming attractiveness for the Scandinavian nonmembers.

Table 3.5 presents the three countries' leading export sectors with regard to the EEC in 1958. Both Norway and Sweden still sold mainly raw

Table 3.4   Overall Export Dependence on the EEC, 1955, 1958, and 1968

	EEC Export Ratio (exports to EEC as % of total exports)	GNP Ratio (exports to EEC as % of GNP)
Sweden		
1955	32.2	6.1
1958	31.0	5.7
1968	27.1	5.2
Norway		
1955	24.4	4.6
1958	27.3	5.0
1968	23.4	5.0
Switzerland		
1955	36.4	7.5
1958	39.2	8.3
1968	36.0	8.3
EEC-Six		
1955	30.9	4.1
1958	30.2	4.1
1968	45.0	7.6

Sources: OEEC, *Statistical Bulletins: Foreign Trade*, Series B, 1960, issues for Sweden, Norway, Switzerland, and "O.E.E.C. Countries Combined" (Paris: OEEC, 1961); OEEC, *Statistical Bulletins: Foreign Trade*, Series IV, 1955, issues for Belgium/Luxembourg, France, Germany, Italy, Netherlands, Norway, Sweden, and Switzerland (Paris: OEEC, 1956); UN COMTRADE database, 1968; and OECD, *National Accounts of OECD Countries 1950–1968* (Paris: OECD, 1970).

materials to the common market, whereas Switzerland supplied manufactures.

The first reduction of intra-Community duties entered into force on 1 January 1959. At the same time, Euratom members abolished among themselves all customs duties and quantitative restrictions on trade in goods falling under the provisions of the nuclear common market. In light of the failure of the negotiations on a free trade area embracing all of Western Europe (see the next section, "The Failure of a Wider European Free Trade Area"), the Council of Ministers decided to extend the first 10 percent reduction to all members of the General Agreement on Tariffs and Trade (GATT). Unlike tariffs, the nontariff barriers to trade (e.g., technical standards, administrative barriers, and transportation regulations) remained comparable both for EEC member states and nonmembers.[39]

On 1 July 1968, the elimination of tariffs, levies, and quantitative restrictions between the EEC member states and the progressive introduction of a Common External Tariff (CET) for imports from third countries was completed. The CET was set at the arithmetical average of the duties applied in the four customs areas (France, Germany, Italy, and the Benelux

Table 3.5   Sector Exports to the EEC, 1958

	Leading Export Sectors to the EEC (SITC number)	Sector Share (sector exports to EEC as % of total exports to EEC)	Sector Export Ratio (sector exports to EEC as % of total sector exports)
Sweden			
Metalliferous ores	(28)	19.1	66.1
Pulp and waste paper	(25)	18.9	41.2
Wood and cork	(24)	12.7	44.2
Norway			
Base metals	(68)	27.8	32.1
Pulp and waste paper	(25)	10.0	27.7
Paper manufactures	(64)	9.0	25.3
Switzerland			
Nonelectrical machinery	(71)	24.5	43.5
Textile manufactures	(65)	10.7	38.1
Professional instruments	(86)	7.7	n.a.
Other manufactures	(8)	16.0	25.4

Sources: OEEC, *Statistical Bulletins: Foreign Trade*, Series IV, 1958, issues for Sweden, Norway, and Switzerland (Paris: OEEC, 1959). Statistics for Switzerland are not available for all SITC divisions. The section of "other manufactures" (SITC 8) comprises, as the main share, "professional instruments, watches and clocks" (SITC 86), the sector share of which is based on OEEC, *Statistical Bulletins: Foreign Trade*, "The Network of Intra-European Trade: Trade by Product in 1958" (Paris: OEEC, 1959).

countries) on 1 January 1957. The effect was roughly to double the Benelux tariffs, to halve those of France and Italy, and to leave those of Germany at approximately the same level. The overall volume of imports from third countries was in general not subject to higher customs duties than before, except for the sensitive products in List G of Annex I of the EEC Treaty, whose common tariffs were established by negotiations in 1960. The tariffs on raw materials were clearly lower than those on manufactures. Table 3.6 shows the average EEC tariffs at the entry into force of the EEC Treaty in 1958 and, for comparison, the CET ten years later, when intra-EEC tariffs were abolished.[40]

Sweden.   In 1958, Sweden's exports to the EEC amounted to a sizable 31 percent (see Table 3.4). Its main exports to the common market concentrated on similar shares of different raw materials, indicating that the Swedish economy overall was quite diversified. With two-thirds of all exported ores destined for the Community, the sectoral export ratio of that product was quite high, whereas pulp and wood reached smaller export ratios (see Table 3.5). Although the EEC tariffs on ores and pulp were low, the duties on wood were rather high (see Table 3.6). Official statements confirm this interpretation. The National Board of Trade established detailed tables of

Table 3.6   Barriers to Trade: EEC Tariffs, 1958 and 1968 (percentage)

Sector (SITC number)		Year	Estimated Average External EEC Tariff
Sweden			
Metalliferous ores	(28)	1958	2–3 (iron ore 0, List G)
		1968	0–1 (iron ore 0)
Pulp and waste paper	(25)	1958	3 (List G)
		1968	1–2
Wood and cork	(24)	1958	10–11 (List G)
		1968	8
Norway			
Base metals	(68)	1958	9–10 (aluminum 5–10, List G)
		1968	6–7 (aluminum 5–9)
Pulp and waste paper	(25)	1958	3 (List G)
		1968	1–2
Paper manufactures	(64)	1958	17
		1968	14–15
Switzerland			
Nonelectrical machinery	(71)	1958	13–14 (List G)
		1968	8–9
Textile manufactures	(65)	1958	17–18
		1968	12–13
Professional instruments	(86)	1958	15–16
		1968	9–10

Sources: The 1958 data are based on *Tariffs and Trade in Western Europe* (London: Political and Economic Planning, 1959), which does not, however, provide complete product coverage and refers to the tariffs of 1 January 1957, and Conférence des Représentants des Etats Membres de la Communauté économique européenne, "Accords concernant l'établissement d'une partie du tarif douanier commun relative aux produits de la liste G prévue au traité instituant la Communauté économique européenne," *Journal officiel des Communautés européennes*, no. 80C (20 December 1960). The 1968 data are based on Council of the European Communities, "Règlement (CEE) no. 950/68 du Conseil, du 28 juin 1968, relatif au tarif douanier commun," *Journal officiel des Communautés européennes*, no. L 172 (22 July 1968).

the EEC's expected "external tariff wall" for Sweden's major import and export commodities.[41] The Common External Tariff would raise the tariff levels in West Germany and the Benelux states, but the tariffs in France and Italy would decrease. The National Board of Trade pointed out: "In this context one should remember that of Sweden's total exports to the Six in 1956 . . . , 40% fell upon West Germany, 32% on the Benelux, 19% on France and 9% on Italy."[42] Hence, there was a potential for trade diversion.

On the sectoral level, the National Board of Trade estimated that the CET would increase tariffs on raw materials to approximately 3 percent, on semimanufactured goods to about 10 percent, on organic chemicals to around 15 percent, and on manufactures to roughly 15–25 percent.[43] Yet exports to the Common Market in 1956 were composed of 57.4 percent raw

materials (including iron and steel products) and only 35.8 percent manufactures.[44] Thus, the trade diversion effects would to some extent be mitigated. Moreover, a positive effect was expected for raw materials such as
paper pulp, timber, and iron ore because of increasing demand, but the
paper and steel industries would have to cope with higher tariffs.[45] The
government underlined that only a third of Sweden's exports were destined
to the EEC-6 and that the main share was raw materials facing "relatively
small barriers to trade," whereas discrimination by the EEC threatened
mainly manufactures, which "in reality amount to no more than . . . 12% of
the total exports."[46] From an aggregate point of view, the importance of
access to the newly founded common market for Sweden's economy in
1958 is best described as medium.

   The Swedish government's unfavorable attitude toward the European
Economic Community was based on concerns regarding neutrality and its
preoccupation with the welfare state.[47] EEC membership would have
involved a marked limitation of Sweden's freedom of action with regard to
socioeconomic policies. Neutrality required a certain degree of self-suffi-
ciency for agricultural products, the right to retain state subsidies for the
defense industry, and a certain freedom concerning trade with third countries. The National Board of Trade pointed out that accession might limit a
member state's possibilities to pursue a strict neutrality policy by the economic structural transformation toward more one-sided production and the
resulting higher dependence on supplies.[48] In the words of the Minister of
Trade, "the problem with joining the Six is not primarily an economic problem: it is instead foremost a political problem."[49] These perceptions put up
a rather high hurdle for Sweden's participation in the EEC.

Norway. In 1958 Norway sold 27.3 percent of its exports to the EEC (see
Table 3.4). The sales of base metals clearly dominated, with a rather high
share of 27.8 percent (see Table 3.5), which, on the average, met medium
levels of tariff barriers (see Table 3.6). Pulp and paper manufactures
reached sector shares of only 9–10 percent and met low and high tariff barriers, respectively. Hence, on average, the Norwegian export sensitivity at
the time seems to be of medium strength. The Norwegian government made
reflections along the same lines: Great Britain, with a share of 20 percent,
was considered the most important single export market, whereas Denmark
and Sweden accounted for 16 percent and the EEC-6 for about 27 percent.[50] Moreover,

> The essential part (ca. three quarters) of Norway's exports to the continen-
> tal customs union goes to Germany and the Benelux where the tariff rates
> as a result of the calculation method will be higher. . . . Incidentally, the
> extent of the discrimination by the Six might be somewhat limited as trade
> in raw materials makes up a relatively big part of Norwegian exports.

Also in the Six manufactures are generally subject to higher customs duties than raw materials and semi-manufactured goods.[51]

Hence, access to the EEC market was of middle-range importance for the Norwegian economy. The government was not inclined to accept the supranational nature of the Community. Hilary Allen discerns two factors for the Norwegians' reluctance to surrender any sovereignty to the EEC: "The first was their fear of endangering the all-important Anglo-Saxon connection," and "the other was simply the Norwegians' wish to retain the fullest possible control over their own domestic affairs, which they had just regained after five years of German occupation."[52] Likewise, "membership was out of the question because of continental economic and social policies which were not compatible with those of Norwegian Social Democracy."[53] In spite of its Euro-compatible alignment policy as a NATO member, Norway in 1958 attributed great importance to political impediments to integration.

Switzerland.   At 39.2 percent, Switzerland's ratio of exports to the new Community was above the EEC average for 1958, and its GNP ratio of 8.3 percent was double the EEC average (see Table 3.4). A considerable share (24.5 percent) of Swiss exports to the Community consisted of nonelectrical machinery, and the EEC absorbed 43.5 percent of this branch's total exports, whereas the shares of textile manufactures (10.7 percent) and professional instruments (7.7 percent) were much smaller (see Table 3.5). All three leading export sectors faced high EEC tariff barriers in 1958 (see Table 3.6). Similar to the Scandinavian countries, the Swiss economy experienced incentives of medium strength in favor of integration: "the EEC states are of considerable importance for Swiss exports; however, the export markets in the rest of the world are even more important since they absorb over 60 percent of our total exports."[54]

The Swiss government clearly identified the political obstacles to membership in the European Economic Community:

> Accession to the EEC would affect our system of direct democracy and partly also the federal structure of our country. In any case, it would be irreconcilable with the constitutionally stipulated democratic decision-making in our country if the protection of the interests of the Swiss people with regard to trade, social, labor, agricultural and fiscal policy would be delegated to organs which are not responsible to it. . . . One of the most important cornerstones of neutrality, namely its predictability, would be harmed and the international confidence in its permanent character undermined.[55]

According to the official reading and the dominant academic doctrine, membership in the EEC was first of all regarded as contradictory to Swiss neutrality. Even the proponents of closer ties with the Community agreed that Switzerland would have to make important reservations to the Rome treaties.[56] With regard to the impact of EEC membership on direct democracy, it has been calculated that out of forty-six federal referenda held between 1945 and 1957, seven would have collided completely with EEC law and eight partially.[57] In other words, one-third of the referenda voted on would have either required modification or would not have been possible. Extending the analysis for another ten years (1945–1967), seventy-seven federal referenda were held, out of which seven fell wholly and eighteen partly into EEC competences.[58] These numbers also amount to a share of one-third of incompatible referenda. In addition, a foreign policy tradition of noninvolvement, a negative recollection of foreign rule, and the Swiss distrust of supranational structures, as opposed to decentralized and federalist ones, contributed to very strong political constraints against accession.

Integration Policy Preferences

The preceding assessment supports the expectation that all three countries will stay outside the Community and aim at a lower level of integration. Switzerland had the strongest economic incentives to join the common market but also faced the highest political impediments. It can thus be expected to be very motivated to look for an alternative form of cooperation with the EEC, whereas Sweden and Norway have less strong motivations to do so.

It seems to be a common feature of the Swedish, Norwegian, and Swiss governments that they assessed the integration efforts of the ECSC-6 in the early 1950s as unrealistic, utopian, and dirigiste. After the failure of the European Defense Community, the success of an ambitious project like the common market seemed rather unlikely to them. In none of the three countries were interest groups pushing to join the common market. Given the general uncertainty of the EEC's success, the export industries basically agreed with their governments' wait-and-see approach. In addition, the trade unions in the EFTA countries, and in particular in Scandinavia, were afraid that joining the common market would jeopardize the high social and economic standards they had obtained for workers.[59]

Sweden. The results of the Messina conference went rather unnoticed in Sweden. A member of the Ministry of Foreign Affairs noted that Sweden, like the other peripheral countries in Europe, was never asked to join the negotiations and that the "policy of neutrality would in any case have prevented us from becoming a member."[60] Besides neutrality, the welfare state goes a long way in explaining the reluctance of Swedish integration policy in the 1950s. "Because the success of the national welfare project was so extremely great in Sweden, it was quite natural that the confidence in the nation-state became greater and less reserved there than maybe elsewhere in Western Europe."[61] The two components of Swedish identity, *folkhemmet* (the people's home) and *alliansfrihet* (freedom from alliances), strengthened each other as the welfare model was formulated in the domestic realm of neutrality, and this choice of security policy reinforced the trust in national solutions in the social and economic field.

The Swedish social democrats preferred a free hand in their economic planning and social reforms. They denounced the capitalism, protectionism, and imperialism of the EEC powers, this "Catholic dominated, reactionary group of Six."[62] Community policies were undoubtedly judged incompatible with Swedish domestic traditions.[63] As expected, Sweden was much more interested in safeguarding its operational sovereignty than in obtaining a voice in the new Community. The search for other, more limited forms of integration set in as soon as it became clear that the EEC was here to stay (see the next two main sections of this chapter).

Norway. As in Sweden, the cooperation of the EEC-6 provoked no significant debate within Norway's *classe politique* or in its economic circles.[64] Celebrating its fiftieth anniversary as an independent nation, Norway had no intention of renouncing its hard-won sovereignty to a supranational, "foreign" institution. The relative lack of Norwegian interest in the EEC changed only when Britain, Norway's most important trading partner, presented plans for a Western European free trade area (see the next section): "Economically Norway was oriented towards the North Atlantic and world markets to a greater degree than towards Europe," and in terms of security, "Norway was wholly dependent upon Britain and to an increasing degree upon the United States."[65]

Norwegian supporters of economic planning and extensive welfare measures were highly skeptical of continental economic policies. This distrust of conservative regimes was reinforced by the awareness of Norway's economic vulnerability within a united Europe: "Overpowering continental cartels might thus interfere with both Norwegian economic development and national control of the economy."[66] A proposal for amending the Norwegian Constitution to allow for the delegation of authority to international institutions was rejected in the Storting in 1956.[67] The Norwegian government showed no immediate reaction to the EEC, but was interested in pursuing alternatives with the other Scandinavian countries and Great Britain.

Switzerland. In December 1956, the Swiss Ministry of Foreign Affairs considered the common market "neither politically nor economically desirable."[68] The Swiss export industry was equally convinced that "giving up an independent policy in customs and monetary matters would inevitably lead to an ever closer fusion of the economic and political institutions such as the financial, social, labor and transport policies" and that "this program is not acceptable for Switzerland."[69] The Swiss Federation of Commerce and Industry criticized the EEC as protectionist, if not "downright socialist."[70] For the Vorort, unlike its Scandinavian counterparts, the Community was not too conservative but rather too "leftist," with its political goals, supranationality, dirigisme, and interventionist policies.[71] The customs union was seen as leading to a loss of treaty-making power and sovereignty and to increasing policy harmonization. Therefore, the Swiss industrial federation preferred bilateral commercial relations.

For both economic and political elites, it seemed hard to imagine that Switzerland should renounce its independent trade and agricultural policies. According to the government, even a partial renunciation of an independent economic policy would cost "a considerable piece of sovereignty."[72] And it would entail greater risks for a small state than for a big one, since the big state possesses "through the weight of its economic and political potential, which has been institutionally reinforced by the weighted voting power granted in the Treaty of Rome, the greater possibility to carry through its interests."[73] A small state like Switzerland would not gain enough voice to compensate for its loss of sovereignty. In order to counterbalance fears that Swiss exports to the Community might be discriminated, the Federal Council chose to support the British initiative for a wider European free trade area.

Switzerland, which was probably most afraid of trade diversion, was following the developments on the continent more closely than Sweden. The Common Market project stirred up the fewest discussions in Norway, which had lower economic incentives to join than the other two countries. In this early stage, none of the three countries inquired about possible membership. Yet the two initiatives for the EEC and the OEEC-wide free trade area (see the next main section) overlapped in time, and the breakdown of the latter led to a third option, the European Free Trade Association (see the last main section of this chapter). It is therefore understandable that in the mid-1950s, the three countries possessed no fully formulated policy toward the Community project. Taking into account this delayed reaction, the expectations of my study seem to be correct. Sweden, Norway, and Switzerland chose to stay outside the European Economic Community and Euratom but began to search for alternative options. The policies of the three countries might have well been different if no alternative to the EEC had emerged so quickly.

The Failure of a Wider European Free Trade Area

In the aftermath of World War II, the U.S. government announced the Marshall Plan for economic aid to all European states. The offer was rejected by the Soviet Union and its Eastern European satellites, as well as by Finland. In 1948, the sixteen Western European countries interested in the European Recovery Program (Austria, Belgium, Denmark, France, Great Britain, Greece, Iceland, Ireland, Italy, Luxembourg, the Netherlands, Norway, Portugal, Sweden, Switzerland, and Turkey) formed the Organization for European Economic Cooperation. The Federal Republic of Germany joined in 1949 and Spain in 1959, and the United States and Canada became associate members in 1950. The OEEC was a purely intergovernmental organization headed by a council representing all the member governments and taking formal decisions by unanimity.

In 1956, the low-tariff countries pushed for reductions of the high tariffs of some member states as a precondition for any further quota liberalization. Upon British initiative, the OEEC Council of Ministers set up a working party to study the possible forms of association, in particular the prospect of a free trade area, between the planned EEC and the other eleven OEEC countries. Its report of January 1957 confirmed that such an OEEC free trade area would indeed be possible.[74] However, different points of view prevailed between the ECSC countries and the United Kingdom's low-tariff supporters with regard to the institutional framework and the issue areas to be covered, especially agriculture and the harmonization of economic, financial, and social policies.

The British government insisted on parallel negotiations in the Community and the OEEC. The ECSC-6 suspected the United Kingdom of attempting to undermine the success of the EEC and went ahead in order to avoid the possibility that the looser arrangement of a free trade area might prove more attractive to some countries. Upon French initiative, in early 1958 the text of the EEC treaty was taken as the basis for the planned OEEC free trade area. The OEEC council declared its determination "to secure the establishment of a European Free Trade Area which would comprise all Member countries of the Organisation; which would associate, on a multi-lateral basis, the European Economic Community with the other Member countries; and which, taking fully into consideration the objectives of the European Economic Community, would in practice take effect parallel with the Treaty of Rome."[75]

The council established an intergovernmental committee under the chairmanship of British paymaster-general Reginald Maudling.[76] The negotiations carried out by the Maudling Committee were under time pressure since the agreement was supposed to enter into force on 1 January 1959, at the time when the Community would take the first steps to dismantle its tariffs and quotas. Even though the British were ready to depart considerably from their original conception, they could not meet the French position with regard to the harmonization of tariffs and policies and certain institutional issues. On the EEC side, the low tariff countries, Germany and the Benelux states, were strongly in favor of the free trade area. Yet, Chancellor Konrad Adenauer chose to support France to make sure that the new government under Charles de Gaulle would ratify the Rome treaties. In November 1958, the French government unilaterally declared the end of the free trade area.[77]

By that time, agreement had been reached on the methods to gradually eliminate tariffs and quotas, the rules regarding the right of establishment, the free movement of capital and international exchange of services, transportation problems, and the provisions relating to restrictive business practices and state aid. Some progress had been made on other questions, such as agriculture; the movement of workers; trade in coal, steel, and products used for nuclear energy; and the special arrangement required for countries in the process of economic development.[78] No agreement was reached on the problems arising from the fact that the free trade area would not have a common external tariff and a common commercial policy, the harmonization and coordination of the domestic social and economic policies, and the institutional questions.

The United Kingdom, the three Scandinavian countries, Switzerland, and Austria—who became known as the "Other Six"—wanted the negotiations to result in a free trade area rather than a customs union. Sweden and Switzerland had relatively low tariffs, and their industrial structures were built on the import of many basic materials and semimanufactured products at very low costs. Norway was also opposed to any arrangement that would mean an increase in tariffs. Portugal's problems were quite different in character, and it was usually grouped with the less-developed countries (Greece, Turkey, Ireland, and Iceland), sometimes referred to as the "Forgotten Five." France demanded protection against certain industries with access to cheap raw materials or power, such as Scandinavian wood pulp and paper industries and Norwegian aluminum and ferro-alloy production, which were based on hydroelectric power. The countries concerned, in particular Sweden, vigorously opposed this claim and defended free competition. With regard to agriculture, the Six wanted a common policy. Denmark was inclined to accept this idea, but Sweden, Norway, Switzerland, Austria, and the United Kingdom were only ready to coordinate agricultural policies. Iceland insisted on full free trade in fish, whereas Norway agreed to limit free trade to industrially processed fish products.

The institutional shape of the project remained incomplete as well.[79] The supreme body would be a council of ministers, and a managing body of senior officials would be responsible for day-to-day work. In principle, the council would decide by unanimity, but in certain cases to be specified, it might take majority decisions. The EEC members themselves would have acted as a unit within the free trade area. Among the open questions were the composition and jurisdiction of the managing body, the creation of juridical, parliamentary, and consultative bodies, and their coordination with the corresponding EEC institutions. Views also diverged on complaint procedures and on how to invoke the escape clauses. On the whole, the free trade project represented an approach with a global scope and an intergovernmental setup and, hence, a medium level of integration.

Incentives for and Impediments to Integration

Table 3.7 shows the export dependence of Sweden, Norway, and Switzerland on the planned free trade area for two years, when the project was first proposed in 1956 and when negotiations broke down in 1958. For all three countries, the importance of the OEEC market was very impressive, and the share of GNP generated by these exports was far above the average of the OEEC or even the EEC states.

The three countries' leading export sectors with regard to the OEEC market are presented in Table 3.8.

Table 3.9 indicates an estimate of the average tariffs that the principal

Table 3.7   Overall Export Dependence on the OEEC, 1956 and 1958

	OEEC Export Ratio (exports to OEEC as % of total exports)	GNP Ratio (exports to OEEC as % of GNP)
Sweden		
1956	69.5	13.6
1958	67.3	12.5
Norway		
1956	64.1	13.0
1958	66.2	12.3
Switzerland		
1956	54.8	11.6
1958	55.8	11.8
EEC		
1956	56.4	7.5
1958	54.0	7.3
OEEC		
1956	51.1	6.6
1958	49.9	6.3

Sources: OEEC, *Statistical Bulletins: Foreign Trade*, "The Network of Intra-European Trade: Trade by Product in 1956" (Paris: OEEC, 1957); OEEC, *Statistical Bulletins: Foreign Trade*, "The Network of Intra-European Trade: Trade by Product in 1958" (Paris: OEEC, 1959); and OECD, *National Accounts of OECD Countries 1950–1968* (Paris: OECD, 1970).

Table 3.8   Sector Exports to the OEEC, 1958

Leading Export Sectors to the OEEC (SITC number)		Sector Share (sector exports to OEEC as % of total exports to OEEC)	Sector Export Ratio (sector exports to OEEC as % of total sector exports)
Sweden			
Pulp and waste paper	(25)	16.8	79.3
Wood and cork	(24)	12.4	93.8
Metalliferous ores	(28)	12.2	91.6
Norway			
Base metals	(68)	23.8	66.7
Pulp and waste paper	(25)	12.1	81.2
Fish	(03)	9.1	43.7
Switzerland			
Nonelectrical machinery	(71)	24.6	62.3
Textile manufactures	(65)	12.1	61.5
Professional instruments	(86)	9.1	n.a.
Other manufactures	(8)	17.0	38.4

Source: OEEC, *Statistical Bulletins: Foreign Trade,* "The Network of Intra-European Trade: Trade by Product in 1958" (Paris: OEEC, 1959). Statistics for Switzerland are not available for all SITC divisions. The section of "other manufactures" (SITC 8) comprises as the main share "professional instruments, watches and clocks" (SITC 86), the sector share of which is based on the OEEC source.

Table 3.9   Barriers to Trade: OEEC Tariffs, 1957 (percentage)

Sector (SITC number)		Estimated Average OEEC Tariff
Sweden		
Pulp and waste paper	(25)	5.0
Wood and cork	(24)	8.0
Metalliferous ores	(28)	1.0
Norway		
Base metals	(68)	8.0
Pulp and waste paper	(25)	5.0
Fish	(03)	n.a.
Switzerland		
Nonelectrical machinery	(71)	14.0
Textile manufactures	(65)	13.0
Professional instruments	(86)	18.0

Source: OEEC, "Alternates of Working Party no. 21 of the Council Group of Trade Exports: Comparison of Member Countries' Tariff Levels for Selected Products: Consolidated List," FTA/WP4(57)36, Paris, 31 October 1957. These data constitute a very rough approximation since they do not comprise all seventeen OEEC members at the time or all the sectors' products.

exports met on the OEEC market in 1957. As in the EEC, on average trade in raw materials faced much lower tariffs in the OEEC area than manufactured goods. Essentially, the trade barriers would have progressively been abolished at the same pace as laid down in the EEC treaty, with special provisions for countries in the course of economic development.

Sweden. In 1956 Sweden was highly dependent on the OEEC area, with 69.5 percent of its total exports going there, accounting for 13.6 percent of GNP (see Table 3.7). As Table 3.8 shows, Sweden's leading exports to the OEEC market consisted of medium shares of raw materials such as pulp, wood, and ores, which went almost exclusively to those countries and faced low to medium tariff levels (see Table 3.9). Several analyses conducted in 1957–1958 by the National Board of Trade and the Committee for Integration Affairs found that Sweden's participation in the free trade area would have favorable effects on the export industries and on the economy's general development.[80] These expectations with regard to the new export market and the high overall export dependence generated strong economic incentives for Sweden to participate in the free trade area, compared to weaker motives to join the EEC.

Parliament underlined that Sweden's foreign policy would be compatible with participation in a large market such as the free trade area but not with membership in an economic and political union, in which joint institutions decided by majority.[81] The foreign minister reiterated that Sweden was still committed to a policy of freedom from alliances, aimed at neutrality in the event of war.[82] With the free trade area's planned weak coordination of social and economic policies, the Swedish welfare model would by no means be jeopardized by participation. In general, the political impediments to joining the OEEC-wide free trade area were very low for Sweden, in contrast to the strong objections raised by EEC membership.

Norway. Norway's export dependence on the OEEC area in 1956 amounted to the high percentage of 64.1 percent, and the share of GNP generated by these exports was 13 percent (see Table 3.7). Within this area, the Scandinavian market and the United Kingdom were of greatest importance. As Table 3.8 shows, Norwegian exports concentrated on raw materials, in particular base metals, pulp, and fish. They met on average medium levels of tariffs (see Table 3.9). Two-thirds of all exported base metals and four-fifths of the pulp and waste paper were sold to the OEEC market, accounting for a rather strong sectoral export sensitivity.

The Norwegian government would have liked to expand the scope of the prospective free trade area by declaring that an exclusion of fish products would imply that about 20 percent of Norway's exports to the OEEC would not benefit from free trade.[83] The liberalization of capital exports was of particular importance to Norwegian industry, with its natural conditions for very capital-intensive production. The fact that the initiative came from the United Kingdom, Norway's most important export market and security partner, made it even more attractive for Norway. Hence, for the government the free trade area was "of fundamental importance to the Norwegian economy."[84] Norway's economic incentives to join the wider free trade area were thus high (not just medium, as in the case of EEC membership).

Because of the lack of supranational institutions, the envisaged free trade area, in contrast to the EEC, posed no problems of "foreign rule" for Norway. Nor did it touch upon the welfare model or mobilize any societal cleavages. In fact, for the Norwegians, "Britain's policy meant that they faced no conflicts between their preference for avoiding supra-national arrangements if possible, their Atlantic orientation, and their tradition of following Britain's lead in European affairs."[85] Norway encountered very low political obstacles against joining the free trade area.

Switzerland. At 54.8 percent, Swiss export dependence on the OEEC area in 1956 was close to the OEEC average, but the share of GNP created by these exports, at 11.6 percent, was double the OEEC average (see Table 3.7). In contrast to Sweden and Norway, Swiss industry sold mainly manufactured goods to OEEC members. Nonelectrical machinery constituted a high share of almost 25 percent, whereas the other leading sectors, textiles and instruments, comprised lower shares (see Table 3.8). Since trade in manufactures encountered tariffs that were more than double of those on raw materials, Swiss exports faced a greater threat of trade diversion than those of the Scandinavian countries (see Table 3.9). Consequently, the Swiss government hoped that the free trade area would ban the threat of economic discrimination resulting from the creation of the EEC.[86] The OEEC-wide free trade area was expected to moderate Switzerland's growing economic dependence on the EEC-6 while not endangering Switzerland's protected agricultural sector. With such a great overall and sectoral export dependence on the OEEC, the importance of market access to the free trade area was high for the Swiss economy (but only medium with regard to the EEC).

Upon joining the OEEC, the Swiss government had declared that its participation must not impinge on neutrality, commit it to decisions to which it had not agreed, or hinder its freedom of action for concluding commercial treaties with countries outside the organization.[87] It admitted a "fundamental aversion to supranational organs" and during the negotiations consistently aimed at maintaining its freedom of action while avoiding any rules of majority decisions.[88] In contrast to a customs union, a free trade area did not raise problems of neutrality, direct democracy, or federalism.

Like Sweden and Norway, Switzerland faced low political impediments to joining the OEEC-wide free trade area.

Integration Policy Preferences

All three countries encountered high economic incentives and very low (or no) political obstacles toward participating in the proposed OEEC-wide free trade area. Following my analysis, they should not hesitate to join this alternative to the Community and hence go for a medium level of integration, in comparison to EEC membership. The governments might also be expected to fight for a "voice" in the free trade area since the maintenance of operational sovereignty becomes less important when economic incentives are high and political impediments to integration are low.

The OEEC negotiations on a free trade area led to coordination among the export-oriented sectors of the Other Six. In April 1958, the principal industrial federations and employers' organizations of Austria, Denmark, Norway, Sweden, Switzerland, and the United Kingdom issued a joint statement on the free trade plans.[89] They recommended to their governments and the Maudling Committee that "all commodities, goods and services should be covered by the Convention with special arrangements regarding products of agriculture and fisheries . . . and that all discrimination based on nationality should be prevented as far as possible."[90] As a compromise between Denmark, Norway, and Britain, they suggested treating a wide range of industrially processed agricultural and fisheries products as industrial products. Moreover, the federations considered it necessary that the transitional periods should follow the Treaty of Rome and abolish trade barriers simultaneously. With regard to policy coordination, they expected a convergence of economic and financial policies but opposed any harmonization of social charges, wages, and working conditions. In addition, the federations favored a liberalization of capital movements, services, and the labor market as well as an intergovernmental institutional setup with an independent secretariat. When the negotiations failed at the end of 1958, the federations carried their deliberations on with regard to a small free trade area among the six non-EEC countries. Like the employers' organizations and the export industries, the labor unions of the six countries supported the creation of a free trade area throughout the negotiations.[91]

Sweden. Except for some typically domestic industries such as textiles, Swedish business took a very favorable attitude toward the prospect of a free trade area. The Federation of Swedish Industries soon became the most active promoter of the scheme, which offered an alternative to both Nordic cooperation, about which the federation was not too enthusiastic, and accession to the EEC. The latter option was not considered realistic: the Swedish export industries needed a geographically broader free trade area, and the Community's political ambitions were not considered compatible with neutrality.[92] For the National Board of Trade, EEC membership was not a desirable alternative to participation in the planned free trade area.[93] When the negotiations of the Maudling Committee deadlocked, the export industries became more willing than the government to adapt to the EEC demands in order to save the market access, yet without directly arguing in favor of joining the Community.[94]

The Swedish government declared that "in view of the fact that a very considerable part of Sweden's external trade is with the United Kingdom and countries of the European continent, it is clear that for Sweden too it is important not to stand outside a free trade area comprising most of the member states of the OEEC."[95] By comparison, accession to the Six was "under no circumstances compatible with the independence in foreign policy backed by the overwhelming majority of our people."[96] The four major parties agreed that adhering to the Rome treaties was out of the question.[97] Practically all economic sectors and political forces in Sweden supported the trade liberalization plans, but full membership in the EEC was believed to impose too many restrictions on the national freedom of action.[98]

As expected, Sweden actively sought full membership in the OEEC free trade area and was prepared to give up a limited amount of sovereignty. By contrast, obtaining a seat and voice in the EEC would have required the surrender of too much operational sovereignty in exchange for smaller economic benefits.

Norway. The initiative for an OEEC-wide free trade area hit the Norwegian commercial and industrial circles rather unexpectedly, but the economic importance of the British market coupled with security considerations made participation in the free trade area negotiations imperative.[99] The Norwegian Trade Council, the Shipowners' Association, and the Bankers' Association supported the project at an early stage, but other interest organizations had greater difficulty in deciding upon a standpoint. The Federation of Norwegian Industries as well as the Federation of Norwegian Craftsmen had a reserved attitude resulting from a split between different branches. The farmers' organizations feared an inclusion of agricultural products that would undermine the Norwegian system of price regulation and subsidization, whereas the fishing industry wanted fish products to receive free trade status.[100] In general, the expectations of the interest groups converged on an acceptance of the free trade plan.[101] The elites hoped that the liberalization of trade and capital movements would allow their economy to shift its production and exports from raw materials, which were exposed to strong market fluctuations, to manufactured products.[102] The Conservative Party showed the most positive attitude toward a free trade area, hoping that it would exert a liberal influence on national policies.

According to the Labor government, technological progress and mass production commanded bigger markets, and the creation of a large free trade area was therefore a "logical consequence" of the increasing economic inter- dependence in Europe.[103] Throughout the negotiations, however, the Norwegian delegation refused to relinquish any sovereignty for a harmo- nization of economic and social policies.[104] In other words, "Norwegian rep- resentatives were extremely unwilling to give up any part of real or imag- ined freedom of action by entering into agreements embodying automatic rules."[105] In the late 1950s, the Norwegian government tried to protect its operational sovereignty and was satisfied with joining the medium-level OEEC free trade area instead of having a say in the supranational EEC.

Switzerland. After the ECSC countries signed the Rome treaties in 1957, the Swiss government strongly favored creating a large free trade area in order to avoid the expected economic discrimination.[106] At the same time, it urged that such a plan should contribute to the development of trade on a global level so as not to undermine the most-favored-nation (MFN) princi- ple. During the negotiations, the government rejected any unification of external tariffs, which would have restricted Switzerland's freedom of action toward third countries, and declared that it did not consider the har- monization of economic, financial, fiscal, or social policies as necessary.[107]

The Swiss Federation of Commerce and Industry supported the free trade area but was very skeptical about its final shape.[108] It was afraid of an illiberal, bureaucratic solution because most of the countries participating in the negotiations were governed by more or less interventionist govern- ments prone to nationalization, and it wished that the area be limited to tar- iff reductions, exclude agriculture, keep competition rules and safeguards to a minimum, and function on the basis of unanimous decisions. Like the political elites, business favored a liberal arrangement that would not endanger neutrality or the autonomy of Swiss commercial and monetary policies.

The Federal Council favored an intergovernmental setting that did not require the surrender of too much sovereignty, and it was tempted "to slow down the efforts of the Six and to tie them into looser organizations like the OEEC, in order to secure a right to a say without having to accept the cor- responding obligations."[109] As expected, Switzerland was willing to partici- pate in the OEEC free trade area but put the emphasis on sovereignty rather than gaining a say in the EEC.

All three governments aimed at full participation in the OEEC's inter- governmental trade arrangement and thus—compared to EEC membership—at a medium level of integration. The elites of Sweden, Norway, and Switzerland were well aware of their economies' dependence on the OEEC market. They were ready to renounce a small part of operational sovereignty in order to obtain attractive economic benefits and some influence in a reorganized Western Europe. The limited scope and structure of the free trade area made binding international cooperation far easier to accept than the "alien" character of the supranational European Economic Community.

The Founding of the European Free Trade Association

As the OEEC negotiations drew to a standstill, the nonmembers of the European Economic Community pondered the effects of the breakdown. The prospect of an early resumption of fruitful negotiations with the EEC was bleak. In June 1959, the "Outer Seven" (Austria, Denmark, Norway, Portugal, Sweden, Switzerland, and the United Kingdom) presented a plan for an industrial free trade area among themselves.[110] In January 1960, hardly more than a year after the idea had been born, the convention was signed in Stockholm and entered into force four months later. Finland had followed the EFTA negotiations as an observer. The Soviet government took a negative attitude not only toward the EEC, which it considered the economic arm of NATO, but also toward EFTA, which it viewed as a transitional solution on the way to full EEC membership.[111] After concluding an agreement on tariff reductions with the Soviet Union, the Finnish government signed an association agreement with the EFTA states in 1961. The so-called FINEFTA basically set up a second free trade area and gave Finland the same rights and obligations.

The Stockholm Convention set out twin targets: to promote economic growth and improve standards of living and to "facilitate the early establishment of a multilateral association for the removal of trade barriers and the promotion of closer economic co-operation between the members of the Organisation for European Economic Co-operation, including the Members of the European Economic Community" (preamble). It was restricted to free trade in industrial goods, covering industrial raw materials, semimanufactures, and manufactures, as well as some specifically listed agricultural and fishing products. The convention put its faith in the adequacy of the origins controls to prevent trade deflections and in the goodwill of the member states to work out any difficulties.[112] The only institution set up was the EFTA Council, meeting either at the ministerial or official level. It can modify most features of the convention by acting unanimously, and it makes recommendations to settle complaints or, by majority decision, authorizes a state to take safeguard measures. The council has established several standing committees such as the Consultative Committee for social partners and a Committee of Members of Parliament. The headquarters and the EFTA Secretariat, which do not have any executive functions comparable to those of the European Commission, were placed in Geneva. In June 2001, the remaining four EFTA members (Switzerland, Norway, Iceland, and Liechtenstein) signed an updated and modernized convention in order to take into account the integration steps of the 1990s.[113] Compared to full EEC membership, EFTA, with its sectoral scope and intergovernmental institutions, constituted a rather low level of integration.

Incentives for and Impediments to Integration

Sweden, Norway, and Switzerland's export dependence on EFTA is indicated in Table 3.10 (which includes, however, all exports, not just the industrial goods covered by the Stockholm Convention). The convention entered into force in 1960, and the gradual abolition of tariffs and quantitative restrictions was to take ten years, with an eye to the liberalization process within the EEC. When the latter decided to accelerate its time schedule, EFTA did the same, and as a result, all tariffs on industrial goods traded among EFTA members were eliminated by 1967.

Table 3.11 presents the three countries' major sectors of exports to the European Free Trade Association (at a 2-digit SITC level[114]) in 1960.

All these products benefited from FTA treatment, provided they ful-

Table 3.10   Overall Export Dependence on EFTA, 1960 and 1967

	EFTA Export Ratio (exports to EFTA as % of total exports)	GNP Ratio (exports to EFTA as % of GNP)
Sweden		
1960	34.4	6.8
1967	43.8	8.2
Norway		
1960	43.5	8.4
1967	47.0	9.7
Switzerland		
1960	15.9	3.5
1967	21.7	4.7
EFTA-7		
1960	19.0	2.9
1967	26.9	4.1

Sources: OECD, *Statistical Bulletins: Foreign Trade,* Analytical Abstracts, Series B, 1960, issues for Sweden, Norway, Switzerland, and "O.E.C.D. Countries Combined" (Paris: OECD, 1961); UN COMTRADE database (SITC, Rev. 1) for the year 1967; and OECD, *National Accounts of OECD Countries 1950–1968* (Paris: OECD, 1970).

London in August 1958 to welcome the creation of a "little" free trade area.[129] At the same time, they demanded the establishment of a consultative EFTA body for the social partners.

Sweden. The Social Democratic government was able to conduct the EFTA negotiations without much debate, and it took a leading role in the process. The Swedish political parties and social partners agreed that a wide free trade area would be the main goal, but since that option was no longer open, an association of the Seven was considered desirable.[130] Very few voices raised the question of EEC membership. The political elites were convinced that the potential economic advantages of the common market would be outweighed by the restrictions on sovereignty and neutrality.[131] In contrast to the Community's customs union with its multitude of common and coordinated policies, EFTA allowed its member states to maintain their national economic, trade, and social policies. In addition, the socialist governments preferred membership in the "red" EFTA to the "black" EEC dominated by conservative governments.[132] Mikael af Malmborg rightly concludes that "EFTA was a clear expression of the British, Swiss, Norwegian and Swedish willingness to firmly defend national sovereignty. However great the differences were between the British with their conception of empire and the Swedes with their welfare state, they could in any case agree on one thing: the importance of maintaining sovereignty."[133]

With full membership in EFTA, Sweden chose a sectoral, intergovernmental, and thus low level of integration, unlike what EEC membership would have required. It was prepared to renounce some of its operational sovereignty to become a member of EFTA, which offered considerable economic benefits.

Norway. In Norway, the Trade Council, the Bankers' Association, and the Association of Commerce and Services recommended ratification of the EFTA Convention, and the Norwegian Confederation of Trade Unions supported ratification with minimal reservations. The Federation of Norwegian Industries and the Federation of Norwegian Craftsmen remained skeptical but did not oppose it.[134] This split in the Federation of Norwegian Industries is evident in its statement that "most of the industrial branches which today manufacture exclusively or mainly for Norwegian consumption have expressed considerable doubts as to the effects Norwegian membership in EFTA would have on them," but "the part of industry manufacturing for export has generally expressed itself in favor of Norwegian association with EFTA."[135] In general, interest groups hoped to expand export possibilities and bypass discrimination from the EEC. Except for the communists, all parties supported the government's integration policy, and the conservatives particularly emphasized that Norway could not afford to stay outside a free trade area of which Great Britain was a member.[136]

By 1960, "European cooperation had developed so far that Norway in one form or another had to engage in its further expansion."[137] When the OEEC-wide free trade area did not succeed, the Norwegian government chose to follow Britain and its own neighbors into EFTA. For the Norwegians, "the commitments entered into involved some limitation on their freedom of action, but in return they gained a voice in international decisions and agreements which would have affected them anyway," and participation was thus seen "as giving them a greater degree of real, if indirect, control over their own affairs."[138] The intergovernmental EFTA was thus a welcome, low-level alternative to the supranational EEC.

Switzerland. The Swiss feared being surrounded by the customs wall of the EEC and early on stressed the common interests of the "Outer" Six or Seven in the OEEC. It has even been presumed that the Swiss suggested the idea of a small free trade area to the British in June 1958.[139] The government summarized its guidelines with regard to EFTA as follows:[140] The Swiss Confederation remains outside institutions with political goals, military alliances, and organizations in which it would have to renounce its treaty-making power. It rejects supranational bodies and the expansion of an organization's tasks by majority voting. In order to avoid having growing economic interdependence restrict its freedom of action or even lead to political dependence, Switzerland seeks to promote trade liberalization on a global level. Unlike the European Communities, membership in EFTA respects these conditions and does not jeopardize neutrality, direct democracy, or federalism. The Swiss parliament agreed with this assessment and added that the Stockholm Convention was "characterized by the absence of all those elements which belong to the constitutive traits of the Rome Treaty and which make our accession to the European Economic Community impossible."[141] After a brief discussion, it decided not to submit EFTA membership to a referendum (which the Swiss constitution at the time did not require for international treaties).

In contrast to the "interventionist" EEC and the OEEC-wide free trade area, the Swiss Federation of Commerce and Industry supported the creation of EFTA actively and without reservations.[142] The liberal EFTA corresponded well to the federation's conception of desirable integration, except for the fact that a wider free trade area would have been preferable. Most industrial branches of the Swiss economy as well as the trade unions approved their country's membership in EFTA.[143] On the political level, all major parties agreed with the government's decision that joining EFTA was the best option to avoid isolation and finally reach an agreement with the EEC.[144]

Like Sweden and Norway, the Swiss government underlined the inter-governmental structure of EFTA and the limited surrender of sovereignty. It pointed out that

> each international treaty implies for a state the voluntary abandonment of a part of its sovereignty which is, in accordance with reciprocity, general-ly compensated for by advantages of the same nature granted by the coun-try or the countries with which the treaty has been concluded. In the Stockholm Convention, the decisions involving new obligations must be taken by unanimity so that we will only be bound by the obligations established in the Convention itself or by those to which we will have later expressly subscribed.[145]

Switzerland obviously preferred EFTA to the EEC since it allowed partici-pation in European integration at a small sovereignty cost.

My expectation that none of the three countries would prefer to remain outside EFTA has been supported. As predicted, Sweden was most actively pushing for the Stockholm Convention, whereas the Norwegian govern-ment was a less eager supporter. Switzerland turned out to be a more ardent actor than might have been expected, given its less powerful eco-nomic incentives. This policy can be explained by the motivation to join EFTA as a second-best alternative and potential bridge to a more attractive agreement with the EEC. In the turmoil of the almost simultaneous negoti-ations of an OEEC-wide free trade area, the EEC, and EFTA, it became evident that the three countries were ready to give up a small part of their operational sovereignty in order to gain the economic benefits of narrow integration.

Conclusion

By the late 1950s, Western Europe was clearly divided between the six members of the supranational European Communities and the states that, after the failure of creating a wider free trade area, founded the intergovern-mental European Free Trade Association. The policies of Sweden, Norway, and Switzerland undoubtedly aimed at limited integration in terms of the scope and degree of institutionalization. Their integration preferences in this period are essentially explained by the proposed hypothesis. That is, a coun-try's integration policy is more reluctant (and operational sovereignty more valued than international voice), when the economic incentives are lower and the political impediments are higher. The EEC encompassed a high level of integration and EFTA a low level restricted to free trade in industrial goods. The OEEC's free trade area was supposed to fall in between yet have an intergovernmental setup. The political problems were inversely related to the level of integration. For all three countries, the wide free trade area was the most economically attractive option, EEC membership promised medium economic benefits, and EFTA generated high incentives for the two Scandinavian countries and medium ones for Switzerland. Hence, a free trade area comprising all of Western Europe would have been their first choice, provided that its final shape would have been acceptable; EFTA was second best; and joining the Communities was out of the question.

In general, the findings seem more accurate for national analyses than for cross-country comparisons. What a country is likely to choose, given the available alternatives, seems plausible, but it is more difficult to anticipate which country will be more interested than the others. For example, Switzerland was very actively supporting EFTA in spite of weaker economic incentives than those of Norway. Another problem is that the integration options of the three countries were to a large extent determined by the EEC-Six. They defined the benchmark of supranational integration, and they let the OEEC negotiations fail. The EEC countries acted and set the pace of the integration process, and the EFTA countries merely reacted to it. This holds also for the next decade, when the bridge-building efforts continued. Among the non-EEC members, the United Kingdom played a pivotal role, which it carried on in the 1960s.

Notes

1. See Diebold, *The Schuman Plan;* and Milward, *The Reconstruction of Western Europe.*
2. See Diebold, *The Schuman Plan,* chap. 21.
3. For the very restricted product coverage of the ECSC, the export ratio is considered high if it exceeds 10 percent, medium if it falls between 5 and 10 percent, and low below 5 percent.
4. UN Statistical Office, "Standard International Trade Classification," UN Statistical Papers, Series M, no. 10, 1951.
5. Gillingham, *Coal, Steel and the Rebirth of Europe, 1945–1955,* p. 319.
6. Mendershausen, "First Tests of the Schuman Plan," pp. 274–277.
7. Diebold, *The Schuman Plan,* pp. 151–152.
8. Lister, *Europe's Coal and Steel Community,* pp. 54–55, 447–449.
9. Olssen, "The Swedish Social Democrats," p. 229.
10. Pamphlet, "Our Foreign Policy," based on an address by the minister for foreign affairs on 5 June 1952 to the Social Democratic Party Congress, in Sweden, Ministry for Foreign Affairs, *Documents on Swedish Foreign Policy: 1952,* New Series I:C:2 (Stockholm: Royal Ministry for Foreign Affairs, 1957), p. 21.
11. Olssen, "The Swedish Social Democrats," p. 228.
12. Diebold, *The Schuman Plan,* p. 522.
13. Pharo, "Norge, EF og europeisk samarbeid," p. 61.
14. Pharo, "The Third Force, Atlanticism and Norwegian Attitudes Towards European Integration," p. 16.
15. Lange, "European Union," pp. 444, 448.

16. Rappard, "L'intégration économique de l'Europe et la Suisse," p. 309.
17. See Schindler, "Vereinbarkeit von EG-Mitgliedschaft und Neutralität," pp. 116–117.
18. Switzerland, Ministry for Foreign Affairs, "Leitsätze des Eidgenössischen Politischen Departementes zum Begriff der Neutralität vom 26. November 1954," in *Verwaltungsentscheide der Bundesbehörden* 24, no. 1 (Bern, 1954): 11.
19. Schaffner, "La Suisse et les grandes organisations économiques internationales," p. 249.
20. af Malmborg, *Den ståndaktiga nationalstaten*, pp. 228–240.
21. See Government statement to the Riksdag on 4 February 1953, in Sweden, Ministry for Foreign Affairs, *Documents on Swedish Foreign Policy: 1953*, New Series I:C:3 (Stockholm: Royal Ministry for Foreign Affairs, 1957), p. 17.
22. Secretary of State Dag Hammarskjöld, quoted in af Malmborg, *Den ståndaktiga nationalstaten*, p. 251.
23. Spierenburg and Poidevin, *Histoire de la Haute Autorité de la Communauté Européenne du Charbon et de l'Acier*, p. 306.
24. Ibid., pp. 769–770.
25. af Malmborg, *Den ståndaktiga nationalstaten*, pp. 260–261.
26. Olssen, "The Swedish Social Democrats," p. 228.
27. Røhne, "De første skritt inn i Europa, pp. 19–20.
28. Ibid., pp. 20–21.
29. Sogner, "The European Idea," pp. 307–327; and Archer and Sogner, *Norway, European Integration and Atlantic Security,* pp. 14–18.
30. Pharo, "The Third Force, Atlanticism and Norwegian Attitudes Towards European Integration," p. 27.
31. Memorandum by Ambassador Arne Skaug of 20 July 1950, quoted in Pharo, "The Third Force, Atlanticism and Norwegian Attitudes Towards European Integration," pp. 26–27.
32. Keel, *Le grand patronat suisse face à l'intégration européenne*, pp. 228–230, 397–398.
33. Fleury, "Le patronat suisse et l'Europe," p. 178.
34. Statement by Federal Councillor Max Petitpierre in Switzerland, Parliament, "Interpellation Egger: Internationale Lage," *Amtliches stenographisches Bulletin der Bundesversammlung: Nationalrat*, Bern, 18 March 1953, pp. 153–154.
35. Spierenburg and Poidevin, *Histoire de la Haute Autorité de la Communauté Européenne du Charbon et de l'Acier,* pp. 298–302, 480–485.
36. Switzerland, Federal Council, *Botschaft des Bundesrates an die Bundesversammlung vom 9. Oktober 1956 über die mit der Europäischen Gemeinschaft für Kohle und Stahl abgeschlossenen Abkommen*, Bern, 9 October 1956.
37. The ECSC's Common Assembly was, like the Court of Justice, expanded to cover the three Communities. The "Merger Treaty" of 1967 established a single Council and a single Commission for all three European Communities. Twenty years later, the Single European Act gave legal recognition to a "European Council" for summit meetings of heads of governments. In 1993, the Maastricht Treaty set up the European Union, with the European Economic Community (renamed the "European Community") as a separate entity within the EU. Moreover, it established an advisory Committee of the Regions and an ombudsman who investigates complaints brought by individuals against maladministration by Community bodies.
38. Wijkman, "Patterns of Production and Trade in Western Europe," pp. 6, 9.

39. Middleton, *Negotiating on Non-Tariff Distortions of Trade*, p. 12.
40. The measurement of tariff levels is notoriously full of difficulties. The tariff data in this study are mere estimates because of different and changing product classifications and because a simple arithmetic average confers the same importance on all tariff lines and may therefore assign a weight to a product that would be disproportionate to its share in trade. Nevertheless, unweighted averages of tariff rates reflect the tariff mentality prevailing in a customs area. The data refer to all the most-favored-nation (MFN) tariff lines and are ad valorem duties (i.e., duties expressed as a fixed percentage of value). See Camps, "Trade Diversion in Western Europe."
41. Sweden, National Board of Trade/Kommerskollegium, *Preliminär PM angående Romstaternas gemensamma yttre tullmur,* Stockholm, 11 January 1958, Fh D 133.
42. Sweden, National Board of Trade/Kommerskollegium, *Diskussionspromemoria angående Sverige och sexstatsmarknaden,* Stockholm, 26 November 1958, Fh 55, H 1/58, p. 5.
43. Ibid., p. 6.
44. Ibid., p. 11.
45. Ibid., pp. 14–38.
46. Minister of Trade Gunnar Lange, in Sweden Parliament, "Meddelande angående Sveriges utrikespolitik," *Riksdagens Protokoll: Andra Kammaren,* no. 7, Stockholm, 11 March 1959, pp. 56–57.
47. Malmborg, *Den ståndaktiga nationalstaten,* pp. 298, 404.
48. Sweden, National Board of Trade/Kommerskollegium, *PM med synpunkter på möjligheten av en svensk anslutning till den europeiska ekonomiska gemenskapen,* Stockholm, 3 June 1957, Fh 17, H 4/57, p. 7.
49. Minister of Trade Gunnar Lange, in Sweden, Parliament, "Meddelande angående Sveriges utrikespolitik," *Riksdagens Protokoll: Andra Kammaren,* no. 7, Stockholm, 11 March 1959, p. 56–57.
50. Norway, Ministry for Foreign Affairs, *Om samtykke til ratifikasjon av konvensjonen av 4. januar 1960 om opprettelse av Det Europeiske Frihandelsforbund med tilknyttet protokoll,* St.prp. nr. 75 (1959–1960), Oslo, 22 January 1960, pp. 32, 34.
51. Ibid., p. 33.
52. Allen, *Norway and Europe in the 1970s,* p. 42.
53. Pharo, "The Norwegian Labour Party," p. 209.
54. Switzerland, Federal Council, *Botschaft des Bundesrates an die Bundesversammlung vom 5. Februar 1960 über die Beteiligung der Schweiz an der Europäischen Freihandels-Assoziation,* Bern, 5 February 1960, p. 848.
55. Ibid., pp. 859–860.
56. See Schindler, "Neutralitätsrechtliche Aspekte eines Beitrittes der Schweiz zur EWG," pp. 217–228. He argues that neutrality reservations would allow only for association with the EEC.
57. Riklin, *Schweizerische Demokratie und EWG,* p. 7.
58. Schindler, "Die Schweiz und die europäische Integration," p. 91.
59. Seidman, *Report on a Study of Trade Union Views on European Economic Community–European Free Trade Area Developments,* pp. 3–4.
60. Testimony by Hubert W. A. de Besche, Chairman of the Senior Officials Group during the negotiations on the Stockholm Convention, in *L'AELE d'hier à demain,* p. 87.
61. af Malmborg, *Den ståndaktiga nationalstaten,* p. 388.

62. Statements by several Swedish officials, quoted in af Malmborg, *Den ståndaktiga nationalstaten*, pp. 298, 303.

63. Ibid., pp. 303, 316, 404, 436–437; and Sweden, National Board of Trade/Kommerskollegium, *PM rörande viss arbetsmarknadsproblem aktualiserade vid förhandlingarna om ett europeiskt frihandelsområde*, Stockholm, 10 January 1958, Fh 31, H 1/58.

64. This lack of interest is reflected in the scarcity of source materials on Norway's integration policy in the 1950s in the foreign ministry archives, in the parliamentary debates as well as in journals. Pharo, "The Norwegian Labour Party," p. 203.

65. Ibid., p. 205.

66. Ibid., pp. 203–204.

67. See Ramberg, "Sovereignty and Cooperation," pp. 49–133. The new Paragraph 93, which was finally adopted in 1962, reads as follows: "In order to secure international peace and security, or in order to promote international law and order and cooperation between nations, the Storting may, by a three-fourth majority, consent that an international organization of which Norway is or becomes a member, shall have the right, within a functionally limited field, to exercise powers which in accordance with this Constitution are normally vested in the Norwegian authorities."

68. Quoted in Enz, "Die Schweiz und die Grosse Europäische Freihandelszone," p. 177.

69. Fleury, "Le patronat suisse et l'Europe," p. 182.

70. du Bois, *La Suisse et le défi européen*, pp. 31–32.

71. Keel, *Le grand patronat suisse face à l'intégration européenne*, pp. 231–241, 398–399.

72. Switzerland, Federal Council, *Botschaft des Bundesrates an die Bundesversammlung vom 5. Februar 1960 über die Beteiligung der Schweiz an der Europäischen Freihandels-Assoziation*, Bern, 5 February 1960, p. 854.

73. Ibid., p. 859.

74. OEEC, *Report on the Possibility of Creating a Free Trade Area in Europe*, prepared for the OEEC Council by a special Working Party, Paris, C(57)5, 1957, p. 27.

75. OEEC, "Resolution of the OEEC Council" of 17 October 1957, in United Kingdom, *Negotiations for a European Free Trade Area: Documents Relating to the Negotiations from July, 1956, to December, 1958* (London: HMSO, Cmnd. 641, 1959), p. 49.

76. See Camps, "The Free Trade Area Negotiations"; Kaiser, *EWG und Freihandelszone;* and Snoy et d'Oppuers, "Les étapes de la coopération européenne et les négociations relatives à une zone de libre échange," pp. 603–623.

77. *Le Monde*, "La querelle reprend sur la zone de libre-échange."

78. OEEC, "Report by the Chairman of the Intergovernmental Committee to the Chairman of the OEEC Council" of 12 December 1958, in United Kingdom, *Negotiations for a European Free Trade Area: Documents Relating to the Negotiations from July, 1956, to December, 1958* (London: HMSO, Cmnd. 641, 1959), pp. 1–6.

79. OEEC, "Summary Report on the Negotiations Concerning the Establishment of a Free Trade Area" of 31 December 1958, in United Kingdom, *Negotiations for a European Free Trade Area: Documents Relating to the Negotiations from July, 1956, to December, 1958* (London: HMSO, Cmnd. 641, 1959), pp. 59–96.

80. af Malmborg, *Den ståndaktiga nationalstaten*, pp. 312–321; and "Sverige och Europamarknaden," pp. 25–42.

81. MP Bertil Ohlin, in Sweden, Parliament, "Meddelande angående Sveriges utrikespolitik," *Riksdagens Protokoll: Andra Kammaren*, no. 7, 11 March 1959, p. 27.

82. Article by the foreign minister in Världshorisont in April 1957, in Sweden, Ministry for Foreign Affairs, *Documents on Swedish Foreign Policy: 1957*, New Series I:C:7 (Stockholm: Royal Ministry for Foreign Affairs, 1959), pp. 27–29.

83. Speech by Minister Arne Skaug, annexed to Norway, Ministry for Foreign Affairs, *Om planene for et europeisk frihandelsområde*, St.meld. nr. 45 (1957), Oslo, 1 March 1957, pp. 22–23.

84. Ibid., p. 10.

85. Allen, *Norway and Europe in the 1970s*, p. 43.

86. Switzerland, Federal Council, *Botschaft des Bundesrates an die Bundesversammlung vom 5. Februar 1960 über die Beteiligung der Schweiz an der Europäischen Freihandels-Assoziation*, Bern, 5 February 1960, pp. 851–863.

87. Switzerland, Federal Council, *Botschaft des Bundesrates an die Bundesversammlung vom 20. August 1948 betreffend den Beitritt der Schweiz zu dem am 16. April 1948 in Paris unterzeichneten Abkommen über die europäische wirtschaftliche Zusammenarbeit*, Bern, 20 August 1948, pp. 1183, 1201.

88. Switzerland, Federal Council, *Botschaft des Bundesrates an die Bundesversammlung vom 5. Februar 1960 über die Beteiligung der Schweiz an der Europäischen Freihandels-Assoziation*, Bern, 5 February 1960, pp. 854–855.

89. Industrial Federations and Employers' Organisations of Austria, Denmark, Norway, Sweden, Switzerland, the United Kingdom, *Free Trade in Western Europe: A Joint Statement by the Industrial Federations and Employers' Organisations of Austria, Denmark, Norway, Sweden, Switzerland, the United Kingdom*, Paris, 14 April 1958.

90. Ibid., p. 4.

91. Seidman, *Report on a Study of Trade Union Views on European Economic Community—European Free Trade Area Developments*.

92. af Malmborg, *Den ståndaktiga nationalstaten*, pp. 298–299, 304.

93. Sweden, National Board of Trade/Kommerskollegium, *PM med synpunkter på möjligheten av en svensk anslutning till den europeiska ekonomiska gemenskapen*, Stockholm, 3 June 1957, Fh 17, H 4/57, p. 21.

94. af Malmborg, *Den ståndaktiga nationalstaten*, pp. 321–322, 357.

95. Statement by the prime minister in the Riksdag on 20 March 1957, in Sweden, Ministry for Foreign Affairs, *Documents on Swedish Foreign Policy: 1957*, New Series I:C:7 (Stockholm: Royal Ministry for Foreign Affairs, 1959), pp. 23–24.

96. Minister of Trade Gunnar Lange, quoted in af Malmborg, *Den ståndaktiga nationalstaten*, p. 323.

97. Ibid., p. 338.

98. af Malmborg, *Den ståndaktiga nationalstaten*, pp. 300–301; and Sweden, Parliament, "Svar på interpellation ang. förhandlingarna om ett europeiskt frihandelsområde," *Riksdagens Protokoll: Andra Kammaren*, 1958:B15, Stockholm, 9 December 1958, pp. 11–46.

99. Berge, "The Expectations of the Government Administration and the Organizations Toward EFTA," p. 139.

100. Hansen, *Det Norske EFTA-sporet i 1950-åra*, pp. 171–314.

101. See the statements annexed to Norway, Ministry for Foreign Affairs, *Om planene for et europeisk frihandelsområde*, St.meld. nr. 45 (1957), Oslo, 1 March 1957, pp. 24–35.

102. Hansen, *Det Norske EFTA-sporet i 1950-åra*, pp. 129–141.

103. Speech by Minister Arne Skaug, annexed to Norway, Ministry for Foreign Affairs, *Om planene for et europeisk frihandelsområde*, St.meld. nr. 45 (1957), Oslo, 1 March 1957, p. 21.

104. Røhne, "De første skritt inn i Europa," p. 52.

105. Quoted in Hansen, *Det Norske EFTA-sporet i 1950-åra*, p. 42.

106. See Enz, "Die Schweiz und die Grosse Europäische Freihandelszone," pp. 157–261.

107. *Neue Zürcher Zeitung*, "Die OEEC-Debatte über die Freihandelszone."

108. Keel, *Le grand patronat suisse face à l'intégration européenne*, pp. 178–201, 401–402.

109. Rudolf Bindschedler, quoted in Enz, "Die Schweiz und die Grosse Europäische Freihandelszone," p. 242.

110. See Camps, "The European Free Trade Association"; and Cook, "EFTA," pp. 72–87.

111. Muoser, *Finnlands Neutralität und die Europäische Wirtschaftsintegration*, pp. 172–173.

112. See Lambrinidis, *The Structure, Function, and Law of a Free Trade Area; EFTA, The Stockholm Convention Examined* (2nd ed. Geneva: EFTA, 1963); and EFTA, *EFTA: The European Free Trade Association* (Geneva: EFTA, 1987).

113. The revised EFTA Convention basically incorporates the rules established between the three EFTA members that are parties to the European Economic Area and the contents of the bilateral agreements between Switzerland and the European Union (e.g., mutual recognition of conformity assessments, the free movement of persons, intellectual property rights, trade in services, public procurement, investments, and concessions for agricultural products). It will be updated on a continuous basis and establish some new committees.

114. UN Statistical Office, "Standard International Trade Classification, Revised," *UN Statistical Papers*, Series M, no. 34, 1961.

115. Sweden, Government, *Kungl. Maj:ts proposition 1960:25 till riksdagen angående godkännande av Sveriges anslutning till konventionen angående upprättandet av Europeiska frihandelssammanslutningen m.m.*, Stockholm, 4 January 1960, pp. 62, 66.

116. Camps, *Britain and the European Community 1955–1963*, p. 220.

117. Speech by the minister of commerce in the Riksdag on 30 March 1959, in Sweden, Ministry for Foreign Affairs, *Documents on Swedish Foreign Policy: 1959*, New Series I:C:9 (Stockholm: Royal Ministry for Foreign Affairs, 1960), p. 22.

118. Sweden, Parliament, Foreign Affairs Committee, *Utrikesutskottets utlåtande 1960:2 i anledning dels av Kungl. Maj:ts proposition angående godkännande av Sveriges anslutning till konventionen angående upprättandet av Europeiska frihandelssammanslutningen, dels ock av motioner väckta i anslutning till sagda proposition*, Stockholm, 17 March 1960, p. 25.

119. Speech by the prime minister on 15 February 1959, in Ministry for Foreign Affairs, *Documents on Swedish Foreign Policy: 1959*, New Series I:C:9 (Stockholm: Royal Ministry for Foreign Affairs, 1960), p. 8.

120. Sweden, Government, *Kungl. Maj:ts proposition 1960:25 till riksdagen angående godkännande av Sveriges anslutning till konventionen angående upprät-*

tandet av Europeiska frihandelssammanslutningen m.m., Stockholm, 4 January 1960, pp. 45–46.

121. Norway, Ministry for Foreign Affairs, *Om samtykke til ratifikasjon av konvensjonen av 4. januar 1960 om opprettelse av Det Europeiske Frihandelsforbund med tilknyttet protokoll*, St.prp. nr. 75 (1959–1960), Oslo, 22 January 1960, pp. 28–29.

122. Ibid., pp. 32–34.

123. Ibid., pp. 38–71.

124. Norway, Parliament, Foreign Affairs and Constitution Committee, *Innstilling fra den utvidede utenriks- og konstitusjonskomité om ratifikasjon av konvensjonen av 4. januar 1960 om opprettelse av Det Europeiske Frihandelsforbund*, St.prp.nr. 75, Innst.S.nr. 157 (1959–1960), Oslo, 16 March 1960, p. 396.

125. Switzerland, Federal Council, *Botschaft des Bundesrates an die Bundesversammlung vom 5. Februar 1960 über die Beteiligung der Schweiz an der Europäischen Freihandels-Assoziation*, Bern, 5 February 1960, p. 888.

126. Ibid., pp. 858–864.

127. Ibid., pp. 891–893.

128. Kreinin, "The 'Outer-Seven' and European Integration," p. 383.

129. See *Gewerkschaftliche Rundschau*, no. 10, 1959, pp. 289–291.

130. af Malmborg, *Den ståndaktiga nationalstaten*, p. 367.

131. Debate in the Riksdag in March 1958, quoted in af Malmborg, *Den ståndaktiga nationalstaten*, p. 358.

132. Katzenstein, "Trends and Oscillations in Austrian Integration Policy Since 1955," p. 188.

133. af Malmborg, *Den ståndaktiga nationalstaten*, p. 386.

134. Berge, "The Expectations of the Government Administration and the Organizations Toward EFTA," pp. 134–176; and Hansen, *Det Norske EFTA-sporet i 1950-åra*, pp. 160–165.

135. Norway, Ministry for Foreign Affairs, *Om samtykke til ratifikasjon av konvensjonen av 4. januar 1960 om opprettelse av Det Europeiske Frihandelsforbund med tilknyttet protokoll*, St.prp. nr. 75 (1959–1960), Oslo, 22 January 1960, Annex 5, p. 3.

136. Røhne, "De første skritt inn i Europa," pp. 58–59.

137. Ramberg, "Sovereignty and Cooperation," p. 113.

138. Allen, *Norway and Europe in the 1970s*, p. 43.

139. Kaiser, *EWG und Freihandelszone*, p. 177.

140. Switzerland, Federal Council, *Botschaft des Bundesrates an die Bundesversammlung vom 5. Februar 1960 über die Beteiligung der Schweiz an der Europäischen Freihandels-Assoziation*, Bern, 5 February 1960, pp. 854–855.

141. MP Willy Bretscher, in Switzerland, Parliament, "Kleine Freihandelszone: Beitritt der Schweiz," *Amtliches stenographisches Bulletin der Bundesversammlung: Nationalrat*, Bern, 16 March 1960, p. 94.

142. Keel, *Le grand patronat suisse face à l'intégration européenne*, pp. 208–223, 403–404.

143. See Veyrassat, *La Suisse et la création de l'AELE (1958–1960)*, pp. 150–191; and the parliamentary ratification debate in Switzerland, Parliament, "Kleine Freihandelszone: Beitritt der Schweiz," *Amtliches stenographisches Bulletin der Bundesversammlung: Nationalrat*, Bern, 16–18 March 1960, pp. 90ff., and Switzerland, Parliament, "Kleine Freihandelszone: Beitritt der Schweiz," *Amtliches stenographisches Bulletin der Bundesversammlung: Ständerat*, Bern, 23 March 1960, pp. 48ff.

144. Roethlisberger, *La Suisse dans l'Association européenne de libre-échange (1960–1966)*, p. 202.

145. President of the Confederation Max Petitpierre in Switzerland, Parliament, "Kleine Freihandelszone: Beitritt der Schweiz," *Amtliches stenographisches Bulletin der Bundesversammlung: Ständerat*, Bern, 23 March 1960, p. 72.

4

The Failures to Reconcile
Europe in the 1960s

By 1962, in fact, it seemed . . . that EFTA might well become a footnote in history. The crucial factor was the reversal of the British stance towards Europe. . . . The issue of enlargement, however, . . . jarred with President de Gaulle's conception of Europe and the EEC.
—Derek W. Urwin, *The Community of Europe*, pp. 101–102

In the 1960s, the common market, in particular the customs union and the Common Agricultural Policy, was still in the making. The membership applications of Norway (together with the United Kingdom, Denmark, and Ireland) in 1961–1962 and 1967, as well as the related requests for association of Sweden and Switzerland (together with Austria), are illustrative of the politics involved. Both attempts at enlargement were initiated by a British move, and both failed due to a French veto.

The 1961–1962 Applications
for Membership and Association

In 1960, Western Europe was split into two rival trading groups: the six European Economic Community (EEC) countries and the seven European Free Trade Association (EFTA) countries. The latter were anxious to begin "bridge building" with the Community, and different ideas on new forms of economic or political cooperation, especially on a customs union, were floated.[1] The British soon realized that membership in the EEC was the indispensable precondition for any real cooperation with the Six. The Community had, upon French initiative, been discussing plans for the establishment of a political union that would coordinate foreign and defense policies, and the British were eager to participate.[2] Moreover, the U.S. government wanted the United Kingdom to join the EEC in order to build up a real Atlantic partnership. The small countries feared that the

United Kingdom might sacrifice EFTA, their most important bargaining tool. Hence, in a "loyalty pledge" agreed upon in London in June 1961, the governments "resolved that the European Free Trade Association . . . would be maintained at least until satisfactory arrangements have been worked out in negotiations to meet the various legitimate interests of all Members of EFTA, and thus enable them all to participate from the same date in an integrated European market."[3]

On 31 July 1961, the British government announced in the House of Commons its decision to open negotiations to join the EEC, thereby acknowledging its intention to take the positions of the Commonwealth and of the EFTA countries into account.[4] The formal application to join the EEC was submitted in Brussels on 10 August 1961, and the applications to join the European Coal and Steel Community (ECSC) and Euratom followed on 28 February 1962. Ireland, which was not a member of EFTA or NATO, had already applied on 31 July 1961. Denmark deposited its application together with Britain, and Norway followed on 2 May 1962. Faced with these membership applications, the neutral EFTA countries asked for special associate arrangements with the EEC. The Swedish and Austrian governments submitted their requests on 12 December 1961, and the Swiss government followed on 15 December 1961. Portugal announced in May 1962 that it also wished to open negotiations with the EEC. Greece had already signed an association agreement on 9 July 1961, discussions were underway with Turkey, and in early 1962 further requests for association were made by the governments of Spain and Malta.

Since the Community did not have the capacity to handle so many requests simultaneously, it decided to concentrate first on the British application. In November 1961, negotiations formally opened. The strongest opposition came from the French president. Charles de Gaulle was advocating an intergovernmental cooperation among states that was easy for the British to accept, but his conception of a European confederation was strictly confined to the Six. If Britain joined, it would be more difficult for France to assume a leading role on the Continent, and the "special relationship" between London and Washington would open the doors to a U.S. "Trojan horse."[5] On 14 January 1963, General de Gaulle announced at a press conference that the British were not yet ready to become a member of the Community. To him, the unresolved question was "whether Great Britain can at present place itself, with the Continent and like it, within a tariff that is truly common, give up all preference with regard to the Commonwealth, cease to claim that its agriculture be privileged and, even more, consider as null and void the commitments it has made with the countries that are part of its free trade area."[6] Obviously, the other five EEC members were very irritated about the unilateral French veto and confirmed their desire for the British to join. The EEC refuted the French assertion that the British government had been unwilling to accept the disciplines of the Treaty of Rome and claimed that the problems could be resolved.[7] However, on 29 January 1963, the negotiations formally ended.

Although de Gaulle's veto did not concern the other three applicants, Norway, Denmark, and Ireland were not prepared to pursue membership without Britain, and only the Austrian government decided to continue the talks about association. Within the Six, the opinion was divided on what, if anything, should be done with regard to Sweden, Switzerland, and Austria. The Commission feared that formal association with the neutral countries would weaken the cohesion of the Community and hamper its political effectiveness. Association was interpreted as intended for economically weak countries on the way to full membership and not for highly industrialized countries like Sweden, Switzerland, and Austria.[8] Moreover, neutrality, except for Austria's "imposed neutrality," was regarded with suspicion by the EEC-6. The European Parliament stated that the neutrals should not be allowed to take the pick of the bunch by being granted the economic advantages of the common market without the restrictions on national freedom of action and the political obligations which the member states had to accept.[9]

In fact, the EEC treaty does not define what constitutes association, but neutrality did not necessarily constitute an obstacle.[10] One of the main difficulties was to find a satisfactory institutional solution.[11] Association generally involves the creation of an association council and a court of arbitration as well as a few committees. "The associated States would naturally be consulted during the elaboration of Community policy and decisions, but the formal decisions would have to be taken first in the E.E.C. Council and later in the Council of Association," and "the associated countries would then have the formal right to vote against them."[12] Association requires far-reaching adaptation and unilateral harmonization with the Community rules without full membership rights. It may be characterized as a global, intergovernmental approach to integration and thus a medium level of integration.

Incentives for and Impediments to Integration

Table 4.1 presents the export dependence of Sweden, Norway, and Switzerland on the EEC for the time of application and the failure of the negotiations.

Except for Switzerland, the export and GDP ratios were slightly lower in 1963 than in the late 1950s as a result of the trade diversion taking place between the EEC and EFTA. For both the Community and EFTA, the gains from intragroup exports outweighed the loss of exports to the other group.[13] The shares would, of course, have increased considerably if the

Table 4.1   Overall Export Dependence on the EEC, 1961 and 1963

	EEC Export Ratio (exports to EEC as % of total exports)	GDP Ratio (exports to EEC as % of GDP)
Sweden		
1961	27.9	5.0
1963	32.0	5.7
Norway		
1961	24.8	4.2
1963	26.9	4.5
Switzerland		
1961	41.2	8.7
1963	42.1	8.6
EEC-6		
1961	36.4	5.1
1963	42.4	5.8

Sources: OECD, *Statistical Bulletins: Foreign Trade,* Analytical Abstracts, Series B, 1961, issues for Sweden, Norway, Switzerland, and "Pattern of Trade of Groups of O.E.C.D. Countries" (Paris: OECD, 1962); UN COMTRADE database for 1963; and OECD, *National Accounts: Main Aggregates 1960–1994,* vol. 1 (Paris: OECD, 1996).

United Kingdom had joined the Community. In 1963 Norway sold 17.8 percent of its exports to Great Britain, Sweden sold 13.9 percent, and Switzerland sold 6.2 percent.[14] The Swiss economy obtained 64 percent of imports from the Community (13.7 percent from EFTA), Sweden 38.9 percent (30.4 percent from EFTA), and Norway 29.8 percent (44.1 percent from EFTA).[15] Table 4.2 identifies the leading export sectors.

Estimates for the average external and internal EEC tariffs in 1963, as well as for 1968, when the EEC customs union was completed, are provided in Table 4.3.[16] Intra-Community tariffs in 1963 were half the rates for imports from third countries. For a state associated with the EEC, the level of tariffs would probably have been the same as for a full member. Tariffs in Western Europe were subject to rapid change, resulting not only from regional integration schemes but also from General Agreement on Tariffs and Trade (GATT) negotiations and national decisions. The timetable for the tariff cuts in the common market and the alignment of national tariffs to the Common External Tariff (CET) had been accelerated several times in the 1960s. Discrimination vis-à-vis the EFTA countries thus steadily increased. On 1 July 1962, the internal EEC tariffs on manufactured goods were reduced by 50 percent and those on agricultural products by 35 percent, three-and-a-half years earlier than foreseen by the Rome treaty. In 1963, the EEC-6 reduced their internal tariffs by another 10 percent and proceeded to the second alignment to the CET. Additional 10 percent cuts took place at the beginning of 1965 and 1966. In mid-1967, another 5 per-

Table 4.2   Sector Exports to the EEC, 1963

Leading Export Sectors to the EEC (SITC, Rev. 1)		Sector Share (sector exports to EEC as % of total exports to EEC)	Sector Export Ratio (sector exports to EEC as % of total sector exports)
Sweden			
Pulp and waste paper	(25)	17.0	46.3
Nonelectrical machinery	(71)	13.5	27.0
Paper manufactures	(64)	13.7	37.2
Norway			
Nonferrous metals	(68)	19.6	33.2
Paper manufactures	(64)	13.3	36.6
Iron and steel	(67)	10.7	36.2
Switzerland			
Nonelectrical machinery	(71)	24.8	44.2
Professional instruments	(86)	9.8	23.7
Textile manufactures	(65)	8.5	41.4

Source: UN COMTRADE database.

cent was deducted from national tariffs, and one year later the last 15 percent was removed and the final CET alignment executed. By comparison, nontariff barriers (NTBs) to trade were not an issue of concern yet at the time.

Sweden. In 1963, the Swedish economy sold almost one-third of its exports to the EEC, accounting for a share of 5.7 percent of GDP (see Table 4.1). Only the EFTA market was more important, with an export ratio of 40.1 percent.[17] The government was aware that Sweden's economy was more integrated into the international division of labor than most of the other European countries.[18] The changes caused by tariff discrimination from the enlarged common market alone were expected to reduce exports by 3 percent; joining would yield a (static) gain of 4 percent of GNP.[19] In 1963, the major export sector with regard to the EEC-6 was pulp and waste paper (17 percent), of which the EEC-6 absorbed almost half, while Sweden's former main exports, metalliferous ores and wood, lost in importance (see Table 4.2). Nonelectrical machinery emerged as a new principal export branch (13.5 percent) in addition to paper manufactures. Among these three medium-sized sector shares, paper manufactures met with a tariff level of 15 percent, followed by nonelectrical machinery with 11 percent (see Table 4.3).[20] The Swedish engineering industry feared that by staying outside the common market, its exports would face tariffs of around 15 percent for steel and metal manufactures and between 3 and 22 percent for machinery.[21] By contrast, raw materials had to cope with relatively low

96 Reluctant Europeans

Table 4.3   Barriers to Trade: EEC Tariffs, 1963 and 1968 (percentage)

		Year	Estimated External Tariffs of the EEC	Estimated Intra-EEC Tariffs
Sweden				
Pulp and waste paper	(25)	1963	2–3	1–2
		1968	1–2	0.0
Nonelectrical machinery	(71)	1963	11	5–6
		1968	8–9	0.0
Paper manufactures	(64)	1963	15	7–8
		1968	14–15	0.0
Norway				
Nonferrous metals	(68)	1963	8–9	4–5
		1968	6–7	0.0
Iron and steel	(67)	1963	15	7–8
		1968	14–15	0.0
Paper manufactures	(64)	1963	10–11	5–6
		1968	7–8	0.0
Switzerland				
Nonelectrical machinery	(71)	1963	11	5–6
		1968	8–9	0.0
Textile manufactures	(65)	1963	14–15	7–8
		1968	12–13	0.0
Professional instruments	(86)	1963	13–14	6–7
		1968	9–10	0.0
Electrical machinery	(72)	1963	14–15	7–8
		1968	11–12	0.0

Sources: The 1963 data are based on GATT, *Protocol to the General Agreement on Tariffs and Trade Embodying Results of the 1960–1961 Tariff Conference*, Annex B (Geneva: GATT, 16 July 1962), GATT's first publication of the consolidated EEC tariff; and C.E.C.A./C.E.E./Euratom, *Tarif douanier des Communautés européennes* (Luxembourg: Service des Publications des Communautés européennes, January 1961). The GATT Protocol incorporates the results of the negotiations under Article 28 GATT, of the Dillon Round (1960–1962) and of other negotiations such as those relating to the accession of new states to the GATT. The 1968 data are based on the Common External Tariff as it entered into force on 1 July 1968, which included a part of the reductions agreed on in the GATT Kennedy Round (1964–1967), Annex to Council of the European Communities, "Règlement (CEE) no. 950/68 du Conseil, du 28 juin 1968, relatif au tarif douanier commun," *Journal officiel des Communautés européennes*, no. L 172 (22 July 1968).

trade barriers, for example, 2–3 percent on pulp and waste paper. This middle-range export dependence and sensitivity made the Swedish government "anxious to participate in a large integrated market and to avoid the risk of Sweden's export industries being exposed to a heavy burden of discrimination."[22]

Jan Magnus Fahlström makes out four groups of arguments in the 1961 public debate on why Sweden should not join the EEC but search for another form of participation: membership would (1) mean joining a club of reactionary regimes, (2) restrain Sweden's traditional welfare policy with full employment and better social benefits, (3) limit the scope of trade policy with regard to third countries and in particular developing countries, and (4) be incompatible with neutrality policy.[23] Integration would lead to "a disarmament of social policy" or at least a slowdown of social progress.[24] The left-wing activists argued that in case of membership, the Community would decide what Sweden could or could not do at home, touching upon such vital issues as the labor market or nationalizations.[25] In the words of a trade union leader, Sweden could not "accept to be bound by a reactionary policy or to West European countries with bourgeois dictatorships."[26]

The government gave three reasons why EEC membership was incompatible with neutrality policy: "in the first place supranational institutions would have the authority to 'direct Swedish trade policy'; secondly, the Treaty of Rome could be interpreted so that it did not permit a member to renounce its obligations in war with the aim of fulfilling the obligations of neutrality; and thirdly, the long-range goal of the EEC was a political union, linked to the Atlantic pact."[27] Since the EEC was viewed as the economic counterpart of NATO, "Sweden would in the eyes of all other countries, though not formally, give up her nonalliance policy and join the Western camp."[28] The trade minister added that even though the "policy of neutrality is deeply rooted in the historical experience of the Swedish people," "there is no reason why Sweden should not be able to participate as an associate in an integrated European market."[29] To conclude, Sweden faced medium-size economic interests and political obstacles toward full integration with the EEC but only low political obstacles toward association.

Norway. Norway's economy exported a share of 26.9 percent to the European Economic Community in 1963 (see Table 4.1), but 42.4 percent went to the EFTA countries.[30] Hence, it was very important whether the other EFTA members, in particular Great Britain, would join the common market: "British and Danish membership in the EEC would put 3/4 of the Norwegian export market into the Community."[31] The government was convinced that a larger Western European market would open up great new export possibilities for Norway, in spite of stronger competition and adjustment problems in the agricultural and fisheries sectors, and that "by staying outside the enlarged Community, we would suffer a significant economic loss."[32] Raw materials still occupied an important position in the Norwegian sales to the EEC in 1963 (see Table 4.2). Nonferrous metals figured prominently, with one-fifth of the economy's total exports to the EEC and one-third of the sector's exports, followed by paper manufactures and iron and qualified steel. The average EEC tariffs for nonferrous metals were 8–9 percent and for paper products 15 percent (see Table 4.3). If Great Britain and other EFTA countries joined the Community, the government expected the tariffs on vital exports to rise to 10 percent for raw aluminum, to 6–10 percent for ferro-alloys, and to 7–17 percent for different kinds of paper.[33] "Nearly 75 percent of the total Norwegian exports would feel the impact of higher tariffs," and because of the exports' special composition, Norway would be among the countries with the highest relative increase in tariffs.[34] In light of the British membership application, the importance of market access for the Norwegian economy was clearly high.

Based on Gallup data, Stein Rokkan found that the debate on the common market brought Norway's societal cleavages out in full daylight: "on the pro-EEC side, the Labor voters, primarily in the cities and outside agriculture and fisheries, the Liberals in the southern and western cities and the Conservatives everywhere," and "on the anti-EEC side, the Left Socialists and the smallholders and fishermen of the Labor party, the Liberals of the eastern cities and to some extent in the western countryside, the Christians of the South and West, and Agrarians practically everywhere."[35] When parliament voted in favor of applying for EEC membership in April 1962, the Norwegian people were about equally split among support and opposition.[36] The announcement of a referendum on EEC membership did not calm the debate but rather intensified it. In the winter of 1962, an ad hoc committee called "Action Against the Common Market" (Aksjon mot norsk medlemskap i Fellesmarkedet) emerged. It received support from persons of all political parties, with a majority of left-wing socialists and agrarians, and from individuals from trade unions and the farmers' and the fishermen's organizations.[37] The "Action Committee" expressed fears that "Norway should be drawn into a political union with a domestic and foreign political tradition unknown to us; that foreign capital would dominate Norwegian industries, agriculture and fisheries; that our economic policy, our employment policy, and social policy would be decided by organs outside Norway; and that we would never be able to withdraw from the Common Market."[38]

Many people feared that EEC membership would deprive Norway of the necessary control over the economy to pursue socialist policies and reforms. "As viewed by many Norwegians, continental economic policies still appeared somewhat antediluvian, and as the Common Market was being organised, it appeared inward-looking to an unacceptable degree."[39] Nevertheless, the Norwegian government carefully noted that the Treaty of Rome foresaw neither a common social policy nor any provisions on full employment and that Norway's strict alcohol policy would not be affected.[40] The Labor government's main opponents in domestic politics, the conservatives, were united with it in according highest priority to the interests of trade and shipping and to maintaining Norway's ties with Britain and its place in the Atlantic alliance. They had the industrial federation and the trade unions on their side.[41] For the elites, British policy was certainly a decisive factor in 1961–1962. It was assumed that Britain could be relied on to resist any unwelcome development of supranational institutions. "Even more important, the Norwegians were confident that an EEC which included Britain would be firmly turned toward the Atlantic, thereby ruling out any danger of their new continental commitments weakening Norway's ties with the United States."[42] One parliamentarian explicitly castigated the opponents' argument that Norway would "come under foreign rule" or suffer "a new occupation" if it joined the EEC.[43]

The Norwegian government thus perceived rather low geohistorical constraints on joining the EEC, provided the United Kingdom would join at the same time. The domestic constraints were at most considered medium, given that the power of the societal cleavages did not fully materialize because of the lack of real negotiations.

Switzerland. With 42.1 percent of its exports going to the European Economic Community in 1963 and a GDP ratio of 8.6 percent (see Table 4.1), Swiss dependence on the EEC must be considered high. By comparison, only 17.7 percent of Swiss exports were sold to the EFTA countries.[44] The government estimated that Switzerland's external trade ratio, calculated per head of its population, was one of the highest ones in the world and considerably above the average of the EEC countries.[45] The composition of Switzerland's leading exports to the common market remained the same compared to the 1950s.[46] One-quarter consisted of nonelectrical machinery, a sector that sold the considerable share of 44.2 percent to the EEC (see Table 4.2). Textile manufactures accounted for a small share of 8.5 percent, and the portion of professional and scientific instruments was equally low, yet more diversified. These major exports encountered tariffs above 10 percent (see Table 4.3), and they were expected to remain relatively high. This constellation made access to the common market important for the Swiss economy.

Neutrality was still regarded as the most fundamental obstacle to EEC membership. "Whereas Switzerland's federalism or direct democracy in case of an accession to the EEC would never have to be renounced but would only be restricted, neutrality cannot be reduced. Half a neutrality is as much as none."[47] If Switzerland had been a member of the EEC, six of the forty federal referenda held between 1958 and 1970 would have collided totally and four partially with Community law.[48] That is, three-quarters of the Swiss referenda would not have been affected. Moreover, EEC membership in the 1960s would mainly have touched upon federal, not cantonal competences.[49] The extent to which association would have restricted direct democracy and federalism depends on the scope of harmonization. Since no agreement had been negotiated, this issue and the impact on neutrality remained blurred. A global approach covering most of the substance of EEC membership would, in principle, have had the same effects as membership itself. It "would involve a significant loss of rights for the parliament and the people in favor of the association council" because "in the areas covered by framework obligations, the parliament would practically only have consultative functions, and the referendum would be excluded as well."[50] The debate about association did not disclose any relevant reinforcing cleavages in Swiss society or even in parliament.

As a result, Switzerland suffered strong political constraints on EEC membership but lower ones on association. From a Swiss point of view, the supranational EEC was "adapted to the political and psychological needs of those European countries which the last war left with the bankrupt state of their political regimes and whose awareness of sovereignty has considerably been weakened," but it did not meet the need of the "politically and spiritually still intact part of Western Europe," such as Switzerland.[51]

Integration Policy Preferences

Market access was of average weight for Sweden but was very important for Switzerland as well as for Norway, if the expectations about the effects of Britain joining the Community are included. The political obstacles to full membership were perceived to be high for Switzerland, medium for Sweden, and low in the case of Norway, provided the UK would join as well. The economic incentives were comparable for membership and association, but the latter would have encountered much weaker political impediments. Based on these findings, both Sweden and Switzerland are expected to aim at limited integration, protecting operational sovereignty, whereas Norway might choose full membership.

Sweden.   On 22 August 1961, Prime Minister Tage Erlander, addressing the national conference of the Metal Industry Workers' Union, declared that full membership in the EEC was out of question for Sweden since it was incompatible with its policy of nonalignment.[52] This so-called Metal Speech (*metall-talet*) was highly significant since it defined the social democratic (and thus governmental) policy toward European integration for almost thirty years. Sweden's freedom from alliances "must be supplemented by a persistent effort to avoid any commitment, even outside the sphere of military policy, which would make it difficult or impossible for Sweden, in the event of a conflict, to choose a neutral course and which would make the world around us no longer confident that Sweden really wanted to choose such a course."[53] In addition, Sweden should not yield sovereignty to supranational institutions governed by majority vote in areas such as economic, social, fiscal, or labor market policy because doing so would restrict its capacity to develop the Swedish welfare state.

The Center Party and the communists concurred with the government's assessment that membership and neutrality were irreconcilable, but the Liberal and Conservative opposition parties argued in favor of accession with certain escape clauses.[54] In the parliamentary debate of October 1961, the Swedish government reaffirmed its choice of association, given the prospect of the United Kingdom, Denmark, and Norway joining the EEC.[55] Thanks to the strong relationship between the social democrats and the Confederation of Trade Unions, the latter fully supported the government's position. Nevertheless, "at various instances representatives of the Confederation expressed some measure of hesitation about the common economic and social policy provided for in the Treaty of Rome."[56] The Swedish farmers, who maintained a strong connection with the Center Party, were afraid of competition from the lower-cost agriculture of the Continent but supported the government's policy in favor of association.

An analysis conducted by the Federation of Swedish Industries and the National Board of Trade showed that all the industrial sectors expected better export opportunities on the continental market in case of Sweden's participation in a European market comprising the EEC and EFTA countries.[57] The Swedish engineering and wood-processing industries, facing relatively high tariffs, particularly advocated integration. The possibility of compensating for the decline in exports resulting from increasing EEC tariff discrimination and the loss of the EFTA preferences through increased sales to other markets was considered rather small.

The three neutral EFTA countries, Austria, Sweden, and Switzerland, held several meetings between July 1961 and June 1962 to discuss the neutrality reservations that they considered necessary for association with the EEC.[58] In order to strengthen their bargaining power vis-à-vis the Community, they stipulated the following joint conditions: (1) the right to retain the treaty-making power with regard to third countries; (2) the right to (partly or wholly) suspend or terminate the association agreement in times of crises or war and to be exempted from economic measures of warlike character in peacetime (e.g., boycotts, embargoes); and (3) the assurance of certain vital supplies in the event of war (in particular, with regard to agricultural policy). The EEC-6 were not too pleased by the three requests for association. They suspected that the neutral countries wanted to reap the (economic) advantages while avoiding any (political) obligations.

Sweden presented its case before the Council of Ministers on 28 July 1962.[59] It put forward the neutrality reservations, suggested an association council and a suitable arbitration procedure, and emphasized that "a neutral country cannot simply be bound by obligations decided by others."[60] For the Swedish government, association "implies essentially that in economic matters the associated country participates in the integrated market" while "retaining its independence on the political level."[61] By contrast, the position of the Swedish Employers' Federation and the Federation of Swedish Industries was that "Sweden has to join the Community, preferably as a member since this would yield possibilities to influence decisions."[62] For the proponents it was clear that "a country will be able to influence its own future more efficiently by being on the established councils and bodies, and thus being able to discuss its difficulties and voting against the policies which it does not like."[63] The opposition equally pointed out that "only membership provides the possibility to participate on an equal footing in the Community's various institutions, while an association does not bring about any influence on the future policies."[64] Yet the social democratic government found that association would best fulfill its two desires of close economic cooperation and a certain political distance.

Hence, Sweden strove for an intermediate level of integration, that is, for a global approach to integration and an intergovernmental institutional setup. Sovereignty became less important relative to the status quo and in view of EEC enlargement but maintained its significance relative to Community membership.

Norway. The United Kingdom's application to join the EEC did not receive an enthusiastic welcome in Norway since it forced the government to address the membership issue. "To remain outside if Great Britain did not join would be acceptable, however difficult," but "to remain outside if Great Britain went in would be directly contrary to Norwegian trading, shipping, and political interests."[65] The decision to enter negotiations with the EEC was preceded by extensive consultations. The Free Trade Committee (Frihandelsutvalget), which was formed in 1960 and comprised representatives from all the relevant ministries and the major economic interest groups, conducted a study on the economic and political implications of EEC membership. It concluded that it was of utmost importance for Norway to participate in an enlarged common market and advised the government to apply for negotiations, preferably for membership instead of association.[66] These negotiations would have to take into account the sensitive areas of agriculture, fisheries, the right of establishment, and the free movement of capital. The Norwegian economy has traditionally imported foreign capital and restricted capital exports since it had to finance big investments in the infrastructure of the extended country and the exploitation of its natural resources, such as hydroelectric power. Another study on the consequences for Norway if it chose to remain aloof of an enlarged Community concluded that isolation would clearly be to its disadvantage.[67]

In a report to parliament in March 1962, the government set out Norway's position in favor of negotiations for EEC membership. It stressed that it would continue to work toward "full employment, strong economic growth and a just income and property distribution" and that stronger development of the Community's political cooperation was in Norway's interest.[68] Parliament considered that staying outside an EEC embracing Britain, Denmark, and an associated Sweden would entail not only economic difficulties but "a break with the foreign policy we have pursued in all those years since World War II."[69] If Britain and Denmark did not join, Norway's policy would have to be reviewed as well. On 28 April 1962, the Storting approved a membership application with a clear majority of more than three-quarters. It also decided to hold a consultative referendum as soon as the negotiations were brought to an end. The governing Labor Party was not united on EEC membership, and there were also clear divisions among the liberals and within the Christian People's Party.[70] Only the conservatives wholly supported membership. The Center Party declared its almost unanimous opposition and argued in favor of association. Strong opposition came also from the far left, the Socialist People's Party and the Communist Party.

All major economic interest groups, except for the farmers' organizations, were in favor of taking up negotiations with the EEC.[71] The Federation of Norwegian Industries and the Confederation of Trade Unions, with its traditionally close relations to the Labor Party, supported the government's decision to apply for membership. The fishermen's organizations welcomed free access to the EEC market for their exports but feared that the other member states would gain admission to Norwegian fishing grounds and companies. In his presentation to the EEC Council of Ministers on 4 July 1962, the Norwegian foreign minister dwelt on the specific problems of agriculture, fisheries, regional policy, and the free movement of capital.[72] The Common Fisheries Policy (CFP) was still in the making, and the Norwegian government wanted to participate in its elaboration.

In 1962, the Norwegian reluctance to enter the EEC was overcome only by two arguments. Firstly, since Norwegian trade, shipping and security interests were so directly related to British interests, it was felt that if the United Kingdom joined, the decision was, in fact, taken out of Norwegian hands. . . . Secondly, it was believed that with such like-minded countries as Great Britain, Sweden and Denmark also joining, the possibility of the development of a supranational authority in the Common Market was reduced.[73]

In contrast to the neutral EFTA countries, the Norwegian government considered association with the EEC undesirable: "If one decides to take up negotiations on association, one should be aware of the fact that in practice one will be as much committed to the EEC decisions as with full membership."[74] Association would offer only limited influence to an industrially advanced country,[75] whereas supranational organs granted small states "real influence."[76] Parliament pointed out that in an interdependent world, the notion of sovereignty should not be overvalued because "even if one were to choose to stay entirely outside, one cannot count on maintaining the same national freedom of action one had before the new Community came into being."[77]

As expected, the economic elites cared more about the anticipated economic benefits, whereas the political elites also took into account political factors such as security and institutional matters. The Norwegian government aimed at a high level of integration and stressed the importance of having a voice in the EEC. After the breakdown of the negotiations between the EEC and Britain, it declared that Norway would not seek membership alone.[78]

Switzerland. On 15 December 1961, the Swiss government asked the Community for "a form of association with the EEC that would leave neutrality, federalism and direct democracy untouched."[79] At the same time, an "Integration Office" was established to improve the cooperation among the different ministries dealing with issues of European integration. Several working groups began to study the implications of association from different angles, led by the Permanent Economic Delegation (Ständige Wirtschaftsdelegation), comprising civil servants as well as representatives of the major economic organizations.[80] The delegation considered that the free movement of persons might require a safeguard clause and that the inclusion of agriculture would pose some problems. With regard to the institutional setup, the Federal Council was aware that "in exchange for nondiscrimination, the EEC will expect us to accept the decisions of the Community which are taken without our participation," and "an association will only make sense for us if we can find a solution that allows us to decide ourselves whether we want to accept the decisions or not."[81]

In its presentation to the EEC ministers on 24 September 1962, the Swiss government underlined again that "in the arrangements to be concluded with the Community Switzerland will have, however, to safeguard her neutrality—guarantee of her independence—her federalist structure and her system of direct democracy."[82] It proposed the establishment of an association council with regular consultations and an arbitration body. Switzerland agreed to adapt its legislation as much as possible to the EEC rules, with due respect to the neutrality reservations. It even suggested harmonizing its tariffs to a great extent with the external tariffs of the Community—a remarkable change of attitude with regard to the Swiss position in the negotiations on a free trade area for the countries in the Organization for European Economic Cooperation and on EFTA.[83]

The Swiss Federation of Commerce and Industry (Vorort) fully supported the government's decision in favor of association instead of EEC membership. On the one hand, it feared the economic isolation of Switzerland, but on the other hand, it insisted, in contrast to the Swedish industrial federation, that joining the Community or even a customs union would not be compatible with neutrality.[84] The Vorort approved of an extensive harmonization with the Community's external tariffs, but it had some reservations regarding the Community's social and agricultural policies and the free movement of workers.[85]

Driven by strong economic incentives but constrained by high political impediments, Switzerland aimed, as expected, at a medium level of integration in the form of association. The economic elites were less supportive of EEC membership than might have been expected. The Swiss government jealously guarded its operational sovereignty, accepting that association would not concede any significant "voice" in the Community's decision-making process. The view prevailed that in a supranational organization, "the sacrifice of sovereignty made by a big state is more theoretical than real because it gains compensation in the influence which it will have on the decisions taken by the common organs. It is confident that nothing will be done against its will. By contrast, a small state's transfer of sovereignty to common organs, in particular one as heterogeneous as Switzerland, exposes it to the risk to be swallowed up or to become a vassal or a satellite."[86] After the French veto in early 1963, the Swiss government decided not to withdraw its request for association or to further pursue it.[87] The economic division of Western Europe persisted after the failed enlargement, but skepticism toward the feasibility of association had grown.[88]

In Sweden, the social democratic government feared that the EEC would undermine its search for social justice and its independent foreign policy. This debate on the impact of integration on the welfare model was less controversial in Norway. The Norwegian elites might have underestimated the power of the domestic opposition, whose alliances drew on societal cleavages and had not yet been fully activated since no negotiations had taken place. For Norway, British membership was a precondition for both political and economic reasons. The discussion in neutral Switzerland focused on the question of whether association or a mere bilateral trade agreement should be chosen, whereas in neutral Sweden the question was one of full membership or association. Moreover, a close link to the EEC was rejected by the leading Swiss industrial federation, but the Federation of Swedish Industries favored full membership. The Swedish export industries hoped that a special protocol would make neutrality compatible with membership, and they argued that only accession would allow having a say in the Community's further development. By contrast, the Swiss political and economic elites stressed the preservation of sovereignty. Switzerland faced stronger political constraints than Sweden.

The 1967 Applications for Membership

The crisis of the European Economic Community, which began with the abortive Fouchet Plan for political cooperation of 1961–1962, deepened with de Gaulle's veto of British membership in 1963. In addition, disagreement arose over defense matters, and in 1966 France withdrew from the NATO military command structure, prompting the relocation of the NATO headquarters from Paris to Brussels. The political crisis hardened in 1965 because of the rejection by France of a series of key proposals: the Commission's request for its own source of revenue, the expansion of the budgetary powers of the European Parliament, and the financing of the new Common Agricultural Policy. A second dispute arose over the French refusal to accept that majority voting should automatically be introduced on a significant range of issues in the Council when the "third stage" of the transitional phase came into effect in January 1966. The French government was not prepared to accept the package deal of an agriculture settlement for an increase in the supranational characteristics of the Community, and it resorted to an "empty-chair" policy, boycotting the meetings of the Council of Ministers. After seven months, a settlement was reached between France and the other five EEC members in the so-called "Luxembourg compromise," which enabled a member state to exercise a veto on matters that it claimed might adversely affect its own vital national interests: "Where, in the case of decisions which may be taken by a majority vote on a proposal from the Commission, very important interests of one or more partners are at stake, the Members of the Council will endeavour, within a reasonable time, to reach solutions which can be adopted by all the Members of the Council while respecting their mutual interests and those of the Community."[89]

These developments and the imminent abolition of tariffs in both EFTA and the EEC led to new discussions about building a bridge between the two trading groups. Even though most EFTA countries were skeptical about the possibility of accession, the United Kingdom launched its second application to the European Communities on 11 May 1967. The decision of the hitherto hostile Labor government was approved in the House of Commons by an overwhelming majority. Once again, Ireland and Denmark followed suit with simultaneous applications. The Norwegian government submitted its request on 24 July 1967. The remaining EFTA states expressed their interest in an arrangement with the Community short of full membership. No mention was made of the 1961 London agreement, but the EFTA ministers pointed out that the industrial free trade achieved among their countries in 1966 must be safeguarded.[90] On 26 July 1967, the Swedish government sent a rather elusive application to the EEC for negotiations that would allow it to participate in the common market while retaining its neutrality. Doubting the chances of a new petition, Switzerland and Austria preferred to wait and see what Sweden would achieve. Austria's attempt to further pursue its association request alone from 1963–1967 had shown that the project was indeed fraught with political difficulties.[91]

On 29 September 1967, the Commission submitted to the Council a preliminary opinion on the applications for membership.[92] It recommended that the Community should pursue its further development and enlargement simultaneously, without trying to determine which of these two aims should take priority. However, at a press conference on 27 November 1967, before the negotiations could get off the ground, the French president delivered his second veto against British entry.[93] Once again, there was anger and disappointment in the other five EEC member states. The British government made clear that there was no question of withdrawing its membership application. Yet the French veto was made official on 19 December 1967, when the deadlock was accepted by the Council of Ministers as final. Denmark, Ireland, and Norway did not pursue membership any further without Britain, and Sweden's "open" application was never dealt with by the Community. Nevertheless, the Council concluded that "the requests for accession presented by the United Kingdom, Ireland, Denmark and Norway, and also the letter from the Swedish Government, remain on the Council's agenda."[94]

Incentives for and Impediments to Integration

Table 4.4 displays the overall export dependence of Sweden, Norway, and Switzerland on the Community in 1967.

Compared to the shares in 1958 and 1963, the export and GDP ratios of 1967 were lower for all three countries because of the gradual establishment of the Community's customs union. Trade creation within EFTA helped to offset this trade diversion. The 1967 export shares to the British

Table 4.4   Overall Export Dependence on the EEC, 1967

	EEC Export Ratio (exports to EEC as % of total exports)	GDP Ratio (exports to EEC as % of GDP)
Sweden	26.8	4.6
Norway	23.3	4.4
Switzerland	36.3	7.8
EEC-6	43.7	6.5

Sources: UN COMTRADE database; and OECD, *National Accounts: Main Aggregates 1960–1994* (Paris: OECD, 1996), vol. 1.

market amounted to 13.3 percent for Sweden, 19.3 percent for Norway, and 7.4 percent for Switzerland.[95] Hence, if the United Kingdom were to join the EEC, the importance of market access would considerably increase for Norway and Sweden. Table 4.5 identifies the sectors with the biggest exports to the EEC.

As reference points for the barriers to trade, Table 4.3 in the previous section provides the tariffs valid in 1968 for the above sectors. Furthermore, as tariffs were continuously lowered in the 1960s, many governments began erecting nontariff barriers to trade and artificially stimulating the production and the export of domestic goods in order to meet foreign competition. The EFTA countries started to focus attention on some of their own NTBs in the mid-1960s, but their invitation to the Community to cooperate on NTBs was unsuccessful.[96]

Sweden.   In 1967, the Swedish economy sold 26.8 percent of its total exports to the EEC-6 (see Table 4.4), and 43.7 percent to the EFTA countries.[97] The significance of the EFTA market was thus greater, but the importance of the Community would have increased with enlargement. The composition of the leading export sectors had hardly changed from 1963 to 1967 (see Tables 4.2 and 4.5). Although the charge on pulp and waste paper was further lowered in 1968 to a mere 1–2 percent, the tariff on nonelectrical machinery still reached 8–9 percent and on paper manufactures as much as 14–15 percent (see Table 4.3). Thus, the government considered that "the tariff discrimination which we encounter today on the EEC markets

Table 4.5   Sector Exports to the EEC, 1967

Leading Export Sectors to the EEC (SITC, Rev. 1)		Sector Share (sector exports to EEC as % of total exports to EEC)	Sector Export Ratio (sector exports to EEC as % of total sector exports)
Sweden			
Pulp and waste paper	(25)	16.6	45.8
Nonelectrical machinery	(71)	15.0	23.1
Paper manufactures	(64)	13.1	38.6
Norway			
Nonferrous metals	(68)	25.8	37.5
Paper manufactures	(64)	9.8	29.1
Iron and steel	(67)	8.7	29.0
Switzerland			
Nonelectrical machinery	(71)	21.8	35.0
Professional instruments	(86)	10.1	20.9
Electrical machinery	(72)	7.9	39.9

Source: UN COMTRADE database.

creates growing problems for important parts of our export industries."[98] Sweden's economic incentives to integrate in 1967 were still in the medium range.

The Swedish government welcomed de Gaulle's resistance against majority decisions and the coordination of foreign policies. "It must . . . be pointed out that developments since 1962 have given some grounds for a more open attitude," as "the efforts to institute supranational ties to determine the actions of the EEC states have become less intense and different views on the political aims of the Six have emerged."[99] If the "danger" of majority voting was eliminated, the argument about the incompatibility of the Swedish welfare model with the continental socioeconomic policies weakened. The Swedish government also reevaluated the need for provisos regarding neutrality but concluded that "the same importance must be attached now as five years ago to the earlier declared neutrality reservations."[100] The real issue then raised was whether a "less supranational" Community would now offer full membership with such reservations. In spite of the changes in the EEC, Sweden's political impediments to integration remained of medium strength.

Norway. In 1967 the Norwegian economy sold 23.3 percent of its exports to the common market (see Table 4.4) and 47 percent to the EFTA countries.[101] As it had five years earlier, the government stressed the importance of foreign trade for Norway, whose export of goods and services made up about 40 percent of GNP; 75 percent of the goods were sold to the EEC and EFTA countries.[102] "When Great Britain, Denmark, and Sweden made known that they will search for a connection with the EEC, Norway could not take a position that might involve that it would stay outside an enlarged EEC."[103] The government thus considered the overall export dependence at stake as high.

The three major export sectors to the common market consisted of a big share of nonferrous metals (25.8 percent) and small shares of iron and steel as well as paper products (see Table 4.5). Nonferrous metals and iron and steel faced average tariffs of 6–8 percent, but paper manufactures had to cope with high duties of 14–15 percent (see Table 4.3). In fact, Norway's most important export in 1966 was not a commodity but a service, shipping, which accounted for over 10 percent of GNP.[104] Since shipping was not yet affected by European integration and basic materials were generally duty-free, "there would appear to be rather less reason for serious complaints in Norway than in some other countries about the present situation with membership of EFTA and exclusion from the EEC."[105] However, the export of typical staple goods with low added value and little product differentiation, such as metals and paper, was considered very sensitive to potential tariff discrimination. Paper, aluminum, ferro-alloys, and magnesium, for instance, were put on the list of exceptions from the offer of tariff reductions made by the EEC in the Kennedy Round of the GATT negotiations. Moreover, the most promising market of growth, frozen fish fillets, confronted a nearly prohibitive EEC tariff.

Having an important and increasing share of exports depending on political decisions (regarding tariffs and duty-free quotas) taken by a group of countries from year to year was not an optimal situation. In 1966, the share of raw materials and semifinished products in Norway's exports still amounted to 70 percent, and finished products had risen to 25 percent.[106] The government stressed that the growth of the Norwegian economy would increasingly depend on the export of finished goods and thus on "the access to a larger duty-free market" and that it would have little chance to find alternative markets.[107] In sum, the Norwegian economy had strong incentives to take part in the common market.

The Labor members who advocated EEC membership hoped for improved control over economic policies, whereas the left-wing socialists still viewed the EEC as a capitalist market economy that would create difficulties for Norway's welfare policy.[108] The Christian Democratic Party and the Center Party feared that the Community might interfere with exploitation of Norway's natural resources and with agricultural, fisheries, or alcohol policies.[109] The Federation of Norwegian Industries and the Confederation of Trade Unions supported the membership request. The latter wished, however, that the government would make it very clear that Norway maintained its system of wage bargaining and of voluntary cooperation between organizations and authorities.[110]

Compared to the early 1960s, the obstacles surrounding Norwegian EEC membership seem to have lost importance as a result of the political developments in Europe. "The very fact that non-aligned Sweden could even consider membership was also regarded by many Norwegians as a reassuring commentary on the EEC's prospects of ever achieving a degree of economic and political integration which might threaten the independence of its member states."[111] With the "Luxembourg compromise," "the idea of the European Economic Community as a largely non-political economic organization with Britain and Denmark as fellow members had gained almost full acceptance in the minds of Norwegian leaders."[112] Consequently, the political issues tended to be less important than they were five years earlier, and the emphasis shifted to a preoccupation with economic advantages.

Switzerland. In 1967, Switzerland exported 36.3 percent to the EEC (see Table 4.4) and 21.6 percent to EFTA.[113] The EEC export ratio had slightly decreased to a medium size since 1963. The major Swiss exports to the EEC in 1967 were dominated by nonelectrical machinery, followed by lower shares of professional instruments and electrical machinery (see Table 4.5). The relevant EEC tariffs, at 8–12 percent, were at the higher end (see Table 4.3). Overall, this export dependence on the Community indicates that market access was of medium importance for the Swiss economy.

Even though the supranational character and the political objectives of the Community as well as the East-West tensions weakened, the Swiss constraints against EEC membership—neutrality, federalism, and direct democracy—persisted unchanged. Any restriction of neutrality was still out of the question. As in the past, federalism and direct democracy would have been affected. Regarding popular rights and cantonal competences, seventy-seven referenda had been held in Switzerland in the time period 1945–1967, of which seven would have been wholly and eighteen partly EEC matters.[114] Moreover, Austria's futile experience in negotiating association revealed the inherent risk of satellization.[115] A consensus prevailed in Swiss politics and society that the obstacles to EEC membership remained high in spite of the new developments in the Community.

Integration Policy Preferences

In 1967, access to the common market was of medium importance for Sweden and Switzerland and slightly greater for Norway. The political constraints on full membership were still very strong for Switzerland and weak for Norway, with Sweden situated in between. Consequently, Sweden would be more likely to go for an intermediate level of integration rather than full membership, trying to combine the protection of its operational sovereignty with the desire to have a say in integration. Switzerland is expected to be satisfied with a low degree of integration that defends its sovereignty, whereas Norway should aim at full membership and a voice in the widened European Communities.

Sweden.   Swedish authorities followed the developments in the European Economic Community very closely.[116] The experience of Austria's *Alleingang* (going it alone) in 1963–1967 taught the other neutral countries that association with the EEC was a difficult matter, in particular with regard to the necessary extent of harmonization and the decisionmaking process.[117] On the same day as the British government announced its decision to apply for membership, the Swedish government declared that it was also prepared to negotiate with the Community.[118] On 28 July 1967, it submitted "a request for negotiations with the Community with a view to enabling Sweden to participate in the extension of the European Economic Community in a form that is compatible with a continued pursuit of the Swedish policy of neutrality."[119] The letter was accompanied by a "verbal addendum," presented by the Swedish ambassador, which expressed

Sweden's willingness to consider any form of participation, including membership:

> For its part, the Swedish Government does not wish to exclude from consideration any of the forms of participation in an enlarged Community which are provided for by the Treaty of Rome. Membership is a form which the Swedish Government already considered to have certain advantages in 1961–62. The decisive factor for the Swedish Government is that our policy of neutrality should remain unchanged and that the reservations resulting from this should be admitted.[120]

Such an "open" application reflected a belief that the Luxembourg compromise and the French policy toward the EEC and NATO made full membership worth exploring, whereas association, after Austria's difficult experience, might not be a good alternative. The social democratic government thus came closer to the long-standing position of the Federation of Swedish Industries and the Swedish Employers' Federation. This strategy was the object of lively discussion in Sweden. In the parliamentary debate on 7 November 1967, the social democratic government told the Riksdag that it kept the form of Swedish participation open "because by doing so we envisage a possibility of entering into discussion and of obtaining greater clarity on the form of participation conceivable for us with our neutrality proviso."[121] On the one hand, "the political features in EEC cooperation have now been pushed into the background," but on the other hand, "an application for membership would in the present situation lessen confidence in our will to uphold the Swedish policy of neutrality because in 1961–62 we had requested negotiations for an association on account of our neutrality."[122]

Yet, in its "preliminary" opinion of 1967 on the membership requests, the EEC Commission stated with regard to Sweden's "open" application that membership with neutrality reservations was not possible.[123] Sweden would have to fully accept the Community's political aims. Furthermore, it clarified that association was actually meant for less developed countries or "cases where the road to membership is blocked because of the international situation of the country concerned."[124]

As anticipated, the Swedish government engaged in a policy directed toward a moderate level of integration. Moreover, the political elites were clearly more favorable toward integration when the political constraints were perceived to have diminished. Obviously, the preservation of operational sovereignty became less relevant as the political obstacles lost in importance. Since association did not offer the expected voice opportunities, Sweden preferred to submit a general "open" application instead of an association request. A change to the Swedish Constitution allowing for a transfer of sovereignty to an international organization had been proposed in 1961 and agreed upon in 1965.[125]

Norway. When Britain renewed its demand for membership in the EEC, a coalition of nonsocialist parties was in office in Norway. The Conservative Party, the Labor Party, and the Liberal Party recommended applying for membership, whereas the Center Party and the Christian Democratic Party were split but came round to support an application. For many former opponents, the real question "was not whether they were now prepared to join the EEC but whether they were prepared to break up the coalition over a question which might well never arise."[126] Backed by the Storting, the government submitted a new request on 21 July 1967 that, like the one five years earlier, was made conditional upon British membership and satisfactory safeguards for the primary sector.

All parties agreed on the importance of Norway's export dependence, yet they disagreed on the impact EEC membership would have on the state's capability to manage the economy.[127] The government had set up a Common Market Committee (Markedsutvalget) in 1966, which investigated the opinions of the major economic interest groups.[128] As in 1963, the main organizations for industry, commerce, crafts, forestry, banking, insurance, and shipping, as well as the trade unions, were all in favor of a membership application, whereas the agricultural and fisheries organizations were still skeptical and asked for special treatment. In general, the support from domestic groups was stronger than five years earlier. None of them asked the government to choose association instead of membership.

In its report to parliament, the Norwegian government basically reiterated the arguments of 1962 and stressed the new developments in the EEC since then.[129] It underlined the economic arguments for membership and the need for special arrangements with regard to both agriculture and fisheries. The Community had still not decided on a Common Fisheries Policy, but it seemed clear that, as a member, Norway would have to open up its fishing grounds to the other EEC countries. With regard to the political goals of the EEC, the Norwegian government welcomed the possibility of participating in the establishment of political cooperation. Parliament agreed with the government's proposal to seek EEC membership and on the whole showed a greater degree of unanimity and a lower level of activity than five years earlier.[130]

Efforts to organize a nationwide anti-EEC campaign did not meet with a big response. Compared to the first EEC debate in 1961–1962, the second round in 1967 amounted to no more than "a quiet summer breeze," perhaps in anticipation of France's veto.[131] The arguments about the loss of sovereignty were less frequent in the 1967 debate, which may be attributed to the weakening of the EEC's supranational character. The economic elites favored EEC membership as they did the first time, and the political elites were more eager and united to join the Community because of the lessened political impediments. They stressed that EEC membership would provide Norway with some influence over policies affecting its economy, that it would strengthen political cooperation with its security partners, and that it was thus reasonable to give up some sovereignty in exchange.[132] In other words, voice had become more important relative to operational sovereignty because political impediments to integration were perceived to be low and economic benefits high.

After the French veto against British membership, the Norwegian government left its application pending. The official policy thus remained to seek membership in the EEC.

Switzerland.   The political changes that occurred between 1961 and 1967 did not lead the Swiss government to renew its association request. Even though the supranational character and the political objectives of the EEC were moderated, the lesson learned from Austria's failure to negotiate an association agreement made that option less attractive. Indeed, the Swiss government was convinced "that the Community was not ready to precede its decision by compulsory pre-consultations with the associates that would have been a precondition for the adoption of far-reaching obligations of harmonization."[133] Association with the EEC "would impose on the one hand many *obligations* on the associated state, *without* on the other hand granting it a *right to participate* in the decisions of the European Economic Community."[134] In other words, with regard to the voice opportunities, full membership would be superior to association. "The associated state would in any case have to take over the EEC legislation and would rapidly be downgraded to a satellite."[135]

For this reason, and given the possibility that France might again veto British membership, Switzerland decided to adopt a wait-and-see policy. Nevertheless, the Swiss government officially declared that its association request of 1961 was never formally withdrawn and could still be reactivated.[136] Moreover, it made clear that it would not exclude a priori any possible solutions, "provided that they contain a right of participation that corresponds to our country's economic significance and are compatible with our state structure."[137] In principle, Switzerland still aimed at a low level of integration. The political constraints had remained strong, but the economic incentives were weaker than in the early 1960s. Since full membership was not an option in 1967 and association offered unsatisfactory voice opportunities in return for a restricted freedom of action, the Swiss government continued to consider the maintenance of operational sovereignty as the better strategy.

Except for the Swiss case, the political impediments to integration seem to have lost some ground compared to the early 1960s, owing to the Community's own "intergovernmentalist" developments. The economic incentives in terms of export dependence were slightly lower as the effects of trade diversion between the EEC and EFTA began to show. Yet for Norway and to a lesser extent for Sweden, the membership application of Britain, a major trading partner, was still significant with regard to the expected economic benefits of access to the EEC market and thus called for reaction.

Conclusion

The 1960s were characterized by two attempts to fix the split of Western Europe into two trading groups. These efforts were not multilateral undertakings, as the predominant paradigm of "building bridges" would have suggested, but a series of bilateral initiatives triggered by the membership applications of the biggest EFTA country, the United Kingdom. In 1963 as well as in 1967, the negotiations for membership or association failed due to French vetoes. In spite of the short period in between, the variation in the integration policies of the three countries has been considerable, ranging from membership and association requests to an "open" application and a "wait-and-see" policy. It seems fair to conclude that in the investigated cases of the 1960s, the suggestion that a country's integration policy is more reluctant when the economic incentives are lower and the political impediments are higher has been substantiated. After these frustrating years, a first rapprochement between the European Communities and the EFTA states was finally reached in the early 1970s.

Notes

1. See Siegler, *Dokumentation der europäischen Integration: 1946–1961*, pp. 424–432.
2. Camps, *Britain and the European Community 1955–1963*, chap. 12. The so-called Fouchet Plan on a political "union of states" was rejected in April 1962. Whereas de Gaulle wanted purely intergovernmental cooperation, the Netherlands and Belgium insisted on introducing some supranational features.
3. EFTA, "Communiqué of the EFTA Ministerial Council in London on 27–28 June 1961," *EFTA Bulletin*, no. 7 (1961): 8.
4. See Camps, *Britain and the European Community 1955–1963*, chaps. 9–14.
5. The so–called Nassau agreement, in which the British placed their nuclear force within NATO in return for U.S. Polaris missiles, offended de Gaulle, who had hoped for an independent European nuclear grouping. Beloff, *The General Says No*, chap. 12.

6. de Gaulle, "Le texte intégral de la conférence de presse tenue par le Général de Gaulle à l'Elysée," p. 2.

7. Commission of the European Communities, *Report to the European Parliament on the State of the Negotiations with the United Kingdom*, Brussels, 26 February 1963.

8. Zeller, "Die bisherige Haltung der EWG gegenüber den Neutralen," pp. 206, 208.

9. Assemblé Parlementaire Européenne, *Rapport fait au nom de la commission politique sur les aspects politiques et institutionnels de l'adhésion ou de l'association à la Communauté*, Rapporteur Mr. Birkelbach, DOC 1962/122, 15 January 1962, pp. 15–16, 19.

10. Plessow, *Neutralität und Assoziation mit der EWG*, pp. 177–179, 211.

11. Ibid., pp. 180–198.

12. Lambert, "The Neutrals and the Common Market," p. 451.

13. EFTA, *The Trade Effects of EFTA and the EEC 1959–1967* (Geneva: EFTA, 1972), pp. 51–56.

14. EFTA, *EFTA Trade 1959–1964* (Geneva: EFTA, 1966), pp. 74, 88, 96.

15. Roethlisberger, *La Suisse dans l'Association européenne de libre-échange (1960–1966)*, pp. 272–274.

16. The fourth sector for Switzerland (electrical machinery) is included with regard to the section on "The 1967 Applications for Membership."

17. EFTA, *EFTA Trade 1959–1964* (Geneva: EFTA, 1966), Table 10 of the Statistical Annex.

18. Speech by the minister of trade before the EEC Council of Ministers on 28 July 1962, in Sweden, Ministry for Foreign Affairs, *Documents on Swedish Foreign Policy: 1962*, New Series I:C:12 (Stockholm: Royal Ministry for Foreign Affairs, 1963), p. 150.

19. Ekström, Myrdal, and Pålsson, *Vi och Västeuropa*, pp. 104–112.

20. Ibid., p. 8; and Odhner, *Sverige i Europa*, p. 39.

21. Sweden, Ministry of Trade and Industry, *Svensk industri och Europamarknaden: Översikt av olika industrigruppers utredningar och bedömningar sammanställd av Industriförbundet och Kommerskollegium* (Stockholm: Handelsdepartementet, 1962), p. 13.

22. Government's message to the Riksdag on 25 October 1961 concerning the efforts to achieve West European integration, in Sweden, Ministry for Foreign Affairs, *Documents on Swedish Foreign Policy: 1961*, New Series I:C:11 (Stockholm: Royal Ministry for Foreign Affairs, 1962), p. 135.

23. Jan Magnus Fahlström, "Sverige och de europeiska marknadsproblemen," *Utrikespolitik*, no. 5, 1961, reprinted in "Europamarknadsdebatten: En antologi," *Studier och debatt*, no. 4 (1961): 198.

24. Bergquist, *Sverige och EEC*, pp. 64, 85, 98.

25. Ekström, Myrdal, and Pålsson, *Vi och Västeuropa*, in particular chap. 3.

26. Quoted in Gidlund, "Nationalstaten och den europeiska integrationen," pp. 105–106.

27. Brodin, Goldmann, and Lange, "The Policy of Neutrality," p. 24; and the government's message to the Riksdag of 25 October 1961, in Sweden, Ministry for Foreign Affairs, *Documents on Swedish Foreign Policy: 1961*, New Series I:C:11 (Stockholm: Royal Ministry for Foreign Affairs, 1962), p. 134.

28. *The European Free Trade Association and the Crisis of European Integration*, p. 123; and Sweden, Ministry of Trade and Industry, *Sverige och EEC: Romfördraget ur svensk synvinkel*. Stockholm: Handelsdepartementet, 1968, p. 20.

29. Speech by the minister of trade before the Düsseldorf Chamber of Commerce on 26 November 1962, in Sweden, Ministry for Foreign Affairs, *Documents on Swedish Foreign Policy: 1962,* New Series I:C:12 (Stockholm: Royal Ministry for Foreign Affairs, 1963), pp. 162–164.

30. EFTA, *EFTA Trade 1959–1964* (Geneva: EFTA, 1966), Table 10 of the Statistical Annex.

31. Hanssen and Sandegren, "Norway and Western European Economic Integration," p. 48.

32. Norway, Ministry for Foreign Affairs, *Om Det Europeiske Økonomiske Fellesskap og de europeiske marketsproblemer,* St.meld. nr. 15 (1961–1962), Oslo, 13 October 1961, pp. 19–32, 54.

33. Ibid., pp. 22–24.

34. Ibid., pp. 53–54.

35. Rokkan, "Geography, Religion, and Social Class," p. 438.

36. Gleditsch and Hellevik, *Kampen om EF,* p. 31; and Kite, *Scandinavia Faces EU,* pp. 157–160.

37. Bjørklund, *Mot strømmen,* chaps. 2–4.

38. Hanssen and Sandegren, "Norway and Western European Economic Integration," p. 52.

39. Pharo, "The Norwegian Labour Party," p. 219.

40. Norway, Ministry for Foreign Affairs, *Om Det Europeiske Økonomiske Fellesskap og de europeiske marketsproblemer,* St.meld. nr. 15 (1961–1962), Oslo, 13 October 1961, pp. 45, 49–50.

41. Allen, *Norway and Europe in the 1970s,* pp. 48–49.

42. Ibid., p. 46.

43. MP Erling Petersen, Norway, Parliament, Foreign Affairs and Constitution Committee, *Stortingets behandling av innstilling fra den utvidede utenriks- og konstitusjonskomite om Norges forhold til Det Europeiske Økonomiske Fellesskap (EEC),* Oslo, 25–28 April 1962 (reprinted from *Stortingsforhandlinger*), p. 2687.

44. EFTA, *EFTA Trade 1959–1964* (Geneva: EFTA, 1966), Table 10 of the Statistical Annex.

45. Switzerland, Federal Council, *Bericht des Schweizerischen Bundesrates an die Bundesversammlung über seine Geschäftsführung im Jahre 1962,* Bern, p. 324.

46. See Roethlisberger, *La Suisse dans l'Association européenne de libre-échange (1960–1966),* pp. 84–94.

47. Schindler, "Spezifische politische Probleme aus Schweizer Sicht," p. 281; and Federal Councillor Friedrich Traugott Wahlen's response in Switzerland, Parliament to "Interpellation Conzett und Tenchio: Stand der europäischen Integration," *Amtliches stenographisches Bulletin der Bundesversammlung: Nationalrat,* Bern, 27 September 1961, p. 423.

48. Riklin, *Schweizerische Demokratie und EWG,* p. 7.

49. Schindler, "Die Schweiz und die europäische Integration," pp. 89–90.

50. Zbinden, "Das EWR-Projekt," p. 241.

51. *Neue Zürcher Zeitung,* "Die Schweiz und die Europäische Wirtschaftsgemeinschaft."

52. "Metal Speech" by Prime Minister Tage Erlander at the Congress of the Swedish Steel and Metalworkers' Union on 22 August 1961, in Sweden, Ministry for Foreign Affairs, *Documents on Swedish Foreign Policy: 1961,* New Series I:C:11 (Stockholm: Royal Ministry for Foreign Affairs, 1962), p. 119.

53. Ibid.

54. See Karlsson, *Partistrategi och utrikespolitik,* pp. 89–112.

55. Prime Minister Tage Erlander in Sweden, Parliament, "Ang. de västeuropeiska integrationssträvandena, m.m.," *Riksdagens Protokoll: Första Kammaren,* no. 27, 25 October 1961, p. 7; and Minister of Trade Gunnar Lange in Sweden, Parliament, "Meddelande rörande de västeuropeiska integrationssträvandena," *Riksdagens Protokoll: Andra Kammaren,* no. 27, 25 October 1961, p. 23.

56. Bergquist, "Sweden and the European Economic Community," p. 9.

57. Sweden, Ministry of Trade and Industry, *Svensk industri och Europamarknaden: Översikt av olika industrigruppers utredningar och bedömningar sammanställd av Industriförbundet och Kommerskollegium* (Stockholm: Handelsdepartementet, 1962).

58. See Roethlisberger, *La Suisse dans l'Association européenne de libreéchange (1960–1966),* pp. 158–162.

59. Speech by the Minister of Trade Gunnar Lange before the EEC Council of Ministers on 28 July 1962, in Sweden, Ministry for Foreign Affairs, *Documents on Swedish Foreign Policy: 1962,* New Series I:C:12 (Stockholm: Royal Ministry for Foreign Affairs, 1963), pp. 146–155.

60. Ibid., p. 154.

61. Government's message to the Riksdag of 25 October 1961 concerning the efforts to achieve Western European integration, in Sweden, Ministry for Foreign Affairs, *Documents on Swedish Foreign Policy: 1961,* New Series I:C:11 (Stockholm: Royal Ministry for Foreign Affairs, 1962), p. 130.

62. Bergquist, "Sweden and the European Economic Community," p. 10. See the "schools of thought" that Bergquist distinguishes in the Swedish EEC debate of 1961–1962: the "Membership School," the "Association School," the "Non-accession School," and the "Anti-accession School." Bergquist, *Sverige och EEC.*

63. Wilhelm Paues, quoted in "Growing Complexities in Sweden," *The Times,* 14 June 1961, reprinted in *The Common Market: A Survey by The Times* (London: Times Publishing Company, 1962), p. 82.

64. MP Knut Ewerlöf in Sweden, Parliament, "Ang. de västeuropeiska integrationssträvandena," *Riksdagens Protokoll: Första Kammaren,* no. 27 (25 October 1961): 12; and MP Gunnar Heckscher in Parliament, "Meddelande rörande de västeuropeiska integrationssträvandena," *Riksdagens Protokoll: Andra Kammaren,* no. 27 (25 October 1961): 36.

65. Hanssen and Sandegren, "Norway and Western European Economic Integration," p. 49.

66. *Uttalelse til Handelsministeren om de europeiske markedsproblemer avgitt av utvalget for saker vedrørende Frihandelsforbundet og nordisk økonomisk samarbeid,* Annex I to Norway, Ministry of Foreign Affairs, *Om Det Europeiske Økonomiske Fellesskap og de europeiske markedsproblemer,* St.meld. nr. 15 (1961–1962), Oslo, 13 October 1961, p. 38.

67. *Utredninger om følger for Norge ved å stå helt utenfor Det Europeiske Økonomiske Felleskap,* Enclosure I to Norway, Ministry of Foreign Affairs, *Om Det Europeiske Økonomiske Fellesskap og de europeiske markedsproblemer,* St.meld. nr. 15 (1961–1962), Oslo, 13 October 1961, pp. 45–73.

68. Norway, Ministry of Foreign Affairs, *Om Norges stilling til Det Europeiske Økonomiske Felleskap og de europeiske samarbeidsbestrebelser,* St.meld. nr. 67 (1961–1962), Oslo, 2 March 1962, p. 14.

69. Norway, Parliament, Foreign Affairs and Constitution Committee, *Innstilling fra den utvidede utenriks- og konstitusjonskomité om Norges forhold til Det Europeiske Økonomiske Fellesskap (EEC) (St.meld. nr. 15 og nr. 67),* Innst.S.nr.

165 (1961–1962), Oslo, 12 April 1962 (reprinted from *Stortingsforhandlinger*), p. 296.

70. See Schou, *Norge og EF,* chaps. 4–9.

71. *Uttalelser og utredninger vedrørende Norges stilling til de europeiske markedsproblemer,* Enclosure I to Norway, Ministry of Foreign Affairs, *Om Det Europeiske Økonomiske Fellesskap og de europeiske marketsproblemer,* St.meld. nr. 15 (1961–1962), Oslo, 13 October 1961.

72. European Economic Community, *Bulletin of the European Economic Community,* no. 8 (1962): 15; and Closse, "Les pays scandinaves et la C.E.E.," pp. 735–753.

73. Miljan, "The Nordic Countries: Europe's Reluctant Partners," p. 128.

74. Minister of Trade Gunnar Lange, quoted in Ekström, Myrdal, and Pålsson, "Spezifische politische Probleme aus schwedischer Sicht," p. 295.

75. *Spørsmålet om tilknytning til Det Europeiske Økonomiske Fellesskap ved assosiering,* Enclosure II to Norway, Ministry of Foreign Affairs, *Om Det Europeiske Økonomiske Fellesskap og de europeiske marketsproblemer,* St.meld. nr. 15 (1961–1962), Oslo, 13 October 1961, pp. 16–22.

76. Foreign Minister Halvard Lange in the Storting on 28 April 1962, quoted in European Economic Community, *Bulletin of the European Economic Community,* no. 6 (1962): 9.

77. Norway, Parliament, *Innstillning fra den utvidede utenriks- og konstitusjonskomité om Norges forhold til Det Europeiske Økonomiske Fellesskap (EEC),* St.meld. nr. 15 og nr. 67, Innst.S.nr. 165 (1961–1962), Oslo, 12 April 1962 (reprinted from *Stortingsforhandlinger*), p. 296.

78. European Economic Community, *Bulletin of the European Economic Community,* no. 4 (1963): 6.

79. Schindler, "Spezifische politische Probleme aus Schweizer Sicht," p. 277; and Switzerland, Federal Council, *Bericht des Schweizerischen Bundesrates an die Bundesversammlung über seine Geschäftsführung im Jahre 1961,* Bern, 1962, p. 281.

80. See Zbinden, "Das EWR-Projekt," pp. 230–242.

81. Exposé by Federal Councillor Hans Schaffner of 20 March 1962, quoted in Zbinden, "Das EWR-Projekt," p. 239.

82. European Communities, *Bulletin of the European Economic Community,* no. 11 (1962): 17. For the full text, see Switzerland, Federal Council, *Bericht des Schweizerischen Bundesrates an die Bundesversammlung über seine Geschäftsführung im Jahre 1962,* Bern, 1963, pp. 323–331.

83. Roethlisberger, *La Suisse dans l'Association européenne de libre-échange (1960–1966),* p. 157.

84. Keel, *Le grand patronat suisse face à l'intégration européenne,* pp. 244–251.

85. Ibid., pp. 251–255.

86. Former Federal Councillor Max Petitpierre, quoted in Binswanger, "Zwischenstaatliche oder übernationale Prinzipien der Integration," p. 101; and *Neue Zürcher Zeitung,* "Die Schweiz und die Europäische Wirtschaftsgemeinschaft."

87. Switzerland, Federal Council, *Bericht des Schweizerischen Bundesrates an die Bundesversammlung über seine Geschäftsführung im Jahre 1963,* Bern, 1964, p. 340.

88. Zbinden, "Das EWR-Projekt," pp. 242–245; and du Bois, *La Suisse et le défi européen,* pp. 65–66.

89. Quoted in Urwin, *The Community of Europe*, p. 114.

90. EFTA, "Communiqué of the Ministerial Meeting of the EFTA Council in London on 28 April 1967," *EFTA Bulletin*, no. 4 (1967): 13. In spite of the resistance from Switzerland, Sweden, Norway, and Portugal, the British had this time ruled out a solidarity clause, arguing that it would make the negotiations in Brussels more difficult. Lie, *A Gulliver Among Lilliputians*, pp. 229–231.

91. See Hamel, "Eine solche Sache würde der Neutralitätspolitik ein Ende machen," pp. 63–80.

92. Commission of the European Communities, *Opinion Submitted on the Applications for Membership Received from the United Kingdom, Ireland, Denmark and Norway*, Brussels, 29 September 1967.

93. de Gaulle, "Les déclarations du Président de la République au cours de la conférence de presse à l'Elysée," p. 3.

94. Commission of the European Communities, *First General Report on the Activities of the Communities 1967*, Brussels, 1968, p. 351.

95. EFTA, *EFTA Trade 1968* (Geneva: EFTA, 1970), Statistical Appendix, Table 84.

96. See Curzon and Curzon, "EFTA Experience with Non-Tariff Barriers," pp. 129–145; and EFTA, *Bâtir l'AELE: Une zone de libre-échange en Europe* (Geneva: EFTA, 1968), chap. 7.

97. EFTA, *EFTA Trade 1959–67* (Geneva: EFTA, 1969), Table 13 of the Statistical Annex.

98. Minister Krister Wickman in Sweden, Parliament, "Sveriges handelspolitik," *Riksdagens Protokoll: Första Kammaren*, no. 40 (7 November 1967): 65.

99. Address by the foreign minister to the special congress of the Social Democratic Party in Stockholm on 23 October 1967, in Sweden, Ministry for Foreign Affairs, *Documents on Swedish Foreign Policy: 1967*, New Series I:C:17 (Stockholm: Royal Ministry for Foreign Affairs, 1968), p. 54.

100. Minister of Trade Gunnar Lange in Sweden, Parliament, "Handelspolitisk debatt," *Riksdagens Protokoll: Andra Kammaren*, no. 40 (7 November 1967): 27, 69.

101. EFTA, *EFTA Trade 1959–67* (Geneva: EFTA, 1969), Table 13 of the Statistical Annex.

102. *Uttalelser vedrørende Norges stilling til de europeiske fellesskap*, Enclosure III to Norway, Ministry for Foreign Affairs, *Om Norges forhold til de europeiske fellesskap*, St.meld. nr. 86 (1966–1967), Oslo, 16 June 1967, p. 97.

103. Ibid., p. 98.

104. *The European Free Trade Association and the Crisis of European Integration*, p. 100.

105. Ibid., p. 101.

106. Norway, Ministry for Foreign Affairs, *Om Norges forhold til de europeiske fellesskap*, St.meld. nr. 86 (1966–1967), Oslo, 16 June 1967, p. 10.

107. Ibid., pp. 13, 21.

108. Schou, *Norge og EF*, pp. 148, 272.

109. Ibid., pp. 188–189, 243, 251.

110. *Uttalelser vedrørende Norges stilling til de europeiske fellesskap*, Enclosure III to Norway, Ministry for Foreign Affairs, *Om Norges forhold til de europeiske fellesskap*, St.meld. nr. 86 (1966–1967), Oslo, 16 June 1967, p. 12.

111. Allen, *Norway and European in the 1970s*, p. 54.

112. Miljan, "The Nordic Countries," p. 128.

precluding the cumulation of origin.[8] Against the desires of the EFTA dele-
gations, "the Community felt throughout the negotiations that free-trade in
the industrial field was the absolute limit of commitments regarding the
nonapplicant countries, which it could make at this stage without too much
risk to its own running and development."[9]

On 22 January 1972, Britain, Norway, Denmark, and Ireland signed
their accession acts for membership in the EEC, the ECSC, and Euratom
and became associated to the negotiations with the other EFTA states.[10] Six
months later, the free trade agreements with the nonapplicants were signed;
one with Finland followed on 5 October 1973. Four national referenda were
held in the ratification process: In May 1972, the Irish supported EC entry;
in September 1972, the Norwegians rejected it; in October 1972, Denmark
approved membership; and in December 1972, the Swiss accepted the free
trade agreements. On 1 January 1973, the United Kingdom, Ireland, and
Denmark became members of the European Communities. At the same
time, the EFTA countries' free trade agreements with the enlarged EEC
entered into force, except for Iceland (1 April 1973), Norway (1 July 1973),
and Finland (1 January 1974). The agreements with the ECSC entered into
force one year later.[11]

A relatively short transitional period until 1 July 1977 was granted to
progressively eliminate duties on industrial goods. This timetable largely
coincided with that in the accession treaties. As an exception for some
products that the EC regarded as "sensitive" (such as paper and certain
metals), duties were temporarily reimposed between the countries leaving
EFTA and those remaining. Tariffs and quotas for these products finally
disappeared by 1984. In contrast to the Treaty of Rome and the EFTA
Convention, the free trade agreements did not contain any provisions on
export restrictions, public procurement, establishment, invisible transac-
tions, or economic and financial policies.[12] On the basis of an evolutionary
clause, the scope of cooperation could be expanded to new fields. The bilateral agreements were overseen by a joint committee, which consisted of the
EEC and the EFTA country, acting by mutual agreement. The joint committee was empowered to make recommendations and take decisions to ensure
the proper functioning of the agreement. The rules of competition (relating
to cartels, dominant positions, and public subsidies) and the escape clauses
were subject to a consultation procedure. Disputes were to be settled by
negotiation since the EC refused to insert an arbitration clause. Finally,
either party could denounce the agreement, which would then cease to
apply after twelve months (three months in the case of Finland).

The Hague summit of December 1969 also generated discussions on a
further deepening of the EEC's integration. The Common Fisheries Policy
was approved in June 1970, only one day before negotiations began with
the four applicant states, each of which had major fishing interests. Its core

was that all EC fishermen should have the right of equal access to all EC waters. The Davignon Report of October 1970 recommended that the coordination of foreign policies should be the first step toward political unification.[13] This process was implemented outside the EC's institutional framework on an intergovernmental basis and became known as European Political Cooperation. In 1974, the practice of summitry was institutionalized by the establishment of the European Council. The idea of Economic and Monetary Union (EMU) was explored in the Werner Report of March 1970.[14] It stressed the need to simultaneously coordinate and harmonize policies, narrow exchange rate margins, integrate capital markets, and establish a common currency with a single central bank. In February 1971, the Council of Ministers finally adopted a modified version of the plan, omitting the institutional elements.[15] However, shortly afterward, these plans were dented severely by a dramatic downturn in the international economic climate. The large payments deficit of the United States, its involvement in the Vietnam War, the collapse of the Bretton Woods system of fixed exchange rates, and the 1973 Yom Kippur War between Israel and neighboring Arab states, with the consequent oil crisis, pushed the Western world into recession and high inflation. Throughout the 1970s, the poor international economic climate left little room for new initiatives, in spite of calls for closer cooperation from the EFTA countries. In June 1978, the Council of Ministers finally agreed that "where additional cooperation beyond the free trade agreements was regarded as desirable by both sides, the Community was prepared to undertake such cooperation."[16]

Incentives for and Impediments to Integration

Table 5.1 shows the Swedish, Norwegian, and Swiss exports to the common market as a share of total exports and of GDP. Negotiations for membership and for bilateral trade agreements began in 1970, and the treaties entered into force in 1973. The implementation of free trade between the EC and the nonacceding EFTA countries was completed in 1984. The considerable increase in the export ratios from 1970 to 1973 was mainly due to the accession of the United Kingdom, Denmark, and Ireland to the European Communities. In 1981, Greece joined the EC as its tenth member state.

Table 5.2 shows the three countries' major exports to the European Communities in 1973.

A principal difference between the two options of industrial free trade and EC membership was their effect on trade in agricultural and fisheries products. Less than 5 percent of the Swedish, Swiss, and Finnish exports to the EC-6 and the UK and 10 percent of the Norwegian exports to those seven countries were made up of food and live animals, whereas nearly half of the Danish exports and more than three-fifths of the Icelandic exports were to be found in this category.[17]

Table 5.1   Overall Export Dependence on the EC, 1970, 1973, and
1984

	EC Export Ratio (exports to EC as % of total exports)	GDP Ratio (exports to EC as % of GDP)
Sweden		
1970	27.6	5.6
1973	50.4	11.7
1984	47.8	14.5
Norway		
1970	29.7	6.0
1973	47.4	10.4
1984	70.0	21.8
Switzerland		
1970	37.2	9.2
1973	45.4	10.5
1984	50.6	14.4
EC		
1970	48.9	8.4
1973	52.6	9.8
1984	52.1	12.8

Sources: UN COMTRADE database; and OECD, *National Accounts: Main Aggregates 1960–1994*, vol. 1 (Paris: OECD, 1996).

Table 5.2   Sector Exports to the EC, 1973

	Leading Export Sectors to the EC (SITC, Rev. 1)	Sector Share (sector exports to EC as % of total exports to EC)	Sector Export Ratio (sector exports to EC as % of total sector exports)
Sweden			
Nonelectrical machinery	(71)	13.3	41.1
Transport equipment	(73)	12.3	37.9
Paper manufactures	(64)	12.1	71.3
Norway			
Nonferrous metals	(68)	19.0	64.9
Transport equipment	(73)	13.3	29.3
Iron and steel	(67)	8.2	60.1
Switzerland			
Nonelectrical machinery	(71)	22.3	42.8
Professional instruments	(86)	9.4	30.7
Electrical machinery	(72)	9.2	49.8

Source: UN COMTRADE database.

On 1 April 1973 (for Norway, 1 July 1973), the EC duties on imports from the EFTA countries were reduced by 20 percent. Country-specific rules were set out for some "sensitive products" such as paper manufactures and some base metals such as aluminum, for which the first reduction was only 5 percent, as well as certain watches. The divergence between EFTA and the EC with regard to nontariff barriers to trade was not yet significant.[18] Table 5.3 shows the average EC tariffs at the entry into force of the free trade agreements in 1973 and at their completion in 1984. The EEC customs union had abolished the Community's internal tariffs by 1968.

Sweden. In 1972, the Swedish economy sold 25.9 percent of its total exports to the EC-6 and 33.8 percent to the four countries that applied to join the Communities.[19] In other words, it had to expect that three-fifths of its exports would be destined to the common market. In fact, in 1973 Sweden sold 50.4 percent of its exports to the enlarged EC, to which Norway had not acceded (see Table 5.1). This high share of exports made up 11.7 percent of the Swedish GDP. Sweden's leading sectoral exports to

Table 5.3   Barriers to Trade: Free Trade Area Tariffs, 1973 and 1984 (percentage)

		Year	Estimated External Tariffs of the EC	Estimated Intra-FTA Tariffs
Sweden				
Nonelectrical machinery	(71)	1973	5–6	4–5
		1984	4–5	0.0
Transport equipment	(73)	1973	7–8	6–7
		1984	6–7	0.0
Paper manufactures	(64)	1973	10–11	10–11
		1984	9–10	0.0
Norway				
Nonferrous metals	(68)	1973	5–6	5–6
		1984	4–5	0.0
Transport equipment	(73)	1973	7–8	6–7
		1984	6–7	0.0
Iron and steel	(67)	1973	6–7	5–6
		1984	5–6	0.0
Switzerland				
Nonelectrical machinery	(71)	1973	5–6	4–5
		1984	4–5	0.0
Professional instruments	(86)	1973	8–9	7–8
		1984	5–6	0.0
Electrical machinery	(72)	1973	8–9	6–7
		1984	5–6	0.0

Sources: Council of the European Communities, "Council Regulation (EEC) no. 1/73 of 19 December 1972 Amending Regulation (EEC) no. 950/68 on the Common Customs Tariff," *Official Journal of the European Communities*, no. L 1 (1 January 1973); and Council of the European Communities, "Council Regulation (EEC) no. 3333/83 of 4 November 1983 Amending Regulation (EEC) no. 950/68 on the Common Customs Tariff," *Official Journal of the European Communities*, no. L 313 (14 November 1983).

the EC comprised three equal 12–13 percent shares of nonelectrical machinery, transportation equipment, and paper manufactures. The substantial amount of 71.3 percent of the latter was sold to the common market (see Table 5.2). Unlike in the 1960s, pulp and waste paper were not among the top three sectors anymore, and the export of transportation equipment had gained in importance. Without some kind of integration, Swedish exports of paper manufactures to the EC would have encountered high tariffs, and the other two sectors would have faced middle-range barriers to trade (see Table 5.3).[20] The government and Parliament agreed that the free trade agreements involved big advantages for the Swedish economy and would have a positive impact on the development of production and employment.[21] A survey conducted by the National Board of Trade confirmed that, in general, Swedish industries expected significant advantages from participation in the common market, such as improved market access and larger exports.[22] Sweden's economic incentives for free trade with the enlarged Communities were fairly strong.

In line with its "open" application of 1967, the Swedish government in early 1970 still pondered the option of EC membership: "it is impossible for us to say whether we want to adhere to the Common Market or associate with it before having precisely determined what the *finalités politiques* mean for the EEC."[23] The crucial question was how the plans for economic and monetary union and for political unification could be reconciled with the Swedish model and neutrality. At that time, Sweden also promoted its concept of the "third way" in developing countries, praising social democracy as the alternative to capitalism and communism. The three pillars of international social democracy were social and economic justice, political détente with disarmament, and international cooperation. The prime minister reiterated that "the fundamental condition to be fulfilled by our EEC policy is for us to be able to continue working for solidarity and social justice."[24] The Swedish model, with its special policies on taxes, welfare, employment, agriculture, tariffs, and the movement of capital, had to be preserved. Once the EC had definitely adopted the Werner and Davignon Reports, in the spring of 1971, the Swedish government reassessed its position:

> The countries which have taken the initiative for co-operation in foreign policy on the basis of the Davignon plan are all members of NATO. The countries that have applied for membership are all—with the exception of Ireland—also members of this military alliance. . . . Co-operation in foreign policy in the form of the Davignon plan cannot be considered compatible with the requirements of a policy of neutrality. . . . Participation by Sweden in an economic and monetary union, which would involve our giving up our national right to make our own decisions in important fields, is not compatible with our policy of neutrality.[25]

In contrast to EC membership, the trade agreements did not contain any commitments that would hinder Sweden's pursuit of an independent foreign policy and maintenance of neutrality or touch on its welfare state.[26] Sweden's political hurdles in the early 1970s were thus very low with regard to the free trade agreements but high with regard to EC membership.

Norway. In 1972, Norway sold 23.8 percent of its exports to the EC-6 and a slightly bigger share of 26.1 percent to the three other candidates for EC membership, the UK, Denmark, and Ireland.[27] Thus, Norway had to expect that half of its total exports would be destined to the common market as of 1973. Indeed, in 1973 the Norwegian economy exported 47.4 percent to the EC-9, accounting for a considerable GDP ratio of 10.4 percent (see Table 5.1). The government pointed out that it was "of great importance to Norway that a satisfactory solution can be found for the problem of the European market."[28]

Norway's major sectoral exports to the European Communities (see Table 5.2) comprised median shares of nonferrous metals and transportation equipment as well as a smaller share of iron and steel. Both metal resources reached substantial ratios of over 60 percent. Compared to the 1960s, paper manufactures lost out to transportation equipment. All three sectors were confronted with medium levels of trade barriers (see Table 5.3). The government noted that "for important Norwegian export goods, like e.g. aluminium, magnesium and ferro-alloys, where Norway does not have any tariff protection, the EC has relatively high tariffs."[29] As an EC member, Norway would have duty-free access to the common market and good prospects of expanding its exports of both traditional natural resources, including fish, and manufactured industrial products.[30] By contrast, in the free trade agreements the transitional period for aluminum, steel, and other "sensitive" metals was extended to 1 January 1980 and for paper to 1 January 1984, instead of the common deadline of 1 July 1977 for most goods.

Agriculture and fisheries provided the basis for settlement in large areas of the country, so it was considered vital to retain that structure. Norwegian farmers were expected to lose more than half of their present income if Community rules were to be applied without reservations.[31] Furthermore, as a typical coastal fishing nation, Norway was afraid that, without special concessions, it might not be able to compete with the bigger ships of the EC members' sea-fishing fleets that would gain access to its waters and might exploit the resources too heavily.

With the discovery of oil in the North Sea in the early 1970s, it became evident that offshore oil exploitation would gain increasing importance. For oil and gas, the EC level of trade barriers was low, but for petrochemical products, tariffs varied between 12 percent and 18 percent, which would "create serious difficulties for the development of a Norwegian chemical industry if Norway will stay outside a duty-free EC area."[32] Finally, shipping was Norway's third biggest industry, and if Britain joined the EC, 60 percent of the Norwegian merchant fleet would be transporting to and from the enlarged Community.[33] All in all, Norway's expectations about the likely consequences of the EC's first enlargement raised its economic incentives to participate to a high level.

As a NATO member, Norway took a positive attitude toward the Davignon Plan for political cooperation.[34] Its foreign policy had traditionally been oriented westward toward Britain and, later, the United States, and from the government's point of view, "World War II had reinforced this tradition."[35] In the summer of 1970, the People's Movement against Norwegian Membership in the Common Market (Folkebevegelsen Mot Norsk Medlemskap i Fellesmarkedet) was launched. It held up the Davignon and Werner Reports as evidence that the European Communities would increasingly infringe upon national sovereignty. The notion of a "union" aroused strong defensive reactions, for in Norway that word was laden with all the historical and emotional overtones acquired through centuries of foreign domination. In short, the People's Movement argued that in case of membership "all the fish would be taken by foreign trawlers. Norwegian agriculture would be ruined. Small industries would be forced out of business or bought up by foreign capital. The north would be depopulated. The country would be invaded by foreign workers, catholic ideas, continental drinking habits, and foreigners buying up their mountain huts, lakes and forests."[36]

The polls about EC membership showed that public opinion in Norway underwent a new mobilization in early 1971, leading to increasing polarization.[37] They also disclosed a clear gap between center and periphery that superseded the left-right conflict characterizing Norwegian politics.[38] Opinions cut across the political parties and created bitter internal struggles, notably in the Labor, Liberal, and Christian Democratic Parties.[39] Again, "the core of the opposition to EEC was composed of an alliance between the radicals in the cities and the farmers and fishermen in the periphery. Equally strange was an alliance in favor of EEC membership by two traditional antagonists, the Conservative Party and the Labor Party (the moderate wing) and their supporting organizations in the labor market, respectively the employers' organizations and the trade unions movement."[40]

The government and Parliament reassured the country that Norway's oil policy, regional policy (*distriktspolitikken*), and social policy would be continued in the Community and that the welfare state would not be affected since the EC considered social policy to be a national area of concern.[41] They perceived the potential political obstacles to membership as being surmountable. In view of the British application, integration was "if not desirable then at least necessary."[42]

Switzerland. In 1972, the Swiss economy sold 36.6 percent of its total exports to the EC-6 and only 11 percent to Denmark, Norway, Britain, and Ireland.[43] Nevertheless, Switzerland had to expect that almost half of its exported goods would go to the enlarged Communities. The Swiss delegation to the EC in November 1970 even spoke of 60 percent.[44] In fact, Switzerland's exports to the EC-9 in 1973 amounted to the relatively high share of 45.4 percent and a GDP ratio of 10.5 percent (see Table 5.1). The president of the Swiss Federation of Commerce and Industry confirmed that "Switzerland's foreign trade is very heavily dependent on the European markets, which made numerous commentators say that our country was, already, one of the most integrated in Europe."[45] The main products destined to be exported to the common market included a big share of nonelectrical machinery and two small segments of professional instruments and electrical machinery (see Table 5.2), which faced medium-level EC tariffs (see Table 5.3). The government calculated that an industrial free trade agreement would wholly or partly cover about 90 percent of Swiss imports from and exports to the enlarged Communities and about 44 percent of the total Swiss exports and that the average of the customs duties that would be saved amounted to 8.6 percent.[46] With such expectations, Switzerland had strong economic incentives to participate in integration.

The Swiss government made clear that its bilateral cooperation with the EC should not affect "the neutrality policy resting on the will of the Swiss people" and that it should "take into account the specifically Swiss moulding of direct democracy and the federal structure of the state," which guaranteed the internal cohesion of the linguistically and religiously heterogeneous population.[47] "For a permanently neutral state like Switzerland it is not possible to accept the political goals of the Communities without calling into question its neutrality policy and losing some of its credibility."[48] Moreover, "the curtailment of direct democracy is difficult to quantify," as the popular rights of initiative and referendum "exert an influence on legislation even if there is no collection of signatures."[49] For many new laws falling within EC competences, the consultation of the Swiss people and cantons might be restricted.

The Swiss government concluded that, in comparison to EC membership, the free trade agreements did not touch on any of the identity-related elements.[50] Switzerland faced strong political constraints against becoming a full member of the European Communities, but low impediments to the conclusion of free trade agreements. The referendum on the free trade agreements in December 1972 did not reveal any relevant cleavages in Swiss society. There were no significant differences in the voting behavior of German- and French-speaking cantons. Of the Swiss German electorate, 72.5 percent voted "yes," as did 74.9 percent in the French-speaking cantons, and all the cantons voted in favor of the free trade agreements.[51]

Integration Policy Preferences

Considering the expected effects of the first EC enlargement, the importance of market access was great for all three countries. The political constraints on full membership were particularly strong for Switzerland. They were equally reassessed as being too high in Sweden, once the EC announced its plans for political and monetary cooperation. Only the Norwegian elites perceived the political obstacles to be surmountable. Based on these findings, I expect that neutral Switzerland and Sweden, in contrast to Norway, will not aim at full EC membership but at a lower level of integration. Norway will value getting some voice, but for Sweden and even more so for Switzerland, sovereignty will remain relatively more important.

Sweden. On 10 November 1970, Sweden informed the EC that it aimed at "the widest possible form of economic cooperation" and proposed "to establish a customs union, subject to a non-harmonization clause concerning commercial policy."[52] The Swedish government was prepared to implement the Common Agricultural Policy and to accept the need of certain economic and social measures to achieve increased freedom of movement of labor, services, and capital. In exchange, "Sweden would, with regard to the future development, expect to be informed and consulted and possibly to be represented at preparatory meetings before final decisions are reached."[53] The minister of trade specified that, of course, "we cannot participate in such forms of co-operation on foreign policy, economic, monetary and other matters which, in our judgement, would jeopardise our possibilities to pursue a firm policy of neutrality."[54] Hence, at the beginning of the process, the government aimed at a medium level of integration.

On 18 March 1971, in light of the developments in the Communities, the Swedish government finally rejected the idea of full EC membership: "Participation by Sweden in the foreign-policy co-operation which has been drawn up on the basis of the Davignon report is not compatible with a policy of unwavering Swedish neutrality"; nor was Sweden's membership in an economic and monetary union based on the Werner plan, "which would mean that important areas of our national right to self-determination would have to be given up."[55] Instead of membership, Sweden asked for a customs union with the EC since it was seeking a "more profound, broader and more intimate collaboration than any other country outside the circle of candidate countries," which presupposed the establishment of "special cooperative bodies" at the level of ministers and parliaments and an opportunity for information and consultations.[56]

The Commission opinion on the relations between the EC and the nonapplicant EFTA countries of June 1971 was, to some extent, an indirect response to the Swedish proposals. It specified that a nonmember could not adopt the CAP, that "ad hoc membership" would create institutional problems, and that a general safeguard clause for neutrality could hardly be controlled without an institutional framework.[57] A special treatment for Sweden might have undermined the European spirit of the countries seeking full membership, given the powerful EC opposition in Great Britain and Norway. The EC Council of Ministers agreed that the nonapplicant EFTA countries could obtain industrial free trade agreements but nothing more.[58] The negotiations began in December 1971, but it was not until June 1972 that the Swedish delegation finally withdrew its request for a customs union.[59]

In the parliamentary debate on the ratification of the free trade agreement in December 1972, the liberal People's Party criticized the fact that Sweden had "a higher level of ambition than Switzerland, Austria, Finland or Portugal" but did not obtain a better agreement.[60] The agrarian Center Party was basically satisfied with the agreement, which preserved neutrality and domestic freedom of action with regard to agricultural, regional, and environmental policies. The social democratic government underlined that the main goals had been reached and that full EC membership with neutrality reservations was simply not feasible.[61] Parliament confirmed that the free trade agreement was "the only formal framework possible for a development of cooperation between Sweden and the Communities."[62] On 12 December 1972, the Riksdag approved the free trade agreement with the endorsement of all parties, except for the communists. The communists' suggestion to hold a referendum on Sweden's agreements with the "reactionary, capitalist and conservative" EC was clearly defeated.[63]

As expected, Sweden was not prepared to give up enough sovereignty to get a voice as a full member of the European Communities, but it was ready to renounce some national freedom of action in exchange for limited influence. The government was aware of this choice as interdependence between nations continued to grow: "This means that small nations must be prepared to give up more and more of their sovereignty. . . . Sovereignty must become gradually limited, not by the use of the tremendous might of the great powers, but by the very exercise of sovereignty, through voluntary agreements dictated by enlightened long-range self-interest. The positive alternative to national sovereignty is international agreements and international structures and regimes."[64]

Since the free trade agreements did not fulfill Swedish ambitions, the government early on suggested extending cooperation with the EC to nontariff barriers to trade, public procurement, energy policy, environmental protection, and research and development.[65] Indeed, several agreements were concluded in these fields, and from 1973 to 1977 Sweden was involved in the EC's exchange rate mechanism.[66]

Norway. On 5 June 1970, the Norwegian government asked parliament to reaffirm its support for the 1967 application for EC membership. It claimed that if Britain and Denmark were joining the common market, Norway would experience considerable problems if it stayed outside.[67] The Storting approved the government's policy on 25 June 1970.[68] The government welcomed the EC's plans for political cooperation and was ready to participate in the elaborations of an Economic and Monetary Union. The main problems in the negotiations involved fisheries, agriculture, and foreign investments in the shipping industry.[69] The agricultural organizations demanded that Norway be excluded from the Common Agricultural Policy and maintain national import controls and price subsidies. The government proposed that the CAP should apply and that the Norwegian farmers would receive monetary compensation amounting to the difference between EC prices and the higher hypothetical domestic price level set in negotiations between the state and agricultural organizations.[70] However, the farmers' organizations opposed this compensation policy.

The fact that the EC adopted its Common Fisheries Policy just when the negotiations with Norway began was very unfortunate for the Norwegians who were for joining the common market. They had argued that it would be possible for Norway to influence the CFP because the Community could hardly ignore the views of Western Europe's largest fishing nation. The opponents of membership claimed that the EC's action showed that the Norwegians would have no say in the EC, even on decisions of such importance to them. As a result, the fishermen's organizations opposed accession if Norway was not granted permanent retention of its exclusive 12-mile fishing zone along the whole coast.[71] The export of fish was vital for the sector, but as an EC member, Norway would lose national control over its fishing resources. After very difficult negotiations, the fisheries agreement was concluded in January 1972.[72] The compromise foresaw a ten-year transitional period in which Norway could retain its exclusive fishing limit. When the time was up, a review would take place. There was thus no legal guarantee that Norway would not have to open up its waters to EC vessels after 1982. The fishermen's national organization unanimously rejected this solution.

The Federation of Norwegian Industries, the Bankers' Association, the Confederation of Trade Unions, the Norwegian Trade Council, the commercial and crafts associations, the Shipowners' Association, and the Norwegian Employers' Federation were in favor of joining the

Communities.[73] The Norwegian Employers' Federation strongly argued that EC membership would ensure continued growth through increased exports without jeopardizing Norway's social system.[74]

Within the nonsocialist coalition government, opinions about EC membership diverged.[75] The conservatives favored membership, the Center Party opposed it, and the Liberal and Christian Democratic Parties were divided on the issue. As a result, the government resigned in March 1971, and the pro-EC Labor Party formed a minority government. The new leaders promised to make a reservation on Norway's position with regard to the Community's most far-reaching plans for economic, monetary, and political union. The Labor government pointed out that "the EEC was not a socialist organization (partly because socialists had left its shaping to conservative and capitalist forces), but it could be turned into one if the socialist parties joined forces with that aim in view."[76] Yet, the Labor Party experienced increasing internal opposition, based primarily on the young socialists' organizations.

The treaty of accession was signed on 22 January 1972. On this occasion, the prime minister underlined that the Norwegian government considered it "a very important task for the Communities to foster social policy and to raise it to ever higher levels" and that it was "equally important to develop regional policy so as to strengthen, with the aid of common resources, the basis of economic activity in the peripheral regions."[77] The government emphasized that a precondition for Norway's accession to the EC was that Great Britain and Denmark would join at the same time. It compared the three options of membership, association, and a mere free trade agreement and concluded that "a trade agreement clearly constitutes a worse alternative for Norway than membership."[78] Prime Minister Trygve Bratteli turned the referendum into a vote of confidence by announcing that the government would resign if EC membership was rejected and that the Labor Party would not assume responsibility for negotiating a free trade agreement. The Conservative Party indicated that it would not do so either because that would be a task for the parties that had opposed membership.

The choice between influence on decisionmaking (*medbestemmelse*) and self-government (*selvstyre*) was a prominent topic in the campaign.[79] For the government, it was clear that if Norway were to remain outside the enlarged European Communities, the latter would nonetheless have direct effects on Norway as a result of the close ties, whereas as a member, Norway could participate in and influence the EC's development.[80] The conservatives also pointed out that "the belief in increased self-government over Norwegian domestic affairs because we concluded a trade agreement instead of membership . . . is to a high degree an illusion."[81]

For Norway, possible membership in the European Communities, even if in certain fields it would limit the formal decisionmaking authority of the

Norwegian political organs, did not imply any real loss of sovereignty but meant that Norway, in cooperation with other countries, gained control or better management over what was determined earlier from outside or what was not under the state's decisionmaking authority. With the influence Norway gained through this form of committed cooperation, it could also create a certain degree of sovereignty in an environment new to the country.[82]

In the referendum held on 24–25 September 1972, the "no" votes won by 53.5 percent, with a turnout of 79 percent. The most striking feature of this result was the clear division between the rural and urban areas. "Voters speaking *landsmål*, supporting teetotalism, or belonging to the fundamentalist Protestant movement—all groups whose strength lay in the rural areas—were more inclined to vote 'no,' whereas people in the large towns who spoke *riksmål* and took a liberal position on moral and religious issues were more frequently found supporting EEC membership."[83]

After weeks of uncertainty, a new minority government comprising the Liberal, Christian Democratic, and Center Parties took office in October 1972. The Liberal Party had split up over the question of a coalition government and those in favor of accession formed a new party, the New People's Party (DNF). The negotiations on a free trade agreement with the EEC revolved around the "sensitive products" (such as paper, aluminum, ferro-alloys, and zinc), fish exports, and shipping, which made up a large share of Norwegian exports to the common market. However, the EC granted only minor modifications to the standard EFTA treaties, and shipping remained outside. When the agreements between Norway, the EEC, and the ECSC were signed on 14 May 1973, the government praised them as "a balanced solution for our industry as a whole" and underlined that Norway maintained its freedom of action in essential areas of economic and social affairs.[84] The Storting approved the agreements by a unanimous vote.[85] On this basis, Norway concluded many bilateral agreements with the EC in the following years, the first one being a fisheries framework agreement.[86]

As predicted, the Norwegian government aimed at full EC membership. However, the negative outcome of the referendum disclosed a gap in the perceptions of the political obstacles between the elites and the people. After this failure, the government chose a low level of integration in the shape of the free trade agreements. Norwegian elites valued very much having a voice in the EC, but the people were less prepared to give up sovereignty in exchange for influence.

Switzerland.   On 10 November 1970, the Swiss delegation explained its position to the EC Council of Ministers.[87] It supported a comprehensive elimination of trade barriers on industrial goods, some limited agreement on agricultural products, and cooperation in areas beyond the free movement of goods (e.g., services, technical barriers to trade, insurance, transportation policy, free movement of workers, energy, and research). In contrast to Sweden, Switzerland did not wish to enter a customs union and ruled out any form of harmonization.

Throughout the negotiations, which began in December 1971, the Swiss delegation kept in close contact with the competent parliamentary commissions, the economic interest groups, and the Permanent Economic Delegation.[88] Even though it did not succeed in introducing provisions on arbitration, public procurement, and nontariff barriers to trade or cooperation on monetary, industrial, regional, or environmental matters, Switzerland was satisfied with the free trade agreements signed on 22 July 1972.[89] A few concessions had to be granted for certain agricultural products and with regard to Italian migrant workers, and a special agreement was concluded for free trade in watches. Overall, the free trade agreements represented the "middle course" between accession and isolation that Switzerland had sought since the 1950s.[90] The pending application for association submitted to the EC in 1961 was hence considered irrelevant.

The government and parliament agreed that the free trade agreements allowed Switzerland to participate in European integration while preserving direct democracy, parliamentary competences, and its neutral foreign policy.[91] They were supported by most political parties and interest groups. Only the extreme right and left opposed the new treaties, and a very few firms advocated EC membership with certain reservations. The farmers' union was relieved that agriculture was basically excluded, and the labor unions judged the agreement acceptable since it did not contain any obligations for harmonization. A survey of the Swiss Federation of Commerce and Industry (Vorort) showed that almost all the firms, without significant differences between sectors, favored free trade in industrial goods.[92] On 3 December 1972, almost three-quarters of the Swiss voters (with a turnout of 52.9 percent) and all the cantons approved the free trade agreements with the European Communities in a referendum. In the following years, Switzerland concluded a long list of other bilateral agreements with the European Communities, particularly in the field of research.[93]

Switzerland's political and economic elites were rather reluctant to give up operational sovereignty since the maintenance of the integration-sensitive political institutions was considered very important. The government recognized that Switzerland's interests went beyond trade because of "the fact that we would be affected to a considerable extent in many other areas by the decisions and developments in the EEC even if we were not to participate in the integration efforts."[94] Hence, already in its opening statement in November 1970, it had made clear that Switzerland wished "to arrive at some form of effective say in decisions taken corresponding to the commitments it is prepared to enter into."[95] The problem lost some of its salience when it turned out that relations with the EEC would be limited to an industrial free trade agreement.[96] In sum, the Swiss government was not prepared to renounce the sovereignty required to join the EC and instead aimed at a low level of market integration.

Even though in the end all three countries obtained similar industrial free trade agreements with the European Communities, the original levels of integration aimed at ranged from low to high, and the intensity of the public debates varied accordingly. Sweden first pursued an "open" approach, whereas Switzerland aimed from the outset at a free trade agreement. After a few months, the Swedish government specified its policy by excluding membership but for some more time continued to insist on establishing a customs union. Only Norway clearly pursued full membership but was forced to lower its ambitions in light of the negative outcome of the referendum.

Conclusion

The early 1970s finally allowed for a rapprochement between the European Communities and the EFTA countries after almost two decades of failures. The result was not a multilateral European free trade area but a series of bilateral solutions. While Britain, Denmark, and Ireland joined the EC, the other EFTA member states each concluded free trade agreements with the enlarged Communities. The European Free Trade Association appeared not as a homogeneous group but rather as a partnership of convenience for the purpose of reaching an acceptable arrangement with the EC. Even though the final outcomes for Sweden, Norway, and Switzerland were almost identical, their preferences and integrationist ambitions had varied considerably. Norway negotiated for full membership, the Swiss government aspired for nothing more than industrial free trade, and the Swedish position was situated in between.

Once more, it became clear that the European Community set the options for the nonmember states' participation in the integration process. Both Norway and Sweden had to modify their policies—Norway as a result of the referendum revealing a gap between the masses and the elites, and Sweden because of the Community's political plans. These incidents illustrate the importance of domestic restraints and of external events for the integration policies of small states.

In the following years, the EFTA countries engaged in no new attempts at joining the EC, whose membership seemed to stagnate until the mid-1980s, owing to "Eurosclerosis." All the same, cooperation between the two sides was further tightened and broadened and finally went beyond industrial free trade to show the first signs of a new multilateralism.

Notes

1. Commission of the European Communities, "Opinion Submitted to the Council Concerning the Applications for Membership from the United Kingdom, Ireland, Denmark and Norway, 1 October 1969," *Bulletin of the European Communities*, Supplement, nos. 9–10 (1969).

2. Council of the European Communities, "Final Communiqué of the Conference in The Hague on 2 December 1969," *Bulletin of the European Communities* 3, no. 1 (1970): 16.

3. Kleppe, "Momentum of Nordic Integration," pp. 147–165. The Finnish president declared that entering a customs union with three states that might soon be joining the EC seemed inadvisable to Finland.

4. See European Communities, *Bulletin of the European Communities* 3, no. 8 (1970): 20–50. For a record of the negotiations see *EFTA Bulletin* from vol. 11, no. 8 (1970) to vol. 14, no. 4 (1973); and Nicholson and East, *From the Six to the Twelve*, chaps. 2–6.

5. See Binswanger and Mayrzedt, *Europapolitik der Rest-EFTA-Staaten,* chap. 2.

6. Commission of the European Communities, "Opinion Submitted by the Commission to the Council on Relations Between the Enlarged Community and those EFTA Member States (including the Associated Finland) Which Have Not Applied for Membership of the Community, 16 June 1971," *Bulletin of the European Communities*, Supplement, no. 3 (1971): 12–14.

7. Binswanger and Mayrzedt, *Europapolitik der Rest-EFTA-Staaten,* chap. 3.

8. That is, a product made partly in one EFTA country and partly in another could not qualify for preferential treatment.

9. Commission of the European Communities, "Agreements with the EFTA States Not Applying for Membership," *Bulletin of the European Communities* 5, no. 9 (1972): 13.

10. See "Ceremonial Conclusion of the Negotiations on Enlargement," *Bulletin of the European Communities* 5, no. 2 (1972): 13–34.

11. Separate treaties were concluded because the ECSC treaty stipulates that the member states will keep their competences in commercial policy. By contrast, the products covered by Euratom were dealt with under the EEC-EFTA agreements.

12. See Norberg, "The Free Trade Agreements of the EFTA Countries with the EC," pp. 77–107; and Wahl, *The Free Trade Agreements Between the EC and EFTA Countries;* Koppensteiner, *Rechtsfragen der Freihandelsabkommen der Europäischen Wirtschaftsgemeinschaft mit den EFTA-Staaten.*

13. Council of the European Communities, "Report by the Foreign Ministers of the Member States on the Problems of Political Unification," *Bulletin of the European Communities*, no. 11 (1970): 9–14.

14. Commission of the European Communities, "Commission Memorandum to the Council on the Preparation of a Plan for the Phased Establishment of an Economic and Monetary Union, 4 March 1970," *Bulletin of the European Communities*, Supplement, no. 3 (1970).

15. European Communities, *Bulletin of the European Communities*, no. 3 (1971): 9–14.

16. Council meeting on 26–27 June 1978, in European Communities, *Bulletin of the European Communities*, no. 6 (1978): 78.

17. Underdal, "Diverging Roads to Europe," p. 67; and EFTA, *EFTA Trade 1973* (Geneva: EFTA, 1975), p. 130.

18. Middleton, "Quelques barrières non tarifaires aux échanges dans l'AELE et la CEE," p. 19. At the end of 1971, about twenty EC directives had been adopted to tackle nontariff barriers to trade in areas such as cars, measuring instruments, and dangerous substances. Dahlström and Söderbäck, *Sveriges avtal med EEC*, pp. 63–64.

19. United Nations, Economic Commission for Europe, "Economic Integration and Export Performance of West European Countries outside the EC," *Economic Studies*, no. 5 (Geneva, 1995): 39; and EFTA, *EFTA Trade 1972* (Geneva: EFTA, 1974), Statistical Appendix, Table 84.

20. In the free trade agreement with the EEC, paper was among the "sensitive products" that faced a transitional period of eleven instead of five years. This competitive disadvantage was partly mitigated by rules allowing various EC countries to establish duty-free paper import quotas. Viklund, *Sweden and the European Community*, pp. 21–22.

21. Sweden, Government, *Kungl. Maj:ts proposition 1972:135 angående avtal med den europeiska ekonomiska gemenskapen, m.m.*, Stockholm, 3 November 1972, p. 35; and Sweden, Parliament, Foreign Affairs Committee, *Utrikesutskottets betänkande nr. 20 med anledning av propositionen 1972:135 angående avtal med de europeiska gemenskaperna m.m. jämte motioner*, Stockholm, 5 December 1972, p. 25.

22. Sweden, Ministry of Trade and Industry, *Inför Sveriges EEC förhandlingar: Fakta och överväganden* (Stockholm: Handelsdepartementet, 1971), Annex 1, pp. 179–194. Skeptical attitudes prevailed only in industries producing shoes, leather goods, and textiles.

23. Interview with the Swedish prime minister Olof Palme in *Le Monde*, "Notre préoccupation centrale est de maintenir l'équilibre qui existe en Europe du Nord," 16 April 1970.

24. Prime Minister Olaf Palme, in Sweden, Parliament, "Allmänpolitisk debatt," *Riksdagens Protokoll*, no. 8 (Stockholm, 19 January 1971): 45.

25. Government statement in the Riksdag on 31 March 1971, in Sweden, Ministry for Foreign Affairs, *Documents on Swedish Foreign Policy: 1971*, New Series I:C:21 (Stockholm: Royal Ministry for Foreign Affairs, 1972), p. 31.

26. Sweden, Government, *Kungl. Maj:ts proposition 1972:135 angående avtal med den europeiska ekonomiska gemenskapen, m.m.*, Stockholm, 3 November 1972, p. 34.

27. United Nations, Economic Commission for Europe, "Economic Integration and Export Performance of West European Countries Outside the EC," *Economic Studies*, no. 5 (Geneva, 1995): 39.

28. Norway, Ministry for Foreign Affairs, *Om Norges forhold til de nordiske og europeiske markedsdannelser*, St.meld. nr. 92 (1969–1970), Oslo, 5 June 1970, p. 54.

29. Norway, Ministry for Foreign Affairs, *Om Norges tilslutning til De Europeiske Fellesskap*, St.meld. nr. 50 (1971–1972), Oslo, 10 March 1972, p. 66.

30. Norway, Ministry for Foreign Affairs, *Om Norges forhold til De Europeiske Fellesskap*, St.meld. nr. 90 (1970–1971), Oslo, 21 May 1971, p. 18.

31. Underdal, "Diverging Roads to Europe," pp. 69–71.

32. Ibid., p. 24.

33. Ibid., p. 45.

34. Norway, Ministry for Foreign Affairs, *Om Norges forhold til de nordiske og europeiske markedsdannelser*, St.meld. nr. 92 (1969–1970), Oslo, 5 June 1970, pp. 33–34; and Norway, Ministry for Foreign Affairs, *Om Norges tilslutning til De*

Europeiske Fellesskap, St.meld. nr. 50 (1971–1972), Oslo, 10 March 1972, pp. 150–155.

35. Norway, Ministry for Foreign Affairs, *Om Norges forhold til De Europeiske Fellesskap,* St.meld. nr. 90 (1970–1971), Oslo, 21 May 1971, pp. 13–14.

36. Allen, *Norway and Europe in the 1970s,* p. 107.

37. Gleditsch and Hellevik, *Kampen om EF,* pp. 32–38, Annex 3.

38. Hellevik, Gleditsch and Ringdal, "The Common Market Issue in Norway," pp. 37–53; Gleditsch, "Generaler og fotfolk i utakt," pp. 795–804; Converse and Valen, "Dimensions of Cleavage and Perceived Party Distances in Norwegian Voting," pp. 148–150; and Valen, "National Conflict Structure and Foreign Politics," pp. 47–82.

39. The Conservative, Center, and Socialist People's Parties were either almost unanimously in favor of or against EC membership. See Schou, *Norge og EF,* chaps. 4–9; and Knudsen, *Den nye Europa-debatten,* chaps. 2–7.

40. Valen, "Norway," p. 215.

41. Norway, Ministry for Foreign Affairs, *Om Norges forhold til de europeiske fellesskap,* St.meld. nr. 90 (1970–1971), Oslo, 21 May 1971, pp. 4–6, 46–56; and Norway, Parliament, Foreign Affairs and Constitution Committee, *Innstillning fra utenriks- og konstitusjonskomitéen om Norges tilslutning til det europeiske fellesskap,* St.meld. nr. 50, Innst.S.nr. 277 (1971–1972), Oslo, 26 May 1972, p. 515.

42. Pharo, "Norge, EF og europeisk samarbeid," Summary.

43. United Nations, Economic Commission for Europe, "Economic Integration and Export Performance of West European Countries Outside the EC," *Economic Studies,* no. 5 (Geneva, 1995): 39; and EFTA, *EFTA Trade 1972* (Geneva: EFTA, 1974), Statistical Appendix, Table 84.

44. Switzerland, Federal Council, "Schweizerische Erklärung an der Zusammenkunft auf Ministerebene zwischen den Europäischen Gemeinschaften und der Schweiz, Brüssel, 10. November 1970," *Bundesblatt* I, no. 4 (Bern, 1971): 62–63.

45. Junod, "Les entreprises suisses et le grand espace économique européen," p. 31.

46. Switzerland, Federal Council, *Botschaft des Bundesrates an die Bundesversammlung vom 16. August 1972 über die Genehmigung der Abkommen zwischen der Schweiz und den Europäischen Gemeinschaften,* Bern, 16 August 1972, p. 721.

47. Switzerland, Federal Council, "Schweizerische Erklärung an der Zusammenkunft auf Ministerebene zwischen den Europäischen Gemeinschaften und der Schweiz, Brüssel, 10. November 1970," *Bundesblatt* I, no. 4 (Bern, 1971): 61–62.

48. Switzerland, Federal Council, *Bericht des Bundesrates vom 11. August 1971 über die Entwicklung der europäischen Integrationsbestrebungen und die Haltung der Schweiz, Bericht zum Postulat Beck (9688) vom 16. März 1967 und zur Motion Furgler (9922) vom 15. März 1968,* Bern, 11 August 1971, p. 107.

49. Ibid., p. 108.

50. Switzerland, Federal Council, *Botschaft des Bundesrates an die Bundesversammlung vom 16. August 1972 über die Genehmigung der Abkommen zwischen der Schweiz und den Europäischen Gemeinschaften,* Bern, 16 August 1972, pp. 730–731.

51. Switzerland, Federal Council, "Bundesratsbeschluss vom 25. Januar 1973 über die Erwahrung des Ergebnisses der Volksabstimmung vom 3. Dezember 1972 betreffend den Bundesbeschluss über die Abkommen zwischen der Schweizerischen

Eidgenossenschaft und der Europäischen Wirtschaftsgemeinschaft sowie den Mitgliedstaaten der Europäischen Gemeinschaft für Kohle und Stahl," *Bundesblatt* I, no. 4 (Bern, 1973): 82.

52. Commission of the European Communities, "Opinion Submitted by the Commission to the Council on Relations Between the Enlarged Community and those EFTA Member States (including the Associated Finland) which Have Not Applied for Membership of the Community, 16 June 1971," *Bulletin of the European Communities,* Supplement, no. 3 (1971): 6.

53. Ibid.

54. Statement by the minister of commerce at the meeting in Brussels between Sweden and the European Communities on 10 November 1970, in Sweden, Ministry for Foreign Affairs, *Documents on Swedish Foreign Policy: 1970,* New Series I:C:20 (Stockholm: Royal Ministry for Foreign Affairs, 1971), p. 60.

55. Speech by Prime Minister Olaf Palme before the Stockholm Labor Union on 18 March 1971, in Sweden, Ministry for Foreign Affairs, *Documents on Swedish Foreign Policy: 1971,* New Series I:C:21 (Stockholm: Royal Ministry for Foreign Affairs, 1972), p. 19.

56. Speech by the minister of commerce at the annual meeting of the Federation of Swedish Industries on 21 April 1971, in Sweden, Ministry for Foreign Affairs, *Documents on Swedish Foreign Policy: 1971,* New Series I:C:21 (Stockholm: Royal Ministry for Foreign Affairs, 1972), pp. 219–220; and Government memorandum to the European Communities on 6 September 1971, in Sweden, Ministry for Foreign Affairs, *Documents on Swedish Foreign Policy: 1971,* New Series I:C:21 (Stockholm: Royal Ministry for Foreign Affairs, 1972), pp. 222–227.

57. Commission of the European Communities, "Opinion Submitted by the Commission to the Council on Relations between the Enlarged Community and those EFTA Member States (including the Associated Finland) which Have Not Applied for Membership of the Community, 16 June 1971," *Bulletin of the European Communities,* Supplement, no. 3 (1971).

58. European Communities, *Bulletin of the European Communities,* nos. 9–10 (1971): 140.

59. See Viklund, *Spelet om frihandelsavtalet,* pp. 42–128.

60. Sweden, Parliament, "Avtal med EEC, m.m.," *Riksdagens Protokoll,* no. 138–139 (Stockholm, 12 December 1972): 10–11.

61. Ibid., pp. 36–42.

62. Sweden, Parliament, Foreign Affairs Committee, *Utrikesutskottets betänkande nr. 20 med anledning av propositionen 1972:135 angående avtal med de europeiska gemenskaperna m.m. jämte motioner,* Stockholm, 5 December 1972, p. 29.

63. Sweden, Parliament, "Avtal med EEC, m.m.," *Riksdagens Protokoll,* no. 138–139 (Stockholm, 12 December 1972): 20–29, 130–131.

64. Address by the prime minister at the National Press Club in Washington on 5 June 1970, in Sweden, Ministry for Foreign Affairs, *Documents on Swedish Foreign Policy: 1970,* New Series I:C:20 (Stockholm: Royal Ministry for Foreign Affairs, 1971), p. 41.

65. Speech by the minister of commerce at the Social Democratic Party Congress on 5 October 1972, in Sweden, Ministry for Foreign Affairs, *Documents on Swedish Foreign Policy: 1972,* New Series I:C:22 (Stockholm: Royal Ministry for Foreign Affairs, 1973), pp. 66–67.

66. See Commission of the European Communities, Treaties Office, *Bilateral*

Relationships, Commitments and Agreements Between EC and EFTA Countries (updated and revised as of January 1989), Brussels, I/119/89, March 1989, pp. 85–98.

67. Norway, Ministry for Foreign Affairs, *Om Norges forhold til de nordiske og europeiske markedsdannelser*, St.meld. nr. 92 (1969–1970), Oslo, 5 June 1970, pp. 54–56.

68. See Vefald, "The 1971 EEC Debate," pp. 280–314.

69. See Allen, *Norway and Europe in the 1970s*, pp. 81–127.

70. Norway, Ministry for Foreign Affairs, *Om Norges forhold til De Europeiske Fellesskap*, St.meld. nr. 90 (1970–1971), Oslo, 21 May 1971, pp. 99, 115–119.

71. Allen, *Norway and Europe in the 1970s*, pp. 97–99.

72. Ibid., pp. 119–127.

73. Norway, Ministry for Foreign Affairs, *Om Norges tilslutning til De Europeiske Fellesskap*, St.meld. nr. 50 (1971–1972), Oslo, 10 March 1972, Annex 4.

74. Aardal, "Economics, Ideology and Strategy," pp. 38–40.

75. Kite, *Scandinavia Faces EU*, pp. 159–160, 165–176.

76. Norway, Ministry for Foreign Affairs, *Om Norges forhold til De Europeiske Fellesskap*, St.meld. nr. 90 (1970–1971), Oslo, 21 May 1971, p. 103.

77. "Ceremonial Conclusion of the Negotiations on Enlargement," *Bulletin of the European Communities*, no. 2 (1972): 32–33.

78. Norway, Ministry for Foreign Affairs, *Om Norges tilslutning til De Europeiske Fellesskap*, St.meld. nr. 50 (1971–1972), Oslo, 10 March 1972, p. 31.

79. See Bjørklund, *Mot strømmen*, chap. 8.

80. Norway, Ministry for Foreign Affairs, *Om Norges forhold til de nordiske og europeiske markedsdannelser*, St.meld. nr. 92 (1969–1970), Oslo, 5 June 1970, p. 54.

81. Norway, Parliament, Foreign Affairs and Constitution Committee, *Innstilling fra utenriks- og konstitusjonskomitéen om ratifikasjon av Avtale mellom Norge og det europeiske økonomiske fellesskap og Avtale mellom Norge og medlemsstatene i det europeiske kull- og stålfellesskap og det europeiske kull- og stålfellesskap*, St.meld. nr. 126, Innst.S.nr. 289 (1972–1973), Oslo, 18 May 1973, p. 965.

82. Norway, Ministry for Foreign Affairs, *Om Norges forhold til De Europeiske Fellesskap*, St.meld. nr. 90 (1970–1971), Oslo, 21 May 1971, pp. 6, 69, 101.

83. Allen, *Norway and Europe in the 1970s*, p. 160. See also Valen, "National Conflict Structure and Foreign Politics," pp. 47–82.

84. Norway, Ministry for Foreign Affairs, *Om samtykke til ratifikasjon av Avtale mellom Norge og det europeiske økonomiske fellesskap og Avtale mellom Norge og medlemsstatene i det europeiske kull- og stålfellesskap og det europeiske kull- og stålfellesskap*, St.meld. nr. 126 (1972–1973), Oslo, 4 May 1973, p. 47.

85. Norway, Parliament, Foreign Affairs and Constitution Committee, *Innstilling fra utenriks- og konstitusjonskomitéen om ratifikasjon av Avtale mellom Norge og det europeiske økonomiske fellesskap og Avtale mellom Norge og medlemsstatene i det europeiske kull- og stålfellesskap og det europeiske kull- og stålfellesskap (St.meld. nr. 126)*, Innst.S.nr. 289 (1972–1973), Oslo, 18 May 1973, pp. 964–969.

86. Commission of the European Communities, Treaties Office, *Bilateral Relationships, Commitments and Agreements Between EC and EFTA Countries*

(updated and revised as of January 1989), Brussels, I/119/89, March 1989, pp. 71–84.

87. Switzerland, Federal Council, "Schweizerische Erklärung an der Zusammenkunft auf Ministerebene zwischen den Europäischen Gemeinschaften und der Schweiz, Brüssel, 10. November 1970," *Bundesblatt* I, no. 4 (Bern, 1971): 59–67.

88. See du Bois, *La Suisse et le défi européen*, pp. 75–94; and Keel, *Le grand patronat suisse face à l'intégration européenne*, pp. 299–322, 356–361, 410–416.

89. See Switzerland, Federal Council, *Botschaft des Bundesrates an die Bundesversammlung vom 16. August 1972 über die Genehmigung der Abkommen zwischen der Schweiz und den Europäischen Gemeinschaften*, Bern, 16 August 1972, pp. 669–712.

90. Ibid., pp. 654, 657, 729.

91. Ibid., p. 655; Switzerland Parliament, "Europäische Wirtschaftsgemeinschaft, Freihandelsabkommen," *Amtliches Bulletin der Bundesversammlung: Nationalrat*, Bern, 20–25 September 1972, pp. 1435, 1438; and Keel, *Le grand patronat suisse face à l'intégration européenne*, pp. 323–350.

92. *Wirtschaftspolitische Aspekte der Europäischen Integration aus schweizerischer Sicht: Ergebnisse einer Untersuchung des Vororts des Schweizerischen Handels- und Industrie-Vereins*, Zürich: Vorort, 1971.

93. See Switzerland, Federal Council, *Bericht des Bundesrates vom 24. August 1988 über die Stellung der Schweiz im europäischen Integrationsprozess*, Bern, 24 August 1988, pp. 193–207; and Commission of the European Communities, Treaties Office, *Bilateral Relationships, Commitments and Agreements Between EC and EFTA Countries (updated and revised as of January 1989)*, Brussels, I/119/89, March 1989, pp. 99–120.

94. Switzerland, Federal Council, *Bericht des Bundesrates vom 11. August 1971 über die Entwicklung der europäischen Integrationsbestrebungen und die Haltung der Schweiz, Bericht zum Postulat Beck (9688) vom 16. März 1967 und zur Motion Furgler (9922) vom 15. März 1968*, Bern, 11 August 1971, p. 103.

95. Switzerland, Federal Council, "Schweizerische Erklärung an der Zusammenkunft auf Ministerebene zwischen den Europäischen Gemeinschaften und der Schweiz, Brüssel, 10. November 1970," *Bundesblatt* I, no. 4 (Bern, 1971): 66.

96. Federal Councilor Ernst Brugger in Switzerland, Parliament, "Europäische Wirtschaftsgemeinschaft, Freihandelsabkommen," *Amtliches Bulletin der Bundesversammlung: Nationalrat*, Bern, 20–25 September 1972, p. 1483.

6

Broadening EC-EFTA
Cooperation in the 1980s

*By 1984 the EFTA-EEC tariff-free zone had been achieved. So what next?
In Luxembourg that year, the French foreign minister . . . suggested that
EFTA and the EEC work towards a "European Economic Space"—a
vaporous concept said to embrace, among other things, a truly free internal market.*   —The Economist, "Survey," p. 44

The so-called Luxembourg process, a new phase of cooperation between
the European Communities (EC) and the European Free Trade Association (EFTA), was triggered in 1984 by the implementation of the free
trade agreements and the European Communities' plans for an internal
market. This period embraces a transition from a bilateral to an increasingly multilateral relationship between the EC and the EFTA countries
and a shift to cooperation beyond free trade. The decade of the 1980s thus
brought about a further rapprochement between the two trading
groups.

The Luxembourg Process

The EC-EFTA free trade area for industrial goods had largely been established by 1 July 1977, and the last tariffs on certain "sensitive" products
were removed by 1984. However, other obstacles, such as public procurement rules, monopolies, technical standards, and regulations remained. In
fact, the economic recessions of the 1970s led to a proliferation of nontariff
barriers (NTBs) to trade in Western Europe. Hence, the EFTA governments
repeatedly called for closer ties with the EC.[1] At the request of the
European Parliament, the European Commission finally sent a communiqué to the Council of Ministers in June 1983 with a list of sectors in
which cooperation could be strengthened.[2] The idea of a common multilateral approach instead of each EFTA country focusing on its bilateral rela-

147

tions with the European Communities was floated in the early 1980s. Swiss and Swedish multinational corporations (e.g., Volvo, Asea, Nestlé, and Ciba-Geigy) had in 1983 been founding members of the European Round Table of Industrialists, which was involved in the preparation for the internal market project.[3]

In June 1985, the Commission presented its "White Paper on Completing the Internal Market," a comprehensive document laying out a step-by-step plan to complete the single market by 1 January 1993.[4] It contained some 300 legislative measures designed to eliminate all physical, technical, and fiscal barriers that could hinder the free functioning of the market. The White Paper program and the EC's Iberian enlargement required certain amendments to the Treaties of Rome, which were set out in the Single European Act (SEA) and took effect on 1 July 1987.[5] The most important change made by the SEA was the introduction of qualified majority decisions in all areas regarding the internal market, except for the provisions relating to fiscal matters and the free movement of persons. It also enhanced the role of the European Parliament in the decisionmaking process; gave formal recognition to the European Council and European Political Cooperation; and introduced provisions on cohesion, research, and environmental policies.

In 1988, the Cecchini Report estimated that the removal of the obstacles that stood in the way of the free flow of goods, services, capital, and persons within the Community would result in an economic welfare gain of about 5.3 percent of the EC's gross domestic product.[6] Technical regulations were identified as the most important category of trade barriers.[7] Moreover, it was estimated that EC imports from third countries would decrease by 2–3 percent in the short term and by 10 percent in the longer run and that most of this reduction would fall on EFTA as the Community's largest and geographically closest trading partner.[8] In light of this threat of trade diversion, the EFTA states intensified their search for cooperation with the Community.

The first joint EC-EFTA ministerial meeting took place in Luxembourg on 9 April 1984 to celebrate the successful implementation of the free trade agreements. The Luxembourg Declaration focused on four issues.[9] First, it supported continued efforts to combat protectionism and encourage free trade in industrial products in Western Europe. To this end, the ministers mentioned the need to cooperate in areas such as the harmonization of standards, elimination of technical barriers, simplification of border formalities, rules of origin, state aid, and public procurement. Second, they stressed their support for pragmatic cooperation going beyond the framework of the EC-EFTA free trade agreements, such as research and development, transportation, agriculture, fisheries, energy, working conditions, social protection, culture, consumer protection, the environment, tourism, and intellectual property. Third, the ministers promised concerted efforts to sustain the economic recovery and reduce the high level of unemployment. Fourth, they advocated increased consultations with regard to an open multilateral trading system. In the Luxembourg Declaration, the concept of a European Economic Space (EES) was proposed for the first time but was not clearly defined. It was characterized as "dynamic" and subsequently also as "homogeneous," which EFTA interpreted as meaning that the same legal rules should apply in all the participating countries and that the EES should develop in step with the Community.[10]

A group of high officials of the EFTA countries and the European Commission was set up with the mandate of organizing and supervising the work of the various expert groups, which eventually covered some thirty areas.[11] The EFTA countries cooperated with the European standards organizations—the European Committee for Standardization (CEN) and the European Committee for Electrotechnical Standardization (CENELEC)—in favor of uniform European standards. In 1987, the first two multilateral agreements between the Community and EFTA as a group were signed on a common transit procedure and on a single administrative document for all trade. One year later, the Lugano Convention on jurisdiction and the enforcement of judgments in civil and commercial matters was concluded. Faster progress was hampered by the fact that the EFTA countries had to agree on a common position in spite of diverging interests and that the Commission insisted on the priority of the Community's internal integration, on the preservation of its decisionmaking autonomy, and on the maintenance of a balance of benefits and obligations.[12] In short, from the EC side, "the triple signal was clear: no parallel, no global approach, no package deals."[13]

As a result, the Luxembourg process was "frustratingly slow, piecemeal, and unstructured and fell far short of EFTA expectations of a parallel development matching the Community's ambitious Internal Market Programme."[14] Specific shortcomings of the free trade agreements included, for example, the absence of a mechanism for settling disputes, the lack of power to impose sanctions in case of excessive subsidies for national industries, the lack of "cumulative origin" for EFTA products, the ambiguity regarding export restrictions, and the direct applicability of the agreements.[15] The abolition of tariffs was partly offset by the increasingly low level of the EC's Common External Tariff (CET); the complicated rules of origin; the lack of recognition of technical standards; and EFTA's exclusion from public procurement, agriculture, capital, services, transport, competition policy, and the free movement of persons. The Luxembourg follow-up had broadened and intensified EC-EFTA cooperation but was still grounded on a sectoral and predominantly bilateral case-by-case approach, which could not keep up with the implementation of the internal market.

Incentives for and Impediments to Integration

Table 6.1 shows the exports of Sweden, Norway, and Switzerland to the EC as a share of total exports and of domestic production. In 1989, the Luxembourg process, launched in 1984, was overtaken by the negotiations that led to the agreement on the European Economic Area (see Chapter 7). In the meantime, the European Communities were further enlarged, when Spain and the former EFTA member Portugal joined in 1986.

The Community's efforts to complete its market meant that the EFTA countries would face welfare losses because of trade diversion and market exclusion, but the EC countries would benefit from such effects as comparative advantages, economies of scale, and increased competition.[16] In fact, the EFTA countries were expected to accumulate much larger potential benefits from participating in the internal market than the average EC country.[17] Table 6.2 identifies those economic sectors of the three countries with the highest shares of exports to the emerging internal market.

In spite of the elimination of tariffs on industrial goods, approximately 25 percent of EC-EFTA trade has been estimated to take place on a nonpreferential basis because of complicated rules of origin.[18] Moreover, the nontariff barriers to trade remaining in the EC market involved costs that the European Commission estimated at 8 percent of the value of intra-EC

Table 6.1   Overall Export Dependence on the EC, 1984, 1989, and 1992

	EC Export Ratio (exports to EC as % of total exports)	GDP Ratio (exports to EC as % of GDP)
Sweden		
1984	47.8	14.5
1989	53.2	14.3
1992	55.7	12.6
Norway		
1984	70.0	21.8
1989	65.1	17.8
1992	66.4	18.5
Switzerland		
1984	50.6	14.4
1989	56.5	16.4
1992	58.9	16.0
EC-10/12		
1984	52.1	12.8
1989	59.7	13.4
1992	61.1	12.6

Sources: UN COMTRADE database; and OECD, *National Accounts: Main Aggregates 1960–1994*, vol. 1 (Paris: OECD, 1996).

Table 6.2   Sector Exports to the EC, 1984

Leading Export Sectors to the EC (SITC, Rev. 1)		Sector Share (sector exports to EC as % of total exports to EEC)	Sector Export Ratio (sector exports to EC as % of total sector exports)
Sweden			
Nonelectrical machinery	(71)	14.0	40.2
Paper manufactures	(64)	13.1	66.6
Transport equipment	(73)	10.6	31.6
Norway			
Petroleum	(33)	44.9	85.0
Gas	(34)	24.4	99.6
Nonferrous metals	(68)	8.0	67.0
Switzerland			
Nonelectrical machinery	(71)	17.5	44.8
Electrical machinery	(72)	10.2	49.4
Miscellaneous manufactures	(89)	7.5	48.9

Source: UN COMTRADE database.

trade.[19] These costs were comparable to the tariffs that the EFTA countries faced in the EC market prior to the free trade agreements.

Sweden.   In 1984, Sweden sold almost half of its exports to the common market, accounting for 14.5 percent of its GDP (see Table 6.1). In the government's eyes, the EC was Sweden's biggest market for goods as well as for services.[20] The leading Swedish exports to the European Communities were the same as ten years earlier: middle-sized, comparable shares of nonelectrical machinery, paper manufactures, and transportation equipment. Only the paper industry sold a high proportion to the EC, with two-thirds of that market (see Table 6.2). Although these exports did not meet any tariffs or quantitative restrictions on the EC market anymore, they were confronted with levels of nontariff barriers to trade that were medium for nonelectrical machinery and transportation equipment and low for paper products.[21] The Commission estimated the gains from the removal of these barriers as a percentage of the EC countries' apparent consumption to be around 3.7 percent for paper products, 13 percent for office machinery, 11.5 percent for mechanical engineering, and 14.5 percent for transportation equipment.[22] They were likely to be comparable for the Swedish economy.

Most of Sweden's trade with the EC was intra-industry trade based on large multinational corporations. Trade diversion and shifting production caused by the EC's internal market were expected to be serious "for a peripherally located country such as Sweden which has a large industrial base consisting of footloose industries dependent on economies of scale."[23]

As a consequence, for each year from 1985 to 1988, Swedish industry doubled its investments in Europe.[24] The high export dependence made Sweden face strong economic incentives to participate in the internal market in the mid-1980s, in particular if the positive expectations about future dynamic effects were included.[25]

The "Golden Age" of the Swedish model ended with the economic crises of the 1970s, and the situation in the early 1980s is best described as a stalemate. The scope and ambitions of the welfare state were reduced and reflected the weight of external pressures.[26] The new economic policies, pursued by both bourgeois and social democratic governments, were designed to stimulate liberalization and deregulation. The assumption of the 1930s that business depended on the domestic labor market was irrevocably changing, and the Scandinavian economies were already undergoing a neoliberal transformation when the EC launched its internal market program.[27] In the mid-1980s, calls for a decentralization of wage bargaining and the deregulation of financial markets announced the exhaustion of the Swedish model. Nevertheless, the government clearly stated that "cuts in social welfare, a poorer external or working environment, weaker consumer protection, an undermining of labour law and concessions on equality between the sexes are prices we are not prepared to pay for closer co-operation with the EC."[28]

European Political Cooperation was considered incompatible with Swedish neutrality because of the obligation to coordinate and elaborate common positions and to undertake such consultations within a group of states that, except for Ireland, belonged to NATO. There was still a strong consensus among all political parties that Sweden must preserve a credible policy of neutrality.[29] This party truce was above all due to the more cautious stance of the conservatives, who had traditionally championed EC membership. For the social democratic government, "neutrality policy makes it certainly impossible to participate in EC cooperation in matters of security and foreign policy, but this should, according to the Swedish view, not prevent us from participating in cooperation in economic and other fields in Western Europe."[30] Påhl Ruin rightly observed that "earlier on, the government was of the opinion that the EC's foreign policy goal made closer cooperation with *the whole* EC impossible" but that now "it emphasizes that it is just the field of security and foreign policy in which Sweden cannot cooperate with the EC—*in all other fields* it was free to do so."[31]

Sweden's integration policy was in the mid-1980s still characterized by "an almost religious belief . . . in the necessity of neutrality and in the . . . superiority of the Swedish welfare model."[32] The political impediments were thus low with regard to the Luxembourg process but still high in relation to full membership in the European Communities.

Norway. At 70 percent, Norway's share of exports to the European Communities was extremely high in 1984, especially in comparison to 47.4 percent in 1973 (see Table 6.1). It accounted for 21.8 percent of the Norwegian GDP, compared to an EC average of only 12.8 percent. This high trade dependence can be explained to a large extent by the discovery and growing exploitation of oil fields in the North Sea. As Table 6.2 shows, Norway's major exports to the EC consisted of two large quotas of petroleum (44.9 percent) and gas (24.4 percent), followed by a small share (8 percent) of nonferrous metals. These three natural resources accounted for more than three-quarters of Norway's exports to the EC. For all of them, the EC was the main export market, with extremely high sector ratios of 67 percent for nonferrous metals, 85 percent for petroleum, and 99.6 percent for gas. In the decade from the mid-1970s to the mid-1980s, Norway did not succeed in transforming the windfall profits from the petroleum sector into internationally competitive nonoil industries but became more and more dependent on high and volatile oil revenues. In fact, in 1984 the share of the oil and gas sector of the Norwegian GDP was 19 percent, of total exports 36.6 percent, and of employment only 0.5 percent.[33]

Exports from Norway's leading sectors to the EC market did not face any tariffs or quantitative restrictions, and they met very low nontariff barriers to trade.[34] The gains from the removal of those barriers as a percentage of the EC countries' apparent consumption were estimated to be around 1.2 percent for gas and petrol and 2.8 percent for ores and metals.[35] Since the Norwegian economy exported mainly petroleum, gas, and energy-intensive goods like metal, wood, and paper products to the European Communities, changes in world prices and comparative advantages were more important than segmented national markets.[36] The major exports were thus not threatened by significant trade barriers, but the elites hoped to promote the diversification of the Norwegian economy and to counter uncertainty about future market access. Moreover, the Community was a customer for 60 percent of Norwegian shipping services.[37] In view of its great export dependence, Norway had strong economic incentives to participate in the internal market in the mid-1980s. The government was convinced that "the establishment of a large single market in Western Europe would bring advantages for the Norwegian economy" and that therefore it was important that cooperation with the EC should develop in parallel with the internal market schedule.[38]

There was a strong consensus among Norwegian elites that another attempt to join the European Communities would have reproduced the dangerous politicization of 1972. By contrast, cooperation under the Luxembourg process and the expected effects of the internal market did not mobilize any societal cleavages.[39] Similarly to Sweden, Norway began to liberalize its welfare model in the early 1980s, yet to a much weaker degree.[40] The main challenge was to reconcile national welfare policies with an increasingly transnational economy. The insight grew that the welfare model would have to be reorganized anyway, whether because of European integration or more encompassing internationalization processes, and in addition, a certain convergence was taking place between the different European welfare systems.[41] In spite of reforms, however, it was still considered that the Norwegian model and in particular its financing would be threatened by too close ties with the European Communities.[42] Others feared that preferential treatment of certain sectors and districts might conflict with EC competition rules; that increased competition might jeopardize the high Norwegian standards of health, safety, and environment; and that increased capital mobility might shift the social partners' balance of power to the disadvantage of workers and trade unions.[43] Owing to its huge oil revenues, Norway has to a large extent escaped the need for significant welfare state rollbacks. As a result, in the mid-1980s Norway still faced strong political constraints on joining the EC but no noteworthy obstacles with regard to participating in the Luxembourg process, which involved neither supranational institutions nor a "union."

Switzerland. At 50.6 percent, the Swiss economy exported a high portion of its foreign sales to the European Communities, and its GDP ratio was still above the EC average (see Table 6.1). The composition of the main sectoral exports to the EC in 1984 was similar in 1973, but the Swiss economy seemed more diversified because the sectors of nonelectrical and electrical machinery as well as miscellaneous manufactures comprised only 35.2 percent of the total Swiss exports to the EC (see Table 6.2). All three sectors sold almost half of their exports to the common market. The European Commission estimated the gains from the removal of trade barriers in those sectors as a percentage of the member countries' apparent consumption to be around 13 percent for office machinery, 11.5 percent for mechanical engineering products, 13.2 percent for electrical goods, and 9.8 percent for other manufactures.[44] Although Swiss exports of electrical machinery faced high levels of nontariff barriers on the EC market, the other two sectors encountered medium levels of NTBs.[45] The government expected economic advantages from participation in the internal market, given the high overall export dependence on the EC.[46]

In its August 1988 report to parliament, the Federal Council argued that "the credibility of the traditional neutrality policy, which we pursue autonomously and at our own discretion, could be called into question by accession to the EC and the adoption of the Community's political objectives" and that the transfer of sovereignty rights to supranational institutions "would also have repercussions on federalism and direct democracy, which both play an important role for Swiss identity."[47] If Switzerland, for instance, had joined the EC in 1973, 31 percent of the laws and federal decisions taken until mid-1987 would have concerned areas that were wholly or partly in Community competence.[48] In addition, popular initiatives in areas regulated by EC law would be barred. The Swiss parliament agreed that aiming at EC membership just for economic reasons was "too high a price for the expected weakening of our national political identity."[49] Unlike EC membership, the government considered that EC-EFTA cooperation under the Luxembourg process "did not affect our neutrality, our direct democracy, or the federal structure of our state."[50]

European politics was discussed much more in the parties' French- and Italian-speaking sections than in their Germanic counterparts.[51] Since EC membership was not on the political agenda, a real mobilization of the public could not be discerned. Nevertheless, several opinion polls of 1988 indicate that the issue divided the "Europhile" French-speaking part of the country from the more skeptical German regions, but "the three institutional pillars (semidirect democracy, neutrality, federalism) remain unwavering and the variations between the two linguistic communities do not exceed 10 percent."[52] The free movement of persons was not yet a topic of cooperation in the 1980s, but several popular initiatives "against the infiltration of foreigners" had been launched in view of the increasing proportion of foreigners living and working in Switzerland (about 15 percent in 1986). These initiatives, which can be interpreted as an expression of the historical Swiss fears of foreign influence, were all rejected by the voters.[53] Switzerland still faced high political impediments to full accession but only low constraints on bilateral and multilateral cooperation with the European Communities.

Integration Policy Preferences

The economic incentives to participate in the EC's internal market were strong for Sweden, Norway, and Switzerland. At the same time, the political constraints on full integration were high for all three countries. Although the gap between the Nordic model and the continental welfare systems was to some extent narrowed, no convergence took place with regard to the institutions that posed problems to a Swiss accession, that is, neutrality, direct democracy, and federalism. Moreover, the phobia of foreign influence in Switzerland and Norway, which was still traumatized by the experience of its 1972 referendum, prevailed. Based on these facts, it can be expected that all three countries would aim at a low level of integration in terms of a sectoral approach to intergovernmental cooperation.

Despite being prepared to give up some operational sovereignty in exchange for economic benefits, they should value maintaining their freedom of action more than obtaining a voice in the European Communities.

Sweden. Even though Sweden was, at the conclusion of the free trade agreements, not satisfied with their scope, "any discussion of establishing a more developed relationship with the EC soon dried up after 1973 as the Palme government pursued a stringent policy of independence from bloc politics."[54] Yet, when the EC decided to complete its internal market in the mid-1980s, the Swedish government was quick to indicate an interest in closer ties with the EC. It intended to "work for the establishment of a common market in Western Europe encompassing all eighteen EFTA and EC countries," to "work for close cooperation with the various EC institutions in all fields except security and foreign policy," and to "strengthen the position of EFTA as a means of achieving this common market."[55] The proposed areas of cooperation comprised the removal of NTBs, equal treatment for Swedish companies, research and development, environmental and consumer protection, transportation, working conditions, movements of capital and persons, and development aid.[56] The parliamentary debate in May 1988 led to a compromise among the four major parties (social democrats, liberals, centrists, conservatives) in favor of the government's stance that EC membership was not an objective.[57] The conservatives were the only party in the Swedish parliament to actually include EC membership in their party program, but they did not insist on it.[58] Only the Greens, who won seats in parliament for the first time in 1988, and the communists opposed closer cooperation with the European Communities.[59]

The business community, particularly the export industries, stepped up its demands for far-reaching cooperation with the EC: Swedish undertakings should have equal opportunities for competition and not fear any discrimination in the internal market.[60] A few voices were raised in favor of EC membership from the Swedish Employers' Federation and the Federation of Swedish Industries, but after intense discussions, they agreed to exclude the issue of membership from all official statements as long as the government would not lower its ambitions.[61] Leading Swedish companies were seeking to establish their own operations inside the EC market in the form of acquisitions, joint ventures, and mergers. To the labor unions, participation in the internal market was an important means of encouraging employment, but concern was expressed that harmonization with EC rules might lead to lower social standards.[62]

The Swedish government aspired to exercise some influence on the implementation of the 1985 White Paper on Completing the Internal Market in reasonable proportion to its commitments. "As nonmembers, we cannot, of course, expect to be permitted to take part in the EC's decisionmaking bodies, but it should be possible to come to suitable arrangements for exchanges of information and for consultation with a view to arriving at common solutions for the entire group of 18 countries on the basis of the Luxembourg Declaration."[63] This hope was not fulfilled, but it soon appeared less urgent because of the static nature of the bilateral and multi-lateral agreements that were reached with the European Communities. In June 1988, the government adopted a directive to secure adequate paral-lelism between Swedish and EC legislation. It stated that every proposed draft legal act or policy in fields related to the internal market must be eval-uated with regard to its compatibility with corresponding EC acts, and any proposal diverging from EC legislation must be justified. "According to the Swedish Government, such harmonisation entails no loss of sovereignty, in that the necessary decisions are taken in Sweden."[64]

By concluding numerous agreements with the European Communities, Sweden pursued a sectoral, intergovernmental approach and hence a low level of integration. In the mid-1980s, it was not yet prepared to renounce enough sovereignty in order to get a voice as a full member, but it gave up some national freedom of action by concluding agreements and unilaterally adapting to EC rules.

Norway. Norway's traditional Atlantic orientation in security and foreign policy gained a stronger European dimension in the early 1980s as European Political Cooperation took shape; the Western European Union (WEU) was reactivated; the Community was enlarged by Greece, Spain, and Portugal; and disagreements between the European NATO members and the United States emerged.[65] On an official visit to Brussels in autumn 1980, the prime minister succeeded in establishing an informal arrange-ment between Norway and EPC, including semiannual meetings with the presidency.[66] It soon became clear, however, that there was no way to fully participate in EPC other than full EC membership. The government deplored that it was likely "to have an increasing impact on all the main areas of Norwegian foreign policy . . . without Norway having any direct influence on the process."[67]

At the same time, the EC's plans for an internal market renewed Norwegian interest in market access. Among the EFTA countries, Norway was the first one to produce a policy paper on the internal market in May 1987.[68] This "European Report" explicitly did not consider the issue of EC membership but was confined to an attempt "to identify the tasks and chal-lenges facing Norway in relation to the EC on the basis of the present form of cooperation."[69] The government pointed out that the free trade agree-ments were insufficient in light of the White Paper program, especially with regard to nontariff barriers to trade, fisheries, and new areas of coop-eration such as research, and that Norway had to adapt to the internal market "as far as possible in order to avoid new trade barriers."[70] This strategy was to be pursued unilaterally, bilaterally, and through EFTA. From the point of view of the Norwegian government, the future EES should "consist of free market access for industrial goods, fish, processed agricultural products and certain services, as well as the implementation of equal terms of competition."[71]

The parliamentary debate on the government's integration policy took place in June 1988.[72] The Labor Party unanimously supported the strategy of active adaptation to the EC's internal market. The Socialist Left Party and the Center Party still opposed membership but accepted closer cooperation with the European Communities. The Christian Democratic Party and the Conservative Party wanted Norway to participate in the EC's internal market on the basis of the free trade agreements. The industries and trade unions supported the government's line without pushing for EC membership.[73] After the "1972 trauma," Norwegian elites contented themselves with pragmatic cooperation.

The conservatives pointed out that Norway might be marginalized because "important decisions of an economic, security policy and foreign policy character are increasingly taken in international fora of cooperation in which Norway does not have the influence which the relevance of the matters for Norway would require."[74] Like Sweden, the Norwegian government required its ministries in June 1988 to ensure that the EC's internal market legislation was taken into account and that any diverging laws must be justified.[75] In fact, "the legislative adaptation to the EC internal market directives appears to be proceeding on a wide scale in the various ministries, in close consultation with export industries and employers' organizations, as well as other interest groups."[76]

Throughout the 1980s, Norway aimed at a low level of integration. Both the political and economic elites supported the government's policy of bilateral and multilateral cooperation with the EC in the Luxembourg process. The economy's need to participate in the internal market was alleviated by the booming oil and gas industries. Preference was given to sovereignty rather than voice, even though extensive unilateral adaptation to EC rules might have started to turn this sovereignty into an illusion.

Switzerland. In January 1984, the Federal Council told parliament that it saw no reason for a change in its integration policy since "the political considerations that have kept us at the time from joining the Community, have not been refuted by the developments since 1972."[77] In March 1986, the Swiss voters overwhelmingly (75.7 percent) rejected their country's membership in the United Nations, which they feared might impair neutrality policy.[78] It took the Swiss longer than any other EFTA country to realize that the internal market project required a new method of cooperation.[79] The impetus for a change of policy in favor of a more global, multilateral approach came in particular from the French- and Italian-speaking regions and the social democrats.[80] Against the background of the EC's southern enlargements, the White Paper, and the introduction of qualified majority decisions, parliament asked the government in 1987 for a detailed report on Switzerland's situation in the European integration process.[81]

The 1988 report discussed several alternatives short of accession to the EC, ranging from reorganization of EFTA, an EC-EFTA customs union, and a global framework agreement to association.[82] The idea of global framework agreements, as they existed for research and development cooperation, was rejected by the Community. Association was excluded by the Swiss because the scope of agreements Switzerland had already concluded with the EC was far larger than those covered by any association agreement the EC had signed with other third countries and because it would not allow participation in the EC's decisionmaking process. A customs union with the EC would endanger Swiss neutrality policy, and a revision of the Stockholm Convention was considered unnecessary. For the first time, EC membership was not flatly excluded, but the Federal Council stressed that the political goals of the EC "*as they present themselves today*" would harm neutrality and that "*under these conditions* accession to the EC can, in today's estimation, not be the goal of Swiss integration policy."[83]

As a result, the Swiss government advocated "an active integration policy" aiming at the establishment of "conditions as similar to the internal market as possible [*binnenmarktähnliche Verhältnisse*]" in which the four freedoms should be realized to different degrees.[84] It met with general approval in both chambers of parliament.[85] None of the parties advocated EC membership. The agrarian Swiss People's Party and the Green Party were the only parties to oppose EC membership, even for the future. The conservative Radical Democratic Party and the Christian Democratic Party, as well as some smaller parties such as the Liberal Party, the Independent Alliance, and the Protestant People's Party, supported intensified cooperation with the EC but did not advocate full membership.[86] The Social Democratic Party appeared to be the most integrationist party, claiming that the value of the national myths of neutrality, federalism, and direct democracy should be reassessed.[87] In contrast to its fellow socialists from the Nordic countries, the Swiss Social Democratic Party expected closer relations with the EC to improve the workers' social conditions.

Like the Social Democratic Party, the labor unions reflected a more pro-European position than the representatives of the industries.[88] The Swiss Federation of Commerce and Industry as well as the Federation of Swiss Employers' Organizations supported the government's sectoral approach and dismissed EC membership as contrary to Switzerland's direct democracy, neutrality, and universality of trade relations.[89] In order to keep the costs of nonmembership as low as possible, the industrial federation postulated an autonomous adaptation to EC rules, the removal of technical barriers to trade, the liberalization of public procurement and services, research and development cooperation, cautious cooperation in the free movement of persons, and the introduction of a European value-added tax. The trade and crafts sector as well as the farmers opposed any far-reaching opening of their protected national market to the EC but supported limited cooperation.[90] In sum, the economic elites favored close ties but did not demand membership because they agreed with the political elites on the importance of the political obstacles.

At parliamentary request, the Federal Council decided in May 1988 to examine all reports and proposals submitted to parliament with regard to their compatibility with European law.[91] Unlike in Sweden and Norway, however, adaptation to EC rules was not to be semiautomatic, nor did deviations require justification. The goal was simply "to ensure the greatest possible compatibility of our legal provisions with those of our European partners in all areas having a transborder dimension (and only in those)."[92] The Swiss government was aware that

> the renunciation of accession to the EC has an institutional price, which today undoubtedly carries more weight than in 1972: Switzerland is thereby excluded from the formal EC decisionmaking process, a process by which, on the other hand, it is more and more affected as a result of the EC enlargements and the extension of EC competences. This is the price that has to be paid for the maintenance of our sovereignty, our foreign policy principles and our federal and democratic institutions.[93]

Moreover, the government pointed out that only an increased desire for voice could change this assessment. For the time being, however, Switzerland was not prepared to renounce the operational sovereignty required to join the EC. As expected, the Swiss government preferred a low level of integration with the European Communities in the mid-1980s.

The bilateral and multilateral EC-EFTA agreements concluded under the Luxembourg process constituted a low level of integration. As expected, Sweden, Norway, and Switzerland aimed at a sectoral scope of integration and an intergovernmental institutional setup. It is striking that in all three countries, a broad consensus prevailed among the political parties and the economic interest groups in favor of pragmatic cooperation. They hoped that the Luxembourg process would allow them to gradually participate in the internal market without becoming full members of the EC.

Conclusion

For once, the preferences of the three countries in the mid-1980s were almost identical. They all hoped to benefit from the internal market almost to the same extent as the EC actors themselves, by concluding a number of bilateral and multilateral agreements and by unilaterally adapting their legislation to that of the *acquis communautaire*. This expectation may account for the relative "inertia" of the economic elites regarding advocacy of EC membership. If the economic benefits could be obtained without having to deal with the political implications of membership, this "third way" was well worth a try.

Sweden, Norway, and Switzerland broadened cooperation with the European Communities beyond trade under the so-called Luxembourg process. Even though this policy still predominantly resulted in bilateral agreements, it constituted a trajectory from bilateral to multilateral cooperation between the two trading groups. EFTA finally began to function as a common platform for dealing with the European Communities. The sector-by-sector approach was heavily geared to the internal market program and prepared the way for a more institutionalized EC-EFTA relationship in the 1990s.

Notes

1. For example, EFTA, "Declaration of the Meeting of the EFTA Heads of Governments and Ministers, Vienna, 13 May 1977." In *Seventeenth Annual Report of the European Free Trade Association 1976–77* (Geneva: EFTA, 1977), p. 53.

2. European Parliament, *Resolution of 11 February 1983 on EEC-EFTA Free Trade Agreements,* Official Journal of the European Communities, no. C 68 (14 March 1983): 88–89; and Commission of the European Communities, *Communication from the Commission to the Council: Closer Cooperation Between the Community and the EFTA Countries,* COM (83) 326 final, Brussels, 6 June 1983, Annex.

3 See Green Cowles, "Setting the Agenda for a New Europe," pp. 501–526.

4. Commission of the European Communities, *Completing the Internal Market: White Paper from the Commission to the European Council,* COM (85) 310 final, 14 June 1985.

5. See de Ruyt, *L'Acte Unique Européen.*

6. Cecchini, Catinat, and Jacquemin, *The European Challenge 1992,* pp. 83–84, 97–98; and Commission of the European Communities, *Research on the "Cost of Non-Europe": Basic Findings,* 16 vols. (Luxembourg: Office for Official Publications of the European Communities, 1988).

7. This finding was based on a 1988 survey of 11,000 businesspeople in the EC. Commission of the European Communities, "The Economics of 1992," *European Economy,* no. 35 (March 1988): 49.

8. Kleppe, "The Single Market and Commercial Relations for Non-Member Countries," p. 153.

9. EFTA and European Communities, "Joint Declaration of the Ministerial Meeting between the European Community and Its Member States and the States of the European Free Trade Association, Luxembourg, 9 April 1984." In *Twenty-Fourth Annual Report of the European Free Trade Association 1984* (Geneva: EFTA, 1985), pp. 53–55.

10. EFTA, *EFTA: The European Free Trade Association* (Geneva: EFTA, 1987), p. 111.

11. Hurni, "EFTA-EC Relations After the Luxembourg Declaration," pp. 88–101; Marschang, *Der "Luxemburg Prozess" als eine Komponente der EFTA-EG-Zusammenarbeit;* and Nell, "EFTA in the 1990s," pp. 340–349.

12. de Clercq, *Speech at the EC-EFTA Ministerial Meeting,* pp. 5–6; and EFTA and European Communities, "Joint Declaration of the Ministerial Meeting Between the European Community, Its Member States and the EFTA States on the Internal Market, Brussels, 2 February 1988." In *Twenty-Eighth Annual Report of the European Free Trade Association 1988* (Geneva: EFTA, 1989), p. 32.

13. Weiss, "EC-EFTA Relations," p. 352.

14. Ibid., p. 352.

15. European Research Associates, *The European Community and EFTA in the 1980s,* p. 5; and *EC/EFTA: The Future European Economic Area,* pp. 13–15.

16. See Krugman, "EFTA and 1992"; and Norman, "1992 and EFTA," pp. 120–139.

17. Norman, "EFTA and the Internal European Market," p. 449; Pintado et al., "Economic Aspects of the European Economic Space," pp. 16–59; and Abrams et al., "The Impact of the European Community's Internal Market on the EFTA," pp. 11–56.

18. Herin, "Rules of Origin and Differences Between Tariff Levels in EFTA and in the EC," p. 6.

19. Commission of the European Communities, "The Economics of 1992," *European Economy,* no. 35 (March 1988): 18.

20. Sweden, Government, *Regeringens proposition 1987/88:66 om Sverige och den västeuropeiska integrationen,* Stockholm, 17 December 1987, pp. 121–122.

21. Commission of the European Communities, *The Sectoral Impact of the Internal Market,* study by Pierre Buigues and Fabienne Ilzkovitz, Brussels, II/335/88-EN, 19 July 1988, Annex II; and Commission of the European Communities, "The Economics of 1992," *European Economy,* no. 35 (March 1988): 51.

22. Pintado et al., "Economic Aspects of the European Economic Space," p. 12.

23. Wijkman, "The Internal Market and EFTA as Viewed from Geneva," p. 63.

24. Ingebritsen, "Coming Out of the Cold," p. 246.

25. Sweden, Government, *Regeringens proposition 1987/88:66 om Sverige och den västeuropeiska integrationen,* Stockholm, 17 December 1987, pp. 4, 8–9, 22, 25.

26. Olsson, *Social Policy and Welfare State in Sweden,* pp. 222–244; and Mjøset, "Nordic Economic Policies in the 1970s and 1980s," p. 449.

27. Hoefer, "Swedish Corporatism in Social Welfare Policy, 1986–1994," pp. 67–80; Andersson and Mjøset, "The Transformation of the Nordic Models," pp. 227–243; and Stephens, "The Scandinavian Welfare States," pp. 43–51.

28. Minister Anita Gradin in reply to parliamentary interpellations on 22 November 1988. In Sweden, Ministry for Foreign Affairs, *Documents on Swedish Foreign Policy 1988* (Stockholm: Royal Ministry for Foreign Affairs, 1990), p. 253.

29. Gidlund, *Partiernas Europa,* pp. 40–43; and Sweden, Parliament, Foreign Affairs Committee, *Utrikesutskottets betänkande 1987/88:24 om Sverige och den västeuropeiska integrationen (prop. 1987/88:66),* Stockholm, 21 April 1988, pp. 10–12, 18–19.

30. Sweden, Government, *Regeringens proposition 1987/88:66 om Sverige och den västeuropeiska integrationen,* Stockholm, 17 December 1987, p. 22.

31. Ruin, *Svensk neutralitetspolitik*, pp. 35–36.
32. Viklund, "Neutraliteten som svensk EG-hinder," p. 256.
33. Austvik, "Norwegian Petroleum and European Integration," pp. 190–192.
34. Commission of the European Communities, *The Sectoral Impact of the Internal Market*, study by Pierre Buigues and Fabienne Ilzkovitz, Brussels, II/335/88-EN, 19 July 1988, Annex II; and Commission of the European Communities, "The Economics of 1992," *European Economy*, no. 35 (March 1988): 51.
35. Pintado et al., "Economic Aspects of the European Economic Space," p. 12.
36. Haaland, "Assessing the Effects of EFTA-EC Integration on EFTA Countries," pp. 382–383.
37. Norway, Ministry for Foreign Affairs, *Om Norge, EF og europeisk samarbeid*, St.meld. nr. 61 (1986–1987), Oslo, 22 May 1987, p. 18.
38. Ibid., p. 33; and Norway, Ministry of Trade and Shipping, *Om enkelte handelspolitiske spørsmål*, St.meld. nr. 63 (1986–1987), Oslo, 22 May 1987, p. 22.
39. Sæter and Knudsen, "Norway," p. 185.
40. Mjøset, "Nordic Economic Policies in the 1970s and 1980s," p. 450; and Mjøset et al., *Norden dagen derpå*, pp. 248–256, 278–282.
41. Gaarder and Christensen, "Den Nordiske Velferdsstatsmodellen i det Nye Europa," pp. 168–196.
42. Reinsvollsveen, "Den europeiske velferdsstat," pp. 119–141.
43. Dølvik et al., *Norsk Økonomi og europeisk integrasjon*, p. 156; and Norway, Parliament, Foreign Affairs and Constitution Committee, *Innstillning fra utenriks- og konstitusjonskomitéen om Norge, EF og europeisk samarbeid*, Innst.S.nr. 244 (1987–1988), Oslo, 26 May 1988, pp. 25, 45–47.
44. Pintado et al., "Economic Aspects of the European Economic Space," p. 12.
45. Commission of the European Communities, *The Sectoral Impact of the Internal Market*, study by Pierre Buigues and Fabienne Ilzkovitz, Brussels, II/335/88-EN, 19 July 1988, Annex II.
46. Switzerland, Federal Council, *Bericht des Bundesrates vom 24. August 1988 über die Stellung der Schweiz im europäischen Integrationsprozess*, Bern, 24 August 1988, pp. 103–120.
47. Ibid., pp. 121–122.
48. Ibid., p. 124. Moreover, at least six initiatives in the same period would not have been possible because of their collision with EC law.
49. MP Heinz Allenspach in Switzerland, Parliament, "Europäische Integration: Bericht," *Amtliches Bulletin der Bundesversammlung: Nationalrat*, Bern, 28 February–1 March 1989, p. 144.
50. Switzerland, Federal Council, "Antwort des Bundesrates auf das Postulat Alder (82.393) vom 8. Oktober 1982 'Beziehungen zur Europäischen Gemeinschaft,'" Annex 3 to "Bericht zur Aussenwirtschaftspolitik 83/2 und Botschaft zu einer internationalen Wirtschaftsvereinbarung vom 11. Januar 1984," *Bundesblatt* I (Bern, 1984): 493.
51. Ayberk, "Les leaders d'opinions suisses et les question européennes," p. 234.
52. Ruffieux and Thurler Muller, "L'opinion publique face à l'intégration européenne," pp. 242–244.
53. Senti, "Switzerland," pp. 225–226.
54. Phinnemore, "The Nordic Countries, the European Community (EC) and the European Free Trade Association (EFTA), 1958–84," p. 44. The nonsocialist

governments ruling from 1976 to 1982 also kept a low profile in integration policy.

55. Sweden, Government, *Regeringens proposition 1987/88:66 om Sverige och den västeuropeiska integrationen,* Stockholm, 17 December 1987, p. 4.

56. Ibid., pp. 25–26, 30–118.

57. Sweden, Parliament, "Sverige och den västeuropeiska integrationen," *Riksdagens Protokoll 1987/88,* no. 114 (Stockholm, 4 May 1988): 4–118.

58. Luif, *Neutrale in die EG?,* pp. 188–191.

59. Viklund, *Sweden and the European Community,* pp. 40–41.

60. Stenberg, "Sweden and the Internal Market," pp. 93–95.

61. Luif, *Neutrale in die EG?,* p. 191.

62. MP Ingemar Eliasson in Parliament, "Sverige och den västeuropeiska integrationen," *Riksdagens Protokoll 1987/88,* no. 114 (4 May 1988): 18.

63. Sweden, Government, *Regeringens proposition 1987/88:66 om Sverige och den västeuropeiska integrationen,* Stockholm, 17 December 1987, pp. 27–28.

64. Evans and Falk, *Law and Integration,* pp. 163–164.

65. Knudsen, "Den nye Europa-debatten," pp. 390–413.

66. Sæter, "Norway: An EFTA Road to Membership?," pp. 121–122. These ad hoc procedures were formalized in March 1988, based on the SEA, in terms of meetings on ministerial and directorial levels. See Foreign Ministry's note of 12 April 1988 annexed to Norway, Parliament, Foreign Affairs and Constitution Committee, *Innstilling fra utenriks- og konstitusjonskomitéen om Norge, EF og europeisk samarbeid,* Innst.S.nr. 244 (1987–1988), Oslo, 26 May 1988, p. 51.

67. Norway, Ministry for Foreign Affairs, *Om Norge, EF og europeisk samarbeid,* St.meld. nr. 61 (1986–1987), Oslo, 22 May 1987, p. 53.

68. Ibid. This "European Report" was supplemented by a bill that dealt in greater detail with trade policy questions. Norway, Ministry of Trade and Shipping, *Om enkelte handelspolitiske spørsmål,* St.meld. nr. 63 (1986–1987), Oslo, 22 May 1987.

69. Norway, Ministry for Foreign Affairs, *Om Norge, EF og europeisk samarbeid,* St.meld. nr. 61 (1986–1987), Oslo, 22 May 1987, p. 3.

70. Ibid., p. 4.

71. Ibid., p. 30.

72. See Knudsen, *Den nye Europa-debatten,* chaps. 2–10; and Norway, Parliament, "Norge, EF og europeisk samarbeid," *Forhandlinger i Stortinget,* St.tid. nos. 262–265, Oslo, 7 June 1988, pp. 3880–3957.

73. Knudsen, "Den nye Europa-debatten," p. 428.

74. Norway, Parliament, *Innstilling fra utenriks- og konstitusjonskomitéen om Norge, EF og europeisk samarbeid,* Innst.S.nr. 244 (1987–1988), Oslo, 26 May 1988, p. 39.

75. Östrem, "La Norvège et la Communauté européenne," p. 11.

76. Sæter and Knudsen, "Norway," pp. 188–189.

77. Switzerland, Federal Council, "Antwort des Bundesrates auf das Postulat Alder (82.393) vom 8. Oktober 1982 'Beziehungen zur Europäischen Gemeinschaft,'" Annex 3 to "Bericht zur Aussenwirtschaftspolitik 83/2 und Botschaft zu einer internationalen Wirtschaftsvereinbarung vom 11. Januar 1984," *Bundesblatt* I (Bern, 1984): 493.

78. Luif, "The European Neutrals and Economic Integration in Western Europe," pp. 14–16.

79. See Steppacher, *Schritte zur Europäisierung der Schweiz,* pp. 64–70, 101–119, 113–117; and Schwendimann, *Herausforderung Europa,* pp. 98–101, 198–209.

80. Langejürgen, *Die Eidgenossenschaft zwischen Rütli und EWR*, pp. 45–57; and Schwendimann, *Herausforderung Europa*, p. 200.

81. Switzerland, Parliament, "Aussenwirtschaftspolitik 1986/2," *Amtliches Bulletin der Bundesversammlung: Nationalrat*, Bern, 4 March 1987, pp. 74–75.

82. Switzerland, Federal Council, *Bericht des Bundesrates vom 24. August 1988 über die Stellung der Schweiz im europäischen Integrationsprozess*, Bern, 24 August 1988.

83. Ibid., pp. 120–131.

84. Ibid., pp. 53, 71, 97, 130–132.

85. Switzerland, Parliament, "Europäische Integration: Bericht," *Amtliches Bulletin der Bundesversammlung: Nationalrat*, Bern, 28 February–1 March 1989, pp. 143–187; and *Amtliches Bulletin der Bundesversammlung: Ständerat*, Bern, 21–22 June 1989, pp. 357–377. See Schwendimann, *Herausforderung Europa*, pp. 209–234; and Steppacher, *Schritte zur Europäisierung der Schweiz*, pp. 123–150.

86. Schwendimann, *Herausforderung Europa*, pp. 225–226.

87. MP Hans Zbinden in Parliament, "Europäische Integration: Bericht," *Amtliches Bulletin der Bundesversammlung: Nationalrat*, Bern, 28 February–1 March 1989, pp. 148–149.

88. Langejürgen, *Die Eidgenossenschaft zwischen Rütli und EWR*, pp. 67–69; and Steppacher, *Schritte zur Europäisierung der Schweiz*, pp. 247–266.

89. *Die Schweizer Wirtschaft vor den Herausforderungen des EG-Binnenmarktes*, pp. 3, 6, 29; and Steppacher, *Schritte zur Europäisierung der Schweiz*, pp. 177–242.

90. Langejürgen, *Die Eidgenossenschaft zwischen Rütli und EWR*, pp. 62–67; Schwendimann, *Herausforderung Europa*, pp. 238–241; and Steppacher, *Schritte zur Europäisierung der Schweiz*, pp. 153–175.

91. Switzerland, Federal Council, *Bericht des Bundesrates vom 24. August 1988 über die Stellung der Schweiz im europäischen Integrationsprozess*, Bern, 24 August 1988, pp. 97, 208–209 (Annex 6).

92. Ibid., p. 132 (emphasis omitted).

93. Ibid., p. 131.

7

The Uniting of
Western Europe in the 1990s

Mr. Delors's offer [of extending the internal market to EFTA] was not an expanded European vision: it was chiefly a bid to prevent the dilution of his existing one. But there is a good chance that Mr. Delors's halfway house will offer most of EFTA too little in return for too much.
—The Economist, "Survey," p. 44

In the late 1980s and early 1990s, Europe witnessed major structural changes that provided a conducive background for a fundamental change in the reluctant Europeans' integration policies. On the one hand, a neoliberal economic climate featured liberalization, deregulation, privatization, and the decline of corporatism, while the European Communities (EC) completed the internal market and embarked upon monetary and political union. On the other hand, the end of the Cold War challenged long-standing national security strategies. The Soviet Union's new policies of glasnost and perestroika ultimately led to its demise and brought down the Iron Curtain. The resultant political uncertainties in Russia and the Yugoslav civil war made membership in the European Communities, if not in NATO or the Western European Union (WEU), more attractive. Even the Central and Eastern European countries began to openly strive for accession.

In the mid-1990s, these transformations finally united Western Europe, after forty years of being split into two trading groups. The EC's internal market was extended to the European Free Trade Association (EFTA) countries through the creation of the European Economic Area (EEA). Nonetheless, Sweden, Switzerland, and Norway, as well as Finland, followed Austria's lead and applied for full membership in what became the European Union (EU) when the Maastricht Treaty entered into force on 1 November 1993. However, only Sweden, Finland, and Austria joined the EU as new members in 1995. The Norwegian people rejected EU membership for the second time, and the Swiss voters' refusal to ratify the EEA

167

agreement kept Switzerland's relations with the EU on the basis of bilateral agreements.

The European Economic Area

The desire for more effective and far-reaching cooperation led to discussions of possible scenarios for future EC-EFTA relations in the late 1980s.[1] Swedish and Norwegian Social Democrats, in particular Prime Minister Gro Harlem Brundtland of Norway, had informally approached their French fellow socialist Jacques Delors, president of the European Commission, on this issue.[2] The idea of institutionalizing EC-EFTA relations was then officially launched by President Delors in a speech to the European Parliament on 17 January 1989. He suggested looking for "a new, more structured partnership with common decision-making and administrative institutions" on the basis of "two pillars," the EC and a strengthened EFTA.[3] In other words, the EC proposed a switch from a sectoral to a global approach of cooperation with intergovernmental (or even quasi-supranational) institutions.

The EFTA governments welcomed the initiative at a summit meeting in Oslo on 14–15 March 1989 and expressed their hope that the negotiations would lead to the "fullest possible realization of free movement of goods, services, capital and persons, with the aim of creating a dynamic and homogeneous European Economic Space."[4] They envisaged consultation procedures, the mutual recognition of equivalent legislation, common decision-making, and a mechanism for the settlement of disputes. Joint expert groups were set up on the free movement of goods, services, capital, and persons, on the so-called flanking and horizontal policies such as education and environment, and on the legal and institutional questions. The Luxembourg process was gradually phased into the new EEA process.

At the outset, neither the EC nor EFTA had a clear concept of the architecture of what was now called the European Economic Area. The scenarios ranged from an association agreement over a customs union to a reorganization of EFTA as a "second pillar" analogous to the EC.[5] Both sides expected the EEA to solve their dilemmas. By offering the EFTA countries an alternative to EC membership, the Community hoped to be able to focus on the completion of the internal market and the intergovernmental conferences on monetary and political union. The EFTA countries hoped to be able to avoid economic discrimination and political satellization by taking part in the internal market.[6] For Norway as well as for neutral Sweden and Switzerland, the EEA seemed to promise a depoliticized version of EC membership.

In order to understand the subsequent change of preferences, it is essential to briefly look at the course and outcome of the EEA negotiations.[7] Based on Delors's speech, the EFTA countries nourished high expectations about equal participation in the internal market. An important first result of the exploratory talks was that the EC's *acquis communautaire* should constitute the legal basis of an agreement. The idea of mutual recognition of equivalent legislation was thus abandoned, and EFTA's strategy had to concentrate on obtaining exceptions from the *acquis.* By "buying the past" and taking over the existing EC legislation, EFTA hoped to be able to influence future EEA rules since "the establishment of a genuine joint decision-making mechanism in substance and form is a basic prerequisite for the political acceptability and the legal effectiveness of an agreement."[8] However, in January 1990, Commission president Delors backtracked and told the EFTA countries that "there will have to be some sort of osmosis between the Community and EFTA to ensure that EFTA's interests are taken into account . . . but this process must stop short of joint decision-making, which would imply Community membership."[9]

Formal negotiations began in June 1990 and lasted until October 1991. A negative opinion of the European Court of Justice required a new round of negotiations.[10] The EEA agreement was finally signed in Porto, Portugal, on 2 May 1992. The far-reaching association more or less fulfilled EFTA hopes regarding its substance,[11] which came close to conveying the status of membership in the Community, but not in respect to the institutional setup.[12] Instead of a "one-pillar" EEA structure with a joint EC-EFTA surveillance body and an independent EEA court, the EFTA countries had to accept a "two-pillar" EC-EFTA structure with their own EFTA court and surveillance authority. Moreover, they were forced to drop their requests for any permanent exceptions from the *acquis* in exchange for short transitional periods and a general safeguard clause.[13]

The EEA agreement covers the four freedoms of the internal market, the EC competition rules, and the so-called horizontal policies (the environment, social policies, consumer protection, statistics, and company law) and flanking policies (e.g., cooperation in research and development, small and medium-sized enterprises, education, tourism, and civil protection). It does not include the Common Commercial Policy and external relations, the Common Agricultural Policy (CAP) and Common Fisheries Policy (CFP), the common transportation policy, regional policy, budget contributions, direct and indirect taxation, economic and monetary policy, the European Atomic Energy Community (Euratom), and political cooperation (that is, the Common Foreign and Security Policy [CFSP], justice, and home affairs). With regard to the less developed EC regions, a Cohesion Fund, financed by EFTA, was established, and concessions in agricultural trade were granted. The sensitive issues of Alpine transit and Nordic fisheries, like trade in agricultural products, had to be dealt with separately in bilateral agreements.

The Commission formally retained its exclusive right to initiative, but the EFTA countries obtained the right to raise a matter of concern at the EEA level at any time (*droit d'évocation*). EFTA experts cannot directly participate in all EC committees but are consulted only in the preparatory stage of new measures. The main discussions take place within the EEA Joint Committee in the so-called decision-shaping phase after the Commission transmits its proposals to the EC Council and to the EFTA states. The EEA Joint Committee meets at least once a month to take formal decisions as close in time as possible to the adoption of the same rules by the Council of Ministers in order to allow for simultaneous application. All decisions are to be taken by consensus, with both the EC and the EFTA side speaking with one voice. The fact that the EFTA countries have to decide under time pressure and that they face a unanimity requirement and the threat of a suspension of related parts of the agreement in case of a collective opting out comes close to a "hidden process of majority voting within EFTA."[14] The EEA Council meets at the ministerial level twice a year to give political impetus to the process. Moreover, an EEA Joint Parliamentary Committee and an EEA Joint Consultative Committee for the economic and social partners have been established as advisory bodies. The Commission reassured the Council of Ministers that the EFTA countries' influence was limited to expressing their views since "at the end of the day, it will be the Community which sets the EEA agenda" and "the common rules of the EEA will be those of the Community's acquis."[15]

The European Commission monitors the application of rules in the EC member states, and the EFTA countries are supervised by the EFTA Surveillance Authority (ESA). The EFTA Court handles disputes between ESA and an EFTA state, disputes between EFTA states, and appeals with regard to ESA decisions in the field of competition. It can also give advisory opinions on the interpretation of EEA rules upon request by national EFTA courts. In order to secure a uniform interpretation of EEA rules, the EEA Joint Committee reviews the development of the case law of the Court of Justice and the EFTA Court. Except for the EFTA Court of Justice, which was established in Geneva and moved to Luxembourg in 1996, all the EEA-related institutions are located in Brussels. These surveillance and enforcement mechanisms have forced EFTA to introduce structures that come close to supranational features. They reinforce the loss of sovereignty that the EFTA countries suffered by taking over the *acquis communautaire*, do not grant a real right of co-decision, and have introduced the principles of primacy and direct effect of EEA law. With its global approach and "quasi-supranational" setup, the EEA agreement represents a medium level of integration.

Switzerland's failure to ratify the EEA agreement in December 1992 postponed its entry into force until 1 January 1994. Liechtenstein, which became a full member of EFTA in September 1991, joined the EEA in May 1995 after finding a solution for the maintenance of the Swiss-Liechtenstein customs and currency union.[16] After only one year of the EEA's existence, Austria, Finland, and Sweden left EFTA and joined the European Union.

Incentives for and Impediments to Integration

Table 7.1 presents the export dependence of Sweden, Norway, and Switzerland on the EC for three different years. The EEA agreement was launched in 1989, concluded in 1992, and entered into force in 1994. All three countries filed their EC membership applications in 1991–1992, and the accession negotiations with Sweden and Norway were concluded in 1994, followed by membership referenda.

The European Economic Area was to extend the internal market to the EFTA countries and confer similar or even greater potential gains than in some EC countries.[17] Without joining the EEA, Sweden, Norway, and

Table 7.1   Overall Export Dependence on the EC, 1989, 1992, and 1994

	EC Export Ratio (exports to EC as % of total exports)	GDP Ratio (exports to EC as % of GDP)
Sweden		
1989	53.2	14.3
1992	55.7	12.6
1994	49.9	15.5
Norway		
1989	65.1	17.8
1992	66.4	18.5
1994	65.1	18.3
Switzerland		
1989	56.5	16.4
1992	58.9	16.0
1994	56.5	15.4
EC-12		
1989	59.7	13.4
1992	61.1	12.6
1994	57.4	12.5

Sources: UN COMTRADE database; and OECD, National Accounts: Main Aggregates 1960–1994, vol. 1 (Paris: OECD, 1996).

Switzerland were expected to experience investment diversion to the EC market, a reduced growth rate, and an "offshoring" of EFTA plants to the EC.[18] Even though 54 percent of EFTA's exports of services already went to the EC in 1989, considerable potential gains were left unexploited.[19] EFTA's consumer gains in the financial services sector alone were estimated to amount to more than 1 percent of GDP.[20] Table 7.2 shows the three countries' leading exports of goods to the EC in 1992.

Sweden. In 1992, Sweden sold 55.7 percent of its exports to the internal market, accounting for 12.6 percent of its GDP and thus a high overall export dependence on the EC (see Table 7.1). With a share of 16.4 percent destined to EFTA, nearly three-quarters of Swedish exports were sold to the EEA countries.[21] The share of exported services as a percentage of GDP had, with 6 percent in 1990, reached the EC average of 6.2 percent.[22] The Swedish economy was not only characterized by a myriad of multinational corporations but also by a large number of companies whose businesses depend on sales to the public sector. "Sweden could therefore be said to be in a particularly strong position to benefit from the opening up of public procurement to foreign companies with the formation of the Internal Market."[23]

The leading sectors still exported medium shares of nonelectrical machinery, paper manufactures, and transportation equipment, but the proportions of exports destined for the EC had markedly increased (see Table 7.2). Both nonelectrical machinery and transportation equipment encoun-

Table 7.2   Sector Exports to the EC, 1992

Leading Export Sectors to the EC (SITC, Rev. 1)		Sector Share (sector exports to EC as % of total exports to EEC)	Sector Export Ratio (sector exports to EC as % of total sector exports)
Sweden			
Nonelectrical machinery	(71)	16.9	52.3
Paper manufactures	(64)	15.1	75.1
Transport equipment	(73)	12.6	46.8
Norway			
Petroleum	(33)	48.9	77.3
Gas	(34)	10.8	98.6
Nonferrous metals	(68)	7.6	73.8
Switzerland			
Nonelectrical machinery	(71)	18.5	55.5
Electrical machinery	(72)	9.9	63.5
Professional instruments	(86)	9.1	45.1

Source: UN COMTRADE database.

tered medium levels of nontariff barriers (NTBs) on the EC market, but paper manufactures faced only low NTBs.[24] The biggest gains were expected for those industries in which the remaining barriers to trade were high, intra-industry trade low, and unexploited economies of scale significant (e.g., certain transport equipment).[25] In general, the government expected the EEA to improve the Swedish economy's efficiency and growth because of more exports, increased competition, and a better investment climate.[26] By contrast, it predicted negative consequences if Sweden stayed outside the EEA.

Swedish firms could not compete equally on the internal market or participate in European research and development cooperation, and they would invest more abroad than in Sweden.[27] Direct investments in the EC increased from 29.9 percent in 1982–1985 to 62.1 percent in 1989–1990, and in 1990, approximately 55 percent of the Swedish investment stock was inside the internal market.[28] The Federation of Swedish Industries argued that Sweden's participation in the internal market would yield an expected growth of 4–6 percent per year.[29] Last but not least, the Swedish economy was hit by a serious recession, shrinking real GDP by 5 percent from 1991 to 1993: "The budget went from a surplus of 4.2 percent at the end of the boom in 1990 to a deficit of 13.4 percent three years later. Government debts spiralled out of control. Some 50,000 firms went bankrupt. The banking system all but collapsed. In a country that thought it had avoided the unemployment plaguing other parts of Europe, half a million people lost their jobs, taking the number out of work or on government programmes toward 14 percent of the workforce."[30] Therefore, Sweden had considerable economic motives to participate in the EEA, in particular if the expected positive effects of cooperation in areas beyond the trade of goods are added. Likewise, the government concluded that "Sweden has a *strong* interest to participate in this agreement."[31]

Already in the 1980s Sweden had embarked on certain corrections of its welfare model such as deregulating financial markets, partially privatizing state enterprises, and introducing tax reform.[32] The economic crisis strongly increased the pressure for restructuring the welfare state. The government did not view the EEA process as a threat to the Swedish model and asserted that "Sweden has been one of the most trade-dependent countries in the world for several decades, but that has not prevented us from moulding a welfare policy of our own, an employment policy of our own, an environment policy of our own."[33] An official study confirmed that EEA membership would not affect Sweden's welfare system.[34] It underlined that Sweden's growing budget deficit and public debt were creating structural changes in its economy, irrespective of whether the country joined the EEA. Compared to Swedish statements in the past, the parliament's insight that "there is reason to believe that Sweden not even with very close cooperation with the EC will have to give up central Swedish values"[35] was quite remarkable. The conservatives and liberals won the 1991 elections with the promise to reduce the tax burden, cut public spending, privatize state-owned companies, and reform the welfare system. For them, "the time for the Nordic model has passed" because "it created societies that were too monopolized, too expensive and didn't give people the freedom of choice they wanted."[36]

At the beginning of the EEA negotiations, the Swedish government remained firm on its earlier decision that EC membership was not compatible with neutrality, in particular because of the formalized obligation to take part in foreign policy consultations. Sweden's political constraints were low with regard to the European Economic Area, whereas they remained of medium strength in relation to full membership in the European Communities, at least until the fall of 1990 (see the next section, "The EC Membership Applications of 1991–1992"). In light of the economic challenges and the end of the East-West conflict, both the welfare model and neutrality lost gradually in importance in the eyes of the Swedish elites.

Norway. In 1992, Norwegian exports were still very dependent on the EC, with two-thirds of all foreign sales going to the Community and a GDP ratio of 18.5 percent (see Table 7.1). The exports to the whole EEA market added up to an impressive share of 80 percent.[37] The government underlined that "almost two thirds of the Norwegian exports of goods went to the EC and about four fifths to the EFTA and EC area. Moreover, all gas exports and about two thirds of the oil exports are destined to the EC area alone. Even if oil and gas are excluded, the EFTA and EC countries together receive about three quarters of Norway's export of goods."[38]

According to Table 7.2, Norway's exports to the EC were still composed of a large quota of petroleum (48.9 percent) and smaller shares of gas and nonferrous metals. Their sector export ratios were extremely high, at three-quarters for nonferrous metals and oil and almost 100 percent for gas, which requires pipeline installations. Yet, these exports faced only low nontariff barriers to trade on the internal market.[39] In sum, "a substantial part of Norway's exports are sold at competitive markets in which barriers to trade are negligible," which means that "the traditional Norwegian export branches may not be much influenced by the completion of the internal market."[40] Nevertheless, the real income effect of integration was anticipated to reach 3.5 percent for trade in goods and services (as compared to an average of 2.7 percent for EFTA as a whole)[41]: "For energy-intensive products, like metals and forest products, it is probably true that the internal market as such does not influence the export possibilities significantly. It is, however, a fact that in a number of these markets antidumping measures or threats of antidumping measures have been used as a kind of nontariff barrier against imports to the EU. With the EEA Agreement, such barriers can no longer be applied against Norwegian exports of, e.g., metals."[42]

Norway's leading export sectors were composed of firms that could not easily be moved abroad. In contrast to Sweden, Norway did not have to face the effects of massive capital flight, even though Norwegian direct investments in the internal market grew heavily from 37.7 percent in 1986–1988 to 62.6 percent in 1989–1990, and in 1990, about 60 percent of Norwegian investment stock was within the EC.[43] The government asserted that the EEA agreement would reduce both the uncertainty of investments in Norway and the differences between export-oriented and domestically oriented sectors of the Norwegian economy.[44] The fisheries sector exported 90 percent of its production and about 60 percent to the EC market, but fisheries accounted for only 6 percent of Norwegian exports in 1991.[45] Within EFTA, free trade in fish was introduced on 1 July 1990. The EEA agreement provided only restricted liberalization of trade in fish, but Norway was granted the right to continue to limit foreign investments in its fishing fleet. Moreover, Norway would profit from the free movement of services because the export of services made up 12 percent of GDP, most of which came from the shipping business.[46] Several studies substantiated the claim that participation in the EEA would clearly increase national income in the long run, compared to a situation in which the Norwegian economy stayed outside the internal market.[47] As a result, Norway had strong economic incentives to integrate in the early 1990s.

Owing to oil revenues, Norway could avoid cutbacks in the welfare state and the high unemployment rates of Sweden and Finland. For the government, it was clear that in order to maintain national welfare, Norway needed access to foreign markets. "Participation in broader economic integration in Europe, such as the EEA Agreement offers, is important in order to contribute to full employment and secure strong growth in the Norwegian economy."[48] A special report showed that in the 1990s the Norwegian model was in some respects better but in others worse than other European welfare systems and that welfare policy remained a national concern both in the EEA and the EC.[49] There were many vested interests in preserving the "Norwegian way of life," including the high levels of social and environmental protection as well as the generous subsidies to the farmers and fishermen that formed part of regional policy in thinly populated areas.

No referendum was called to ratify the EEA agreement, which involved neither supranational institutions nor any "union" and hence hardly mobilized societal cleavages. In a 1992 opinion poll, 44 percent of the Norwegians supported the EEA agreement, 15 percent favored applying for EC membership, and 16 percent voted against both options.[50] Accordingly,

Norway faced weak political impediments with regard to participating in the EEA but still greater obstacles to joining the EC.

Switzerland. In 1992, the Swiss economy exported a high portion of 58.9 percent of its foreign sales to the European Communities, accounting for an impressive GDP ratio of 16 percent (see Table 7.1). Total Swiss sales to the EEA market made up about two-thirds of all exports (65.2 percent).[51] Switzerland was thus highly dependent on the EC (and EEA) market. The sectoral composition of the main exports to the EC had not changed much since 1984, comprising a medium portion of nonelectrical machinery and low shares of electrical machinery and professional and scientific instruments (see Table 7.2). Both types of machinery sold important quantities of their exports to the internal market, but professional instruments were more globally oriented. Electrical machinery faced high levels of NTBs on the EC market, and nonelectrical machinery faced medium levels, whereas precision and optical instruments as well as clocks and watches met only low barriers.[52] In spite of this seeming diversification, the "future development of Swiss industry seems quite sensitive to the EC common market program" as "import and export sensitive sectors account for about 70 percent of industrial value added and employment."[53]

A study commissioned by the government estimated that integration either via EEA or EC membership would yield a onetime increase in real GDP of 4–6 percent or, over a ten-year period, an annual growth rate of 0.4–0.6 percent.[54] Although export industries would profit from improved market access, domestically oriented sectors would have to face stronger import competition. For the Federal Council, "the most tangible cost of non-participation would be a competitive disadvantage for our industries which export to the EC," Swiss "companies would relocate a greater part of their production to the EC," and "Switzerland's position as a host country for direct investments from the EC would be dealt a blow."[55] In fact, Switzerland's direct investments in the EC market increased sharply from 28.6 percent in 1982–1985 to 71 percent in 1986–1988. In contrast to Sweden's investments, Swiss investments fell again to 39.7 percent as the EEA began to take shape in 1989–1990, and in 1990, about 48 percent of the Swiss investment stock was in the internal market.[56] The Swiss export share of services as a percentage of GDP reached 7.4 percent in 1990, and consumer gains from integrating financial services alone were estimated to yield a big share of 2.8 percent of Swiss GDP.[57] By and large, the Swiss economy experienced high economic incentives to join the European Economic Area in the early 1990s.

Direct democracy and federalism were at the forefront of the concerns about Switzerland's accession to the EEA. The primacy of EEA law would restrict the right of initiative not only of parliament, government, and cantons but also of the people. Together with the direct effect of certain EEA rules, it might affect the voters' right of referendum, both on federal and cantonal levels.[58] For the political elites, repercussions of the EEA "would be stronger than those of a case-by-case approach, but they would be less important than the ones in case of Swiss accession to the Community."[59] In November 1990, the Federal Council declared that EEA membership was safe both from the point of view of neutrality law and neutrality policy.[60]

Because of its political importance, the government decided to submit the EEA treaty to a referendum requiring a double majority (that is, a majority of the cantons and of the population as a whole). The "yes" and "no" camps were more or less entrenched in the two major linguistic areas and reflected "a division between the center and the periphery which appears in all votes that touch on central values of Helvetic identity."[61] On 6 December 1992, a high voter turnout of 78.3 percent rejected the EEA agreement by 50.3 percent of the voters and sixteen out of twenty-three cantons. Forty-four percent of the Swiss Germans and 77 percent of the *Romands* voted for the EEA agreement. In the French-speaking part, 86 percent of the city dwellers and 71 percent of the countryside voted "yes," compared to 53 percent in the German-speaking cities and 39 percent of the countryside. The linguistic cleavage accounted for about 70 percent of the variance between "yes" and "no," whereas the urban-rural factor had a much weaker effect.

The quasi-supranational nature of the EEA and the lack of voice had raised fears of foreign influence.[62] They were reinforced by the prospect of the free movement of persons in the EEA because of the fact that the Swiss economy offered high wages and its population spoke three EC languages. In 1989, the share of foreigners in Switzerland's population amounted to 16 percent, and three-quarters of them were EC and EFTA nationals. Given Switzerland's high wages and multiple languages, there was a general anxiety that, once the legal restrictions were lifted, "a further increase of the foreign population could affect Switzerland's autonomy and identity."[63] The Federal Council argued that a large influx of additional immigration was not to be expected in the EEA and that a liberalization of the acquisition of property, notably holiday homes, by foreigners would not give rise to strong foreign demand.[64] The government was aware that "the rejection of foreign judges has, in our country, an almost mythological significance" but claimed that it could "say with good reason that with this EEA treaty we are in no way submitting to a foreign judge."[65]

At the beginning of the EEA process, the Swiss elite perceived still very strong political constraints against becoming a full member of the European Communities but relatively low impediments to the prospect of a European Economic Area. For the Federal Council, the EEA was "the only option which in today's situation takes into account, on the one hand, the acceleration of the EC integration process and the EC's growing influence in Europe, and on the other hand, the essential peculiarities of the institutional, economic and social organization of our country."[66]

Integration Policy Preferences

In light of the completion of the EC's internal market, the economic incentives for participation in the European Economic Area turned out to be strong for all three countries. They were more compelling for Sweden than for Norway and Switzerland. In 1989–1990, when the EEA was launched, Sweden and Norway faced political obstacles of intermediate importance, but they were still considered high in Switzerland. As the next section, The EC Membership Applications of 1991–1992, will show, the values attributed to them decreased soon afterward, yet at different speeds. These findings led me to expect that all three countries would first aim at a medium level of integration in terms of a global approach to intergovernmental (or at most quasi-supranational) cooperation with the EC. They would be prepared to give up some operational sovereignty in exchange for economic benefits and a (limited) voice. I anticipated that Switzerland would be the most reluctant of the three countries, followed by Norway.

Sweden.   Since the late 1980s, the Swedish government has pursued a policy of active adaptation to the EC, including important economic reforms. It actively supported the EEA from its inception and aimed at as far-reaching a solution as possible (e.g., a customs union). In the eyes of parliament, the EEA agreement should strive for "a balance of rights and obligations" and "a reasonable degree of participation" in the decisionmaking process in proportion to the required commitments.[67] In spite of its policy change in favor of EC membership in October 1990 (see section entitled "The EC Membership Applications of 1991–1992"), the government repeatedly confirmed that "Sweden's stated aim of applying for EC membership has not in any way diminished our interest in the EEA agreement."[68]

In general, the EEA negotiations did not give rise to an extensive public debate in Sweden. The Federation of Swedish Industries, the Swedish Employers' Federation, and the major trade unions supported the EEA agreement.[69] In the ratification debate in November 1992, the EEA agreement was approved by all the political forces, except for the (formerly communist) Left Party.[70] From the government's point of view, "even if the EEA Agreement entails important advantages for our economy . . . that agreement cannot in the long run constitute an alternative to full membership in the EC."[71] The EEA was not sufficient in the long run since it would not grant the same co-decision rights as full membership, nor would it encompass the same areas of cooperation.[72] EFTA's ambitions with regard to the EEA decisionmaking process had not been met, and "a balance between the commitments in substance and the corresponding influence on the formulation of rules can only be reached through membership."[73] Sweden, like the other EFTA countries, had to evaluate "whether the maintenance of national sovereignty in the areas covered by the internal market programme, as well as the flanking and horizontal policies, is crucial enough for the country to be excluded from the internal market; and whether the maintenance of sovereignty in areas not included in the EEA Treaty (such as customs tariffs, taxation, agriculture, and monetary policy) outweighs the lack of true influence on the decision-making process in the EEA."[74]

With the EEA agreement, the Swedish government aimed at a medium level of integration based on a broad consensus among the economic and political elites. As the economic incentives became stronger and the political impediments weaker, however, the acquisition of voice gained in importance compared to the maintenance of operational sovereignty.

Norway. In late 1989, the Norwegian parliament approved specific aims for the EEA process: full access to the internal market for the Norwegian business sector; elimination of rules of origin and of antidumping measures; free access for the export of fish products; common rules of competition in the EEA; high standards regarding social and regional policies and environmental issues; full participation in EC cooperation in fields such as environmental protection, research and development, and social, educational, and consumer issues; and, finally, the establishment of the necessary EFTA institutions.[75] Like Sweden, the Norwegian government kept the option of an EC-EFTA customs union open. In the fall of 1990, the nonsocialist coalition government under Prime Minister Jan Syse collapsed after only one year in office because the Center Party feared that Norway was giving away too much in the EEA negotiations. Labor leader Gro Harlem Brundtland formed a new government and declared that EC membership was not an issue as long as Norway was preoccupied with the EEA negotiations.

The government's report on the EEA agreement of May 1992 stressed that Norwegian interests would best be taken care of by joining the EEA, which created a huge single market; offered improved market access for fish; preserved restrictions on foreign investments in fishing vessels; opened up public procurement; maintained Norway's regional policy; granted Norwegian shipping equal access to the EC market; and strengthened European cooperation beyond the free movement of goods, services, capital, and persons without the transfer of any legislative powers to EEA organs.[76] The Progress, Center, Christian Democratic, and Socialist Left Parties demanded a referendum on the EEA, but parliament rejected their demand.[77] The Conservative Party and the Labor Party were strongly in favor of the EEA agreement, whereas the Christian Democratic Party and the Progress Party supported it less enthusiastically, and the Socialist Left and Center Parties opposed it. In addition, the Conservative Party insisted that Norway should apply for EC membership as soon as possible. On 16 October 1992, the Storting adopted the agreement by a majority of 130 to 35, thereby for the first time applying Paragraph 93 of the Constitution, which requires a parliamentary majority of three-quarters for the transfer of sovereignty powers.[78]

The Confederation of Norwegian Business and Industry (NHO) strongly welcomed the EEA Agreement, as did the Norwegian Trade Council, the Association of Norwegian Banks, the Association of Commerce and Services, and the Norwegian Shipowners' Association.[79] Some of the interest groups, like the NHO, indicated that the EEA could only be a step on the way to EC membership. The petroleum industry was not a strong advocate of integration since oil and gas could be sold to the internal market regardless of Norway's integration status. The Norwegian Confederation of Trade Unions considered the EEA Agreement as "satisfying" and expected the government to take the necessary steps to protect Norwegian working conditions, wage levels, and social standards. The fishery sector was divided between the export-oriented fish-processing industries, represented by the Federation of Norwegian Fishing Industry (Fiskerinæringens Landsforening), and the Norwegian Fish Farmers' Association (Norske Fiskeoppdretteres Forening), both of which wanted the EEA's free market access, and the Norwegian Fishermen's Union (Norges Fiskarlag), which felt threatened by the prospect of EC boats fishing in Norwegian waters. The Norwegian Farmers' Union and the Norwegian Farmers and Smallholders' Union (Norges Bondelag and Norges Bonde- og Småbrukarlag) opposed any adaptation to EC rules. Unlike Sweden, the Norwegian state had not liberalized its agricultural and regional policies and continued to heavily subsidize agriculture and peripheral regions.[80]

The Norwegian government clearly aimed at a medium level of integration. The political constraints were still too strong to aim at full integration at the expense of sovereignty. A report by the Foreign Ministry stated that the EEA "decisionmaking process will give Norway and the other EFTA countries an opportunity to influence the formulation of new rules," but EC membership will provide "a much stronger influence than the EEA Agreement can give."[81] In contrast to Austria, Sweden, Finland, and Switzerland, the Norwegian government held out until the EEA agreement was ratified by the Storting before turning toward EC membership.

Switzerland. In November 1990, the Federal Council maintained that the primordial goal of Swiss integration policy was the conclusion of "an agreement that gives us access to the EC internal market and concedes a general right to participate in the procedures for decision-shaping and decision-taking in the future EEA, and which allows our country to essentially preserve its particularities."[82] It admitted, however, that the EC membership option was gaining in attraction, given the difficulties of the EEA process, the collapse of the bipolar security structure, and the strengthening of the EC's "federalist" features such as subsidiarity.[83]

The Swiss Federation of Commerce and Industry (Vorort) welcomed the EEA initiative in 1989. It desired a removal of technical barriers in EC-EFTA trade, a simplification of rules of origin, liberalization of public procurement and of trade in services (e.g. banking, insurance, transport), and participation in the EC's research and education programs.[84] The Vorort did not push for EC membership, which would have involved a loss of treaty-making power and restrictions on national institutions in exchange for increased interventionism and regulation.[85] The Swiss Union of Small and Medium Enterprises (SGV) supported the EEA negotiations but hoped that the free trade area would not come too close to EC membership.[86] The Federation of Swiss Employers' Organizations, as well as the Vorort and the SGV, supported the free movement of persons in order to ensure the necessary recruitment for the Swiss economy.[87] The Swiss Confederation of Trade Unions (SGB) required, in addition, that the "inhumane" status of foreign seasonal workers (*saisonniers*) be abolished and that the legal situation of transborder commuters be improved.[88] In general, the trade unions hoped that the EEA rules would improve social conditions for workers in Switzerland. Only the Swiss Farmers' Union rejected the EEA agreement, even though agriculture was almost completely excluded. The farmers were afraid that the EEA might eventually lead them into the EC's Common Agricultural Policy, cutting Swiss prices and subsidies.

At the beginning of the EEA negotiations, the government's four coalition parties supported the process.[89] Yet, when it became clear that the Community would not grant the EFTA states equal rights in the EEA decisionmaking process and that the other EFTA countries were eager to join the EC, the Swiss elites reassessed their preferences in light of the new European architecture and the end of the East-West conflict. The Social Democratic Party and, for a while, the Christian Democratic Party began to favor EC membership, but the agrarian Swiss People's Party drifted toward opposition to both EEA and EC membership. After the draft EEA treaty was agreed upon in Luxembourg on 22 October 1991, the Federal Council announced that it now opted for the double strategy of pursuing both EEA membership and, as a long-term goal, accession to the European Communities (see the next section, "The EC Membership Applications of 1991–1992").[90]

In its bill to parliament, the government concluded that the substance of the EEA treaty corresponded to its expectations, but the institutional structure did not.[91] Compared to EC membership, the EEA would impose fewer obligations but would also grant fewer rights and should thus be seen as a step toward Switzerland's future accession to the EC.[92] In the summer of 1992, the EEA agreement gained vast support in the two chambers of parliament, with 62 percent in the National Council (Nationalrat) and 85 percent in the State Council (Ständerat).[93] Although the treaty was almost unanimously accepted by the French-speaking deputies, the German-speaking parliamentarians were more divided. The EEA agreement was supported by the Social Democratic Party, the conservative Radical Democratic Party, and the Christian Democratic Party as well as by the Liberal Party, the Independent Alliance, and the Protestant People's Party. The opposition was composed of the agrarian Swiss People's Party—the only "no" party in the government—the Green Party, the left-wing Labor Party, and three small right-wing populist groups (the Swiss Democrats, the Freedom Party, and the Lega dei Ticiniesi).

The "no" campaign under the leadership of the Action Committee for Independent and Neutral Switzerland "tried to dramatize the debate with emotional arguments about the loss of sovereignty and neutrality, the decline of direct democracy, the threat of massive immigration and the resulting rise of unemployment, the decrease of wages, and so on," while the government's information campaign suffered from a one-sided focus on economic aspects.[94] Nevertheless, in September 1992, Swiss voters accepted the establishment of a new railway system crossing the Alps, the New Alpine Rail Axes, an important element in the bilateral transit agreement between Switzerland and the EC, which itself was not submitted to a referendum. The transit agreement was concluded separately from the EEA agreement because the Federal Council, under pressure from the cantons most affected by Alpine transit traffic, rejected the EC demand of allowing 40-ton foreign trucks on Swiss roads. The treaty allowed Switzerland to keep the 28-ton limit for trucks while promoting combined road-railways traffic. In spite of this positive harbinger, the Swiss voters and cantons refused to ratify the EEA agreement on 6 December 1992.

More than any other EFTA country, the Swiss government was disappointed about the institutional shortcomings of the EEA. In the fall of 1990, it had still stressed that Switzerland would not transfer any legislative powers and that the EEA agreement in reality would not entail a greater loss of sovereignty than an *alleingang* (going it alone) requiring unilateral adaptation to EC rules.[95] By contrast, if Switzerland did not join the EEA, "the greater freedom of action would face fewer possibilities for influence for Switzerland in the process of European integration," and "this loss of influence would not be offset by Switzerland's possibility to escape the EC's pressure for adaptation."[96] However, at the end of the negotiation process, the Federal Council had to admit that the EEA institutions granted a right to consultation but not to co-decision making.[97]

In 1989–1990, strong economic incentives and political impediments made Switzerland aim at no more than a medium level of integration in the form of the European Economic Area. It had weaker ambitions than Sweden and Norway and, in fact, was often the EFTA country to put on the brakes during the EEA negotiations. The Swiss government tried hard to obtain more voice for the required loss of operational sovereignty. The economic interest groups and the export industries in particular strongly supported the EEA agreement but were rather reluctant to openly push for EC membership. The outcome of the 1992 referendum revealed a gap in the perceptions of the political constraints on integration between the Swiss elites and the masses, given that "identity is at the heart of the refusal of the majority of Swiss to integrate with the EEA."[98]

As expected, Sweden and Norway were more forthcoming than the Swiss hardliners, aiming at a global scope of integration and a quasi-supranational institutional setup in the EEA agreement. All three countries wanted to join the European Economic Area, and all were disappointed by its lack of voice. Ironically, the Commission's intransigent position in the EEA negotiations contributed to the EFTA countries' decisions to apply for EC membership—a development that it had originally sought to avoid. Under these circumstances, the concept had lost its value for the EFTA states as an alternative to EC accession and instead became a means of preparing for it.

The EC Membership Applications of 1991–1992

At the outset, the EFTA countries perceived the EEA as a "third way" between marginalization and full membership in the European Communities. Considering the extensive substance of the final EEA agreement and the rather limited influence it conferred, accompanied by the need to transform EFTA into a "mini-EC," EC membership became a more viable option. In July 1989 Austria was the first EFTA country to apply for EC membership with an explicit neutrality reservation.[99] Later that year, the communist regimes in Central and Eastern Europe began to collapse. In December 1989, the European Commission advised the Council of Ministers to reject Turkey's membership application of August 1987. Nevertheless, in July 1990, Cyprus and Malta applied for accession to the European Communities. In October 1990, the two Germanies were united, and the territory of the former German Democratic Republic became part of the EC. In July 1991, Sweden submitted its EC membership application. In view of this demand, the unsatisfactory outcome of the EEA, and the collapse of the Soviet Union, in March 1992 the Finnish government applied to join the EC without a neutrality reservation. The Swiss government announced its EC membership application in May 1992, when the EEA agreement was signed, and Norway followed in November 1992.

In December 1991, the European Council in Maastricht had agreed on the Treaty on European Union, which envisaged turning the Community into an Economic and Monetary Union and adding the pillars of a Common Foreign and Security Policy and cooperation in the fields of justice and home affairs. In June 1992, Danish voters rejected the Maastricht Treaty by a narrow margin (50.7 percent "no" votes), whereas the Irish approved it by a majority of two to one. In September 1992, the French people narrowly accepted the Treaty with 51 percent in favor.[100] The internal market came into existence on 1 January 1993, and the EC began to consider the membership applications of the EFTA states. After being granted the requested opt-out clauses (e.g., defense, the single currency), the Danes supported the Treaty with a majority of 56.7 percent in a second referendum in May 1993, and the European Union finally entered into force on 1 November 1993.

Since Switzerland had rejected the EEA agreement in a referendum in late 1992, its EC bid was not followed up by the government. The membership negotiations with the remaining four candidate EFTA countries were relatively speedy since, by virtue of the EEA agreement, an important part of the *acquis communautaire* was already in place in the applicant countries.[101] Various transitional periods were granted, for example, with regard to the acquisition of secondary residences by foreigners or restrictions on the ownership of Norwegian fishing vessels by nonnationals. The applicants were allowed to keep their higher standards and level of protection of public health and environment, and the EU would endeavor to raise its own standards. Sweden and Norway also obtained an exception from the prohibition of the traditional tobacco product *snus* (moist, orally taken snuff), but they were not allowed to export it to the other member states. A compromise was found on alcohol policies that required the Nordic countries to abolish the states' monopolies on the importation, production, and wholesale distribution of alcohol but allowed them to maintain the monopoly on the retail sales, provided it did not discriminate against products from other member states. Moreover, the Nordic countries were allowed to retain their free trade agreements with the Baltic states until the EU negotiated similar agreements. A solution was developed to accommodate arctic and subarctic agriculture into the CAP and to widen the EU's regional policy objectives to include northern criteria such as low population density. Agreement on fisheries between Norway and the EU was difficult to reach because of the fact that Spain and Portugal had to be fully integrated into the Common Fisheries Policy a few years ahead of the date envisaged in their accession treaties.

The accession acts were signed at the European Council summit in Corfu, Greece, on 24 June 1994. The national referenda were held in the order of the likelihood in which the different electorates were expected to vote in favor of membership.[102] On 12 June 1994, the Austrians overwhelmingly approved EU membership with 66.6 percent in favor and a turnout of 82.3 percent. Finland followed on 16 October 1994 with 56.9 percent "yes" votes and a turnout of 74 percent. On 13 November 1994, a majority of 52.3 percent of the Swedish electorate voted in favor of joining the Union, but two weeks later the same percentage of Norwegian voters had rejected EU membership. Hence, on 1 January 1995, only Sweden, Finland, and Austria joined the European Union as full members, whereas Norway remained an EFTA member in the European Economic Area, together with Iceland and Liechtenstein.

Incentives for and Impediments to Integration

When the accession acts were signed in 1994, the shares of exports to a market comprising all the EU and EFTA countries amounted to 66.3 percent for Sweden, 79.1 percent for Norway, and 63.5 percent for Switzerland.[103] Since the free trade agreements had eliminated industrial tariffs and the EEA agreement had removed most nontariff barriers to trade, factors beyond market access gained in importance. In fact, the estimated net welfare effects of moving from EEA to EU membership, which could result from Community budget transfers, the common agricultural, commercial, and fisheries policies, and the elimination of border controls, were relatively small and depended primarily on the initial national protection of agriculture.[104] Expectations about the credibility, stability, and permanence of the EEA or about the effectiveness of national policies outside the EU gained in importance.

Sweden. As set out in the first section of this chapter, Sweden had strong economic incentives to participate in integration in the early 1990s. In addition to the EEA, EU membership would require Sweden to adopt the Common Customs Tariff and the EC's nontariff measures, such as quotas, voluntary export restraints, or antidumping actions vis-à-vis third countries, which for certain products were higher than the Swedish barriers to trade, but these differences were considered small.[105] The net impact of changes in trade barriers, agricultural policy, and transfers to and from the Community budget were estimated to amount to 0.22 percent of Swedish GDP.[106] In contrast to these static effects, the government expected the dynamic effects of EU membership to be more crucial.[107] Accession would permanently secure Swedish participation in the internal market, increase the level of investments, and exert a tangible psychological effect on promoting Swedish business. Several studies confirmed that EU membership would clearly benefit Sweden's economy.[108] The following statement underlines the fundamental change of Swedish reasoning in comparison to earlier decades: "The smallness and openness restrict Sweden's possibilities to pursue a policy which is radically different from the rest of the world. . . . For the development and welfare of Sweden, access to foreign markets without discrimination is therefore of decisive importance. At the same time, dependence on big companies forces Sweden to pay attention to alternative options for investments and export markets which the companies face."[109]

In fact, the EEA negotiations had not been able to stop the massive outward flow of capital. The share of Swedish direct investment assets in the Community increased fivefold from 42 billion Swedish crowns (38.2 percent of total foreign assets) in 1986 to 215 billion (64 percent of total foreign assets) in 1992.[110] The Federation of Swedish Industries made it clear that "the EEA cannot match industry's strong demand for a satisfying investment climate."[111] Sweden experienced its most serious recession since the 1930s. Unemployment grew from an already above-average 4 percent in 1989 to 12 percent in 1992, and the position of the Swedish economy declined from one of the largest budgetary surpluses relative to GDP among the countries in the Organization for Economic Cooperation and Development to one of the biggest deficits.[112] Under these circumstances, the Swedish government might have regarded EU membership as a means to halt the exodus of capital and the rise of unemployment:

> The EEA Agreement grants the companies access to the Swedish economy's most important export market. EU membership guarantees that this access will last. Stability is a key factor. The EEA Agreement has in this respect clear limitations:
>
> * It can be terminated at one year's notice.
> * It can be undermined—eroded—if the EFTA countries do not agree on the introduction of new rules.
> * Interest in the EEA could fade away when the EU's membership widens.[113]

A commission of independent experts appointed by the government to analyze the economic crisis concluded that the Swedish model "resulted in institutions and structures that today constitute an obstacle to economic efficiency and economic growth because of their lack of flexibility and their one-sided concerns for income safety and distribution, with limited concern for economic incentives."[114] EU membership would contribute to the reforms necessary for restoring a well-functioning market economy.[115] The government told parliament that the traditional goals of Swedish economic policy, such as high employment, a reliable welfare system, growth, low inflation, regional leveling-out, and a healthy environment were considerably easier to achieve if Sweden joined the EU than if it stayed outside.[116] Given these concerns, Sweden had rather strong economic incentives to join the EU in spite of the EEA.[117] At the time of application, the fate of the European Economic Area had not yet been decided, but it seemed that only EU membership could improve business confidence in the Swedish economy.

Not surprisingly, the political controversy about EU membership focused on how Sweden could maintain its policy of neutrality and to what extent the Swedish model would change. Sweden spent 40 percent of its GDP on social protection in 1992, compared to an average of 27.1 percent in the European Union.[118] The social democratic government argued that the real threat to welfare policy was a weak economy and that integration would safeguard the Swedish model.[119] In 1990, the Swedish Employers' Confederation had abandoned centralized wage bargaining, one year later it withdrew from the boards of all state agencies, and from 1993 on, negotiations were carried out at the sectoral level between national employers' associations and national trade unions.[120] Since the 1980s, Sweden had continually adjusted to EC legislation through liberalization and privatization. The financial market was opened, and foreign exchange controls were removed. Swedish agricultural policy was completely overhauled in favor of deregulation. Swedish farmers—unlike those in Norway—showed a weak support for EU membership.[121] In fact, Andreas Bieler argues that Sweden's accession must be analyzed on the background of the structural change often referred to as globalization (that is, transnationalization of production and finance in connection with neoliberal ideas).[122]

In late October 1990, the government proclaimed that, given the end of the Cold War, "Swedish membership in the EC, while maintaining Swedish neutrality, is in our national interest."[123] Parliament supported this view, even though the Community was developing a Common Foreign and Security Policy.[124] After the elections in the fall of 1991, the new conservative government went a step further by declaring that

> differences in historical experience were only one of the reasons why Sweden belonged to the circle of reluctant Europeans for so many years. Another reason was Sweden's continued economic and social success. . . . Although there was no direct connection, there tended to be a mental correlation of the policy of neutrality in the field of security and the economic and social policies of the "Swedish middle way" . . . between East and West. . . . It goes without saying that there is no longer any room for this sort of policies. No one wants to be a compromise between a system which has turned out to be a success and another that has turned out to be a historic catastrophe.[125]

In May 1992, the main parties in parliament formulated the following compromise on the future of neutrality policy: "Sweden's non-participation in military alliances, with the aim of making it possible for our country to be neutral in the event of war in our vicinity, remains unchanged."[126] The notion of neutrality was being phased out in Swedish official discourse and was increasingly replaced by military nonalignment. "This doctrine is now dignified as the 'hard core' of Swedish *defence* policy, as distinguished from a *foreign and security* policy outlook which will become much more adaptively oriented towards Europe."[127] Hence, the European Commission was able to note in its 1992 opinion on Sweden's membership application that there seemed to exist a consensus regarding full participation in the CFSP, but with "reservations in the Swedish position relative to the eventual framing of a common defence policy and, in an even more marked way, regarding the possible establishment in time of a common defence."[128] The government expected EU membership to increase the "possibilities to work for goals and interests that traditionally were important in Swedish foreign policy . . . without risking that the national identity would be wiped out."[129] An official comparison of the positions of Sweden and those of the EU countries taken in the CFSP framework exhibited "a fundamental agreement of opinions."[130] Hence, after forty years, Sweden finally perceived its political impediments to full membership in the European Union to be low.

Norway. When Norway decided to join the EEA, it had a strong economic motivation to do so (see the section on "The European Economic Area"). However, the net effects of moving from EEA to EC membership were estimated to amount to no more than 0.94 percent of Norway's GDP.[131] A study by Norway's Statistics Office confirmed that EU membership would, in the medium term, have relatively small effects on production and employment and that agriculture and food industries would face considerable restructuring.[132] The adoption of the Common Commercial Policy vis-à-vis third countries might in some cases lead to higher barriers to trade, but these difficulties were viewed as small.[133] With regard to industries and services, the additional gains of EU membership were not considered to be very significant, except for the food industries relying on the agricultural and fishing sectors, the shipping industry, and the impact of monetary union.[134] In contrast to Sweden and Finland, the Norwegian oil economy did not look to EU membership as a means to recover from a severe recession, but it would lead to a higher level of income for Norway in the long run than the EEA agreement.[135] Joining the European Union with the other Nordic countries would offer better market access to Norwegian exports, reduce uncertainty about the fate of the EEA, increase Norway's attractiveness for investments, and facilitate diversification of the economy.

Based on these analyses, the government argued that EU membership

the Swedish crown. In its *Report on Measures to Stabilize the Economy and to Limit the Growth of Public Expenditure* of 26 October 1990, the government suggested reducing the state bureaucracy, partly privatizing the state sector, and cutting sickness benefits and food prices. In two sentences, it announced that "Swedish membership in the EC while maintaining Swedish neutrality is in our national interest" and that "the government will work for a new decision by Parliament on the policy towards Europe, which more clearly and in more positive wording clarifies Sweden's ambitions to become a member of the European Community."[161] Only two weeks earlier, the foreign minister had told parliament that it was "wrong and unwise to raise the membership question" and that the parties should stick to their earlier consensus not to bring up that issue in light of the uncertain security situation in Europe and the EC plans for political union.[162] The timing of this remarkable volte-face was obviously affected by the recession and the vast capital flight that boosted the economic incentives for accession.

In November 1990, the four largest parties agreed that "Sweden should strive to become a member of the European Community, while maintaining its neutrality policy."[163] After the end of the Cold War, the government considered that "Swedish membership in the European Community is now compatible with the retention of a policy of neutrality."[164] On 12 December 1990, parliament endorsed the decision to join the EC by an overwhelming majority (287 to 40), with only the Left and Green Parties voting against it.[165] On 14 June 1991, the Swedish government, with the support of all the major parties, decided to submit its membership application, which it formally did on 1 July 1991.

The elections of September 1991 produced a new nonsocialist four-party coalition government committed to EC membership. At the opening of the accession negotiations on 1 February 1993, it declared that "Sweden fully shares the political objectives and principles, the so-called *finalités politiques*, of the Treaty on the European Union," even though "Sweden's policy of non-participation in military alliances remains unchanged."[166] The final decision to participate in Economic and Monetary Union was left open.[167] In contrast to the Conservative Party and the Liberal People's Party, the Center and Christian Democratic Parties, both members of the coalition government, had strong "no" profiles among their voters, as did the Social Democratic Party.[168]

The accession act was signed on 24 June 1994. Parliament decided that a referendum should be held on the membership question, and all political parties agreed that they would respect the outcome. From the government's point of view, the result of the accession negotiations largely corresponded to its initial positions.[169] For the Federation of Swedish Industries, EU membership would guarantee a more comprehensive and stable relationship than the EEA agreement while eliminating the risk of marginalization.[170] In August 1994, the coalition government presented its bill on membership in the European Union.[171] The required changes to the Swedish Constitution needed to be endorsed by two successive parliaments with a general election in between. In September 1994, the Social Democratic Party returned to power, and the bill was welcomed by all parliamentary parties, with the exception of the Left and Green Parties.[172]

In the referendum campaign, the "yes" side emphasized economic arguments for accession and the possibility of directing the Union as a whole toward a more extensive welfare state model, whereas the skeptics argued that EU membership was incompatible with neutrality and a threat to the welfare state.[173] More than 83 percent of the Swedish voters participated in the referendum on 13 November 1994, and 52.3 percent voted "yes," as opposed to 46.8 percent voting "no" and 0.9 percent blank votes.[174]

Obtaining a voice in the new Europe became increasingly important, while the traditional political obstacles lost in importance and the economic incentives intensified. For the government, the membership application was based on "the insight that we have been and will be more and more dependent on the decisions taken in the EU" and that the intended "firm cooperation based on common sovereignty with other states need not be in contrast to concerns for the right of national self-determination."[175] It had realized that "in a Europeanized and internationalized environment, political power transforms its nature: power is a question of both governing oneself and making oneself less sensitive to the others as well as exerting control over or influence on others."[176] In other words, "a country can through participation in an international organization exchange a part of its own formal independence for influence in the organization" without losing in total power.[177] Parliament supported the view that in the age of globalization, accession to the European Union would reduce Sweden's sovereignty but in return increase its influence:

> This apparently paradoxical state of things is a consequence of the fact that the scope for national determination shrinks because decisions which we have agreed upon in a democratic order can sometimes appear to be difficult to implement as a result of the links to international developments. This continuous weakening of Sweden's influence, and thereby of democracy, in our own country can be counteracted if also we have the right to vote in Europe and we take our place at the EU's table as a nation having equal rights.[178]

With a remarkably broad consensus among the Swedish elites, the government aimed at full integration. The interest groups supported EU membership in consideration of the economic benefits, and the political elites were anxious to secure Swedish influence on the EU's future policy through "a controlled surrender of sovereignty with a view to obtaining a common negotiated sovereignty."[179] Sweden's "third way" identity had lost much of its meaning as the welfare model and foreign policy gradually converged with the rest of Europe.

Norway. On 16 November 1992, after a long period of hesitation, Prime Minister Brundtland told parliament that Norway was confronted with a new situation because of the transformations in Central and Eastern Europe and the Soviet Union, the completion of the European Community's internal market, and the fact that Sweden and Finland had applied for EC membership. "The government thinks that Norway has the greatest freedom of action by, on the one hand, joining the EEA Agreement and, on the other hand, applying for EC membership so that we can negotiate and possibly become a member together with countries with which we share common interests."[180] A few days later, on 25 November 1992, the Norwegian government submitted its membership application to the European Communities with the approval of the Storting. At the opening of the accession negotiations on 5 April 1993, the minister of trade emphasized that Norway wanted to keep control over its natural resources and find acceptable solutions for the fisheries, agricultural, and regional policies, taking into account Norway's special geographic, climatic, and demographic situation.[181]

The Labor Party, the Conservative Party, and the Progress Party advocated accession, but all other parties opposed it.[182] As had happened twenty years earlier, the political parties were split on the membership question, except for the Conservative Party, the Center Party, and the Socialist Left Party. For the Labor Party, EU membership would establish stable economic conditions, thus guaranteeing employment and strengthening the basis of the welfare state, and it would be in line with Norway's foreign and defense policies. The Conservative Party considered membership of vital importance to ensure Norway's security, employment, and welfare and to gain a say in international decisions. The Center Party opposed EU membership because it refused to move power away from Norway's democratic organs to the bureaucratic politicians in Brussels and because it saw important goals threatened, such as full employment, a fair distribution between groups and districts, and environmental protection. With similar arguments, the Christian Democratic Party recommended voting "no" because the EU would weaken the democratic tradition and increase the distance between citizens and decisionmakers, and the Socialist Left Party feared that accession would threaten the achievements of the Nordic model. Given that

Norway's economic interests were taken care of in the EEA and its defense policy in NATO, the Liberal Party thought that Norway would lose more in the Storting than it could gain in Brussels.

In the September 1993 elections, the Center Party, with its unwavering anti-EU stance, was the clear winner and became Norway's second-largest party. It capitalized on the Norwegians' identification with the farmer as the "real" Norwegian and "freedom fighter" against foreign domination.[183] The grassroots movement Nei til EU (No to EU) had been launched in late 1990, and by the time the government applied for membership, it was organized on a nationwide basis. Like its 1972 predecessor, it had a very broad membership of about 140,000 members (compared to the 35,000 members of the Europabevegelsen, or the "Europe movement").[184] On the "yes" side, the Labor Party and the Conservative Party became important actors arguing in favor of Norway's influence in the EU, its participation in the CFSP and WEU, and guaranteed market access.[185] On the "no" side, self-government and local democracy were clearly the crucial arguments, followed by concerns about employment and the primary sector. The welfare state took a less prominent place in the debate than it had in the past.

Upon conclusion of the accession negotiations, the government was of the opinion that it had struck a good deal, including the sensitive issues of fisheries and agriculture.[186] Norway had to only slightly increase the EU's cod quota beyond the EEA agreement, and Norwegian seafood would obtain immediate free access to EU markets. After a transitional period, Norway would have to allow EU citizens to purchase Norwegian boats, give up its 12-mile exclusive fishing zone along the coast, and hand over the right to manage fish resources to the Union, but the EU would maintain the sustainable Norwegian management policy in northern waters. The agricultural settlement foresaw an extension of the Common Agricultural Policy to Norway, with special support for certain areas. The EU also allowed for subsidies to arctic and subarctic farmers and sparsely populated regions. With regard to offshore oil and gas development, agreement was achieved that Norway would retain full jurisdiction over its natural resources. The Norwegian government was afraid that the value of the EEA agreement would be diminished if Sweden, Finland, and Austria joined the EU, and it wanted to participate in the development of a European security and defense policy.[187]

Several organizations spoke out in favor of EU membership, such as the powerful Confederation of Norwegian Business and Industry, the Norwegian Trade Council, the Association of Norwegian Banks, the Norwegian Shipowners' Association, and the Association of Commerce and Services.[188] The export industries stressed that the EEA agreement did not offer the same competitive conditions as EU membership regarding certain products, the investment climate, or border controls. Both the fish-processing and fish-farming industries were in favor of membership since it offered free access to the major export market. By contrast, the fishermen's organizations fervently opposed accession, as did the farmers who feared that their income and the equality between different societal groups and districts would be affected. The trade unions were reluctant to get involved on either side. For a long time, the Norwegian Confederation of Trade Unions abstained from taking a position, until a narrow majority at a special meeting in September 1994 finally voted to oppose EU membership, in contrast to its attitude in 1972.[189]

On 28 November 1994, 52.2 percent of the Norwegians voted against joining the European Union, with a very high voter turnout of 88.8 percent. The regional continuity in the referendum results of 1972 and 1994 was striking. The same counties had a majority against EU membership in 1994 as in 1972, with only one exception.[190] Even though the international and European context had changed fundamentally, Nordic countries were joining the EU, and Norway had obtained a relatively "good deal," the Norwegian skepticism of supranational integration prevailed. Once again, the European issue showed its ability to open up old territorial and cultural cleavages that cut across the functional and economic divisions in Norwegian society.[191] Still, the aftermath of the 1994 referendum was less serious than the traumatizing experience of 1972. The Labor government had not threatened to resign in case of a "no," and the political parties did not suffer any significant shifts in voter support.[192] The government aimed at limiting the damage through close cooperation with the EU in the framework of the EEA, the CFSP, and justice and home affairs. In other words, Norway pursued a policy of "eager adjustment" to the European Union.[193] Thanks to the Nordic passport union, it managed to participate in the Schengen agreements eliminating border controls. Moreover, Norway stressed its association with the WEU, pushed for a political dialogue within the EEA, and sought for bilateral contacts in areas such as fisheries and energy.[194]

With regard to the choice of strategy, it was clear for the government that "only by means of binding international cooperation, which leads to common solutions in cases where national solutions are inadequate, can we fully cope with common challenges such as unemployment, environmental degradation, security, and development of the welfare state" and that by remaining outside the EU, Norway would be limiting its own freedom of action.[195] "By means of cooperation in which states adopt common rules applicable across borders, so that they exercise in the community parts of the authority which they before exercised for themselves, each state recovers possibilities to govern that otherwise would have been lost through increased internationalization."[196]

The support of the economic and political actors turned out to be more or less as expected, even though many parties were split on the membership issue. The government aimed at full integration, but the Norwegian people did not follow the assessment of their elites that voice had become more important relative to the maintenance of operational sovereignty. For many voters, the additional economic incentives were too weak and the remaining political obstacles too strong to join the European Union. Norway thus returned to the pursuit of a medium level of integration in the EEA.

Switzerland. Since October 1991, the Federal Council officially considered the EEA an important step on the way to full membership in the European Communities. By that time, most political parties had changed their minds in favor of accession. The Socialist Party, Conservative Party, Liberal Party, and Christian Democratic Party recommended EC membership, whereas the Green Party and a majority of the Swiss People's Party opposed it. In contrast to the other EFTA countries, the first umbrella organization to advocate EC membership in October 1990 was not the export industry's federation, but the Swiss Confederation of Trade Unions.[197] The application was filed soon after the signing of the EEA agreement in May 1992. The government justified its change of policy in a separate bill to parliament that was presented on the same day as the bill on ratification of the EEA agreement.[198] It tried to show that in an interdependent world, sovereignty and independence were becoming relative notions: "If we want to participate in the elaboration of rules and policies which will affect us more and more (whether we want it or not), and if we want to have the opportunity to cooperate with those states which are closest to us on an equal footing, there is no other way than accession to the EC."[199]

After the negative EEA referendum in December 1992, the Swiss government decided to keep the option of EC membership open, but given the domestic political situation, to "freeze" the application for the time being. Switzerland's relations with the European Union were maintained on the legal basis of the 1972 free trade agreements. In 1993, the government suggested a domestic reform and "revitalization" program for the Swiss economy, with continued adaptation to Community rules as well as bilateral negotiations with the European Union on sixteen areas of interest.[200] These bilateral negotiations, which enjoyed the broad support of most parties and economic interest groups, finally began in December 1994 on the seven issue areas of air traffic, land transportation, agriculture, free movement of persons, public procurement, research, and technical barriers to trade.[201] The bargaining process was fraught with problems, and the seven treaties were finally signed in June 1999. The European Union had made it clear from the outset that Switzerland could not pick and choose but had to take (or leave) the whole package deal. The government argued that they would stabilize Switzerland's economic relations with the EU and considerably improve the investment climate while not touching on its "legislative autonomy."[202] In May 2000, the Swiss people approved the bilateral agreements by a clear majority of 67.2 percent.

By aiming at EC membership, the Swiss elites were, at least for a few months, pursuing a high level of integration. As in Norway, the people did not follow the government's changed perceptions about the significance of the political obstacles to supranational integration. After the rejection of the EEA agreement, which could be interpreted as a "no" to EC membership, Swiss policy again aimed at a low level of integration by means of bilateral sectoral agreements.

As prospective members of the European Economic Area, Sweden, Norway, and Switzerland enjoyed most of the economic benefits of integration regarding the removal of trade barriers, but not necessarily secure market access and effective national policies. In other words, the main challenge was no longer gaining access to the internal market but attracting investments and obtaining some influence on relevant policy decisions. These economic factors were less compelling for Norway and Switzerland than for the crisis-ridden Swedish economy. Even though Norway was more export-dependent, its relative wealth and export structure made it less susceptible to dependency pressures.[203] Both Switzerland and Norway have developed niche economies (petroleum and financial services), would be net payers to the EC budget, and, because of high adjustment costs (e.g., agriculture), probably would enjoy the economic benefits of membership only in the long run.

The importance of political constraints was decreasing faster in Sweden than in the other two states, but in all three cases, the lack of voice—in spite of the great loss of operational sovereignty in the EEA— played an important role in the decisions to apply for full EC membership. The desire to have a say in future policy formation was a driving force behind the EFTA countries' membership bids. The elites but not yet the majority of the publics realized that in the new Europe and in a globalizing world economy, operational sovereignty alone did not allow for efficient policymaking. This finding is consistent with the claim that the more "political" an integration option, the more influence on preference formation is enjoyed by the political elites. As the effectiveness of national policies that diverge from Community policies became more and more questionable, they came to the conclusion that in a closely integrated and interdependent Europe, "a very important distinction . . . is that between *formal* sovereignty, in the sense of legal control over policy parameters, and the *actual* ability to control the goal variables. The latter depends, of course, on the former but also on the openness of the economy and the country's power to influence decision-making on a supranational level, in this case the policies of the EU."[204]

Conclusion

In 1991–1992, at a time when the Cold War was over and the European Communities were engaged in the construction of a political, economic, and monetary union, Sweden, Norway, and Switzerland finally applied for full membership. In all three countries, the elites realized that their increasing dependence on the EC and the toll of globalization weakened the effectiveness of their national policies, whereas unilateral adaptation to EC rules safeguarded their "independence" only in name. Hence, they shifted their strategy from defending sovereignty to acquiring more voice to achieve their domestic and international goals. However, the Swiss and Norwegian voters did not follow their governments' lead. Sweden joined the European Union in 1995, Norway remained an EFTA member in the European Economic Area, and Switzerland concluded bilateral agreements with the EU. For Norway and Switzerland, the Union had not yet become similar enough to their countries in terms of policies and institutions, and the need for domestic reforms was not strong enough to reconsider cherished national traditions and overcome fears of foreign influence. Material incentives were critical in the EU membership debate, yet images of the "self" and the European "other" mattered as well, in particular as long as the national economic and security policies remained successful. Norway and Switzerland had to cope with much stronger domestic constraints and problems of national identity than Sweden. The Swedes were more willing to view EU membership as a way of protecting identity, whereas the Norwegians and Swiss, with a history of resisting foreign rule and centralization of authority, stubbornly held on to the idea of separateness from the Union, which they perceived as a threat to their national identities.

Notes

1. See Jamar and Wallace, *EEC-EFTA: More Than Just Good Friends?;* Jacot-Guillarmod, ed., *L'avenir du libre-échange en Europe;* and Robinson and Findlater, *Creating a European Economic Space,* pp. 17–89.

2. Eide, "Europa-debatten i Arbeiderpartiet," p. 413; Michalski and Wallace, *The European Community,* p. 94; and Hveem, "The EEA and the Nordic Countries," p. 6.

3. Delors, "Statement on the Broad Lines of Commission Policy," pp. 17–18.

4. EFTA, "Declaration of the Meeting of the EFTA Heads of Government, Oslo, 14–15 March 1989," in *Twenty-Ninth Annual Report of the European Free Trade Association 1989* (Geneva: EFTA, 1990), p. 36.

5. See Wijkman, "Policy Options Facing EFTA"; and Wallace and Wessels, "Towards a New Partnership."

6. Schwok, "L'AELE face à la Communauté européenne," pp. 15–53.

7. See Gstöhl, "EFTA and the European Economic Area or the Politics of Frustration," pp. 337–349; Pedersen, *European Union and the EFTA Countries*, pp. 33–63; and Dupont, "Domestic Politics, Information and International Bargaining," pp. 208–301.

8. EFTA, "Communiqué of the Meeting of the EFTA Council at Ministerial Level, Geneva, 11–12 December 1989," in *Twenty-Ninth Annual Report of the European Free Trade Association 1989* (Geneva: EFTA, 1990), p. 51.

9. Delors, "Introduction of the Commission's Programme for 1990 by the President of the Commission of the European Communities," p. 9.

10. European Court of Justice, "Opinion of the Court, 14 December 1991 (Opinion 1/91)," *Official Journal of the European Communities*, no. C 110 (29 April 1992): 1–15; and European Court of Justice, "Opinion of the Court, 10 April 1992 (Opinion 1/92)," *Official Journal of the European Communities*, no. C 136 (26 May 1992): 1–12.

11. See Norberg, "The Agreement on a European Economic Area," pp. 1171–1198; Reinisch, "The European Economic Area," pp. 279–309; and O'Keeffe, "The Agreement on the European Economic Area," pp. 1–27.

12. See Reymond, "Institutions, Decision-Making Procedure and Settlement of Disputes in the European Economic Area," pp. 449–480; and Gittermann, *Das Beschlussfassungsverfahren des Abkommens über den Europäischen Wirtschaftsraum.*

13. Calls for transitional periods were put forward in areas such as higher standards for health, safety, and environmental protection; the foreign ownership of land and of Finnish forests; and the free movement of persons in Switzerland and Liechtenstein. See United Kingdom, House of Lords, Select Committee on the European Communities, *Relations Between the Community and EFTA*, 14th Report with Evidence, Session 1989–1990, London: HMSO, HL Paper 55-I and 55-II, 22 May 1990, pp. 13–15, 33.

14. Hösli, "Decision-Making in the EEA and EFTA States' Sovereignty," p. 490.

15. Andriessen, "EFTA Negotiations."

16. See Gstöhl, "Successfully Squaring the Circle," pp. 163–176.

17. Abrams et al., "The Impact of the European Community's Internal Market on the EFTA," p. 54; and Haaland and Norman, "Global Production Effects of European Integration," p. 81.

18. *Is Bigger Better?*, pp. 9–16, 27–32.

19. Andersson, Järvenpaa, and Leskelä, "EFTA Countries' Trade in Services," p. 37; and EFTA, "Effects of '1992' on the Services Sectors of the EFTA Countries."

20. Gardener and Teppett, "The Impact of 1992 on the Financial Services Sectors of EFTA Countries," p. 12.

21. *EFTA Trade 1992* (Geneva: EFTA, 1994), p. 45.

22. EFTA, "Effects of '1992' on the Services Sectors of the EFTA Countries," p. 15.

23. Sweden, Ministry for Foreign Affairs, *Sverige och den västeuropeiska*

integrationen: Sammanfattning av Konsekvensutredningarna, "Samhällsekonomi," Stockholm, 1994, p. 5.

24. Commission of the European Communities, "The Impact of the Internal Market by Industrial Sector: The Challenge for the Member States." *European Economy: Social Europe,* special edition (1990): 24; and EFTA, "Effects of '1992' on the Manufacturing Industries of the EFTA Countries," pp. 282–285.

25. Lundberg, "Konsekvenser för svensk industri av EGs inre marknad," pp. 60–61; and Flam and Horn, "Ekonomiska konsekvenser för Sverige av EGs inre marknad."

26. Sweden, Ministry for Foreign Affairs, *Sverige och den västeuropeiska integrationen: Ekonomiska konsekvenser av ett svenskt medlemskap i EG/EU,* Stockholm, 1993, pp. 32–37.

27. Sweden, Government, *Regeringens proposition 1991/92:170 om Europeiska Ekonomiska Samarbetsområdet (EES), Del 1, Bilaga 1,* Stockholm, 27 May 1992, pp. 27–28.

28. Leskelä, "EFTA Countries' Foreign Direct Investment," pp. 27–28.

29. Ohlsson, *Industrin inför EGs 90tal,* p. 187.

30. *The Economist,* "Sweden," p. 47.

31. Sweden, Government, *Regeringens proposition 1991/92:170 om Europeiska Ekonomiska Samarbetsområdet (EES), Del 1, Bilaga 1,* Stockholm, 27 May 1992, p. 46.

32. Stephens, "The Scandinavian Welfare States," pp. 43–51; Olsson, *Social Policy and Welfare State in Sweden,* pp. 349–381; and Ingebritsen, *The Nordic States and European Unity,* pp. 58–72.

33. Speech by Prime Minister Ingvar Carlsson at a conference of trade union chairs from the EFTA countries in Stockholm, 23 January 1990, in Sweden, Ministry for Foreign Affairs, *Documents on Swedish Foreign Policy 1990* (Stockholm: Royal Ministry for Foreign Affairs, 1991), pp. 25–26.

34. Sweden, Ministry for Foreign Affairs, *Sverige och den västeuropeiska integrationen: Sammanfattning av Konsekvensutredningarna,* "Social välfärd och jämställdhet," Stockholm, 1994, pp. 10–12.

35. Sweden, Parliament, Foreign Affairs Committee, *Utrikesutskottets betänkande 1990/91:UU8 Sverige och den västeuropeiska integrationen,* Stockholm, 22 November 1990, p. 59.

36. Prime Minister Carl Bildt, quoted in *International Herald Tribune,* "Scandinavians Defrost Anti-European Attitudes," p. 2.

37. *EFTA Trade 1992* (Geneva: EFTA, 1994), p. 45.

38. Norway, Ministry for Foreign Affairs, *Om samtykke til ratifikasjon av Avtale om Det europeiske økonomiske samarbeidsområde (EØS), undertegnet i Oporto 2. mai 1992,* St.prp.nr. 100 (1991–1992), Oslo, 15 May 1992, pp. 9, 363.

39. Commission of the European Communities, "The Impact of the Internal Market by Industrial Sector: The Challenge for the Member States," *European Economy: Social Europe,* special edition (1990), p. 24; and EFTA, "Effects of '1992' on the Manufacturing Industries of the EFTA Countries," pp. 282–285.

40. EFTA, "Effects of '1992' on the Manufacturing Industries of the EFTA Countries," p. 222; and Halvorsen, "European Integration and the Effects on Regional Development in Norway," p. 61.

41. Haaland, "Assessing the Effects of EFTA-EC Integration on EFTA Countries," pp. 394, 397.

42. Haaland, "Norway," p. 693.

43. Leskelä, "EFTA Countries' Foreign Direct Investment," pp. 27–28. In the

early 1990s, the largest Norwegian industries (such as Statoil or Norsk Hydro) still invested more in Norway than in the EC market. Ingebritsen, *Scandinavia in Europe*, pp. 158–160.

44. Norway, Ministry for Foreign Affairs, *Om samtykke til ratifikasjon av Avtale om Det europeiske økonomiske samarbeidsområde (EØS), undertegnet i Oporto 2. mai 1992*, St.prp.nr. 100 (1991–1992), Oslo, 15 May 1992, pp. 44–51, 357–410.

45. Ibid., pp. 16–18, 130–141.

46. "Effects of '1992' on the Services Sectors of the EFTA Countries," p. 15; and Juel, "Norway and Free Trade in Services."

47. Norway, Ministry for Foreign Affairs, *Norge ved et veivalg: Virkninger av ulike former for tilknytning til Det Europeiske Fellesskap*, Europautredngingen Hovedrapport, Oslo, 1992; and Norway, Ministry for Foreign Affairs, *Norsk økonomi og næringsliv ved ulike tilknytninsformer til EF*, Delrapport til Europautredningen, Oslo, 1992, pp. 48–49, 175–176.

48. Norway, Ministry for Foreign Affairs, *Om samtykke til ratifikasjon av Avtale om det europeiske økonomiske samarbeidsområde (EØS), undertegnet i Oporto 2. mai 1992*, St.prp.nr. 100 (1991–1992), Oslo, 15 May 1992, p. 55.

49. Norway, Ministry for Foreign Affairs, *Norsk velferd og europeisk samarbeid*, Delrapport til Europautredningen, Oslo, 1992.

50. Ingebritsen, *Scandinavia in Europe*, pp. 187–188.

51. *EFTA Trade 1992* (Geneva: EFTA, 1994), p. 45.

52. Except for medic-surgical equipment, for which the NTBs were rated high. Commission of the European Communities, "The Impact of the Internal Market by Industrial Sector: The Challenge for the Member States," *European Economy: Social Europe*, special edition (1990), p. 24; and EFTA, "Effects of '1992' on the Manufacturing Industries of the EFTA Countries," pp. 282–285.

53. EFTA, "Effects of '1992' on the Manufacturing Industries of the EFTA Countries," p. 308.

54. Hauser and Bradke, *EWR-Vertrag, EG-Beitritt, Alleingang*, pp. 78–81.

55. Switzerland, Federal Council, *Botschaft des Bundesrates vom 18. Mai 1992 über die Genehmigung des Abkommens über den Europäischen Wirtschaftsraum*, Bern, 18 May 1992, pp. 68–69.

56. Leskelä, "EFTA Countries' Foreign Direct Investment," *EFTA Trade 1990* (Geneva: EFTA, 1991), pp. 27–28.

57. EFTA, "Effects of '1992' on the Services Sectors of the EFTA Countries," p. 15; and Gardener and Teppett, "The Impact of 1992 on the Financial Services Sectors of EFTA Countries," p. 12.

58. Lombardi, "Verwirklichung des EWR-Abkommens durch Bund und Kantone," pp. 721–740.

59. Statement by Ambassador Jakob Kellenberger on 3 November 1989, reprinted in Jacot-Guillarmod, ed., *L'avenir du libre-échange en Europe*, p. 502 (emphasis omitted).

60. Switzerland, Federal Council, *Informationsbericht des Bundesrates über die Stellung der Schweiz im europäischen Integrationsprozess vom 26. November 1990*, Bern, 26 November 1990, p. 59.

61. Kriesi et al., *Analyse de la votation fédérale du 6 décembre 1992*, p. 33.

62. Langejürgen, *Die Eidgenossenschaft zwischen Rütli und EWR*, p. 98; and *Neue Zürcher Zeitung*, "Politischer Durchbruch ohne die Schweiz."

63. Senti, "Switzerland," p. 226.

64. Switzerland, Federal Council, *Botschaft des Bundesrates vom 18. Mai*

1992 über die Genehmigung des Abkommens über den Europäischen Wirtschaftsraum, p. 67; and Hauser and Bradke, *EWR-Vertrag, EG-Beitritt, Alleingang*, Bern, 18 May 1992, pp. 25–43, 238.

65. Statement by Federal Councilor Arnold Koller in Switzerland, Parliament, "EWR-Abkommen," *Amtliches Bulletin der Bundesversammlung: Ständerat*, Bern, 22–24 September 1992, p. 824.

66. Switzerland, Federal Council, *Informationsbericht des Bundesrates über die Stellung der Schweiz im europäischen Integrationsprozess vom 26. November 1990*, Bern, 26 November 1990, p. 62.

67. Sweden, Parliament, Foreign Affairs Committee, *Utrikesutskottets betänkande 1990/91:UU8 Sverige och den västeuropeiska integrationen*, Stockholm, 22 November 1990, pp. 17, 24–26.

68. Speech by Foreign Minister Sten Andersson in Oslo on 12 February 1991, in Sweden, Ministry for Foreign Affairs, *Documents on Swedish Foreign Policy 1991* (Stockholm: Royal Ministry for Foreign Affairs, 1992), p. 49; and Sweden, Ministry for Foreign Affairs, *Sweden, the EC and Security Policy: Developments in Europe. Statement to the Riksdag by the Prime Minister on 14 June 1991, on Sweden's Application for Membership of the European Community*, Stockholm, 14 June 1991, p. 12.

69. Sweden, Government, *Regeringens proposition 1991/92:170 om Europeiska Ekonomiska Samarbetsområdet (EES), Del 1, Bilaga 1*, Stockholm, 27 May 1992, p. 23.

70. See Sweden, Parliament, "Europeiska ekonomiska samarbetsområdet," *Riksdagens Protokoll 1992/93*, no. 26 (Stockholm, 18 November 1992): 1–31. After the 1991 elections, the Green Party, which opposed the EEA agreement, had no seats in parliament anymore, and a new populist party, the Discontent Party, was represented for the first time.

71. Minister for European Affairs Ulf Dinkelspiel, in Sweden, Parliament, "Europeiska ekonomiska samarbetsområdet," *Riksdagens Protokoll 1992/93*, no. 26 (Stockholm, 18 November 1992): 34.

72. Sweden, Government, *Regeringens proposition 1991/92:170 om Europeiska Ekonomiska Samarbetsområdet (EES), Del 1, Bilaga 1*, Stockholm, 27 May 1992, pp. 2–4.

73. Ibid., pp. 43–44.

74. Hösli, "Decision-Making in the EEA and EFTA States' Sovereignty," p. 488.

75. Norway, Parliament, *Innstilling fra finanskomitéen om norsk tilpasning til EFs indre marked*, St.meld.nr. 1, kap. 3, Innst.S.nr. 38 (1989–1990), Oslo, 28 November 1989, pp. 11–12.

76. Norway, Ministry for Foreign Affairs, *Om samtykke til ratifikasjon av Avtale om det europeiske økonomiske samarbeidsområde (EØS), undertegnet i Oporto 2. mai 1992*, St.prp.nr. 100 (1991–1992), Oslo, 15 May 1992, pp. 411–412.

77. Norway, Parliament, "Samtykke til ratifikasjon av Avtale om Det europeiske økonomiske samarbeidsområdet (EØS)," *Forhandlinger i Stortinget*, St.tid. nos. 12–22 (Oslo, 15–16 October 1992): 170–179.

78. Norway, Ministry for Foreign Affairs, *Om samtykke til ratifikasjon av Avtale om Det europeiske økonomiske samarbeidsområde (EØS), undertegnet i Oporto 2. mai 1992*, St.prp.nr. 100 (1991–1992), Oslo, 15 May 1992, pp. 42–43, 335–347.

79. See Annex 3 to Norway, Ministry for Foreign Affairs, *Om samtykke til ratifikasjon av Avtale om Det europeiske økonomiske samarbeidsområde (EØS)*,

undertegnet i Oporto 2. mai 1992, St.prp.nr. 100 (1991–1992), Oslo, 15 May 1992, p. 427–482.

80. Ingebritsen, *Scandinavia in Europe*, pp. 158–178.

81. Norway, Ministry for Foreign Affairs, *Europeisk samarbeid—styring og demokrati*, Delrapport til Europautredningen, Oslo, 1992, pp. 55–56.

82. Switzerland, Federal Council, *Informationsbericht des Bundesrates über die Stellung der Schweiz im europäischen Integrationsprozess vom 26. November 1990*, Bern, 26 November 1990, p. 16.

83. Ibid., pp. 66–67.

84. Veyrassat, "L'économie suisse face à 1992," pp. 181–183.

85. Langejürgen, *Die Eidgenossenschaft zwischen Rütli und EWR*, pp. 131–144, 180–184.

86. Steppacher, *Schritte zur Europäisierung der Schweiz*, pp. 231–232.

87. Ibid., pp. 242–246.

88. Ibid., pp. 245, 250–255; and Aeschbach, "Le marché européen vu par les syndicats," pp. 191–193.

89. Langejürgen, *Die Eidgenossenschaft zwischen Rütli und EWR*, pp. 105–130, 169–179.

90. Ibid., pp. 77–104, 151–160.

91. Switzerland, Federal Council, *Botschaft des Bundesrates vom 18. Mai 1992 über die Genehmigung des Abkommens über den Europäischen Wirtschaftsraum*, Bern, 18 May 1992, p. 49.

92. Ibid., p. 59.

93. Switzerland, Parliament, "EWR-Abkommen," *Amtliches Bulletin der Bundesversammlung: Nationalrat*, Bern, 24–26 August 1992, pp. 1290–1397; and Switzerland, Parliament, "EWR-Abkommen," *Amtliches Bulletin der Bundesversammlung: Ständerat*, Bern 22–24 September 1992, pp. 781–838.

94. Sciarini and Listhaug, "Single Cases or a Unique Pair?," pp. 418–419; and Huth-Spiess, *Europäisierung oder "Entschweizerung"?*, chap. 3; and Goetschel, *Zwischen Effizienz und Akzeptanz*.

95. Switzerland, Federal Councilor Arnold Koller in Parliament, "EWR-Abkommen," *Amtliches Bulletin der Bundesversammlung: Nationalrat*, Bern, 24–26 August 1992, pp. 1378–1379.

96. Switzerland, Federal Council, *Informationsbericht des Bundesrates über die Stellung der Schweiz im europäischen Integrationsprozess vom 26. November 1990*, Bern, 26 November 1990, p. 68.

97. Switzerland, Federal Council, *Botschaft des Bundesrates vom 18. Mai 1992 über die Genehmigung des Abkommens über den Europäischen Wirtschaftsraum*, Bern, 18 May 1992, pp. 49–51.

98. Schwok, "Switzerland," p. 24.

99. Leitner, "Der Weg nach Brüssel," pp. 87–108; and Schneider, *Alleingang nach Brüssel*.

100. Michalski and Wallace, *The European Community*, pp. 67–78.

101. See Jorna, "The Accession Negotiations with Austria, Sweden, Finland and Norway"; and Granell, "The European Union's Enlargement Negotiations with Austria, Finland, Norway and Sweden."

102. See Kaiser et al., "Die EU-Volksabstimmungen in Österreich, Finnland, Schweden und Norwegen"; and Bjørklund, "The Three Nordic 1994 Referenda Concerning Membership in the EU."

103. OECD, *Monthly Statistics of Foreign Trade*, March 1995 (Paris: OECD, 1995), p. 89.

104. Baldwin and Flam, "Enlargement of the European Union," pp. 3–15.

105. See UNCTAD, *Implications of the Dynamism of Large Economic Spaces: Major New Developments in Large Economic Spaces and Regional Integration Processes and Their Implications*, Statistical Annex (Geneva: UNCTAD), TD/B/SEM.1/2/Add.1, 28 November 1995, pp. 13–22; and Sveriges Industriförbundet, "EGs handelspolitik och svensk industri," *Industriförbundets serie om Sverige och EG* no. 9 (Stockholm: Industrilitteratur, 1993), pp. 8–16.

106. Baldwin and Flam, "Enlargement of the European Union," pp. 3–15; and Flam, "From EEA to EU," pp. 457–466.

107. Sweden, Ministry for Foreign Affairs, *Sverige och den västeuropeiska integrationen: Ekonomiska konsekvenser av ett svenskt medlemskap i EG/EU, Mars 1993*, Stockholm, 1993, pp. 45–137; and Wetterberg, *Vad kostar det att stå utanför?*, pp. 10–11.

108. See Sweden, Ministry for Foreign Affairs, *Sweden and Europe, Committee of Enquiry: Consequences of the EU for Sweden—the Economy. Summary and Conclusions* (Stockholm: Statens offentliga utredningar SOU, no. 6, 1994); Sweden, Ministry for Foreign Affairs, *Sveriges medlemskap i den Europeiska Unionen* (Stockholm: Departementsserien, no. 48, Ds 1994); and Sweden, Ministry for Foreign Affairs, *Sverige och den västeuropeiska integrationen: Inför ett svenskt EG/EU-medlemskap, Hösten 1993*, Stockholm, 1993.

109. Sweden, Ministry for Foreign Affairs, *Sverige och den västeuropeiska integrationen: Sammanfattning av Konsekvensutredningarna*, "Slutsatser," Stockholm, 1994, p. 3.

110. Falk, Lauronen, and Lindell, *Direct Investment in 1998*, pp. 42–43.

111. Sweden, Sveriges Industriförbundet, *Världen, EU och Sverige* (Stockholm: Industrilitteratur, 1994), p. 97.

112. Miles, "The European Union and the Nordic Countries," p. 324; and Lachman et al., "Challenges to the Swedish Welfare State," pp. 3–30.

113. Sweden, Ministry for Foreign Affairs, *Sverige och den västeuropeiska integrationen: Sammanfattning av Konsekvensutredningarna*, "Samhällsekonomi," Stockholm, 1994, pp. 5–6.

114. Lindbeck et al., *Turning Sweden Around*, p. 17.

115. Ibid., p. 86.

116. Sweden, Government, *Regeringens proposition 1994/95:19 Del 1 om Sveriges medlemskap i den Europeiska unionen*, Stockholm, 11 August 1994, p. 47.

117. This assessment is confirmed by an analysis of voting behavior in the membership referendum. Oskarson and Ringdal, "The Arguments," pp. 152–153.

118. Miles, "The European Union and the Nordic Countries," p. 33.

119. Speech by Minister of Trade Anita Gradin in the parliamentary debate on Europe on 11 December 1990, in Sweden, Ministry for Foreign Affairs, *Documents on Swedish Foreign Policy 1990* (Stockholm: Royal Ministry for Foreign Affairs, 1991), pp. 295–296; and Sweden, Ministry for Foreign Affairs, *Sverige och den västeuropeiska integrationen: Sammanfattning av Konsekvensutredningarna*, "Social välfärd och jämställdhet," Stockholm, 1994, p. 17.

120. See de Geer, *The Rise and Fall of the Swedish Model*.

121. Ringdal and Valen, "Structural Divisions in the EU Referendums," pp. 188–189.

122. Bieler, *Globalisation and Enlargement of the European Union*, in particular pp. 70–87, 102–121. His analysis follows a neo-Gramscian perspective focusing on (transnational) social forces that are engendered by the production process.

123. Sweden, Government, *Regeringens skrivelse 1990/91:50 om åtgärder för*

att stabilisera ekonomin och begränsa tillväxten av de offentliga utgifterna, Stockholm, 26 October 1990, p. 5.

124. Sweden, Parliament, Foreign Affairs Committee, *Utrikesutskottets betänkande 1990/91:UU8 Sverige och den västeuropeiska integrationen,* Stockholm, 22 November 1990, pp. 20–23.

125. Speech by Prime Minister Carl Bildt in Bonn on 13 November 1991, in Sweden, Ministry for Foreign Affairs, *Documents on Swedish Foreign Policy 1991* (Stockholm: Royal Ministry for Foreign Affairs, 1992), p. 96.

126. Sweden, Parliament, Foreign Affairs Committee, *Utrikesutskottets betänkande 1991/92:UU17 Säkerhet och nedrustning,* Stockholm, 28 April 1992, p. 17; and Sweden, Parliament, Foreign Affairs Committee, *Utrikesutskottets betänkande 1991/92:UU24 Sverige och EG,* Stockholm, 28 April 1992.

127. Carlsnaes, "Sweden Facing the New Europe," p. 85.

128. Commission of the European Communities, "Sweden's Application for Membership: Commission Opinion, 31 July 1992," *Bulletin of the European Communities,* Supplement, no. 5 (1992): 22–23.

129. Sweden, Ministry for Foreign Affairs, *Sverige och den västeuropeiska integrationen: Sammanfattning av Konsekvensutredningarna,* "Utrikes- och säkerhetspolitik," Stockholm, 1994, pp. 5–6.

130. Sweden, Ministry for Foreign Affairs, *Historiskt vägval: Följderna för Sverige i utrikes- och säkerhetspolitiskt hänseende av att bli, respektive inte bli medlem i Europeiska Unionen* (Stockholm: Statens offentliga utredningar SOU, no. 8 Betänkande, 1994), p. 36.

131. Baldwin and Flam, "Enlargement of the European Union," pp. 3–15; and Flam, "From EEA to EU," pp. 457–466.

132. Bowitz et al., *Norsk medlemskap i EU,* p. 9.

133. Ibid., pp. 15–17, 35–39.

134. Norway, Ministry for Foreign Affairs, *Norge ved et veivalg: Virkninger av ulike former for tilknytning til det europeiske fellesskap,* Europautredngingen Hovedrapport, Oslo, 1992, p. 124.

135. Ibid., p. 141.

136. Norway, Ministry for Foreign Affairs, *Om medlemskap i Den europeiske union,* St.meld. nr. 40 (1993–1994), Oslo, 3 June 1994, chap. 7; and Dølvik et al., *Norsk Økonomi og europeisk integrasjon.*

137. Fossli, "Survey Norway"; and Ingebritsen, *The Nordic States and European Unity,* p. 139.

138. *Financial Times,* "Oslo Fears Being Europe's Odd Man Out."

139. Norway, Ministry for Foreign Affairs, *Norsk velferd og europeisk samarbeid,* Delrapport til Europautredningen, Oslo, 1992, p. 13.

140. Norway, Ministry for Foreign Affairs, *Om medlemskap i den europeiske union,* St.meld. nr. 40 (1993–1994), Oslo, 3 June 1994, p. 70.

141. Norway, Ministry of Trade and Shipping, "Handelsminister Grete Knudsen: EU-medlemskap den beste garanti for fortsatt utvikling av våre velferdsordninger," *Pressemelding,* no. 109/1993, Oslo, 3 June 1993.

142. Norway, Ministry for Foreign Affairs, *Om medlemskap i Den europeiske union,* St.meld. nr. 40 (1993–1994), Oslo, 3 June 1994, pp. 61–64, 336–350.

143. Jenssen, Listhaug, and Pettersen, "Betydningen av gamle og nye skiller."

144. Bjørklund, "The Three Nordic 1994 Referenda Concerning Membership in the EU," p. 31; and Bjørklund, "Sentrum mot periferi," pp. 51–52.

145. Ringdal, "Velgernes argumenter," pp. 45–64; and Oskarson and Ringdal, "The Arguments," pp. 152–157.

146. Bjørklund, "The Three Nordic 1994 Referenda Concerning Membership in the EU," p. 30.

147. Ludlow, "Public Opinion in the Nordic Candidate Countries," p. 17.

148. Switzerland, Federal Council, *Bericht des Bundesrates vom 18. Mai 1992 über einen Beitritt der Schweiz zur Europäischen Gemeinschaft*, Bern, 18 May 1992, pp. 162–168.

149. Ibid., p. 115.

150. Ibid., pp. 23–27, 146–160, 176.

151. Schindler, "Auswirkungen der EG auf die schweizerische Staatsstruktur," p. 8.

152. *Neue Zürcher Zeitung*, "Die Einbusse an direkter Demokratie."

153. Widmer and Buri, "Brüssel oder Bern," pp. 371–386; and Zbinden, "Die Unterschiede in der Perzeption der europäischen Integration zwischen der Deutschschweiz und der Romandie," pp. 42–46.

154. Langejürgen, *Die Eidgenossenschaft zwischen Rütli und EWR*, p. 86.

155. Switzerland, Federal Council, *Bericht des Bundesrates vom 18. Mai 1992 über einen Beitritt der Schweiz zur Europäischen Gemeinschaft*, Bern, 18 May 1992, pp. 114–123.

156. "Bericht zur Neutralität," Annex to Switzerland, Federal Council, *Bericht des Bundesrates vom 29. November 1993 über die Aussenpolitik der Schweiz in den 90er Jahren*, Bern, 29 November 1993, pp. 82–88.

157 Luif, *On the Road to Brussels*, pp. 207–210; and Kite, "Scandinavia Faces EU," pp. 176–180.

158. "La demande d'adhésion de la Suède," pp. 503–504, 536–539.

159. Bieler, "Globalization, Swedish Trade Unions and European Integration."

160. Michalski and Wallace, *The European Community*, p. 104.

161. Sweden, Government, *Regeringens skrivelse 1990/91:50 om åtgärder för att stabilisera ekonomin och begränsa tillväxten av de offentliga utgifterna* (Stockholm: Finansdepartement, 26 October 1990), p. 5.

162. Foreign Minister Sten Andersson in Sweden, Parliament, "Allmänpolitisk debatt: Europafrågor," *Riksdagens Protokoll 1990/91*, no. 6 (Stockholm, 10 October 1990): 24–25, 32.

163. Sweden, Parliament, Foreign Affairs Committee, *Utrikesutskottets betänkande 1990/91:UU8 Sverige och den västeuropeiska integrationen*, Stockholm, 22 November 1990, p. 22.

164. Speech by Foreign Minister Sten Andersson in Oslo on 12 February 1991, in Sweden, Ministry for Foreign Affairs, *Documents on Swedish Foreign Policy 1991* (Stockholm: Royal Ministry for Foreign Affairs, 1992), p. 48; and Minister of Trade Anita Gradin in the parliamentary debate on 11 December 1990, in Sweden, Ministry for Foreign Affairs, *Documents on Swedish Foreign Policy 1990* (Stockholm: Royal Ministry for Foreign Affairs, 1991), p. 293.

165. Sweden, Parliament, "Information från regeringen om EG-ansökan," *Riksdagens Protokoll 1990/91*, no. 132 (14 June 1991): 8–16.

166. Minister of European Affairs and Foreign Trade Ulf Dinkelspiel, in Sweden, Ministry for Foreign Affairs, *Documents on Swedish Foreign Policy 1993* (Stockholm: Royal Ministry for Foreign Affairs, 1994), pp. 30–31.

167. Ibid., p. 31; and Sweden, Ministry for Foreign Affairs, *Sverige och den västeuropeiska integrationen: Inför ett svenskt EG/EU-medlemskap, Hösten 1993*, Stockholm, 1993, pp. 14–21.

168. Huldt, "Sweden and European Community-Building 1945–92," pp. 126–127; and Kite, "Scandinavia Faces EU," pp. 181–190.

169. Sweden, Ministry for Foreign Affairs, *Sveriges medlemskap i den europeiska unionen* (Stockholm: Departementsserien, no. 48, Ds 1994); and Sweden, Government, *Regeringens proposition 1994/95:19 Del 1 om Sveriges medlemskap i den Europeiska Unionen,* Stockholm, 11 August 1994, Parts 2 and 3.

170. Statement by the Federation of Swedish Industries with regard to the government's bill on EU membership, reprinted in Sweden, Ministry for Foreign Affairs, *Sveriges medlemskap i den Europeiska Unionen: Remissyttranden över departementspromemoriam (Ds 1994:48)* (Stockholm: Departementsserien, no. 104, Ds 1994).

171. Sweden, Government, *Regeringens proposition 1994/95:19 Del 1 om Sveriges medlemskap i den europeiska unionen,* Stockholm, 11 August 1994.

172. Parliament, "Remissdebatt," *Riksdagens Protokoll 1994/95,* no. 7 (Stockholm, 11 October 1994): 19–100; and Sweden, Parliament, "Allmänpolitisk debatt: EU-frågan," *Riksdagens Protokoll 1994/95,* no. 11 (Stockholm, 19 October 1994): 1–118. The Green Party had regained parliamentary representation in the 1994 elections.

173. Widfeldt, "Sweden and the European Union," pp. 108, 110.

174. Miles, *Sweden and European Integration,* pp. 248–255.

175. Government, *Regeringens proposition 1994/95:19 Del 1 om Sveriges medlemskap i den Europeiska unionen,* Stockholm, 11 August 1994, p. 31.

176. Sweden, Ministry for Foreign Affairs, *Om Sveriges inflytande i den europeiska unionen: Bilaga 5 till EG-konsekvensutredningen, Samhällsekonomi* (Stockholm: Fritzes, 1993), p. 18.

177. Sweden, Ministry for Foreign Affairs, *Sverige och den västeuropeiska integrationen: Sammanfattning av Konsekvensutredningarna,* "Suveränität och demokrati," Stockholm, 1994, pp. 2–3.

178. Sweden, Parliament, Foreign Affairs Committee, *Utrikesutskottets betänkande 1994/95:UU5 Sveriges medlemskap i Europeiska unionen,* Stockholm, 1 December 1994, p. 29.

179. Sweden, Ministry for Foreign Affairs, *Om Sveriges inflytande i den europeiska unionen: Bilaga 5 till EG-konsekvensutredningen, Samhällsekonomi* (Stockholm: Fritzes, 1993), pp. 11–12, 26.

180. Norway, Prime Minister Gro Harlem Brundtland, "Redegjørelse av statsministeren om Regjeringens vurderinger og begrunnelse for at Norge bør søke medlemskap i EF," *Forhandlinger i Stortinget,* St.tid. no. 74, Oslo, 16 November 1992, p. 1127.

181. "Handelsminister Bjørn Tore Godals innlegg i forbindelse med åpeningen av Norges medlemskapsforhandlinger med EF i Luxembourg, 5. april 1993," Annex 3 to Norway, Ministry for Foreign Affairs, *Om medlemskap i Den europeiske union,* St.meld. nr. 40 (1993–1994), Oslo, 3 June 1994, pp. 432–436.

182. See Norway, Ministry for Foreign Affairs, "The Norwegian Political Parties' Attitude to EU," *Norway Information,* Oslo, November 1994; and Kite, "Scandinavia Faces EU," pp. 165–176.

183. Haaland Matláry, "'And Never the Twain Shall Meet?'" pp. 46–47.

184. Jenssen, "Ouverturen," pp. 18–19. See Archer and Sogner, *Norway, European Integration and Atlantic Security,* pp. 69–74.

185. Ringdal, "Velgernes argumenter," pp. 45–64.

186. See the press releases of the different ministries, Norway, Ministry of Foreign Affairs, "Norge-EU: Om forhandlingsresultatet," *Pressehefte,* Oslo, 16 March 1994; see also Archer and Sogner, *Norway, European Integration and Atlantic Security,* pp. 57–66.

187. Norway, Ministry for Foreign Affairs, *Om medlemskap i Den europeiske union*, St.meld. nr. 40 (1993–1994), Oslo, 3 June 1994, pp. 77, 83.

188. Annex 5 to Norway, Ministry for Foreign Affairs, *Om medlemskap i den europeiske union*, St.meld. nr. 40 (1993–1994), Oslo, 3 June 1994, pp. 444–476.

189. Archer and Sogner, *Norway, European Integration and Atlantic Security*, p. 71.

190. Statistics Norway, *Folkeavstemningen 1994 om norsk medlemskap i EU: The 1994 Referendum on Norwegian Membership of the EU*, Oslo: Statistisk sentralbyrå, 1995, p. 19.

191. Kite, "Scandinavia Faces EU," pp. 158–164.

192. Jenssen, "Etterspill," pp. 187–203.

193. Eide, "Adjustment Strategy of a Non-Member," pp. 69–104.

194. Archer and Sogner, *Norway, European Integration and Atlantic Security*, pp. 137–158.

195. Norway, Minister of Trade and Shipping Grete Knudsen, *Handelsministerens redegjørelse i Stortinget 20. april 1994 om resultatet av EU-forhandlingene*, Oslo, 20 April 1994, pp. 20–21; and Norway, Prime Minister Gro Harlem Brundtland, "Redegjørelse av statsministeren om Regjeringens vurderinger og begrunnelse for at Norge bør søke medlemskap i EF," *Forhandlinger i Stortinget*, St.tid. no. 74, Oslo, 16 November 1992, p. 1126.

196. Norway, Ministry for Foreign Affairs, *Om medlemskap i den europeiske union*, St.meld. nr. 40 (1993–1994), Oslo, 3 June 1994, pp. 65, 351.

197. Steppacher, *Schritte zur Europäisierung der Schweiz*, pp. 254–255.

198. Switzerland, Federal Council, *Bericht des Bundesrates vom 18. Mai 1992 über einen Beitritt der Schweiz zur Europäischen Gemeinschaft*, Bern, 18 May 1992, pp. 11–20.

199. Ibid., p. 176.

200. Switzerland, Federal Council, *Botschaft des Bundesrates vom 24. Februar 1993 über das Folgeprogramm nach der Ablehnung des EWR-Abkommens*, Bern, 24 February 1993.

201. See *Accords bilatéraux Suisse-UE*.

202. Switzerland, Federal Council, *Botschaft vom 23. Juni 1999 zur Genehmigung der sektoriellen Abkommen zwischen der Schweiz und der EG*, Bern, 23 June 1999, pp. 4–5.

203. Moses and Jenssen, "Nordic Accession," p. 240.

204. Lundberg, "Finland," p. 716.

8

Conclusion:
Some Implications

The major challenges facing the Union are to make it fit for enlargement; to accommodate the different views on the appropriate scope and depth of European integration; and to close the democratic deficit to revive public support for the Union. The principle task of reform should be to accommodate the different demands of heterogeneous European interests by introducing more flexibility without risking the gains achieved through previous integration efforts.
—Centre for Economic Policy Research, *Flexible Integration,* p. 9

A Solution to the Puzzle

Sweden, Norway, and Switzerland are small, export-dependent countries that for a long time have been able but not willing to join the European Communities (EC). In response to the need for market access, they have participated in European integration, but until the early 1990s they consistently aimed at a lower level than full membership in the European Communities. I set out to explain in this book why they have been so reluctant to participate in supranational integration. I argued that economic interests alone do not sufficiently explain integration preferences but rather coexist with, and are often dominated by, political constraints. Improved access to export markets may lose its temptation when domestic institutions, societal cleavages, foreign policy traditions, and experiences of foreign rule that touch on feelings of national identity come into play. The importance attached to political factors has indeed varied over time, as has the intensity of economic interests. Variation has also been found in the elites' preferences regarding the mixture of operational sovereignty and international voice opportunities entailed in different integration options.

The results of the case studies in Chapters 3 to 7 are condensed in two

Table 8.1   Findings for the Targeted Level of Integration

	Full Integration	Global Approach	Sectoral Integration
Supranational Institutions	*High* Full EC membership	*High*	*Medium*
Quasi-supranational Institutions	*High*	*Medium* Extended association with EC European Economic Area	*Medium*
Intergovernmental Institutions	*Medium*	*Medium* OEEC free trade area Association with EC	*Low* EFTA Bilateral agreements with EC

tables. Table 8.1 shows (in *italics*) the levels of integration at which the three countries aimed over the past fifty years. Their scope of integration and degree of institutionalization have ranged from low to high.

Table 8.2 summarizes the findings for the explanatory variables, that is, for the economic incentives for Sweden (S), Norway (N), and Switzerland (CH) to participate in an integration scheme and the political impediments to full EC membership. In order to facilitate a comparison with the findings for the dependent variable in Table 8.1, the level of integration as expected by the hypothesis is indicated in *italics*.

As a comparison of the two tables shows, the argument has to a very high degree been confirmed. The few cases that have not been straightforward can be accounted for. For example, Swiss policy toward the European Coal and Steel Community (ECSC) turned out to be slightly more active than expected due to the fact that the indicators used in this study do not include import dependence. Switzerland was not interested in the ECSC as an export market but as a secure supplier of coal and steel. Moreover, the policies toward the newly launched European Economic Community taken as isolated cases, might have looked like no action rather than aiming at limited integration. The founding of the EEC in 1958 overlapped with the initiative for a free trade area encompassing the Organization for European Economic Cooperation (OEEC), and the breakdown of the latter led to the European Free Trade Association (EFTA) (see Chapter 3 for a discussion of all four cases). Switzerland, Sweden, and Norway were among the most eager supporters of both a wide and a narrow free trade area in Western Europe. From this broader perspective, the policies with regard to the three projects are well in line with the hypothesis.

A similar overlap of options occurred in the early 1990s regarding the

Table 8.2   Findings for the Incentives and Impediments to Integration

	High economic incentives	Medium economic incentives	Low economic incentives
Low political impediments	*High* EC application, 1961 (N) EC application, 1967 (N) EC "application," 1970 (N) EC applications, 1991–1992 (S, N, CH)	*Medium*	*Medium/Low*

Medium political impediments	*Medium*
	 "Open" application (S until
	   March 1971)
	 European Economic Area,
	   1989 (S, N, CH)
		Medium/Low
		 Association request,
		   1961 (S)
		 "Open" application,
		   1967 (S)
			Low

High political impediments	*Medium/Low*
	 EFTA, 1960 (S, N)
	 OEEC free trade area,
	   1956–1958 (S, N, CH)
	 Association request,
	   1961 (CH)
	 Free trade agreements,
	   1972–1973 (S, N, CH)
	 Luxembourg process,
	   1984 (S, N, CH)
	 Bilateral agreements,
	   1999 (CH)
		Low
		 ECSC, 1950 (S)
		 EEC, 1958 (S, N, CH)
		 EFTA, 1960 (CH)
			None/Low
			 ECSC, 1950 (N, CH)

three countries' step from the European Economic Area (EEA) to an application for full membership in the European Communities (see Chapter 7). The nature of the European Economic Area generated new concerns besides export dependence. Once equal treatment in the internal market was achieved through the EEA, other factors such as attracting investments, the security of market access, and gaining full access to the EC's decisionmaking process became more compelling. The reasoning on sovereignty and voice clearly points in such a direction. The cases of the 1990s trace in an impressive way how the elites but not necessarily the masses realized that in the era of globalization and in a highly integrated Europe, operational sovereignty alone could not guarantee the accomplishment of national goals anymore.

My primary objective in the book has been to analyze each country's path-dependent policy over time. The hypothesis is geared to intracountry analyses rather than cross-country comparisons. Table 8.2 shows the development of national integration policies over time. For Sweden, the economic incentives to integrate with the European Communities have never been rated as weak. From a medium strength in the 1950s and 1960s, they increased to a high level in the 1990s, whereas the importance of the political impediments ran through all three stages of the scale. Depending, inter alia, on the EC's development, the constraints were considered strong in the 1950s, weaker in the 1960s, and significant again in the 1970s, before they began to decline in the late 1980s as the external environment changed. For Norway, the economic stimuli continuously intensified over time, but perceptions of the political obstacles were marked by great variation. Norway applied for EC membership twice in the 1960s following the British lead and again in 1992 in the wake of the Swedish and Finnish applications. The negative referenda in 1972 and 1994, however, proved the elites' viewpoints wrong. For Switzerland, the economic incentives to integrate have also steadily increased over time. At the same time, the political constraints remained strong until the early 1990s.

It seems that Norway and Switzerland had to cope with much stronger domestic constraints and more issues of national identity than did Sweden. Swedish society does not have to deal with domestic cleavages or wounds left by a history of foreign rule. External events such as the end of the East-West bloc confrontation and an increasingly interdependent economy played a greater role. Once the Swedish model and foreign policy had lost their exceptionalism, membership in the European Union (EU) no longer threatened any cherished national institutions and traditions. Surprisingly, at least for the Scandinavian countries, the cases revealed more oscillation in the importance attributed to political impediments than in the economic incentives to integrate. That is, a steady increase in the material motives was not accompanied by a steady decrease in the weight of ideational factors.

Sufficient observations have been generated to substantiate the claim that the less important market access is and the stronger the domestic and geohistorical constraints are, the lower the level of integration aimed at in terms of the scope of integration and the degree of institutionalization. The three small EFTA countries have, in spite of good economic reasons to integrate, for a long time been reluctant to join the European Union because they suffered high political impediments to do so. Moreover, they tended to value the maintenance of operational sovereignty more than the acquisition of international voice opportunities.

Policy Implications

The varying willingness of states to further integrate is likely to become more salient as future enlargements multiply the member states' heterogeneity and integration deepens into more sensitive issue areas. Therefore, the question arises, what could the Swiss and Norwegian governments or other candidate countries do to realize their declared goal of EU membership? I think that an approach to mitigate reluctance should comprise both certain "materialist" policies and aspects of "identity politics." Norway and Switzerland should try to reduce resistance from protected, domestically oriented sectors of their economies by implementing necessary reforms such as the liberalization measures required in the framework of the World Trade Organization. For example, both of them need to adapt their agricultural policies, and Norway needs to diversify its economy, which is heavily dependent on oil resources that will not last forever.

To convince voters, the political elites must not only confront well-organized economic interest groups but introduce new ideas into the national discourse. EU membership can only be sold to Norwegian and Swiss voters as a reinforcement of national identity. The proponents must fight the perception that they are less Norwegian or Swiss, and they have to demonstrate that European identity does not replace but complements and enriches national identity. After all, Article 6(3) of the Treaty on European Union demands that "the Union shall respect the national identities of its Member States." In 1992 the Swedish foreign minister pointed out that politicians must take the lead in explaining to their citizens why "modern Europeans must be able to handle a triple identity—regional, national and European" and must "show the public that these three identities are not only compatible but also desirable."[1] For example, the government argued that the future of the Swedish welfare state was better guaranteed inside the European Union.

However, skepticism does not disappear with accession to the European Union, as the cases of Britain and Denmark show. Membership is likely to exert a "socialization effect"—socialization being the process by which actors internalize norms that influence how they perceive themselves and their interests—since "the experience of integration and the presence of European institutions affect the ways state preferences and strategies are defined."[2] Certain political domestic or geohistorical constraints that have grown over centuries are, however, hard to "socialize away." Therefore, I doubt Christine Ingebritsen's statement that "Sweden is as committed to pan-Europeanism as Finland is."[3] The brief membership periods of Sweden and Finland have indeed revealed very different attitudes, for instance, in relation to the single currency. The Swedish state may have joined the European Union, but the Swedish society has not yet come to terms with membership.[4]

Switzerland might consider institutional reforms that render federalism and direct democracy more compatible with EU membership. As a result of the EEA negotiations, for example, the rights of the cantons to participate in Swiss foreign policy were formalized in law and enshrined in Article 55 of the revised constitution in 1999. Fears about restrictions on Swiss federalism and direct democracy might be further countered by reference to the emerging "federalism" of the European Union (in terms of subsidiarity, regionalism, integration at different speeds, and plans for a European constitution) and the EU's efforts to reduce its "democratic deficit." The impact of societal cleavages could be decreased by a reassessment of national myths and maybe revised history schoolbooks that show that traditions survive only if they adapt. Swiss neutrality, for example, has been questioned by a recent debate about Switzerland's role during World War II, which was triggered by the issue of dormant bank accounts of Holocaust victims in Swiss banks and by new research after the opening of various archives (e.g., with regard to the Swiss refugee policy). This public discussion has contributed to a change in the conception of Swiss history that may make neutrality look less like an obstacle to integration.[5] In 2000, the government declared that neutrality should be reduced to its legal core and that the new leitmotiv was "security through cooperation."[6]

For Norwegians it seems important to demonstrate that EU membership does not threaten welfare policies and support for peripheral regions or require any cultural leveling. In fact, nonparticipation might seriously affect important monetary, energy, or security interests. In times of heightened interdependence, it is increasingly difficult to curb foreign influence by simply staying aloof. In the aftermath of their European referenda in the 1990s, the integration policies of Norway and Switzerland have one-sidedly focused on self-determination (or operational sovereignty) at the neglect of co-determination (or voice). Both countries have tried to become "shadow members" of the EU by implementing extensive unilateral adaptation to the *acquis communautaire* and concluding bilateral agreements with the Union. They are well advised to increase public awareness of the sovereignty-voice trade-off described in this study. In fact, in its foreign policy report of 2000, the Swiss Federal Council asserted that staying outside the EU would run the risk of increasing foreign determination, whereas accession would entail influence and hence "a gain of sovereignty."[7] In the same year, a Norwegian report on European integration concluded that Norway was increasingly concerned by processes and rules that were determined in EU forums in which it was not fully represented and that the safeguarding of Norwegian interests would require that "Norway's voice be heard to the greatest extent possible."[8]

For the time being, the Swiss Federal Council pursues further bilateral negotiations with the European Union in order to supplement the sectoral agreements of 1999 in areas such as services, processed agricultural products, the environment, education, the fight against fraud, taxation on interest, and cooperation on domestic security. Nonetheless, the Federal Council is determined to revive Switzerland's 1992 EU application in the coming years.[9] In 1999, it issued a report that compared the different policy options of continuing the status quo, concluding more bilateral agreements with the EU, joining the EEA, and acceding to the EU.[10] This report was intended to initiate a public debate so that the government can decide whether domestic support exists for taking up accession negotiations with the EU. In a special section, it answered a collection of questions posed by citizens. With regard to concerns about Swiss identity, the government stated that "European identity does not develop at the cost of national, regional or local identities" and that "joining the EU would allow Switzerland to bring its identity and specific cultural characteristics to bear, where decisions affecting it are taken."[11] Norway's integration report of December 2000 was also intended to invite the people to discuss European policy and thus left the question of membership open.[12] Given the deficiencies of the EEA, in particular with regard to the second and third EU pillars (but also the monetary union and fisheries and energy policies), and given the fact that the EEA will further lose in importance as a result of EU enlargements to the east, the Norwegian government might launch another membership bid in a few years.

The most obvious help the European Union can offer reluctant Europeans is to allow for more flexibility in both the deepening and widening processes. In accession negotiations, it should take politically sensitive issues into account, as was to some extent done in the case of Norway's second attempt to join in 1994. In light of the number and heterogeneity of the applicant countries from Central, Eastern, and Southern Europe, the traditional method of enlargement, which requires candidates to accept the *acquis communautaire* except for some transitional periods, might have to be adapted. Without flexible solutions, the choice is between a very long waiting period before full membership or early membership with very long transitional periods. Any strategy of flexible or "incremental" enlargement might create interesting precedents for Norway and Switzerland. Finally, the EU should strive for a fair treatment of small states. Skepticism has again surfaced in the dispute over bilateral "sanctions" against Austria after a right-wing party entered the government coalition in early 2000 (but not in the case of Italy one year later), as well as in the quarrel over the distribution of seats and weighing of votes in the intergovernmental conference in 2000.

In this study, I also hint at the increasing importance of certain principles that the Union has acknowledged in the past few years, such as subsidiarity, the strengthening of the regions, transparency, openness, and flexibility. They allow nation-states to keep certain competences that help them to reconcile the effects of integration and globalization with identity-generating national traditions. The principle of flexibility has been institutionalized in the Amsterdam Treaty and permits a group of member states to pursue closer cooperation within the first and third EU pillars, provided that a number of conditions are met.[13] These prerequisites are facilitated in the Treaty of Nice, which also introduces the possibility of closer cooperation in the second pillar's Common Foreign and Security Policy. Therefore, reluctant member states are not necessarily obliged to participate in all new integration efforts, which might make membership more attractive to Norway and Switzerland.

Theoretical Implications

Besides its empirical implications, the book's contributions and limitations as well as the ground for future research need to be considered.

Some Contributions

In this book, some thirty policy decisions across three countries and five decades are assembled and coded in order to elucidate the question why and under what conditions small, open economies—and thus the most likely candidates for EU membership—resist supranational integration. Through an analysis of material interests in market integration and of ideational interests in protecting national identity, a solution to the puzzle is provided. In the volume, the analytical focus shifts from integration theory to integration policy theory in a way that allows readers to study both successes and failures of integration efforts. The book adds to the understanding of European integration studies by extending the liberal approach to preference formation beyond commercial and geopolitical interests. Unlike studies in liberal intergovernmentalism, ideational factors are taken seriously; and unlike those with constructivist approaches, material interests that help shed light on the timing and contents of policy decisions are not dismissed.

In a broader context of international relations theory, the framework of analysis points to a possible combination of systemic, societal, and state-centered approaches by tracing integration policy to structural constraints and opportunities, demands of domestic actors and national elites, and the state's institutional structure. It brings thus international relations, which addresses politics across countries by treating them as fundamentally similar, and comparative politics, which deals with politics within countries by neglecting the common context in which they operate, closer to one another. For a long time, international relations scholars "have paid too little attention to how a combination of domestic and international processes shape preferences"[14] and that, especially in integration policy, "the origins of national preferences should be understood as an interaction of national interests and identity."[15] My approach to explaining the formation of national preferences takes this criticism into account and considers domestic and international, economic and political factors. With an interest-based approach that "factors in" identity, I situate this book in the contemporary debate about interests and ideas in international relations.

Finally, the long-term study shows how national elites redefine their positions on how to deal with the classic dilemma between sovereignty and interdependence. Internationalization erodes the effectiveness of national policies and thus the ability to unilaterally accomplish policy objectives. As a result, preferences may shift from operational sovereignty to international voice opportunities.

Some Limitations

Besides contributions to the theoretical debates already mentioned, a number of shortcomings of the book have to be acknowledged. My ambition was not to develop a theory that predicts the integration policy of a country. It is questionable whether predictable theories can be constructed at all in social sciences. The aspiration was rather to create a framework of analysis that allows understanding of a nonmember's policy toward a regional integration scheme like the European Union. The hypothesis herein helps to describe and explain but provides only cautious forecasts. Moreover, I focus not on policy outcomes but on the formation of national preferences, and more precisely on the change in elites' preferences. Hence, I am not primarily interested in why Sweden finally joined the European Union in 1995 but Norway and Switzerland have not yet done so. Instead of carrying out a real cross-country comparison, I wished to scrutinize the national policy developments over time.

In the study, I rely primarily on descriptive methods of preference assessment, drawing on statistics and documents. Using these sources of evidence remains an interpretative exercise that is encumbered with the usual problems of obtaining accurate information about intentions and motivations. In order to improve reliability, I tried to cross-check them from different, "triangular" sources, such as statements by officials of national governments, parliaments, interest groups, parties, EFTA, the EC, and the interpretations of knowledgeable observers, including academics and journalists.

My approach might be challenged for its macro-interpretation, which relies on the aggregate variables of economic incentives and political impediments. Most indicators measure the variables' concepts, the importance of market access and of domestic and geohistorical constraints, only indirectly or partly. Obviously, other (or additional) indicators could have been chosen, such as economic performance, import dependence, or public resistance. To a large extent, I neglect party politics in the sense that a change of government could cause a change of integration policy. Such a focus on the micro-dynamics of domestic politics does not seem an appropriate tool for explaining the broader question of the EFTA countries' long-term, persistent pattern of reluctance toward integration. The approach taken here is more in line with the traditions of international relations and comparative politics than with foreign policy analysis and its focus on decisionmaking processes. Party politics might be relevant for the timing of a membership application, but political impediments, through their links to national identity, hardly disappear with a change of government. This holds true even more in corporatist systems and for popular referenda. Nonetheless, an inclusion of party politics would certainly add explanatory power.

Furthermore, referendum campaigns are vital for the mobilization of societal cleavages and, together with elections and public opinion polls, for the revelation of elite-mass gaps on issues of integration policy. This mechanism calls for further investigation, even though in this study I actually focus on the level of integration aimed at by the elites, not the actual outcome such as the result of a referendum or of negotiations. Given reelection constraints and instruments of direct democracy, elites must take public opinion into account. The model might well gain by including considerations about, on the one hand, the role of elites in shaping public opinion and, on the other hand, about the impact of public opinion on policy.

The discussion of economic elites might be further refined to take conflicting interests within sectors and associations into account. For example, the concentration on export industries tends to disregard the interests of domestically oriented sectors. This restriction is justified by the fact that the EFTA countries have traditionally been free traders with strong export sectors and that the focus was on aggregate (net) economic incentives to integrate. Yet the EFTA countries have to a certain degree maintained dual economies with protected agricultural sectors, cartels, and monopolies. Treating political elites as de facto single actors also leaves room for refinements. Even though corporatist systems attempt to reconcile domestic conflicts, the opposition of agrarian or radical parties, for instance, could be further investigated. Transnational actors, such as nongovernmental organizations and transgovernmental coalitions, are less instrumental. They play a more important role in the deepening of EU integration than in enlargement, and in corporatist countries transnational groups have, in general, fewer channels through which they can access the political and social system.[16]

Another limitation of the study is its concentration on the EFTA countries' points of view. The approach is context-dependent in the sense that

the cases concern the policies of Western European democracies with highly industrialized market economies. Last but not least, the study focuses on
the "demand" side of integration and neglects the "supply" side question of
why an existing community would admit new members.[17] These limitations
leave ample space for future research and for the expansion of the approach
to enhance explanatory power.

Possible Extensions of the Model

Generalizations about the analytical framework can be made with regard to
cases and variables, as well as with regard to an extension from preference
formation to bargaining, in order to explain not only the level of integration
aimed at but also the outcomes of integration policies. First, an adjustment
to the situation of "nonreluctant" candidates requires an additional operationalization of important political incentives, such as the strengthening of
democratic and market transitions, security interests, or great power aspirations. In spite of many Central and Eastern European countries' desire to
"return to Europe" and strong economic incentives to join the EU, a recent
European Commission study confirms the weight of the identity dimension
in the current enlargements "because the applicant countries' national identities have been forged on the basis of (often) difficult, (sometimes) dramatic, historical experiences."[18] Second, the perspective may be changed from
the nonmember's point of view to the one of an integration-skeptical EU
member state such as Great Britain and Denmark (see Chapter 1) or
Sweden since 1995. In intra-EU politics, supranational actors play a more
important role, and, as a result of the long-term "socialization process,"
member states may partly form their preferences endogenously.[19] Then
again, Jeffrey Checkel claims that in corporatist states (such as Sweden,
Norway, and Switzerland), European norms are diffused primarily through
societal pressure and only secondarily through elite social learning.[20] Third,
cases of integration outside Europe (e.g., the North American Free Trade
Agreement, the Southern Cone Common Market, and the Association of
South-East Asian Nations) might be considered.

Fourth, the model could be extended to cover not just preference formation but also the stage of bargaining (as well as the ratification and
implementation of an integration agreement). In order to reveal why one
specific solution prevailed over another, the strategic interaction needs to
be included, as liberal intergovernmentalism suggests.[21] Modeling international negotiations is a formidable task because the process has little structure and involves many variables. In the noncoercive, institutionalized context of negotiations among democratic governments, the three most pivotal
variables influencing governments' strategic calculations seem to be the
relative bargaining power of the actors, the level of information or uncer-

tainty, and the role of institutions.[22] To analyze the process, a two-level game approach could be used, in which at the national level, "domestic groups pursue their interests by pressuring the government to adopt favorable policies, and politicians seek power by constructing coalitions among those groups," and at the international level, "governments seek to maximize their own ability to satisfy domestic pressures, while minimizing the adverse consequences of foreign developments."[23]

Conclusion

In this volume, I set out to help develop integration policy theory in order to understand what shapes national preferences with regard to European integration. An "intellectual deficit" seems to prevail regarding the widening of integration schemes: "indeed, it is an oddity of the literature on the EU, and more generally on (west) European integration, that so little effort has been made to theorize about the enlargement of the EU"[24] and about the impact of integration on nonmembers. I present the ever-closer relationship between the European Union and Sweden, Norway, and Switzerland as a path-dependent process. The three countries would have fulfilled the eligibility criteria of Community/Union membership, but for a long time they aimed at limited integration in various forms. They have generally been able but—in spite of (mounting) economic incentives—not willing to join a supranational community. The potential domestic and geohistorical constraints that caused this reluctance are closely linked to ideas about sovereign statehood. The importance attributed to those elements of national identity has varied over the five decades. Although economic elites, in particular export-oriented sectors, were more favorable toward integration, when market access was important, political elites additionally required the political impediments to be low.

Furthermore, it has been argued that the lower the economic incentives and the higher the political impediments, the more valuable the maintenance of operational sovereignty relative to the acquisition of international voice opportunities. The importance of sovereignty has, for instance, varied in relation to how similar or how different the features of an integration scheme were perceived to be from national features. In the 1990s, the degree of liberalization and integration in Europe had reached a stage at which the effectiveness of national policies that are not in line with EU policies were increasingly questioned and unilateral adaptation to the *acquis* was considered necessary by nonmember states. Obtaining a voice in the more and more powerful European Union has thus gained in importance at the expense of a sovereignty that has progressively been challenged by integration and globalization processes.

Still, economic considerations may well fade when domestic institutions and foreign policy legacies that touch on feelings of national identity come into play. Conceptions of the national "self" featuring institutional, societal, geopolitical, or historical elements that are hardly compatible with EU membership call for careful investigation. Myths about national exceptionalism, heroic fights for independence and resistance, or certain features of the political systems may produce awkward EU members. Future enlargement rounds will further increase the Union's heterogeneity and thus deeply affect not only its effectiveness but its very character. The varying willingness of states to integrate is thus becoming a more and more salient policy issue that needs to be understood.

Notes

1. af Ugglas, "Sweden at the Heart of Europe," p. 8.
2. Sandholtz, "Membership Matters," pp. 404–405.
3. Ingebritsen, *The Nordic States and European Unity*, p. 188.
4. Miles, "Conclusion," p. 234.
5. *Neue Zürcher Zeitung*, "Erosion des traditionalistischen Neutralitätsbildes."
6. Switzerland, Federal Council, *Aussenpolitischer Bericht 2000, Präsenz und Kooperation: Interessenwahrung in einer zusammenwachsenden Welt*, Bern, 15 November 2000, p. 27, Annex, pp. 21–22.
7. Ibid., p. 44.
8. Norway, Ministry for Foreign Affairs, *Om Norge og Europa ved inngangen til et nytt århundre*, St.meld. nr. 12 (2000–2001), Oslo, 1 December 2000, chap. 12.
9. However, the Federal Council is not in a hurry. In March 2001, 76.7 percent of the Swiss voters followed its advice to reject an initative that demanded immediate accession negotiations. *Financial Times*, "Swiss vote Against Early Talks About Joining EU."
10. Switzerland, Federal Council, *Schweiz-Europäische Union: Integrationsbericht 1999*, Bern, 3 February 1999. The report was accompanied by several studies on the economic and legal-institutional implications of EU membership.
11. Ibid., pp. 319–323.
12. Norway, Ministry for Foreign Affairs, *Om Norge og Europa ved inngangen til et nytt århundre*, St.meld. nr. 12 (2000–2001), Oslo, 1 December 2000.
13. Articles 40, 43–45 of the Treaty on European Union and Article 11 of the Treaty of Rome. See Gstöhl, "The European Union After Amsterdam."
14. Keohane and Nye, "Power and Interdependence Revisited," p. 753.
15. Ingebritsen and Larson, "Interest and Identity," pp. 208–209.
16. Risse-Kappen, "Transnational Relations, Domestic Structures, and International Institutions."
17. Mattli claims that a union may accept new members in order to increase its international bargaining power, to economize on investment transaction costs, or to offset negative externalities threatening the union's security, stability, or prosperity. Mattli, *The Logic of Regional Integration*, chaps. 5–7.
18. European Commission, "Survey of National Identity and Deep-Seated

Attitudes Towards European Integration in the Ten Applicant Countries of Central and Eastern Europe," *Forward Studies Unit Working Paper,* Brussels, 1998, p. 5.

19. See Sandholtz, "Membership Matters"; and Smyrl, "When (and How) Do the Commission's Preferences Matter?"

20. Checkel, "Social Construction and Integration," pp. 552–553.

21. See Moravcsik, *The Choice for Europe,* chap. 1.

22. Relative bargaining power is defined as the ability to change the perceived win-sets (i.e., those agreements that would gain the necessary domestic support) so as to make preferred negotiation outcomes more likely. A negotiator can exercise power, inter alia, by actions that worsen the other side's no-agreement alternatives and/or improve her own, by creating additional joint gains, or by making credible commitments within the zone of possible agreements. Sebenius, "Challenging Conventional Explanations of International Cooperation," pp. 340–343.

23. Putnam, "Diplomacy and Domestic Politics," p. 434. The likelihood of an international agreement depends on the distribution of international power and on the win-set, which in turn is determined by domestic coalitions and preferences, domestic institutions or actors involved in the ratification practices, and the negotiator's strategies.

24. Wallace, "EU Enlargement," p. 149.

Acronyms & Abbreviations

AUNS	Action Committee for Independent and Neutral Switzerland (Aktion für eine unabhängige und neutrale Schweiz)
CAP	Common Agricultural Policy
CEN	Comité Européen de Normalisation (European Committee for Standardization)
CENELEC	Comité Européen de Normalisation Electrotechnique (European Committee for Electrotechnical Standardization)
CET	Common External Tariff
CFP	Common Fisheries Policy
CFSP	Common Foreign and Security Policy
CNG	Swiss Confederation of Christian Trade Unions (Christlichnationaler Gewerkschaftsbund der Schweiz)
COMTRADE	Commodity Trade Statistics Database (United Nations Statistics Division)
CVP	Swiss Christian Democratic Party (Christlichdemokratische Volkspartei)
DNA	Norwegian Labor Party (Det Norske Arbeiderparti)
DNF	Norwegian New People's Party (Det Nye Folkeparti)
EC	European Communities (includes the European Community, the ECSC, and Euratom)
ECSC	European Coal and Steel Community
EDC	European Defense Community
EEA	European Economic Area
EEC	European Economic Community
EES	European Economic Space
EFTA	European Free Trade Association
EMU	European Monetary Union

EPC	European Political Cooperation
ESA	EFTA Surveillance Authority
EU	European Union
Euratom	European Atomic Energy Community
EVP	Swiss Protestant People's Party (Evangelische Volkspartei)
FDP	Swiss Radical Democratic Party (Freisinnig-Demokratische Partei)
FINEFTA	Finland-EFTA Association
FP	Swedish Liberal People's Party (Folkpartiet Liberalerna)
FRP	Norwegian Progress Party (Fremskrittspartiet)
FTA	free trade agreement
GATT	General Agreement on Tariffs and Trade
GDP	gross domestic product
GNP	gross national product
GPS	Swiss Green Party (Grüne Partei Schweiz)
IGC	intergovernmental conference
KD	Swedish Christian Democratic Party (Kristdemokraterna, formerly Kristdemokratiska Samhällspartiet, or KDS)
KDS	Swedish Christian Democratic Party (Kristdemokratiska Samhällspartiet)
KRF	Norwegian Christian Democratic Party (Kristelig Folkepartiet)
LDU	Swiss Independent Alliance (Landesring der Unabhängigen)
LO-Norway	Confederation of Trade Unions in Norway (Landsorganisasjonen i Norge)
LO-Sweden	Confederation of Trade Unions in Sweden (Landsorganisationen i Sverige)
LPS	Swiss Liberal Party (Liberale Partei Schweiz)
MFN	most-favored nation
MP	member of parliament
NA	National Action (Switzerland, Nationale Aktion)
NAF	Norwegian Employers' Federation (Norsk Arbeidsgiverforening)
NATO	North Atlantic Treaty Organization
NEAT	New Alpine Rail Axes (Neue Eisenbahn Alpen Transversale)
NHO	Confederation of Norwegian Business and Industry (Næringslivets Hovedorganisasjon)
NI	Federation of Norwegian Industries (Norges Industriforbund)

NKP	Norwegian Communist Party (Norges Kommunistiske Parti)
NTB	nontariff barrier
NYD	Swedish Discontent Party (Ny Demokrati)
OECD	Organization for Economic Cooperation and Development (formerly OEEC)
OEEC	Organization for European Economic Cooperation
PDA	Swiss Labor Party (Partei der Arbeit)
RV	Norwegian Red Electoral Alliance (Rød Valgallianse)
SACO	Swedish Confederation of Professional Associations (Sveriges Akademikers Centralorganisation)
SAF	Swedish Employers' Federation (Svenska Arbetsgivareföreningen)
SAP	Swedish Social Democratic Party (Sveriges Socialdemokratiska Arbetareparti)
SBV	Swiss Farmers' Union (Schweizerischer Bauernverband)
SD	Swiss Democratic Party (Schweizer Demokraten, formerly Nationale Aktion, or NA)
SEA	Single European Act
SEM	Single European Market
SF	Norwegian Socialist People's Party (Sosialistisk Folkpartiet)
SGB	Swiss Confederation of Trade Unions (Schweizerischer Gewerkschaftsbund)
SGV	Swiss Union of Small and Medium Enterprises (Schweizerischer Gewerbeverband)
SHIV	Swiss Federation of Commerce and Industry (Schweizerischer Handels- und Industrie-Verein, or Vorort)
SI	Federation of Swedish Industries (Sveriges Industriförbund)
SITC	Standard International Trade Classification
SMUV	Swiss Watchmakers' and Metalworkers' Union (Schweizerischer Metall- und Uhrenarbeitnehmer-Verband)
SP	Norwegian Center Party (Senterpartiet)
SPS	Swiss Social Democratic Party (Sozialdemokratische Partei Schweiz)
SV	Norwegian Socialist Left Party (Sosialistisk Venstreparti, formerly Sosialistisk Folkpartiet, or SF)
SVP	Swiss People's Party (Schweizerische Volkspartei)

TCO	Swedish Confederation of Salaried Employees (Tjänstemännens Centralorganisation)
VPK	Swedish Left Party Communists (Vänsterpartiet Kommunisterna)
VSA	Swiss Federation of Salaried Employees (Vereinigung Schweizerischer Angestelltenverbände)
WEU	Western European Union
ZSAO	Federation of Swiss Employers' Organizations (Zentralverband Schweizerischer Arbeitgeber-Organisationen)

Bibliography

Contents

Books and Articles

Aardal, Bernt Olav. "Economics, Ideology and Strategy: An Analysis of the EC-Debate in Norwegian and Danish Organizations 1961–72." *Scandinavian Political Studies* 6, no. 1 (1983): 27–49.

Abrams, Richard K., et al. "The Impact of the European Community's Internal Market on the EFTA." *Occasional Paper* no. 74. Washington, D.C.: International Monetary Fund, 1990.

Accords bilatéraux Suisse-UE (commentaires). Bilaterale Abkommen Schweiz-EU (Erste Analysen), ed. by Daniel Felder and Christine Kaddous. Basel: Helbing and Lichtenhahn, 2001.

Aeschbach, Karl. "Le marché européen vu par les syndicats: dimension sociale et liberté des personnes." In *La Suisse et son avenir européen: une analyse des positions suisses face à l'intégration de l'Europe*, ed. by Roland Ruffieux and Annik Schachtschneider Morier-Genoud. Lausanne: Payot, 1989, pp. 187–193.

af Malmborg, Mikael. *Den ståndaktiga nationalstaten: Sverige och den västeuropeiska integrationen 1945–1959*. Lund: Lund University Press, 1994.

af Ugglas, Margaretha. "Sweden at the Heart of Europe." Address by the Swedish Minister of Foreign Affairs at Chatham House, London, 26 November 1992.

Allen, Hilary. *Norway and Europe in the 1970s*. Oslo: Universitetsforlaget, 1979.

Alt, James E., and Michael Gilligan. "The Political Economy of Trading States: Factor Specificity, Collective Action Problems and Domestic Political Institutions." *The Journal of Political Philosophy* 2, no. 2 (1994): 165–192.

Anderson, Christopher J., and Karl C. Kaltenthaler. "The Dynamics of Public Opinion Toward European Integration, 1973–93." *European Journal of International Relations* 2, no. 2 (1996): 175–199.

Andersson, Jan Otto, and Lars Mjøset. "The Transformation of the Nordic Models." *Cooperation and Conflict* 22, no. 4 (1987): 227–243.

Andersson, Peter, Sirpa Järvenpaa, and Jukka Lesk selä. "EFTA Countries' Trade in Services." *EFTA Trade 1991*. Geneva: EFTA, 1993: 29–39.

Andriessen, Frans. "EFTA Negotiations." Intervention in the General Affairs Council, 29–30 July 1991.

Archer, Clive, and Ingrid Sogner. *Norway, European Integration and Atlantic Security*. Oslo: PRIO International Peace Research Institute. London: Sage, 1998.

Aschinger, Franz E. "Zurücktreten des Assoziationsgedankens in der Schweiz." In *Die Neutralen in der europäischen Integration: Kontroversen, Konfrontationen, Alternativen*, ed. by Hans Mayrzedt and Hans Christoph Binswanger. Wien: Wilhelm Braumüller, 1970, pp. 354–357.

Atlantic Tariffs and Trade. London: Political and Economic Planning, Allen and Unwin, 1962.

Austvik, Ole Gunnar. "Norwegian Petroleum and European Integration." In *Norway and the European Community: The Political Economy of Integration*, ed. by Brent F. Nelsen. Westport: Praeger, 1993, pp. 181–209.

Avery, Graham, and Fraser Cameron. *The Enlargement of the European Union*. Sheffield: Sheffield Academic Press, 1998.

Ayberk, Ural. "Les leaders d'opinion suisses et les question européennes." In *La Suisse et son avenir européen: Une analyse des positions suisses face à l'intégration de l'Europe*, ed. by Roland Ruffieux and Annik Schachtschneider Morier-Genoud. Lausanne: Payot, 1989, pp. 227–236.

Baldwin, Richard E., and Harry Flam. "Enlargement of the European Union: The Economic Consequences for the Scandinavian Countries." *CEPR Occasional Paper* no. 16. London: Centre for Economic Policy Research, 1994.

Banchoff, Thomas. "German Identity and European Integration." *European Journal of International Relations* 3, no. 3 (1999): 259–289.

Beloff, Nora. *The General Says No: Britain's Exclusion from Europe*. London: Penguin Books, 1963.

Berge, Olav. "The Expectations of the Government Administration and the Organizations Toward EFTA." In *Fears and Expectations: Norwegian Attitudes Toward European Integration*, ed. by Nils Örvik. Oslo: Universitetsforlaget, 1972, pp. 134–176.

Berglund, Sten, and Ulf Lindström. *The Scandinavian Party System(s): A Comparative Study*. Lund: Studentlitteratur, 1978.

Bergquist, Mats. *Sverige och EEC: En statsvetenskaplig studie av fyra åsiktsriktningars syn på svensk marknadspolitik 1961–1962*. Stockholm: Norstedt, 1970.

———. "Sweden and the European Economic Community." *Cooperation and Conflict* 4, no. 1 (1969): 1–12.

Bergström, Hans. "Sweden's Politics and Party System at the Crossroads." *West European Politics* 14, no. 3 (1991): 8–30.

Bieler, Andreas. *Globalisation and Enlargement of the European Union: Austrian and Swedish Social Forces in the Struggle over Membership*. London: Routledge, 2000.

———. "Globalization, Swedish Trade Unions and European Integration: From Europhobia to Conditional Support." *Cooperation and Conflict* 34, no. 1 (1999): 21–46.

Binswanger, Hans Christoph. "Zwischenstaatliche oder übernationale Prinzipien der Integration: Aus Sicht der Kleinstaaten." In *Die Neutralen in der europäischen Integration: Kontroversen, Konfrontationen, Alternativen*, ed. by Hans Mayrzedt and Hans Christoph Binswanger. Wien: Wilhelm Braumüller, 1970, pp. 91–106.

Binswanger, Hans Christoph, and Hans Manfred Mayrzedt. *Europapolitik der Rest-EFTA-Staaten: Perspektiven für die siebziger Jahre*. Zürich: Schulthess, 1972.

Bjørklund, Tor. *Mot strømmen: Kampen mot EF 1961–1972*. Oslo: Universitetsforlaget, 1982.

———. "Sentrum mot periferi: Norsk EF-strid belyst ut fra ulike sentrum-periferi modeller." In *EF, Norge og 1990-årene: Seks artikler om EF-sakens betydning i norsk politikk*, ed. by Nils Asbjørnsen and Gunnar Vogt. Oslo: Institutt for Statsvitenskap, 1993.

———. "The Three Nordic 1994 Referenda Concerning Membership in the EU." *Cooperation and Conflict* 31, no. 1 (1996): 11–36.

Blankart, Franz A. "Considérations sur la politique européenne de la Suisse." *Cadmos*, no. 38 (1987): 22–38.

Bloom, William. *Personal Identity, National Identity and International Relations*. Cambridge: Cambridge University Press, 1990.

Bonjour, Edgar. *Geschichte der schweizerischen Neutralität: Vier Jahrhunderte eidgenössischer Aussenpolitik*. Vols. 1–6. Basel: Helbing and Lichtenhahn, 1965–1970.

Bowitz, Einar, et al. *Norsk medlemskap i EU: En makroøkonomisk analyse*. Oslo: Statistisk sentralbyrå, Rapporter 25, 1994.

Brodin, Katarina, Kjell Goldmann, and Christian Lange. "The Policy of Neutrality: Official Doctrines of Finland and Sweden." *Cooperation and Conflict* 3, no. 1 (1968): 18–51.

Bulmer, Simon. "Britain and European Integration: Of Sovereignty, Slow Adaptation, and Semi-Detachment." In *Britain and the European Community: The Politics of Semi-Detachment*, ed. by Stephen George. Oxford: Clarendon Press, 1992, pp. 1–29.

———. "Domestic Politics and European Community Policy-Making." *Journal of Common Market Studies* 21, no. 4 (1983): 349–363.

Camps, Miriam. *Britain and the European Community 1955–1963*. Princeton: Princeton University Press, 1964.

———. "The European Free Trade Association: A Preliminary Appraisal." *PEP Occasional Paper* no. 4. London: Political and Economic Planning, 1959.

———. "The Free Trade Area Negotiations." *PEP Occasional Paper* no. 2. London: Political and Economic Planning, 1959.

———. "Trade Diversion in Western Europe." *PEP Occasional Paper* no. 9. London: Political and Economic Planning, 1960.

Carlsnaes, Walter. "Sweden Facing the New Europe: Whither Neutrality?" *European Security* 2, no. 1 (1993): 71–89.

Cecchini, Paolo, Michel Catinat, and Alexis Jacquemin. *The European Challenge 1992: The Benefits of a Single Market*. Aldershot: Wildwood House, 1988.

Centre for Economic Policy Research. *Flexible Integration: Towards a More Effective and Democratic Europe*. London: Centre for Economic Policy Research, 1995.

———. *Is Bigger Better? The Economics of EC Enlargement*. London: Centre for Economic Policy Research, 1992.

Checkel, Jeffrey T. "Social Construction and Integration." *Journal of European Public Policy* 6, no. 4 (1999): 545–560.

Checkel, Jeffrey T., and Andrew Moravcsik. "A Constructivist Research Program in EU Studies?." *European Union Politics* 2, no. 2 (2001): 219–249.

Christensen, Tom, and Morten Egeberg. "Organized Group-Government Relations in Norway: On the Structured Selection of Participants, Problems, Solutions, and Choice Opportunities." *Scandinavian Political Studies* 2, no. 3 (1970): 239–259.

Closse, Willy. "Les pays scandinaves et la C.E.E." *Chronique de politique étrangère* 17, no. 6 (1964): 697–768.

Club de Bruxelles. *EC/EFTA: The Future European Economic Area*. Study written by the Club de Bruxelles under the direction of Patrick Baragiola. Brussels: Club de Bruxelles, 1991.

Coftier, A. "L'adhésion de la Suisse à la Communauté européenne vue sous l'angle de la neutralité." *Revue de droit international et de droit comparé*, no. 2 (1998): 119–172.

The Common Market: A Survey by The Times. London: Times Publishing Company, 1962.

Converse, Philip E., and Henry Valen. "Dimensions of Cleavage and Perceived Party Distances in Norwegian Voting." *Scandinavian Political Studies* 6 (1971): 107–152.

Cook, Philip C. "EFTA: The Origins and History of the European Free Trade Association." Ph.D. diss., University of Georgia, 1968.

Curzon, Gérard, and Victoria Curzon. "EFTA Experience with Non-Tariff Barriers." In *Europe's Free Trade Area Experiment: EFTA and Economic Integration*, ed. by Hugh Corbet and David Robertson. Oxford: Pergamon Press, 1970, pp. 129–145.

Dahlström, Gösta, and Britt-Marie Söderbäck. *Sveriges avtal med EEC: En faktasammanställning*. Stockholm: Rabén and Sjögren, 1977.

de Clercq, Willy. "Speech at the EC-EFTA Ministerial Meeting." Interlaken, 20 May 1987.

de Gaulle, Charles. "Les déclarations du Président de la République au cours de la conférence de presse à l'Elysée." *Le Monde*, 29 November 1967, pp. 3–4.

———. "Le texte intégral de la conférence de presse tenue par le Général de Gaulle à l'Elysée." *Le Monde*, 16 January 1963, pp. 2–3.

de Geer, Hans. *The Rise and Fall of the Swedish Model: The Swedish Employers' Confederation, SAF, and Industrial Relations over Ten Decades*. London: Carden, 1992.

de Ruyt, Jean. *L'Acte Unique Européen: Commentaire*. 2nd ed. Brussels: Editions de l'Université de Bruxelles, 1989.

de Stercke, Gilles. "La Suède." In *L'Union européenne et les défis de l'élargissement*, ed. by Mario Telò, Brussels: Université de Bruxelles, 1994, pp. 159–175.

Delors, Jacques. "Introduction of the Commission's Programme for 1990 by the President of the Commission of the European Communities." *Bulletin of the European Communities*, Supplement no. 1 (1990): 5–16.

———. "Statement on the Broad Lines of Commission Policy, Strasbourg, 17 January 1989." *Bulletin of the European Communities*, Supplement no. 1 (1989): 5–19.

Die Schweizer Wirtschaft vor den Herausforderungen des EG-Binnenmarktes: Eine praxisorientierte Lageanalyse. Zürich: Vorort, 1988.

Diebold, William. *The Schuman Plan: A Study in Economic Cooperation 1950–1959*. New York: Praeger, 1959.

Dølvik, Jon Erik, et al. *Norsk Økonomi og europeisk integrasjon*. Oslo:

Fagbevegelsens senter for forskning, utredning og dokumentasjon, FAFO-rapport, no. 130, 1991.

Dörfer, Ingemar. "Scandinavia and NATO: À la carte." *The Washington Quarterly* 9, no. 1 (1986): 15–30.

du Bois, Pierre. *La Suisse et le défi européen: 1945–1992.* Lausanne: Favre, 1989.

Dupont, Cédric. "Domestic Politics, Information and International Bargaining: Comparative Models of Strategic Behavior in Non-Crisis Negotiations." Ph.D. diss., University of Geneva, Institut universitaire de hautes études internationales, 1994.

Economist, The. "Survey: Europe's Internal Market," 8 July 1989.

———. "Sweden: Still in Convalescence," 14 October 1995, 47–48.

Eide, Espen Barth. "Adjustment Strategy of a Non-Member: Norwegian Foreign and Security Policy in the Shadow of the European Union." *Cooperation and Conflict* 31, no. 1 (1996): 69–104.

———. "Europa-debatten i Arbeiderpartiet: Forholdet mellom 'konføderale' og 'føderale' posisjoner." *Internasjonal Politikk* 48, no. 3 (1990): 403–418.

Eikestøl, Oddbjørn. "Vest-europeisk integrasjon etter 1945." In *Vil Norge overleve i EEC? Hva er EEC og hvilke konsekvenser vil medlemskap få for Norge?* Ed. by Per M. Arnstad et al. Oslo: Cultura Forlag, 1971, pp. 13–25.

Ekström, Tord, Gunnar Myrdal, and Roland Pålsson. "Spezifische politische Probleme aus schwedischer Sicht." In *Die Neutralen in der europäischen Integration: Kontroversen, Konfrontationen, Alternativen,* ed. by Hans Mayrzedt and Hans Christoph Binswanger. Wien: Wilhelm Braumüller, 1970, pp. 288–302.

———. *Vi och Västeuropa: Uppfordran till eftertanke och debatt.* Stockholm: Rabén and Sjögren, 1962.

Enz, Annette. "Die Schweiz und die Grosse Europäische Freihandelszone." *Studien und Quellen,* no. 16 (1990–1991): 157–255.

Epiney, Astrid, and Karine Siegwart. "Direkte Demokratie und Europäische Union: Ein Problemaufriss." In *Direkte Demokratie und Europäische Union/Démocratie directe et Union européenne,* ed. by Astrid Epiney and Karine Siegwart. Freiburg: Universitätsverlag Freiburg Schweiz, 1997, pp. 117–139.

Esping-Andersen, Gøsta. *Politics Against Markets: The Social Democratic Road to Power.* Princeton: Princeton University Press, 1985.

Esping-Andersen, Gøsta, and Walter Korpi. "From Poor Relief to Institutional Welfare States: The Development of Scandinavian Social Policy." In *The Scandinavian Model: Welfare States and Welfare Research,* ed. by Robert Erikson, Erik Jørgen Hansen, Stein Ringen, and Hannu Uusitalo. Armonk: M. E. Sharpe, 1987, pp. 39–74.

"Europamarknadsdebatten: En antologi." *Studier och debatt,* no. 4 (1961).

European Free Trade Association, The, and the Crisis of European Integration: An Aspect of Atlantic Crisis? Study Group of the Graduate Institute of International Studies. Geneva: Graduate Institute of International Studies, 1968.

European Research Associates. *The European Community and EFTA in the 1980s: What Trade and Industrial Strategy for Western Europe in an Increasingly Hostile Economic Environment?* Brussels: ERA, 1984.

Evans, Andrew, and Per Falk. *Law and Integration: Sweden and the European Community.* Stockholm: Norstedts, 1991.

Falk, Maria, Kati Lauronen, and Kajsa Lindell. *Direct Investment in 1998: Assets and Income.* Stockholm: Sveriges Riksbank, Financial Statistics Department, 1999.

Feller, Markus, et al. "Zusammenfassung und Versuch einer Synthese der wissenschaftlichen Diskussion." In *Schweizerische Identität und Europäische Integration: Elemente schweizerischer Identität: Hemmnisse oder entwicklungsfähige Grundlagen für eine Annäherung an Europa?* Ed. by Ewald R. Weibel and Markus Feller. Bern: Paul Haupt, 1992, pp. 15–48.

Financial Times. "Oslo Fears Being Europe's Odd Man Out," 28 November 1992.

———. "Swiss Vote Against Early Talks about Joining EU," 5 March 2001.

Flam, Harry. "From EEA to EU: Economic Consequences for the EFTA Countries." *European Economic Review* 39, nos. 3–4 (1995): 457–466.

Flam, Harry, and Henrik Horn. "Ekonomiska konsekvenser för Sverige av EGs inre marknad: En översikt av tillämplig ekonomisk teori och empiri." In *Svensk ekonomi och Europaintegrationen,* Bilaga 2. Stockholm: Ekonomiska Rådet, 1989.

Fleury, Antoine. "Le patronat suisse et l'Europe: du Plan Marshall aux Traités de Rome." In *L'Europe du patronat: De la guerre froide aux années soixante,* ed. by Michel Dumoulin, René Girault and Gilbert Trausch. Bern: Peter Lang, 1993, pp. 165–189.

Fossli, Karen. "Survey Norway: Contemplating Europe." *Financial Times,* 24 June 1994, p. 4.

Gaarder, Andreas, and Øyvind Christensen. "Den Nordiske Velferdsstatsmodellen i det Nye Europa." In *Hva Skjedde med Norden? Fra Selvbevissthet til Rådvillhet,* ed. by Iver B. Neumann. Drammen: Cappelen, 1992, pp. 148–198.

Gardener, Edward P. M., and Jonathan L. Teppett. "The Impact of 1992 on the Financial Services Sectors of EFTA Countries." *Occasional Paper* no. 33. Geneva: EFTA, Economic Affairs Department, revised version 1992.

George, Alexander L., and Timothy J. McKeown. "Case Studies and Theories of Organizational Decision Making." In *Advances in Information Processing in Organizations,* ed. by Lee S. Sproull and Patrick D. Larkey, vol. 2. Greenwich, Conn.: JAI Press, 1985, pp. 21–58.

Gewerkschaftliche Rundschau, no. 10 (1959). Bern: Schweizerischer Gewerkschaftsbund.

Gidlund, Gullan. *Partiernas Europa.* Stockholm: Natur och Kultur, 1992.

Gidlund, Janerik. "Epilog." In *Den nya politiska konserten: Identitet, suveränitet och demokrati i den Europeiska integrationen,* ed. by Janerik Gidlund. Malmö: Liber-Hermods, 1993, pp. 194–203.

———. "Nationalstaten och den europeiska integrationen." In *Ett nytt Europa: Identitet och suveränitet i den europeiska integrationen,* ed. by Janerik Gidlund and Sverker Sörlin. Stockholm: SNS Förlag, 1991, pp. 65–127.

Gillingham, John. *Coal, Steel and the Rebirth of Europe, 1945–1955: The Germans and French from Ruhr Conflict to Economic Community.* Cambridge: Cambridge University Press, 1991.

Gittermann, Martin. *Das Beschlussfassungsverfahren des Abkommens über den Europäischen Wirtschaftsraum.* Baden-Baden: Nomos, 1998.

Gleditsch, Nils Petter. "Generaler og fotfolk i utakt: EF-avgjørelsen i de tre skandinavske land." *Internasjonal Politikk,* no. 4b (1972): 795–804.

Gleditsch, Nils Petter, and Ottar Hellevik. *Kampen om EF.* Oslo: NAVF, 1977.

Goetschel, Laurent. *Zwischen Effizienz und Akzeptanz: Die Information der Schweizer Behörden im Hinblick auf die Volksabstimmung über den EWR-Vertrag vom 6 Dezember 1992.* Bern: Paul Haupt, 1994.

Goldmann, Kjell. "The Swedish Model of Security Policy." *West European Politics* 14, no. 3 (1991): 122–143.

Gorman, Lyn, and Marja-Liisa Kiljunen. *The Enlargement of the European Community: Case-Studies of Greece, Portugal and Spain*. Spanish original edited by José Luis Sampedro and Juan Antonio Payno. London: Macmillan, 1983.

Granell, Francisco. "The European Union's Enlargement Negotiations with Austria, Finland, Norway and Sweden." *Journal of Common Market Studies* 33, no. 1 (1995): 117–141.

Green Cowles, Maria. "Setting the Agenda for a New Europe: The ERT and EC 1992." *Journal of Common Market Studies* 33, no. 4 (1995): 501–526.

Grindheim, Jan Erik. "Die Europäische Union: Von der funktionalen zur territorialen Integration?" In *Schweizer Eigenart—eigenartige Schweiz: Der Kleinstaat im Kräftefeld der europäischen Integration*, ed. by Wolf Linder, Prisca Lanfranchi and Ewald R. Weibel. Bern: Haupt, 1996, pp. 145–167.

Gstöhl, Sieglinde. "EFTA and the European Economic Area, or the Politics of Frustration." *Cooperation and Conflict* 29, no. 4 (1994): 333–366.

———. "The European Union After Amsterdam: Towards a Theoretical Approach to (Differentiated) Integration." In *The State of the European Union*. Vol. 5: *Risks, Reform, Resistance, and Revival*, ed. by Maria Green Cowles and Michael Smith. Oxford: Oxford University Press, 2000, pp. 42–63.

———. "Successfully Squaring the Circle: Liechtenstein's Membership of the Swiss and European Economic Area." In *Free Trade Agreements and Customs Unions: Experiences, Challenges and Constraints*, ed. by Madeleine O. Hösli and Arild Saether. Brussels/Maastricht: Tacis European Commission and European Institute of Public Administration, 1997, pp. 163–176.

———. "Switzerland, Norway and the EU: The Odd Ones Out?" *EURYOPA: Articles et conférences*, no. 2. Genève: Institut européen de l'Université de Genève, 1996.

Haaland, Jan I. "Assessing the Effects of EFTA-EC Integration on EFTA Countries: The Position of Norway and Sweden." *Journal of Common Market Studies* 28, no. 4 (1990): 379–400.

———. "Norway: The Trade Effects of European Integration." *The World Economy* 17, no. 5 (1994): 683–695.

Haaland, Jan I., and Victor D. Norman. "Global Production Effects of European Integration." In *Trade Flows and Trade Policy After "1992,"* ed. by L. Alan Winters. Cambridge: Cambridge University Press, 1992, pp. 67–88.

Haaland Matláry, Janne. "'And Never the Twain Shall Meet?' Reflections on Norway, Europe and Integration." In *The Nordic Countries and the EC*, ed. by Teija Tiilikainen and Ib Damgaard Petersen. Copenhagen: Copenhagen Political Studies Press, 1993, pp. 43–63.

Haas, Ernst B. "The Limits of Liberal Nationalism in Western Europe." In *The New Europe Asserts Itself: A Changing Role in International Relations*, ed. by Beverly Crawford and Peter W. Schulze. Berkeley: University of California, 1990, pp. 307–352.

———. *The Uniting of Europe: Political, Social and Economical Forces 1950–1957*. London: Stevens and Sons, 1958.

Haga, Otto Egil. *Identity and Inclination Towards Integration: A Comparative Study of Austria and Norway*. University of Oslo: Department of Political Science, Hovedfagsoppgave, 1995.

Halvorsen, Knut. "European Integration and the Effects on Regional Development in Norway." In *Visions and Strategies in European Integration: A North*

European Perspective, ed. by Lars Lundqvist and Lars Olof Persson. Berlin: Springer 1993, pp. 61–78.

Hamel, Stephan. "Eine solche Sache würde der Neutralitätspolitik ein Ende machen: Die österreichischen Integrationsbestrebungen 1961–1972." In *Österreich und die europäische Integration 1945–1993*, ed. by Michael Gehler and Rolf Steininger. Wien: Böhlau, 1993, pp. 55–86.

Hancock, M. Donald. "Sweden, Scandinavia and the EEC." *International Affairs* 48, no. 3 (1972): 424–437.

Hansen, Svein Olav. *Det Norske EFTA-sporet i 1950-åra: En studie av Norges Europa-politikk, med særlig vekt på perioden 1956–1960*. Oslo: University of Oslo, Department of History, Hovedfagsoppgave, 1990.

Hanssen, Halle Jörn, and Kaare Sandegren. "Norway and Western European Economic Integration." *Cooperation and Conflict* 4, no. 1 (1969): 47–62.

Hauser, Heinz, and Sven Bradke. *EWR-Vertrag, EG-Beitritt, Alleingang: Wirtschaftliche Konsequenzen für die Schweiz*. Chur: Rüegger, 1991.

Heclo, Hugh, and Henrik Madsen. *Policy and Politics in Sweden: Principled Pragmatism*. Philadelphia: Temple University Press, 1987.

Heer, Friedrich. *Der Kampf um die österreichische Identität*. Wien: Hermann Böhlaus, 1981.

Hellevik, Ottar, Nils Petter Gleditsch, and Kristen Ringdal. "The Common Market Issue in Norway: A Conflict between Center and Periphery." *Journal of Peace Research* 12, no. 1 (1975): 37–53.

Herin, Jan. "Rules of Origin and Differences Between Tariff Levels in EFTA and in the EC." *Occasional Paper* no. 13. Geneva: EFTA, Economic Affairs Department, 1986.

Hoefer, Richard. "Swedish Corporatism in Social Welfare Policy, 1986–1994: An Empirical Examination." *Scandinavian Political Studies* 19, no. 1 (1996): 67–80.

Hösli, Madeleine. "Decision-Making in the EEA and EFTA States' Sovereignty." *Aussenwirtschaft*, no. 4 (1990): 463–494.

———. "Trade Flows in Western Europe: The Experience of the European Community and of the European Free Trade Association." In *Free Trade Agreements and Customs Unions: Experiences, Challenges and Constraints*, ed. by Madeleine O. Hösli and Arild Saether. Brussels/Maastricht: Tacis European Commission and European Institute of Public Administration, 1997, pp. 145–162.

Huldt, Bo. "Sweden and European Community-Building 1945–92." In *Neutral States and the European Community*, ed. by Sheila Harden. London: Brassey's, 1994, pp. 104–143.

Hurni, Bettina. "EFTA-EC Relations After the Luxembourg Declaration." In *Facing the Change in Europe: EFTA Countries' Integration Strategies*, ed. by Kari Möttölä and Heikki Patomäki. Helsinki: Finnish Institute of International Affairs, 1989, pp. 88–101.

Huth-Spiess, Petra. *Europäisierung oder "Entschweizerung"? Der Abstimmungskampf der Schweiz um den Beitritt zum Europäischen Wirtschaftsraum*. Bern: Peter Lang, 1996.

Hveem, Helge. "The EEA and the Nordic Countries: End Station or Transition to EC Membership?" *Jean Monnet Chair Paper*. Florence: European University Institute, 1992.

Hylland Eriksen, Thomas. *Ethnicity and Nationalism: Anthropological Perspectives*. London: Pluto Press, 1993.

————. *Typisk norsk: Essays om kulturen i Norge.* Oslo: C. Huitfeldt Forlag, 1993.

Industrial Federations and Employers' Organisations of Austria, Denmark, Norway, Sweden, Switzerland, the United Kingdom. *Free Trade in Western Europe: A Joint Statement by the Industrial Federations and Employers' Organisations of Austria, Denmark, Norway, Sweden, Switzerland, the United Kingdom.* Paris, 14 April 1958.

Ingebritsen, Christine. "Coming Out of the Cold: Nordic Responses to European Union." In *Europe's Ambiguous Unity: Conflict and Consensus in the Post-Maastricht Era,* ed. by Alan W. Calfruny and Carl Lankowski. Boulder: Lynne Rienner, 1997, pp. 239–256.

————. *The Nordic States and European Unity.* Ithaca: Cornell University Press, 1998.

————. "Scandinavia in Europe: The Politics of Markets and Security." Ph.D. diss., Cornell University, 1993.

Ingebritsen, Christine, and Susan Larson. "Interest and Identity: Finland, Norway and European Union." *Cooperation and Conflict* 32, no. 2 (1997): 207–222.

International Herald Tribune. "Scandinavians Defrost Anti-European Attitudes," 24 February 1992, p. 2.

Jacot-Guillarmod, Olivier. "Conséquences, sur la démocratie suisse, d'une adhésion de la Suisse à la Communauté européenne." In *EG-Recht und schweizerische Rechtsordnung: Föderalismus, Demokratie, Neutralität, GATT und europäische Integration,* ed. by Olivier Jacot-Guillarmod, Dietrich Schindler, and Thomas Cottier. Basel: Helbing and Lichtenhahn, 1990, pp. 39–79.

————. "Conséquences, sur le fédéralisme suisse, d'une adhésion de la Suisse à la Communauté européenne." In *EG-Recht und schweizerische Rechtsordnung: Föderalismus, Demokratie, Neutralität, GATT und europäische Integration,* ed. by Olivier Jacot-Guillarmod, Dietrich Schindler and Thomas Cottier, Basel: Helbing and Lichtenhahn, 1990, pp. 7–37.

————, ed. *L'avenir du libre-échange en Europe: Vers un Espace économique européen?* Zürich: Schulthess Polygraphischer Verlag; Bern: Stämpfli, 1990.

Jamar, Joseph, and Helen Wallace, eds. *EEC-EFTA: More Than Just Good Friends? CEE-AELE: Mariage en vue?* Bruges: De Tempel, Tempelhof, 1988.

Jenssen, Anders Todal. "Etterspill." In *Brussel midt imot: Folkeavstemningen om EU,* ed. by Anders Todal Jenssen and Henry Valen. Gyldendal: Ad Notam, 1996, pp. 187–203.

————. "Ouverturen." In *Brussel midt imot: Folkeavstemningen om EU,* ed. by Anders Todal Jenssen and Henry Valen. Gyldendal: Ad Notam, 1996, pp. 13–29.

Jenssen, Anders Todal, Ola Listhaug, and Per Arnt Pettersen. "Betydningen av gamle og nye skiller." In *Brussel midt imot: Folkeavstemningen om EU,* ed. by Anders Todal Jenssen and Henry Valen. Gyldendal: Ad Notam, 1996, pp. 143–163.

Jerneck, Magnus. "Sweden: The Reluctant European?" In *The Nordic Countries and the EC,* ed. by Teija Tiilikainen and Ib Damgaard Petersen. Copenhagen: Copenhagen Political Studies Press, 1993, pp. 23–42.

Jorna, Marc. "The Accession Negotiations with Austria, Sweden, Finland and Norway: A Guided Tour." *European Law Review* 20, no. 2 (1995): 131–158.

Juel, Steinar. "Norway and Free Trade in Services." In *Norway and the European Community: The Political Economy of Integration,* ed. by Brent F. Nelsen. Westport: Praeger, 1993, pp. 115–137.

Junod, E. "Les entreprises suisses et le grand espace économique européen." In *La*

Suisse devant l'élargissement de la Communauté économique européenne. Geneva: Institut universitaire de hautes études internationales, 1971, 28–42.

Kaiser, Karl. *EWG und Freihandelszone: England und der Kontinent in der europäischen Integration.* Leiden: A. W. Sythoff, 1963.

Kaiser, Wolfram, et al. "Die EU-Volksabstimmungen in Österreich, Finnland, Schweden und Norwegen: Verlauf, Ergebnisse, Motive und Folgen." *Forschungsberichte,* no. 23. Wien: Institut für Höhere Studien, 1995.

Karlsson, Michael. *Partistrategi och utrikespolitik: Interna motiveringar och dagspressens agerande i Catalina-affären 1952 och EEC-frågan 1961/62.* Stockholm: Stockholms universitet, Statsvetenskapliga institutionen, 1995.

Katzenstein, Peter J. *Corporatism and Change: Austria, Switzerland, and the Politics of Industry.* Ithaca: Cornell University Press, 1984.

———. "Introduction: Alternative Perspectives on National Security." In *The Culture of National Security: Norms and Identity in World Politics,* ed. by Peter J. Katzenstein. New York: Columbia University Press, 1996, pp. 1–32.

———. "The Small European States in the International Economy: Economic Dependence and Corporatist Politics." In *The Antinomies of Interdependence: National Welfare and the International Division of Labor,* ed. by John Gerard Ruggie. New York: Columbia University Press, 1983, pp. 91–130.

———. *Small States in World Markets: Industrial Policy in Europe.* Ithaca: Cornell University Press, 1985.

———. "Trends and Oscillations in Austrian Integration Policy Since 1955: Alternative Explanations." *Journal of Common Market Studies* 14, no. 2 (1975): 171–197.

Keel, Guido Adalberto. *Le grand patronat suisse face à l'intégration européenne.* Bern: Peter Lang, 1980.

Keohane, Robert O. "Ideas Part-way Down." *Review of International Studies* 26, no. 1 (2000): 125–130.

Keohane, Robert O., and Joseph S. Nye. "Power and Interdependence Revisited." *International Organization* 41, no. 4 (1987): 725–753.

Kite, Cynthia. "Scandinavia Faces EU: Debates and Decisions on Membership 1961–1994." Ph.D. diss., University of Umeå, 1996.

Kleppe, Per. "Momentum of Nordic Integration." In *Europe's Free Trade Area Experiment: EFTA and Economic Integration,* ed. by Hugh Corbet and David Robertson. Oxford: Pergamon Press, 1970, pp. 147–165.

———. "The Single Market and Commercial Relations for Non-Member Countries: Views from the EFTA Countries." *Journal of Development Planning,* no. 21 (1992): 147–161.

Knudsen, Bård Bredrup. "Den nye Europa-debatten." In *Den nye Europa-debatten: Partiene og Norges forhold til EF mot år 2000,* ed. by Bård Bredrup Knudsen. Drammen: Cappelen, 1989, pp. 390–449.

———. "Norsk Europa-politikk, EF og de historiske og kulturelle rammebetingelser." In *Den nye Europa-debatten: Partiene og Norges forhold til EF mot år 2000,* ed. by Bård Bredrup Knudsen. Drammen: Cappelen, 1989, pp. 15–85.

———, ed. *Den nye Europa-debatten: Partiene og Norges forhold til EF mot år 2000.* Drammen: Cappelen, 1989.

Knutsen, Oddbjørn. "Political Cleavages and Political Realignment in Norway: The New Politics Thesis Reexamined." *Scandinavian Political Studies* 9, no. 3 (1986): 235–263.

Koppensteiner, Hans-Georg. *Rechtsfragen der Freihandelsabkommen der*

Europäischen Wirtschaftsgemeinschaft mit den EFTA-Staaten. Wien: Orac, 1987.

Kreinin, Mordechai E. "The 'Outer-Seven' and European Integration." *American Economic Review* 50, no. 3 (1960): 370–386.

Kreissler, Felix. *L'Autriche, treizième des Douze: Entre "nostalgies" et "obsolescences," quelle identitè?* Rouen: University of Rouen, 1993.

Kriesi, Hanspeter. *Le système politique suisse.* Paris: Economica, 1995.

———. "The Structure of the Swiss Political System." In *Patterns of Corporatist Policy-Making,* ed. by Gerhard Lehmbruch and Philippe C. Schmitter. London: Sage, 1982, pp. 133–161.

Kriesi, Hanspeter, et al. *Analyse de la votation fédérale du 6 décembre 1992.* Berne: Institut de recherche pratique GfS/Département de science politique de l'Université de Genève, 1993.

———. *Le clivage linguistique: Problèmes de compréhension entre les communautés linguistiques en Suisse.* Bern: Office fédéral de la statistique, 1996.

———. *New Social Movements in Western Europe: A Comparative Analysis.* Minneapolis: University of Minnesota Press, 1995.

Kristinsson, Gunnar Helgi. "Iceland: Vulnerability in a Fish-based Economy." *Cooperation and Conflict* 22, no. 4 (1987): 245–253.

Kronsell, Annica, and Erika Svedberg. "The Duty to Protect: Gender in the Swedish Practice of Conscription." *Cooperation and Conflict* 36, no. 2 (2001): 153–176.

Krugman, Paul. "EFTA and 1992." *Occasional Papers* no. 23. Geneva: EFTA, Economic Affairs Department, 1988.

Kurzer, Paulette. *Business and Banking: Political Change and Economic Integration in Western Europe.* Ithaca: Cornell University Press, 1993.

Kvavik, Robert B. *Interest Groups in Norwegian Politics.* Oslo: Universitetsforlaget, 1976.

"La demande d'adhésion de la Suède." Special issue of *Revue du Marché Commun et de l'Union Européenne,* no. 359 (1992).

Lachman, Desmond, et al. "Challenges to the Swedish Welfare State." *Occasional Paper* no. 130. Washington, D.C.: International Monetary Fund, 1995.

L'AELE d'hier à demain: EFTA from Yesterday to Tomorrow, ed. by the European Free Trade Association, Institut universitaire d'études européennes (IUEE) and Fondation Archives européennes, under the direction of Pierre du Bois and Bettina Hurni. Geneva: EFTA, IUEE, 1987.

Laffan, Brigid. "Sovereignty and National Identity." In *Ireland and EC Membership Evaluated,* ed. by Patrick Keatinge. London: Pinter, 1991, pp. 187–189.

Lambert, J. R. "The Neutrals and the Common Market." *The World Today* 18, no. 10 (1962): 444–452.

Lambrinidis, John S. *The Structure, Function, and Law of a Free Trade Area: The European Free Trade Association.* London: Stevens and Sons, 1965.

Lange, Halvard M. "European Union: False Hopes and Realities." *Foreign Affairs* 28, no. 3 (1950): 441–450.

Langejürgen, Ralf. *Die Eidgenossenschaft zwischen Rütli und EWR: Der Versuch einer Neuorientierung der Schweizer Europapolitik.* Zürich: Rüegger, 1993.

Lawler, Peter. "Scandinavian Exceptionalism and European Union." *Journal of Common Market Studies* 35, no. 4 (1997): 565–594.

Legro, Jeffrey W. *Cooperation under Fire: Anglo-German Restraint During World War II.* Ithaca: Cornell University Press, 1995.

Leitner, Gregor. "Der Weg nach Brüssel: Zur Geschichte des österreichischen EG-Beitrittsantrages vom 17 Juli 1989." In *Österreich und die europäische*

Integration 1945–1993, ed. by Michael Gehler and Rolf Steininger. Wien: Böhlau, 1993, pp. 87–108.

Le Monde. "La querelle reprend sur la zone de libre-échange," 16–17 November 1958.

———. "Notre préoccupation centrale est de maintenir l'équilibre qui existe en Europe du Nord," 16 April 1970.

Leskelä, Jukka. "EFTA Countries' Foreign Direct Investment." *EFTA Trade 1990.* Geneva: EFTA, 1991, pp. 21–29.

Lie, Bjarne. "A Gulliver Among Lilliputians: A History of the European Free Trade Association 1960–1972." Cand. Philos. thesis, University of Oslo, 1995.

Lijphardt, Arend, and Markus M. L. Crepaz. "Corporatism and Consensus Democracy in Eighteen Countries: Conceptual and Empirical Linkages." *British Journal of Political Science* 21, no. 2 (1991): 235–246.

Lindbeck, Assar, et al. *Turning Sweden Around.* Cambridge: MIT Press, 1994.

Lindgren, Raymond E. *Norway-Sweden: Union, Disunion, and Scandinavian Integration.* Princeton: Princeton University Press, 1959.

Lisein-Norman, Margaretha. *La Suède face à l'intégration européenne.* Bruxelles: Institut d'études européennes, 1975.

Lister, Louis. *Europe's Coal and Steel Community: An Experiment in Economic Union.* New York: Twentieth Century Fund, 1960.

Ljung, Bengt. "The EFTA Countries' European Integration Policies: In Search for a Place in Europe." Master's thesis, Johns Hopkins University, 1991.

Logue, John. "The Legacy of Swedish Neutrality." In *The Committed Neutral: Sweden's Foreign Policy*, ed. by Bengt Sundelius. Boulder: Westview Press, 1989, pp. 35–65.

Lombardi, Aldo. "Verwirklichung des EWR-Abkommens durch Bund und Kantone." In *Accord EEE: Commentaires et réflexions. EWR-Abkommen: Erste Analysen. EEA Agreement: Comments and Reflexions*, ed. by Olivier Jacot-Guillarmod. Zürich: Schulthess Polygraphischer Verlag; Bern: Stämpfli, 1992, pp. 721–770.

Ludlow, Peter. "Public Opinion in the Nordic Candidate Countries: An Overview." In "The Fourth Enlargement: Public Opinion in the Nordic Candidate Countries." *CEPS Paper* no. 56. Brussels: Centre for European Policy Studies, 1994, pp. 1–27.

Luif, Paul. "The European Neutrals and Economic Integration in Western Europe." *Annuaire Européen. European Yearbook 1987.* Published under the Auspices of the Council of Europe 35, Dordrecht: Martinus Nijhoff, 1989, pp. 1–25.

———. *Neutrale in die EG? Die westeuropäische Integration und die neutralen Staaten.* Wien: Braumüller, 1988.

———. *On the Road to Brussels: The Political Dimension of Austria's, Finland's and Sweden's Accession to the European Union.* Wien: Braumüller, 1995.

Lundberg, Lars. "Finland: Economics and Politics of EU Accession: A Comment." *The World Economy* 17, no. 5 (1994): 715–718.

———. "Konsekvenser för svensk industri av EGs inre marknad." In *Svensk industri inför EG '92.* Stockholm: Statens Industriverk, 1989, pp. 51–62.

Magee, Stephen P., William A. Brock, and Leslie Young. *Black Hole Tariffs and Endogenous Political Theory: Political Economy in General Equilibrium.* Cambridge: Cambridge University Press, 1989.

Marcussen, Martin, et al. "Constructing Europe? The Evolution of French, British and German Nation State Identities." *Journal of European Public Policy* 6, no. 4 (1999): 614–633.

Marschang, Elisabeth. "Der 'Luxemburg-Prozess' als eine Komponente der EFTA-EG-Zusammenarbeit." Ph.D. diss., University of Innsbruck, 1992.

Mattli, Walter. *The Logic of Regional Integration: Europe and Beyond*. Cambridge: Cambridge University Press, 1999.

Melich, Anna. "Identité nationale." In *Les valeurs des Suisses*, ed. by Anna Melich. Bern: Peter Lang, 1991, pp. 13–58.

Mendershausen, Horst. "First Tests of the Schuman Plan." *The Review of Economics and Statistics* 35 (1953): 269–288.

Michalski, Anna, and Helen Wallace. *The European Community: The Challenge of Enlargement*. London: Royal Institute of International Affairs, 1992.

Middleton, Robert. *Negotiating on Non-Tariff Distortions of Trade: The EFTA Precedents*. London: Trade Policy Research Centre, 1975.

———. "Quelques barrières non tarifaires aux échanges dans l'AELE et la CEE." *EFTA Bulletin* 13, no. 9 (1972): 18–19.

Miles, Lee. "Conclusion: Polishing the 'Membership Diamond.'" In *Sweden and the European Union Evaluated*, ed. by Lee Miles. London: Continuum, 2000, pp. 231–248.

———. "The European Union and the Nordic Countries: Impacts on the Integration Process." In *The State of the European Union 3: Building a European Polity?* Ed. by Carolyn Rhodes and Sonia Mazey. Boulder: Lynne Rienner, 1995, pp. 317–334.

———. *Sweden and European Integration*. Aldershot: Ashgate, 1997.

Miljan, Toivo. "The Nordic Countries: Europe's Reluctant Partners." In *The European Community and the Outsiders*, ed. by Peter Stingelin. Don Mills: Longman, 1973, pp. 117–136.

———. *The Reluctant Europeans: The Attitudes of the Nordic Countries Towards European Integration*. Montreal: McGill-Queen's University Press, 1977.

Milner, Henry. *Sweden: Social Democracy in Practice*. Oxford: Oxford University Press, 1989.

Milward, Alan S. *The Reconstruction of Western Europe: 1945–51*. London: Methuen, 1984.

Mjøset, Lars. "Nordic Economic Policies in the 1970s and 1980s." *International Organization* 41, no. 3 (1987): 403–456.

Mjøset, Lars, et al. *Norden dagen derpå: Den nordiske økonomisk-politiske modellene og deres problemer på 70- og 80-tallet*. Oslo: Universitetsforlaget, 1986.

Moravcsik, Andrew. *The Choice for Europe: Social Purpose and State Power from Messina to Maastricht*. Ithaca: Cornell University Press, 1998.

———. "Preferences and Power in the European Community: A Liberal Intergovernmentalist Approach." *Journal of Common Market Studies* 31, no. 4 (1993): 473–524.

———. "Taking Preferences Seriously: A Liberal Theory of International Politics." *International Organization* 51, no. 4 (1997): 513–553.

Moses, Jonathon W., and Anders Todal Jenssen. "Nordic Accession: An Analysis of the EU Referendums." In *Forging an Integrated Europe*, ed. by Barry Eichengreen and Jeffry Frieden. Ann Arbor: University of Michigan Press, 1998, pp. 211–246.

Muoser, Toni. *Finnlands Neutralität und die Europäische Wirtschaftsintegration*. Baden-Baden: Nomos, 1986.

Nef, Rolf. "Die Schweizer Referendumsdemokratie." *Der Bürger im Staat* 38, no. 1 (1988): 53–60.

Nell, Philippe G. "EFTA in the 1990s: The Search for a New Identity." *Journal of Common Market Studies* 28, no. 4 (1990): 327–358.

Nelson, Douglas. "Endogenous Tariff Theory: A Critical Survey." *American Journal of Political Science* 32, no. 3 (1988): 796–837.

Neue Zürcher Zeitung. "Aktivere Aussenpolitik der Schweiz?" 30 January 1967.

———. "Die Einbusse an direkter Demokratie," 11 October 1995.

———. "Die OEEC-Debatte über die Freihandelszone," 14 February 1957.

———. "Die Schweiz und die Europäische Wirtschaftsgemeinschaft," 5 September 1961.

———. "Erosion des traditionalistischen Neutralitätsbildes," 10 July 1997.

———. "Politischer Durchbruch ohne die Schweiz," 15 May 1991.

Neumann, Iver B. "The Nordic States and European Unity." *Cooperation and Conflict* 36, no. 1 (2001): 87–94.

Nicholson, Frances, and Roger East. *From the Six to the Twelve: The Enlargement of the European Communities.* Harlow: Longman, 1987.

Norberg, Sven. "The Agreement on a European Economic Area." *Common Market Law Review* 29, no. 6 (1992): 1171–1198.

———. "The Free Trade Agreements of the EFTA Countries with the EC: Experiences and Problems." *Svensk Juristtidning* (1988): 77–107.

Norman, Victor D. "EFTA and the Internal European Market." *Economic Policy*, no. 9 (1989): 423–465.

———. "1992 and EFTA." In *European Integration: Trade and Industry*, ed. by L. Alan Winters and Anthony J. Venables. Cambridge: Cambridge University Press, 1991, pp. 120–139.

North, Douglass C. *Institutions, Institutional Change and Economic Performance.* Cambridge: Cambridge University Press, 1990.

Nydegger, Alfred. "Die Einstellung der drei EFTA-Neutralen gegenüber der EWG." *Wirtschaft und Recht* 14 (1962): 3–15.

Odhner, Clas-Erik. *Sverige i Europa.* Stockholm: Rabén and Sjögren, 1962.

Ohlsson, Lennart. *Industrin inför EGs 90tal: En strategisk effektanalys.* Stockholm: Industriförbundets Förlag, 1989.

O'Keeffe, David. "The Agreement on the European Economic Area." *Legal Issues of European Integration*, no. 1 (1992): 1–27.

Olsen, Johan. *Organized Democracy: Political Institutions in a Welfare State—the Case of Norway.* Oslo: Univeritetsforlaget, 1983.

Olssen, Ulf. "The Swedish Social Democrats." In *Socialist Parties and the Question of Europe in the 1950s*, ed. by Richard T. Griffiths. Leiden: E. J. Brill, 1993, pp. 221–238.

Olsson, Sven E. *Social Policy and Welfare State in Sweden.* 2nd ed. Lund: Arkiv, 1993.

Ørvik, Nils. "Från halvneutralitet till halvallians." *Internationella Studier*, no. 1 (1990): 31–44.

Oskarson, Maria, and Kristen Ringdal. "The Arguments." In *To Join or Not to Join: Three Nordic Referendums on Membership in the European Union*, ed. by Anders Todal Jenssen, Pertti Pesonen, and Mikael Gilljam. Oslo: Scandinavian University Press, 1998, pp. 149–167.

Østergård, Uffe. "Peasants and Danes: The Danish National Identity and Political Culture." *Comparative Studies in Society and History* 34, no. 1 (1992): 3–27.

Östrem, Inger-Lise. "La Norvège et la Communauté européenne: D'une appartenance de fait à une appartenance de droit?" *Revue du Marché Commun et de l'Union Européenne*, no. 364 (1993): 8–23.

Pedersen, Thomas. *European Union and the EFTA Countries: Enlargement and Integration.* London: Pinter, 1994.

Petersen, Nikolaj. "Denmark and the European Union 1985–96: A Two-Level Analysis." *Cooperation and Conflict* 31, no. 2 (1996): 185–210.

Petersmann, Hans G. *Die Souveränität des Britischen Parlaments in den Europäischen Gemeinschaften.* Baden-Baden: Nomos, 1972.

Petersson, Olof, and Henry Valen. "Political Cleavages in Sweden and Norway." *Scandinavian Political Studies* 2, no. 1 (1979): 313–331.

Pfetsch, Frank. "Tensions in Sovereignty: Foreign Policies of EC Members Compared." In *European Foreign Policy: The EC and Changing Perspectives in Europe,* ed. by Walter Carlsnaes and Steve Smith. London: Sage, 1994, pp. 120–137.

Pharo, Helge. "Norge, EF og europeisk samarbeid." *Internasjonal Politikk,* no. 6 (1988): 41–67.

———. "The Norwegian Labour Party." In *Socialist Parties and the Question of Europe in the 1950s,* ed. by Richard T. Griffiths. Leiden: E. J. Brill, 1993: 201–220.

———. "The Third Force, Atlanticism and Norwegian Attitudes Towards European Integration." *EUI Working Papers,* no. 255. Florence: European University Institute, 1986.

Phinnemore, David. "The Nordic Countries, the European Community (EC) and the European Free Trade Association (EFTA), 1958–84." In *The European Union and the Nordic Countries,* ed. by Lee Miles, London: Routledge, 1996, pp. 32–46.

Pintado, Xavier, et al. "Economic Aspects of the European Economic Space." *Occasional Papers* no. 25. Geneva: EFTA, Economic Affairs Department, 1988.

Plessow, Utta. *Neutralität und Assoziation mit der EWG: Dargestellt am Beispiel der Schweiz, Schwedens und Österreichs.* Köln: Carl Heymanns Verlag, 1967.

Pollack, Mark. "International Relations Theory and European Integration." *Journal of Common Market Studies* 39, no. 2 (2001): 221–244.

Prebensen, Chris. *Norway and NATO.* Oslo: Royal Ministry for Foreign Affairs, 1974.

Putnam, Robert D. "Diplomacy and Domestic Politics: The Logic of Two-Level Games." *International Organization* 42, no. 3 (1988): 427–460.

Rae, Douglas W., and Michael Taylor. *The Analysis of Political Cleavages.* New Haven: Yale University Press, 1970.

Ramberg, Trygve. "Sovereignty and Cooperation." In *Fears and Expectations: Norwegian Attitudes Toward European Integration,* ed. by Nils Örvik. Oslo: Universitetsforlaget, 1972, pp. 49–133.

Rappard, William E. "L'intégration économique de l'Europe et la Suisse: Le problème envisagé du point de vue politique." *Schweizerische Zeitschrift für Volkswirtschaft und Statistik,* no. 4 (1952): 301–311.

Redmond, John. *The Next Mediterranean Enlargement of the European Community: Turkey, Cyprus and Malta?* Aldershot: Dartmouth, 1993.

Reinisch, August. "The European Economic Area." *The Journal of Social, Political and Economic Studies* 18, no. 3 (1993): 279–309.

Reinsvollsveen, Gerd. "Den europeiske velferdsstat: hva nå?." In *Og atter nei? Norge og EF,* ed. by Rolf Berg. Oslo: Pax, 1989, pp. 119–141.

Reymond, Christophe. "Institutions, Decision-Making Procedure and Settlement of Disputes in the European Economic Area." *Common Market Law Review* 30, no. 3 (1993): 449–480.

Riklin, Alois. *Schweizerische Demokratie und EWG*. Zürich: Schweizerischer Aufklärungs-Dienst (SAD), Arbeitsheft W8, 1972.

Ringdal, Kristen. "Velgernes argumenter." In *Brussel midt imot: Folkeavstemningen om EU*, ed. by Anders Todal Jenssen and Henry Valen. Gyldendal: Ad Notam, 1996, pp. 45–64.

Ringdal, Kristen, and Henry Valen. "Structural Divisions in the EU Referendums." In *To Join or Not to Join: Three Nordic Referendums on Membership in the European Union*, ed. by Anders Todal Jenssen, Pertti Pesonen, and Mikael Gilljam. Oslo: Scandinavian University Press, 1998, pp. 168–193.

Risse, Thomas. "A European Identity? Europeanization and the Evolution of Nation-State Identities." In *Transforming Europe: Europeanization and Domestic Change*, ed. by Maria Green Cowles, James Caporaso, and Thomas Risse. Ithaca: Cornell University Press, 2001, pp. 198–216.

Risse-Kappen, Thomas. "Exploring the Nature of the Beast: International Relations Theory and Comparative Policy Analysis Meet the European Union." *Journal of Common Market Studies* 34, no. 1 (1996): 53–80.

———. "Public Opinion, Domestic Structure, and Foreign Policy in Liberal Democracies." *World Politics* 43, no. 4 (1991): 479–512.

———. "Transnational Relations, Domestic Structures, and International Institutions: A Conceptual Framework." Paper prepared for delivery at the Annual Meeting of the American Political Science Association, Chicago, 3–6 September 1992.

Robinson, Mary, and Jantien Findlater. *Creating a European Economic Space: Legal Aspects of EC-EFTA Relations*. Dublin: Irish Centre for European Law, 1990.

Roethlisberger, Eric. *La Suisse dans l'Association européenne de libre-échange (1960–1966): Sept années d'intégration économique dans un cadre européen restreint*. Neuchâtel: La Baconnière, 1969.

Røhne, Nils A. "De første skritt inn i Europa: Norsk Europa-politikk fra 1950." *Forsvarsstudier* no. 5. Oslo: Institutt for forsvarsstudier, 1989.

Rokkan, Stein. "Geography, Religion, and Social Class: Crosscutting Cleavages in Norwegian Politics." In *Party Systems and Voter Alignments: Cross-National Perspectives*, ed. by Seymour M. Lipset and Stein Rokkan. New York: Free Press, 1967, pp. 367–444.

Rokkan, Stein, and Henry Valen. "Regional Contrasts in Norwegian Politics: A Review of Data from Official Statistics and from Sample Surveys." In *Mass Politics: Studies in Political Sociology*, ed. by Erik Allardt and Stein Rokkan. New York: Free Press, 1970, pp. 190–247.

Ruffieux, Roland, and Anne-Lise Thurler Muller. "L'opinion publique face à l'intégration européenne: que disent et ne disent pas les sondages?" In *La Suisse et son avenir européen: une analyse des positions suisses face à l'intégration de l'Europe*, ed. by Roland Ruffieux and Annik Schachtschneider Morier-Genoud. Lausanne: Payot, 1989, pp. 237–252.

Ruin, Påhl. *Svensk neutralitetspolitik: Hur har den bedrivits i EG-frågan?* University of Lund: Department of Political Science, Trebetygsuppsats, 1988.

Ruth, Arne. "The Second New Nation: The Mythology of Modern Sweden." *Dædalus* 113, no. 2 (1984): 53–96.

Sæter, Martin. "Norway and the European Union: Domestic Debate Versus External Reality." In *The European Union and the Nordic Countries*, ed. by Lee Miles. London: Routledge, 1996, pp. 133–149.

———. "Norway: An EFTA Road to Membership?" In *EFTA and the EC:*

Implications of 1992, ed. by Finn Laursen. Maastricht: European Institute of Public Administration, 1990, pp. 115–133.

Sæter, Martin, and Olav F. Knudsen. "Norway." In *The Wider Western Europe: Reshaping the EC/EFTA Relationship*, ed. by Helen Wallace. London: Pinter, Royal Institute of International Affairs, 1991, pp: 179–193.

Sandholtz, Wayne. "Membership Matters: Limits of the Functional Approach to European Institutions." *Journal of Common Market Studies* 34, no. 3 (1996): 403–429.

Särlvik, Bo. "Sweden: The Social Bases of the Parties in a Developmental Perspective." In *Electoral Behavior: A Comparative Handbook*, ed. by Richard Rose. New York: Free Press, 1974, pp. 371–434.

Schaffner, Hans. "La Suisse et les grandes organisations économiques internationales." *Revue économique et sociale* 13, no. 4 (1955): 241–259.

Schindler, Dietrich. "Auswirkungen der EG auf die schweizerische Staatsstruktur." *Wirtschaftspolitische Mitteilungen*, no. 2 (1990): 1–18.

––––––. "Die Lehre von den Vorwirkungen der Neutralität." In *Festschrift für Rudolf Bindschedler*, ed. by Emanuel Diez, Jean Monnier, Jörg P. Müller, Heinrich Reimann, and Luzius Wildhaber. Bern: Stämpfli, 1980, pp. 563–582.

––––––. "Die Schweiz und die europäische Integration: Völkerrechtliche und staatsrechtliche Aspekte." In *Die Schweiz und die europäische Integration*. Zürich: Schweizerische Kreditanstalt, 1968, pp. 73–95.

––––––. "Neutralitätsrechtliche Aspekte eines Beitrittes der Schweiz zur EWG." *Wirtschaft und Recht*, no. 4 (1959): 217–228.

––––––. "Spezifische politische Probleme aus Schweizer Sicht." In *Die Neutralen in der europäischen Integration: Kontroversen, Konfrontationen, Alternativen*, ed. by Hans Mayrzedt and Hans Christoph Binswanger. Wien: Wilhelm Braumüller, 1970, pp. 277–287.

––––––. "Vereinbarkeit von EG-Mitgliedschaft und Neutralität." In *EG-Recht und schweizerische Rechtsordnung: Föderalismus, Demokratie, Neutralität, GATT und europäische Integration*, ed. by Olivier Jacot-Guillarmod, Dietrich Schindler, and Thomas Cottier. Basel: Helbing and Lichtenhahn, 1990, pp. 81–137.

Schmid, Carol L. *Conflict and Consensus in Switzerland*. Berkeley: University of California Press, 1981.

Schmitter, Philippe C. "Three Neo-functional Hypotheses about International Integration." *International Organization* 23, no. 1 (1969): 161–166.

Schneider, Heinrich. *Alleingang nach Brüssel: Österreichs EG-Politik*. Bonn: Europa Union Verlag, 1990.

Schou, Tove Lise. *Norge og EF: En undersøgelse af ydre og indre faktorers påvirkning af de norske partiers stillingtagen til spørgsmålet om Norges forhold til EF 1961–1972*. Copenhagen: Københavns Universitets Institut for Samfundsfag, Forlaget Politiske Studier, 1980.

Schwendimann, Thomas. *Herausforderung Europa: Integrationspolitische Debatten in Österreich und in der Schweiz 1985–1989*. Frankfurt/Main: Peter Lang, 1993.

Schwok, René. "L'AELE face à la Communauté européenne: un risque de satellisation." *Revue d'intégration européenne. Journal of European Integration* 13, no. 1 (1989): 15–53.

––––––. "Switzerland: The European Union's Self-appointed Pariah." In *Prospective Europeans: New Members for the European Union*, ed. by John Redmond. New York: Harvester Wheatsheaf, 1994, pp. 21–39.

Sciarini, Pascal, and Ola Listhaug. "Single Cases or a Unique Pair? The Swiss and Norwegian 'No' to Europe." *Journal of Common Market Studies* 35, no. 3 (1997): 407–438.

Sebenius, James K. "Challenging Conventional Explanations of International Cooperation: Negotiation Analysis and the Case of Epistemic Communities," *International Organization* 46, no. 1 (1992): 323–365.

Seidman, Bert. *Report on a Study of Trade Union Views on European Economic Community–European Free Trade Area Developments*. Paris, 1960.

Seip, Anne-Lise. "Nation-building Within the Union: Politics, Class and Culture in the Norwegian Nation-State in the Nineteenth Century." *Scandinavian Journal of History* 20, no. 1 (1995): 35–50.

Senti, Richard. "Switzerland." In *The Wider Western Europe: Reshaping the EC/EFTA Relationship*, ed. by Helen Wallace, London: Pinter, Royal Institute of International Affairs, 1991, pp. 215–230.

Siegler, Heinrich. *Dokumentation der europäischen Integration: 1946–1961, unter besonderer Beachtung des Verhältnisses EWG-EFTA*. Bonn: Verlag für Zeitarchive, 1961.

Skodvin, Magne. *Norden eller NATO? Utenriksdepartementet og alliansespørsmålet 1947–1949*. Oslo: Universitetsforlaget, 1971.

Smith, Anthony D. *National Identity*. Reno: University of Nevada Press, 1991.

Smyrl, Marc. "When (and How) Do the Commission's Preferences Matter?" *Journal of Common Market Studies* 36, no. 1 (1998): 79–99.

Snoy et d'Oppuers, Baron J. "Les étapes de la coopération européenne et les négociations relatives à une zone de libre échange." *Chronique de politique étrangère* 12, nos. 5–6 (1959): 569–623.

Sogner, Ingrid. "The European Idea: The Scandinavian Answer. Norwegian Attitudes Towards a Closer Scandinavian Economic Cooperation 1947–1959." *Scandinavian Journal of History* 18, no. 4 (1993): 307–327.

Sollohub, Maria. "National Identity and the Norwegian EC Debate." Master's thesis, University of Southampton, 1991.

Spierenburg, Dirk, and Raymond Poidevin. *Histoire de la Haute Autorité de la Communauté Européenne du Charbon et de l'Acier: une expérience supranationale*. Brussels: Bruylant, 1993.

Steinberg, Jonathan. *Why Switzerland?* Cambridge: Cambridge University Press, 1976.

Stenberg, Hans. "Sweden and the Internal Market: Situating Some Problems." *Legal Issues of European Integration*, no. 1 (1989): 89–107.

Stephens, John S. "The Scandinavian Welfare States: Achievements, Crisis, and Prospects." In *Welfare States in Transition: National Adaptations in Global Economies*, ed. by Gøsta Esping-Andersen. London: Sage, 1996, pp. 32–65.

Steppacher, Burkard. *Schritte zur Europäisierung der Schweiz: Politisches System und Wirtschaftsverbände in den Jahren 1985 bis 1990*. Frankfurt/Main: Peter Lang, 1992.

Stråth, Bo. *Folkhemmet mot Europa: Ett historiskt perspektiv på 90-talet*. Falun: ScandBook, 1993.

Sundelius, Bengt. "Committing Neutrality in an Antagonistic World." In *The Committed Neutral: Sweden's Foreign Policy*, ed. by Bengt Sundelius, Boulder: Westview Press, 1989, pp. 1–13.

"Sverige och Europamarknaden." *Studier och debatt*, no. 3, 1957.

Sveriges Industriförbundet. "EGs handelspolitik och svensk industri."

Books and Articles   247

Industriförbundets serie om Sverige och EG no. 9. Stockholm: Industrilitteratur, 1993.

———. *Världen, EU och Sverige: En handelspolitisk betraktelse.* Stockholm: Industrilitteratur, 1994.

Tanner, Albert, and Denis von Burg. "Arbeitsgruppe 'Politische Aspekte schweizerischer Identität.'" In *Schweizer Eigenart—eigenartige Schweiz: Der Kleinstaat im Kräftefeld der europäischen Integration,* ed. by Wolf Linder, Prisca Lanfranchi, and Ewald R. Weibel. Bern: Haupt, 1996, pp. 281–289.

Tariffs and Trade in Western Europe. London: Political and Economic Planning, 1959.

Tiilikainen, Teija. *Europe and Finland: Defining the Political Identity of Finland in Western Europe.* Aldershot: Ashgate, 1998.

The Times. "Equal Footing with Great Power Groups: Full Text of Mr. Macmillan's Case for the Common Market," 8 October 1962, p. 8.

Underdal, Arild. "Diverging Roads to Europe." *Cooperation and Conflict* 10, nos. 1–2 (1975): 65–76.

Urwin, Derek W. *The Community of Europe: A History of European Integration Since 1945.* 2nd ed. London: Longman, 1995.

Valen, Henry. "National Conflict Structure and Foreign Politics: The Impact of the EEC Issue on Perceived Cleavages in Norwegian Politics." *European Journal of Political Research* 4, no. 1 (1976): 47–82.

———. "Norway: 'No' to EEC." *Scandinavian Political Studies* 8 (1973): 214–226.

Valen, Henry, and Stein Rokkan. "Norway: Conflict Structure and Mass Politics in a European Periphery." In *Electoral Behavior: A Comparative Handbook,* ed. by Richard Rose. New York: Free Press, 1974, pp. 315–370.

van Ham, Peter. *The EC, Eastern Europe and European Unity: Discord, Collaboration and Integration Since 1947.* London: Pinter, 1993.

Vefald, Olav. "The 1967 EEC Debate." In *Fears and Expectations: Norwegian Attitudes Toward European Integration,* ed. by Nils Örvik. Oslo: Universitetsforlaget, 1972, pp. 207–279.

———. "The 1971 EEC Debate." In *Fears and Expectations: Norwegian Attitudes Toward European Integration,* ed. by Nils Örvik. Oslo: Universitetsforlaget, 1972, pp. 280–314.

Veyrassat, Paul. *La Suisse et la création de l'AELE (1958–1960).* Neuchâtel: La Baconnière, 1969.

———. "L'économie suisse face à 1992: Perspectives et priorités." In *La Suisse et son avenir européen: Une analyse des positions suisses face à l'intégration de l'Europe,* ed. by Roland Ruffieux and Annik Schachtschneider Morier-Genoud. Lausanne: Payot, 1989, pp. 177–185.

Viklund, Daniel. "Neutraliteten som svensk EG-hinder." In *Europa och Sverige: EF-frågan inför 90-talet,* ed. by Carl B. Hamilton et al. 2nd ed. Stockholm: SNS, 1989, pp. 253–260.

———. *Spelet om frihandelsavtalet: En kritisk studie i svensk utrikespolitik 1959–1972.* Stockholm: Rabén och Sjögren, 1977.

———. *Sweden and the European Community: Trade, Cooperation and Policy Issues.* Stockholm: Swedish Institute, 1989.

von Dosenrode, Sören Zibrandt. "Denmark: The Testing of a Hesitant Membership." In *Adapting to European Integration: Small States and the European Union,* ed. by Kenneth Hanf and Ben Soetendorp. New York: Longman, 1998, pp. 52–68.

von Dosenrode-Lynge, Sören Zibrandt. *Westeuropäische Kleinstaaten in der EG und EPZ.* Chur: Rüegger, 1993.

Wahl, Nils. *The Free Trade Agreements Between the EC and EFTA Countries: Their Implementation and Interpretation: A Case Study.* Stockholm: Juristförlaget, 1988.

Wallace, Helen. "EU Enlargement: A Neglected Subject." In *The State of the European Union.* Vol. 5: *Risks, Reform, Resistance, and Revival,* ed. by Maria Green Cowles and Michael Smith, Oxford: Oxford University Press, 2000, pp. 149–163.

Wallace, Helen, and Wolfgang Wessels. "Towards a New Partnership: The EC and EFTA in the Wider Western Europe." *Occasional Papers* no. 28. Geneva: EFTA, Economic Affairs Department, 1989.

Wallace, William. "Foreign Policy and National Identity in the United Kingdom." *International Affairs* 67, no. 1 (1991): 65–80.

———. "Small European States and European Policy-Making: Strategies, Roles, Possibilities." In *Between Autonomy and Influence: Small States and the European Union.* Oslo: ARENA Report, no. 1, 1999, pp. 11–26.

Walsh, James I. "National Preferences and International Institutions: Evidence from European Monetary Integration." *International Studies Quarterly* 45, no. 1 (2001): 59–80.

Weber, Max. *Gesammelte Aufsätze zur Religionssoziologie I.* Tübingen: J. C. B. Mohr, 1920.

Weiss, Friedl. "EC-EFTA Relations: Towards a Treaty Creating a European Economic Space." *Yearbook of European Law 1989.* Vol. 9. Oxford: Oxford University Press, 1990, 329–365.

Wendt, Alexander. "Collective Identity Formation and the International State." *American Political Science Review* 88, no. 2 (1994): 384–396.

Wessels, Wolfgang. "Deepening Versus Widening: Debate on the Shape of EC-Europe in the Nineties." In *The European Union in the 1990s: Ever Closer and Larger?* Ed. by Wolfgang Wessels and Christian Engel. Bonn: Europa Union Verlag, 1993, pp. 17–56.

Wetterberg, Gunnar. *Vad kostar det att stå utanför? En konsekvensutredning av ett eventuellt nej till svenskt EG-medlemskap.* Stockholm: Stiftelsen Ja till Europa, 1993.

Widfeldt, Anders. "Sweden and the European Union: Implications for the Swedish Party System." In *The European Union and the Nordic Countries,* ed. by Lee Miles. London: Routledge, 1996, pp. 101–116.

Widmer, Thomas, and Christof Buri. "Brüssel oder Bern: Schlägt das Herz der 'Romands' eher für Europa?" In *Die Schweiz und Europa: La Suisse et l'Europe: Schweizerisches Jahrbuch für Politische Wissenschaft* 32. Bern: Haupt, 1992, pp. 363–387.

Wijkman, Per Magnus. "The Internal Market and EFTA as Viewed from Geneva." In *EFTA and the EC: Implications of 1992,* ed. by Finn Laursen. Maastricht: European Institute of Public Administration, 1990, pp. 61–70.

———. "Patterns of Production and Trade in Western Europe: Looking Forward After Thirty Years." *Occasional Papers* no. 32. Geneva: EFTA, Economic Affairs Department, 1990.

———. "Policy Options Facing EFTA." *Occasional Papers* no. 22. Geneva: EFTA, Economic Affairs Department, 1988.

Wirtschaftspolitische Aspekte der Europäischen Integration aus schweizerischer

Sicht: Ergebnisse einer Untersuchung des Vororts des Schweizerischen Handels- und Industrie-Vereins. Zürich: Vorort, 1971.

Worre, Torben. "Danish Public Opinion and the European Community." *Scandinavian Journal of History* 20, no. 3 (1995): 209–227.

Zbinden, Martin. "Das EWR-Projekt: eine Wiederholung des Assoziationsversuches von 1961 bis 1963?" In *Die Schweiz und Europa. La Suisse et l'Europe. Schweizerisches Jahrbuch für Politische Wissenschaft* 32, Bern: Haupt, 1992, pp. 221–248.

———. "Die Unterschiede in der Perzeption der europäischen Integration zwischen der Deutschschweiz und der Romandie." *Traverse: Zeitschrift für Geschichte,* no. 3, 1994: 40–63.

Zeller, Willy. "Die bisherige Haltung der EWG gegenüber den Neutralen." In *Die Neutralen in der europäischen Integration: Kontroversen, Konfrontationen, Alternativen,* ed. by Hans Mayrzedt and Hans Christoph Binswanger. Wien: Wilhelm Braumüller, 1970, pp. 202–219.

Zimmerman, William. "Issue Area and Foreign-Policy Process: A Research Note in Search for a General Theory." *American Political Science Review* 67, no. 4 (1973): 1204–1212.

Zürn, Michael. "Assessing State Preferences and Explaining Institutional Choice: The Case of Intra-German Trade." *International Studies Quarterly* 41, no. 2 (1997): 295–320.

Documents of the European Communities/European Union

Assemblé Parlementaire Européenne. *Rapport fait au nom de la commission politique sur les aspects politiques et institutionnels de l'adhésion ou de l'association à la Communauté.* Rapporteur Mr. Birkelbach, DOC 1962/122, 15 January 1962.

Commission of the European Communities. "Agreements with the EFTA States Not Applying for Membership." *Bulletin of the European Communities* 5, no. 9 (1972): 11–21.

———. "Commission Memorandum to the Council on the Preparation of a Plan for the Phased Establishment of an Economic and Monetary Union, 4 March 1970." *Bulletin of the European Communities,* Supplement, no. 3 (1970).

———. *Communication from the Commission to the Council: Closer Cooperation Between the Community and the EFTA Countries.* COM (83) 326 final, Brussels, 6 June 1983, Annex.

———. *Completing the Internal Market: White Paper from the Commission to the European Council.* COM (85) 310 final, Brussels, 14 June 1985.

———. "The Economics of 1992: An Assessment of the Potential Economic Effects of Completing the Internal Market of the European Community." *European Economy,* no. 35 (March 1988).

———. *General Report on the Activities of the Communities.* Brussels, several years.

———. "The Impact of the Internal Market by Industrial Sector: The Challenge for the Member States." *European Economy: Social Europe,* special edition (1990).

———. "Opinion Submitted by the Commission to the Council on Relations

Between the Enlarged Community and those EFTA Member States (including the Associated Finland) Which Have Not Applied for Membership of the Community, 16 June 1971." *Bulletin of the European Communities*, Supplement, no. 3 (1971).

———. *Opinion Submitted on the Applications for Membership Received from the United Kingdom, Ireland, Denmark and Norway.* Brussels, 29 September 1967.

———. "Opinion Submitted to the Council Concerning the Applications for Membership from the United Kingdom, Ireland, Denmark and Norway, 1 October 1969." *Bulletin of the European Communities*, Supplement, nos. 9–10 (1969).

———. *Report to the European Parliament on the State of the Negotiations with the United Kingdom.* Brussels, 26 February 1963.

———. *Research on the "Cost of Non-Europe": Basic Findings.* 16 vols. Luxembourg: Office for Official Publications of the European Communities, 1988.

———. *The Sectoral Impact of the Internal Market.* Study by Pierre Buigues and Fabienne Ilzkovitz. Brussels, II/335/88-EN, 19 July 1988.

———. "Sweden's Application for Membership: Commission Opinion," 31 July 1992. *Bulletin of the European Communities*, Supplement, no. 5 (1992).

———. "Survey of National Identity and Deep-Seated Attitudes Towards European Integration in the Ten Applicant Countries of Central and Eastern Europe." *Forward Studies Unit Working Paper*, 1998.

———, Treaties Office. *Bilateral Relationships, Commitments and Agreements Between EC and EFTA Countries (updated and revised as of January 1989).* Brussels, I/119/89, March 1989. Updated version: European Commission. *Annotated Summary of Agreements Linking the Communities with Non-Member Countries (as of 31 December 1993).* Brussels, IA/104/94, June 1994.

C.E.C.A./C.E.E./Euratom. *Tarif douanier des Communautés européennes.* Luxembourg: Service des Publications des Communautés européennes, January 1961.

Conférence des Représentants des Etats Membres de la Communauté économique europénne. "Accords concernant l'établissement d'une partie du tarif douanier commun relative aux produits de la liste G prévue au traité instituant la Communauté économique européenne." *Journal officiel des Communautés européennes*, no. 80C, 20 December 1960.

Council of the European Communities. "Council Regulation (EEC) no. 1/73 of 19 December 1972 amending Regulation (EEC) no. 950/68 on the Common Customs Tariff." *Official Journal of the European Communities*, no. L 1, 1 January 1973.

———. "Council Regulation (EEC) no. 3333/83 of 4 November 1983 Amending Regulation (EEC) no. 950/68 on the Common Customs Tariff." *Official Journal of the European Communities*, no. L 313, 14 November 1983.

———. "Final Communiqué of the Conference in The Hague on 2 December 1969." *Bulletin of the European Communities* 3, no. 1 (1970): 11–16.

———. "Règlement (CEE) no. 950/68 du Conseil, du 28 juin 1968, relatif au tarif douanier commun." *Journal officiel des Communautés européennes*, no. L 172, 22 July 1968.

———. "Report by the Foreign Ministers of the Member States on the Problems of Political Unification." *Bulletin of the European Communities*, no. 11 (1970): 9–14.

European Communities. *Bulletin of the European Communities*, several issues.

European Court of Justice. "Opinion of the Court, 14 December 1991 (Opinion 1/91)." *Official Journal of the European Communities*, no. C 110, 29 April 1992, pp. 1–15.

———. "Opinion of the Court, 10 April 1992 (Opinion 1/92)." *Official Journal of the European Communities*, no. C 136, 26 May 1992, pp. 1–12.

European Economic Community. *Bulletin of the European Economic Community,* several issues.

European Parliament. "Resolution of 11 February 1983 on EEC-EFTA Free Trade Agreements." *Official Journal of the European Communities,* no. C 68, 14 March 1983, pp. 88–89.

Documents of the European Free Trade Association (EFTA)

EFTA. *Annual Report of the European Free Trade Association.* Geneva: EFTA, various years.

———. *Bâtir l'AELE: Une zone de libre-échange en Europe.* Geneva: EFTA, 1968.

———. "Communiqué of the EFTA Ministerial Council in London on 27–28 June 1961." *EFTA Bulletin,* no. 7 (1961), p. 8.

———. "Communiqué of the Meeting of the EFTA Council at Ministerial Level, Geneva, 11–12 December 1989." In *Twenty-Ninth Annual Report of the European Free Trade Association 1989.* Geneva: EFTA, 1990, pp. 50–53.

———. "Communiqué of the Ministerial Meeting of the EFTA Council in London on 28 April 1967." *EFTA Bulletin,* no. 4 (1967):13.

———. "Declaration of the Meeting of the EFTA Heads of Governments and Ministers, Vienna, 13 May 1977." In *Seventeenth Annual Report of the European Free Trade Association 1976–77.* Geneva: EFTA, 1977, pp. 52–56.

———. "Declaration of the Meeting of the EFTA Heads of Governments, Oslo, 14–15 March 1989." In *Twenty-Ninth Annual Report of the European Free Trade Association 1989.* Geneva: EFTA, 1990, pp. 35–38.

———. "Effects of '1992' on the Manufacturing Industries of the EFTA Countries." *Occasional Paper* no. 38, special edition. Geneva: EFTA, Economic Affairs Department, 1992.

———. "Effects of '1992' on the Services Sectors of the EFTA Countries." *Occasional Paper* no. 49, special edition. Geneva: EFTA, Economic Affairs Department, 1994.

———. *EFTA Bulletin.* Geneva: EFTA, several years.

———. *EFTA: The European Free Trade Association.* Geneva: EFTA, 1987.

———. *EFTA Trade.* Geneva: EFTA, several years.

———. *The Stockholm Convention Examined.* 2nd ed. Geneva: EFTA, 1963.

———. *The Trade Effects of EFTA and the EEC 1959–1967.* Geneva: EFTA, 1972.

EFTA and European Communities. "Joint Declaration of the Ministerial Meeting Between the European Community and Its Member States and the States of the European Free Trade Association, Luxembourg, 9 April 1984." In *Twenty-Fourth Annual Report of the European Free Trade Association 1984.* Geneva: EFTA, 1985, pp. 53–55.

———. "Joint Declaration of the Ministerial Meeting Between the European Community, Its Member States and the EFTA States on the Internal Market,

Brussels, 2 February 1988." In *Twenty-Eighth Annual Report of the European Free Trade Association 1988*. Geneva: EFTA, 1989, pp. 31–33.

Documents of Norway

Ministry for Foreign Affairs. *Europeisk samarbeid—styring og demokrati*. Delrapport til Europautredningen, 1992.

———. "Norge-EU: Om forhandlingsresultatet." *Pressehefte*. Oslo, 16 March 1994.

———. *Norge ved et veivalg: Virkninger av ulike former for tilknytning til Det Europeiske Fellesskap*. Europautredngingen Hovedrapport, Oslo, 1992.

———. *Norsk økonomi og næringsliv ved ulike tilknytningsformer til EF*. Delrapport til Europautredningen, Oslo, 1992.

———. *Norsk velferd og europeisk samarbeid*. Delrapport til Europautredningen, 1992.

———. "The Norwegian Political Parties' Attitude to EU." *Norway Information*. Oslo, November 1994.

———. *Om Det Europeiske Økonomiske Fellesskap og de europeiske marketsproblemer*. St.meld. nr. 15 (1961–62), Oslo, 13 October 1961.

———. *Om medlemskap i Den europeiske union*. St.meld. nr. 40 (1993–94), Oslo, 3 June 1994.

———. *Om Norge, EF og europeisk samarbeid*. St.meld. nr. 61 (1986–87), Oslo, 22 May 1987.

———. *Om Norge og Europa ved inngangen til et nytt århundre*. St.meld. nr. 12 (2000–2001), Oslo, 1 December 2000.

———. *Om Norges forhold til De Europeiske Fellesskap*. St.meld. nr. 86 (1966–67), Oslo, 16 June 1967.

———. *Om Norges forhold til De Europeiske Fellesskap*. St.meld. nr. 90 (1970–71), Oslo, 21 May 1971.

———. *Om Norges forhold til de nordiske og europeiske markedsdannelser*. St.meld. nr. 92 (1969–70), Oslo, 5 June 1970.

———. *Om Norges stilling til Det Europeiske Økonomiske Fellesskap og de europeiske samarbeidsbestrebelser*. St.meld. nr. 67 (1961–62), Oslo, 2 March 1962.

———. *Om Norges tilslutning til De Europeiske Fellesskap*. St.meld. nr. 50 (1971–72), 10 March 1972.

———. *Om planene for et europeisk frihandelsområde*. St.meld. nr. 45 (1957), Oslo, 1 March 1957.

———. *Om samtykke til ratifikasjon av Avtale mellom Norge og Det Europeiske Økonomiske Fellesskap og Avtale mellom Norge og medlemsstatene i Det Europeiske Kull- og Stålfellesskap og Det Europeiske Kull- og Stålfellesskap*. St.meld. nr. 126 (1972–73), Oslo, 4 May 1973.

———. *Om samtykke til ratifikasjon av Avtale om Det europeiske økonomiske samarbeidsområdet (EØS), undertegnet i Oporto 2. mai 1992*. St.prp.nr. 100 (1991–92), Oslo, 15 May 1992.

———. *Om samtykke til ratifikasjon av konvensjonen av 4. januar 1960 om opprettelse av Det Europeiske Frihandelsforbund med tillknyttet protokoll*. St.prp. nr. 75 (1959–60), Oslo, 22 January 1960.

Ministry of Trade and Shipping. *Om enkelte handelspolitiske spørsmål*. St.meld. nr. 63 (1986–87), Oslo, 22 May 1987.

———. "Handelsminister Grete Knudsen: EU-medlemskap den beste garanti for

Documents of Sweden   253

fortsatt utvikling av våre velferdsordninger." *Pressemelding*, no. 109/1993. Oslo, 3 June 1993.

———. *Handelsministerens redegjørelse i Stortinget 20. April 1994 om resultatet av EU-forhandlingene.* Oslo, 20 April 1994.

Parliament. "Norge, EF og europeisk samarbeid." *Forhandlinger i Stortinget.* St.tid. nos. 262–265 (Oslo, 7 June 1988): 3880–3957.

———. "Samtykke til ratifikasjon av Avtale om Det europeiske økonomiske samarbeidsområdet (EØS)." *Forhandlinger i Stortinget.* St.tid. nos. 12–22 (Oslo, 15–16 October 1992): 169–341.

Parliament, Finance Committee. *Innstillning fra finanskomitéen om norsk tilpasning til EFs indre marked,* St.meld.nr. 1, kap. 3, Innst.S.nr. 38 (1989–90), Oslo, 28 November 1989.

Parliament, Foreign Affairs and Constitution Committee. *Innstilling fra den utvidede utenriks- og konstitusjonskomité om ratifikasjon av konvensjonen av 4. januar 1960 om opprettelse av Det Europeiske Frihandelsforbund,* St.prp.nr. 75, Innst.S.nr. 157 (1959–60), Oslo, 16 March 1960.

———. *Innstillning fra den utvidede utenriks- og konstitusjonskomité om Norges forhold til Det Europeiske Økonomiske Fellesskap (EEC),* St.meld. nr. 15 og nr. 67, Innst.S.nr. 165 (1961–62), Oslo, 12 April 1962 (reprinted from *Stortingsforhandlinger).*

———. *Innstillning fra utenriks- og konstitusjonskomitéen om Norges forhold til de europeiske fellesskap,* St.meld. nr. 86, Innst.S.nr. 289 (1966–67), Oslo, 5 July 1967.

———. *Innstillning fra utenriks- og konstitusjonskomitéen om Norges tilslutning til Det Europeiske Fellesskap,* St.meld. nr. 50, Innst.S.nr. 277 (1971–72), Oslo, 26 May 1972.

———. *Innstillning fra utenriks- og konstitusjonskomitéen om ratifikasjon av Avtale mellom Norge og Det Europeiske Økonomiske Fellesskap og Avtale mellom Norge og medlemsstatene i Det Europeiske Kull- og Stålfellesskap og Det Europeiske Kull- og Stålfellesskap,* St.meld. nr. 126, Innst.S.nr. 289 (1972–73), Oslo, 18 May 1973.

———. *Innstillning fra utenriks- og konstitusjonskomitéen om Norge, EF og europeisk samarbeid.* Innst.S.nr. 244 (1987–88), Oslo, 26 May 1988.

———. *Stortingets behandling av innstilling fra den utvidede utenriks- og konstitusjonskomite om Norges forhold til Det Europeiske Økonomiske Fellesskap (EEC).* Oslo, 25–28 April 1962 (reprinted from *Stortingsforhandlinger).*

Prime Minister Gro Harlem Brundtland. "Redegjørelse av statsministeren om Regjeringens vurderinger og begrunnelse for at Norge bør søke medlemskap i EF." *Forhandlinger i Stortinget.* St.tid. no. 74 (Oslo, 16 November 1992): 1125–1132.

Statistics Norway. *Folkeavstemningen 1994 om norsk medlemskap i EU: The 1994 Referendum on Norwegian Membership of the EU.* Oslo: Statistisk sentralbyrå, 1995.

Documents of Sweden

Government. *Kungl. Maj:ts proposition 1960:25 angående godkännande av Sveriges anslutning till konventionen upprättandet av Europeiska frihandelssammanslutningen, m.m.* Stockholm, 4 January 1960.

———. *Kungl. Maj:ts proposition 1972:135 angående avtal med den europeiska ekonomiska gemenskapen, m.m.* Stockholm, 3 November 1972.

———. *Regeringens proposition 1987/88:66 om Sverige och den västeuropeiska integrationen.* Stockholm, 17 December 1987.

———. *Regeringens skrivelse 1990/91:50 om åtgärder för att stabilisera ekonomin och begränsa tillväxten av de offentliga utgifterna.* Stockholm: Finansdepartement, 26 October 1990.

———. *Regeringens proposition 1991/92:170 om Europeiska Ekonomiska Samarbetsområdet (EES).* Stockholm, 27 May 1992.

———. *Regeringens proposition 1994/95:19 Del 1 om Sveriges medlemskap i den Europeiska Unionen.* Stockholm, 11 August 1994.

Ministry for Foreign Affairs. *Documents on Swedish Foreign Policy.* Stockholm: Royal Ministry for Foreign Affairs, several years.

———. *Historiskt vägval: Följderna för Sverige i utrikes- och säkerhetspolitiskt hänseende av att bli, respektive inte bli medlem i europeiska unionen.* Stockholm: Statens offentliga utredningar SOU, no. 8 Betänkande, 1994.

———. *Om Sveriges inflytande i den europeiska unionen: Bilaga 5 till EG-konsekvensutredningen, Samhällsekonomi.* Stockholm: Fritzes, 1993.

———. *Sverige och den västeuropeiska integrationen: Ekonomiska konsekvenser av ett svenskt medlemskap i EG/EU, Mars 1993.* Stockholm, March 1993.

———. *Sverige och den västeuropeiska integrationen: Inför ett svenskt EG/EU-medlemskap, Hösten 1993.* Stockholm, December 1993.

———. *Sverige och den västeuropeiska integrationen: Sammanfattning av Konsekvensutredningarna.* Stockholm, March 1994.

———. *Sveriges medlemskap i den Europeiska Unionen.* Stockholm: Departementsserien, no. 48, Ds 1994.

———. *Sveriges medlemskap i den Europeiska Unionen: Remissyttranden över departementspromemorian (Ds 1994:48).* Stockholm: Departementsserien, no. 104, Ds 1994.

———. *Sweden and Europe, Committee of Enquiry: Consequences of the EU for Sweden—the Economy. Summary and Conclusions.* Stockholm: Statens offentliga utredningar SOU, no. 6, 1994.

———. *Sweden, the EC and Security Policy: Developments in Europe. Statement to the Riksdag by the Prime Minister on 14 June 1991, on Sweden's Application for Membership of the European Community.* Stockholm, 14 June 1991 (published in Ministry for Foreign Affairs, *Information*, no. 2, 1991.)

Ministry of Trade and Industry. *Europeiska ekonomiska gemenskapen, del VI: Redogörelse för Romfördragets tillämpning under tiden 1 april 1966–30 juni 1968 utarbetad inom Kommerskollegium.* Stockholm: Handelsdepartementet, 1969.

———. *Inför Sveriges EEC förhandlingar: Fakta och överväganden.* Stockholm, 1971.

———. *Svensk industri och Europamarknaden: Översikt av olika industrigruppers utredningar och bedömningar sammanställd av Industriförbundet och Kommerskollegium.* Stockholm, 1962.

———. *Sverige och EEC: Romfördraget ur svensk synvinkel.* Stockholm, 1968.

National Board of Trade/Kommerskollegium. *Diskussionspromemoria angående Sverige och sexstatsmarknaden.* Stockholm, 26 November 1958, Fh 55, H 1/58.

———. *PM med synpunkter på möjligheten av en svensk anslutning till den europeiska ekonomiska gemenskapen.* Stockholm, 3 June 1957, Fh 17, H 4/57.

———. *PM rörande vissa arbetsmarknadsproblem aktualiserade vid förhandlin-*

garna om ett europeiskt frihandelsområde. Stockholm, 10 January 1958, Fh 31, H 1/58.

———. *Preliminär PM angående Romstaternas gemensamma yttre tullmur.* Stockholm, 11 January 1958, Fh D 133.

———. *Sveriges officiella statistik: Handel berättelse för år 1952, del I.* Stockholm, 1954.

Parliament. "Allmänpolitisk debatt," *Riksdagens protokoll,* no. 8 (Stockholm, 19 January 1971).

———. "Allmänpolitisk debatt: Europafrågor." *Riksdagens Protokoll 1990/91,* no. 6 (Stockholm, 10 October 1990): 3ff.

———. "Allmänpolitisk debatt: EU-frågan." *Riksdagens Protokoll 1994/95,* no. 11, Stockholm, 19 October 1994, pp. 1–118.

———. "Ang. de västeuropeiska integrationssträvandena, m.m." *Riksdagens Protokoll: Första Kammaren,* no. 27 (Stockholm, 25 October 1961): 4ff.

———. "Avtal med EEC, m.m." *Riksdagens Protokoll,* nos. 138–139 (Stockholm, 12 December 1972): 3ff.

———. "Europeiska ekonomiska samarbetsområdet." *Riksdagens Protokoll 1992/93,* no. 26 (Stockholm, 18 November 1992): 1–165.

———. "Handelspolitisk debatt." *Riksdagens Protokoll: Andra Kammaren,* no. 40 (Stockholm, 7 November 1967): 25ff.

———. "Information från regeringen om EG-ansökan." *Riksdagens Protokoll 1990/91,* no. 132 (Stockholm, 14 June 1991): 4–16.

———. "Meddelande angående Sveriges utrikespolitik." *Riksdagens Protokoll: Andra Kammaren,* no. 7 (Stockholm, 11 March 1959): 18–108.

———. "Meddelande rörande de västeuropeiska integrationssträvandena." *Riksdagens Protokoll: Andra Kammaren,* no. 27 (Stockholm, 25 October 1961): 20ff.

———. "Remissdebatt." *Riksdagens Protokoll 1994/95,* no. 7 (Stockholm, 11 October 1994): 19–100.

———. "Svar på interpellation ang: Förhandlingarna om ett europeiskt frihandelsområde." *Riksdagens Protokoll: Andra kammaren,* 1958:B15 (Stockholm, 9 December 1958): 11–46.

———. "Sveriges handelspolitik," *Riksdagens Protokoll: Första Kammaren,* no. 40 (Stockholm, 7 November 1967): 37ff.

———. "Sverige och den västeuropeiska integrationen." *Riksdagens Protokoll 1987/88,* no. 114 (Stockholm, 4 May 1988): 4–118.

Parliament, Foreign Affairs Committee. *Utrikesutskottets betänkande nr. 20 med anledning av propositionen 1972:135 angående avtal med de europeiska gemenskaperna m.m. jämte motioner.* Stockholm, 5 December 1972.

———. *Utrikesutskottets betänkande 1990/91:UU8 Sverige och den västeuropeiska integrationen.* Stockholm, 22 November 1990.

———. *Utrikesutskottets betänkande 1987/88:24 om Sverige och den västeuropeiska integrationen (prop. 1987/88:66).* Stockholm, 21 April 1988.

———. *Utrikesutskottets betänkande 1991/92:UU17 Säkerhet och nedrustning.* Stockholm, 28 April 1992.

———. *Utrikesutskottets betänkande 1991/92:UU24 Sverige och EG.* Stockholm, 28 April 1992.

———. *Utrikesutskottets betänkande 1994/95:UU5 Sveriges medlemskap i europeiska unionen.* Stockholm, 1 December 1994.

———. *Utrikesutskottets utlåtande 1960:2 i anledning dels av Kungl. Maj:ts proposition angående godkännande av Sveriges anslutning till konventionen angående upprättandet av Europeiska frihandelssammanslutningen, m.m., dels ock av motioner väckta i anslutning till sagda proposition.* Stockholm, 17 March 1960.

Documents of Switzerland

Eidgenössische Oberzolldirektion. *Jahresstatistik des Aussenhandels der Schweiz.* Vol. 1. Bern, 1952, 1958.

Federal Council. "Antwort des Bundesrates auf das Postulat Alder (82.393) vom 8. Oktober 1982 'Beziehungen zur Europäischen Gemeinschaft.'" Annex 3 to "Bericht zur Aussenwirtschaftspolitik 83/2 und Botschaft zu einer internationalen Wirtschaftsvereinbarung vom 11. Januar 1984." *Bundesblatt I*, Bern, 1984, pp. 457–494.

———. *Aussenpolitischer Bericht 2000—Präsenz und Kooperation: Interessenwahrung in einer zusammenwachsenden Welt.* Bern, 15 November 2000.

———. *Bericht des Bundesrates vom 11. August 1971 über die Entwicklung der europäischen Integrationsbestrebungen und die Haltung der Schweiz. Bericht zum Postulat Beck (9688) vom 16. März 1967 und zur Motion Furgler (9922) vom 15. März 1968.* Bern, 11 August 1971.

———. *Bericht des Bundesrates vom 24. August 1988 über die Stellung der Schweiz im europäischen Integrationsprozess.* Bern, 24 August 1988.

———. *Bericht des Bundesrates vom 18. Mai 1992 über einen Beitritt der Schweiz zur Europäischen Gemeinschaft.* Bern, 18 May 1992.

———. *Bericht des Bundesrates vom 29. November 1993 über die Aussenpolitik der Schweiz in den 90er Jahren. Anhang: Bericht zur Neutralität.* Bern, 29 November 1993.

———. *Bericht des Schweizerischen Bundesrates an die Bundesversammlung über seine Geschäftsführung.* Bern, several years.

———. *Botschaft des Bundesrates an die Bundesversammlung vom 20. August 1948 betreffend den Beitritt der Schweiz zu dem am 16. April 1948 in Paris unterzeichneten Abkommen über die europäische wirtschaftliche Zusammenarbeit.* Bern, 20 August 1948.

———. *Botschaft des Bundesrates an die Bundesversammlung vom 9. Oktober 1956 über die mit der Europäischen Gemeinschaft für Kohle und Stahl abgeschlossenen Abkommen.* Bern, 9 October 1956.

———. *Botschaft des Bundesrates an die Bundesversammlung vom 5. Februar 1960 über die Beteiligung der Schweiz an der Europäischen Freihandels-Assoziation.* Bern, 5 February 1960.

———. *Botschaft des Bundesrates an die Bundesversammlung vom 16. August 1972 über die Genehmigung der Abkommen zwischen der Schweiz und den Europäischen Gemeinschaften.* Bern, 16 August 1972.

———. *Botschaft des Bundesrates vom 18. Mai 1992 über die Genehmigung des Abkommens über den Europäischen Wirtschaftsraum.* Bern, 18 May 1992.

———. *Botschaft des Bundesrates vom 24. Februar 1993 über das Folgeprogramm nach der Ablehnung des EWR-Abkommens.* Bern, 24 February 1993.

———. *Botschaft des Bundesrates vom 23. Juni 1999 zur Genehmigung der sektoriellen Abkommen zwischen der Schweiz und der EG.* Bern, 23 June 1999.

———. "Bundesratsbeschluss vom 25. Januar 1973 über die Erwahrung des Ergebnisses der Volksabstimmung vom 3. Dezember 1972 betreffend den

Bundesbeschluss über die Abkommen zwischen der Schweizerischen Eidgenossenschaft und der Europäischen Wirtschaftsgemeinschaft sowie den Mitgliedstaaten der Europäischen Gemeinschaft für Kohle und Stahl." *Bundesblatt* I, no. 4, Bern, 1973, pp. 81–82.

―――. *Informationsbericht des Bundesrates über die Stellung der Schweiz im europäischen Integrationsprozess vom 26. November 1990.* Bern, 26 November 1990.

―――. *Schweiz-Europäische Union: Integrationsbericht 1999.* Bern, 3 February 1999.

―――. "Schweizerische Erklärung an der Zusammenkunft auf Ministerebene zwischen den Europäischen Gemeinschaften und der Schweiz, Brüssel, 10. November 1970." *Bundesblatt* I, no. 4 (Bern, 1971): 59–67.

Ministry for Foreign Affairs. "Leitsätze des Eidgenössischen Politischen Departementes zum Begriff der Neutraliät vom 26. November 1954." In *Verwaltungsentscheide der Bundesbehörden* 24, no. 1 (Bern, 1954): 9–13.

Parliament. "Aussenwirtschaftspolitik 1986/2." *Amtliches Bulletin der Bundesversammlung: Nationalrat,* Bern, 4 March 1987, pp. 74–91.

―――. "Europäische Integration: Bericht." *Amtliches Bulletin der Bundesversammlung: Nationalrat,* Bern, 28 February–1 March 1989, pp. 143–187, and *Amtliches Bulletin der Bundesversammlung: Ständerat,* Bern, 21–22 June 1989, pp. 357–377.

―――. "Europäische Wirtschaftsgemeinschaft, Freihandelsabkommen." *Amtliches Bulletin der Bundesversammlung: Nationalrat,* Bern, 20–25 September 1972, pp. 1434ff.

―――. "EWR-Abkommen." *Amtliches Bulletin der Bundesversammlung: Nationalrat,* Bern, 24–26 August 1992, pp. 1290–1397.

―――. "EWR-Abkommen." *Amtliches Bulletin der Bundesversammlung: Ständerat,* Bern, 22–24 September 1992, pp. 781–838.

―――. "Interpellation Conzett und Tenchio: Stand der europäischen Integration." *Amtliches stenographisches Bulletin der Bundesversammlung: Nationalrat,* Bern, 27 September 1961, pp. 418–425.

―――. "Interpellation Egger: Internationale Lage." *Amtliches stenographisches Bulletin der Bundesversammlung: Nationalrat,* Bern, 18 March 1953, pp. 141–165.

―――. "Interpellation Weber Max: Auswirkungen der Kennedy-Runde." *Amtliches Bulletin der Bundesversammlung: Nationalrat,* Bern, 27 June 1967, pp. 297–304.

―――. "Kleine Freihandelszone: Beitritt der Schweiz." *Amtliches stenographisches Bulletin der Bundesversammlung, Nationalrat,* Bern, 16–18 March 1960, pp. 90ff.

―――. "Kleine Freihandelszone: Beitritt der Schweiz." *Amtliches stenographisches Bulletin der Bundesversammlung: Ständerat,* Bern, 23 March 1960, pp. 48ff.

Other Documents

GATT (General Agreement on Tariffs and Trade). *Protocol to the General Agreement on Tariffs and Trade Embodying Results of the 1960–1961 Tariff Conference.* Geneva: GATT, 16 July 1962.

OECD (Organization for Economic Cooperation and Development). *Monthly Statistics of Foreign Trade*, March 1995. Paris: OECD, 1995.

——. *National Accounts: Main Aggregates 1960–1994*, Vol. 1. Paris: OECD, 1996.

——. *National Accounts of OECD Countries 1950–1968*. Paris: OECD, 1970.

OEEC (Organization for European Economic Cooperation). "Alternates of Working Party no. 21 of the Council Group of Trade Exports: Comparison of Member Countries' Tariff Levels for Selected Products: Consolidated List," FTA/WP4(57)36, Paris, 31 October 1957.

——. *Report on the Possibility of Creating a Free Trade Area in Europe*. Prepared for the OEEC Council by a special Working Party. Paris, C(57)5, 1957.

——. *Statistical Bulletins: Foreign Trade*. "The Network of Intra-European Trade: Trade by Product in 1956." Paris: OEEC, 1957.

——. *Statistical Bulletins: Foreign Trade*. "The Network of Intra-European Trade: Trade by Product in 1958." Paris: OEEC, 1959.

OEEC/OECD (Organization for European Economic Cooperation/Organization for Economic Cooperation and Development). *Statistical Bulletins: Foreign Trade*, Series B. Paris: OEEC/OECD, several years.

——. *Statistical Bulletins: Foreign Trade*, Series IV. Paris: OEEC/OECD, several years.

——. *Statistical Bulletins: Foreign Trade*, Analytical Abstracts. Paris: OEEC/OECD, several years.

United Kingdom. *Negotiations for a European Free Trade Area: Documents Relating to the Negotiations from July, 1956, to December, 1958*. London: HMSO, Cmnd. 641, 1959.

United Kingdom, House of Lords, Select Committee on the European Communities. *Relations Between the Community and EFTA*. 14th Report with Evidence, Session 1989–1990. London: HMSO, HL Paper 55-I and 55-II, 22 May 1990.

United Nations. *Statistical Papers: Commodity Trade Statistics*, Series D, New York, several years.

——. *UN COMTRADE database*, several years.

United Nations, Economic Commission for Europe. "Economic Integration and Export Performance of West European Countries Outside the EC." *Economic Studies*, no. 5, Geneva, 1995.

United Nations, Statistical Office. "Standard International Trade Classification." *UN Statistical Papers*, Series M, no. 10, 1951.

——, "Standard International Trade Classification, Revised," *UN Statistical Papers*, Series M, no. 34, 1961.

United Nations Conference on Trade and Development (UNCTAD). *Implications of the Dynamism of Large Economic Spaces: Major New Developments in Large Economic Spaces and Regional Integration Processes and Their Implications*. Geneva: UNCTAD, Statistical Annex TD/B/SEM.1/2/Add.1, 28 November 1995.

Index

About the Book

Analyzing some thirty policy decisions across three countries and five decades, Sieglinde Gstöhl considers why some countries continue to be "reluctant Europeans."

Typically, small, highly industrialized states are expected to be more likely to integrate than are larger or less advanced countries. Why, then, did Norway, Sweden, and Switzerland choose for so long not to join the European Communities? And what accounts today for their differing levels of integration? Gstöhl argues that economic interests alone do not sufficiently explain attitudes toward integration but rather coexist with—and are often dominated by—domestic political and geohistorical constraints. The lure of improved access to EU markets may fade in the shadow of domestic institutions and societal cleavages, foreign policy traditions, and experiences of foreign rule that touch on feelings of national identity. Thoroughly addressing these issues, *Reluctant Europeans* offers key insights into the problems associated with deepening integration in an enlarging European Union.

Sieglinde Gstöhl is assistant professor of international relations at the Institute of Social Sciences at Humboldt University Berlin.